SATCHEL

SATCHEL

The Life and Times of an American Legend

LARRY TYE

RANDOM HOUSE

NEW YORK

LR77

Library of Congress Cataloging-in-Publication Data
Tye, Larry.
Satchel : the life and times of an American legend / Larry Tye.
p. cm.
ISBN 978-1-4000-6651-3
1. Paige, Satchel, 1906–1982.   2. Baseball players—United States—Biography.
I. Title.
GV865.P3T94 2009
796.357092—dc22   2008044858

Printed in the United States of America on acid-free paper

www.atrandom.com

24689753

Book design by Christopher M. Zucker

To Buck O'Neil, Silas Simmons, and the other
Negro League veterans who enthusiastically shared with
me their stories about Satchel but did not live to see them told

IT WAS A FASTBALL WRAPPED IN A RIDDLE that first drew me to Satchel Paige. I was an adolescent baseball fanatic and had grown up hearing that Satchel was the most overpowering and artful pitcher who ever lived. The stories were enchanting but they were not backed up by the won-lost records, earned run averages, and other vital statistics that students of the game like me needed to decide for ourselves. I wanted to know more.

It was that same blend of icon and enigma that drew me back to Satchel thirty-five years later. I was writing a book on the Pullman porters called *Rising from the Rails,* and the venerable African American railroad men I interviewed reignited my memories and my interest. They had watched Satchel play in his heyday in the 1930s, had talked to him when he rode the train, and told riveting tales of his feats on the diamond and off. Yet the more I probed, the clearer it became how thin their knowledge was of this towering talent. Everyone knew about him but no one really knew him.

That is understandable. Satchel Paige was a black man playing in an obscure universe. Few records were kept or stories written of his games in the strictly segregated Negro Leagues, fewer still of his barnstorming through America's sandlots and small towns. Did he really win three games in a single day and two thousand over a career? Was he confident enough in his strikeout pitch to actually order his outfielders to abandon their posts? Could he really have been better than Walter Johnson, Cy Young, and the other all-time marvels of the mound? In a game where box scores and play-by-play accounts encourage such comparisons, the hard data on Satchel was elusive. That helps explain why, while fourteen full-fledged biographies have been published of Babe Ruth and eleven of Mickey Mantle, there is only one on Satchel Paige, who was at least as important to baseball and America.

To fill in that picture I tracked down more than two hundred veteran Negro Leaguers and Major Leaguers who played with and against Satchel. His teammate and friend Buck O'Neil told me about the Satchel he knew—a pitcher who threw so hard that catchers tried to soften the sting by cushioning their gloves with beefsteaks, with control so precise that he used a hardball to knock lit cigarettes out of the mouths of obliging teammates. Hank Aaron had his own Satchel stories, as did Bob Feller, Orlando Cepeda, Whitey Herzog, and Silas Simmons, a patriarch of black baseball whom I spoke with the day he turned 111. I talked to Leon Paige and other relatives in Mobile. In Kansas City, I heard Robert Paige and his siblings publicly share for the first time their recollections of their father. I retraced Satchel's footsteps from the South to the Midwest to the Caribbean, visiting stadiums where he had pitched, rooming houses where he stayed, and restaurants where he ate in an era when a black man was lucky to find any that would serve him. I watched him in the movies and read everything written about him in books, magazines, and newspapers, thousands of articles in all. Researchers helped me recheck statistics and refute or confirm his claims on everything from how many games he won (probably as many as he said) to how many times he struck out the mighty Josh Gibson (not quite as many as he boasted).

Along the way I untangled riddles such as the one about how old Satchel was. It was the most argued statistic in sports. The answer depended on who was asking and when. In 1934 the *Colored Baseball & Sports Monthly* reported that Satchel was born in 1907. In 1948 he was born in 1901 (The Associated Press), 1903 (*Time*), 1908 (*The Washington Post, The New York Times,* and *The Sporting News*), and 1904 (his mother). The Cleveland Indians hedged their bets after signing him in 1948, writing in their yearbook that Satchel was born "on either July 17, Sept. 11, Sept. 18 or Sept. 22, somewhere between 1900 and 1908." *Newsweek* columnist John Lardner took him back further, saying that Satchel "saved the day at Waterloo, when the dangerous pull-hitter, Bonaparte, came to bat with the bases full."

The mystery over Satchel's age mattered because age matters in baseball. It is a way to compare players, and to measure a player's current season against his past performance. No ballplayer gave fans as much to debate about, for as long, as Satchel Paige. At first he was Peter Pan—forever young, confoundingly fast, treacherously wild. Over time his durability proved even more alluring. After a full career in the Negro Leagues he broke through to the Majors in 1948, helping propel the Cleveland Indians to the World Series at the over-the-hill age of forty-two. He still holds the record as the game's oldest player, an honor earned during one last go-round at an inconceivable fifty-nine. He started pitching professionally when Babe Ruth was on the eve of his sixty-home-run season in 1926; he was still playing when Yankee Stadium, "The House That Ruth Built," was entering its fifth decade in 1965. Over that span Satchel Paige pitched more baseballs, for more fans, in more ballparks, for more teams, than any player in history.

When kids who watched Satchel early in his career watched him a generation later with their kids and grandkids, it was natural to wonder how old the pitcher was. Satchel obliged with tales that grew more fantastic with each retelling. Proof of his birth date was in the family bible. Unfortunately, his grandfather was reading that bible under a chinaberry tree when a wind kicked up, blowing the Good Book into the path of the family goat, who ate it. His draft record showed he was born September 26, 1908, his Social Security card had August 15, 1908, and his passport file indicated February 5, 1908. The three dates shared one thing: all were supplied by Satchel.

The truth was simpler and more complex. Pinning down Satchel's date of birth should have been a straightforward matter of checking public records in his native Mobile, but in the post-Reconstruction Confederacy it was easier to track the bloodline of a packhorse than of a Negro citizen. Until 1902, descendants of slaves in Mobile were included in neither the city census nor the city directory. Even when they finally did enter into the accounting, it was with caveats. Like Satchel and his eleven sisters and brothers, most blacks were delivered not in an operating room at the hospital but in a bedroom at home, so health authorities had to rely on the family's filing notice of the birth. Recordings that did make it into the official directories were accompanied by a *B* for black or a *C* for colored.

All that might have made Satchel doubt whether Mobile officials ever got word of his birth and accurately registered it. Or it might have until he signed with Cleveland in 1948, and owner Bill Veeck did what Satchel could have done—and may have—years earlier. Veeck traveled to Mobile to get to the bottom of the elusive age issue. He contacted Satchel's mom, Lula, who dispatched Satchel's nephew Leon Paige to accompany the Indians' owner and his entourage to the County Health Department. "They saw his birth certificate," Leon says. "They knew [Lula] had twelve children and they knew when they were born." In Satchel's case, the registry was clear: the baby was a boy, his race was Colored, and his date of birth was July 7, 1906.

So why the ruses?

Satchel knew that, despite being the fastest, winningest pitcher alive, being black meant he would never get the attention he deserved. That was easy to see in the backwaters of the Negro Leagues but it remained true when he hit the Majors at age forty-two, with accusations flying that his signing was a mere stunt. He needed an edge, a bit of mystery, to romance sportswriters and fans. Longevity offered the perfect platform. "They want me to be old," Satchel said, "so I give 'em what they want. Seems they get a bigger kick out of an old man throwing strikeouts." He feigned exasperation when reporters pressed to know the secret of his birth, insisting, "I want to be the onliest man in the United States that nobody knows nothin' about."

In fact he wanted just the opposite: Satchel masterfully exploited his lost birthday to ensure the world would remember his long life.

It was not a random image Satchel crafted for himself but one he knew played perfectly into perceptions whites had back then of blacks. It was a persona of agelessness and fecklessness, one where a family's entire history could be written into a faded bible and a goat could devour both. The black man in the era of Jim Crow was not expected to have human proportions at all, certainly none worth documenting in public records or engraving for posterity. He was a phantom, without the dignity of a real name (hence the nickname Satchel), a rational mother (Satchel's mother was so confused she supposedly mixed him up with his brother), or an age certain ("Nobody knows how complicated I am," he once said. "All they want to know is how old I am."). That is precisely the image that nervous white owners relished when they signed the first black ballplayers. Few inquired where the pioneers came from or wanted to hear about their struggles. In these athletes' very anonymity lay their value.

Playing to social stereotypes the way he did with his age is just half the story of Satchel Paige, although it is the half most told. While many dismissed him as a Stepin Fetchit if not an Uncle Tom, this book makes clear that he was something else entirely—a quiet subversive, defying Uncle Tom and Jim Crow. Told all his life that black lives matter less than white ones, he teased journalists by adding or subtracting years each time they asked his age, then asked them, "How old would you be if you didn't know how old you were?" Relegated by statute and custom to the shadows of the Negro Leagues, he fed Uncle Sam shadowy information on his provenance. Yet growing up in the Deep South he knew better than to flaunt the rules openly, so he did it opaquely. He made his relationships with the press and the public into a game, using insubordination and indirection to challenge his segregated surroundings.

His stagecraft was so successful that it amazed even him. He pitched spectacularly enough, especially when his teams were beating the best of the white big leaguers, that white sportswriters showed up to watch black baseball. He proved that black fans would fill ballparks, even when those parks had concrete seats and makeshift walls, and that white fans would turn out in droves to see black superstars. He barnstormed in the United States and in the Caribbean alongside Dizzy Dean, Bob Feller, and other Caucasian champions, winning them over to him and to the notion that Negro Leaguers could really play ball. He drew the spotlight first to himself, then to his all-black Kansas City Monarchs team, and inevitably to the Monarchs' rookie second baseman, Jackie Robinson.

The truth is that Satchel Paige had been hacking away at Jim Crow decades before the world got to know Jackie Robinson. Satchel laid the groundwork for Jackie the way A. Philip Randolph, W.E.B. DuBois, and other early civil rights leaders did for Martin Luther

King, Jr. Paige was as much a poster boy for black baseball as Louis "Satchmo" Armstrong was for black music and Paul Robeson was for the black stage—and much as those two became symbols of their art in addition to their race, so Satchel was known not as a great black pitcher but as a great pitcher. In the process Satchel Paige, more than anyone, opened to blacks the national pastime and forever changed his sport and this nation.

CONTENTS

CHRONOLOGY

JULY 7, 1906: Leroy Robert Paige is born in Mobile, Alabama.

1912: Enrolls at all-black W. H. Council School.

1918: Sentenced to Alabama Reform School for Juvenile Negro Law-Breakers.

1923: Released from reform school.

1924: Starts pitching for semi-professional Mobile Tigers.

1926: Signs with first professional team, the Chattanooga White Sox, with stint at end of season for the New Orleans Black Pelicans.

1927: Leaves Chattanooga for the Birmingham Black Barons, his first team in the black Majors. He stays for parts of four seasons.

1929: Plays winter ball with Cuba's Santa Clara Leopards.

1930: Joins the Baltimore Black Sox, then rejoins Birmingham.

1931: Plays for the Nashville Elite Giants and Cleveland Cubs before joining the Pittsburgh Crawfords for first of six seasons.

1931: Pitches first season in the California Winter League, where he will return for eight winters during the 1930s and '40s.

1933: Joins Bismarck, North Dakota, team for part of season, and comes back two years later.

1933: First of two brief baseball tours in Venezuela.

1934: Pitches for House of David team at Denver Post Tournament.

1934: Marries Janet Howard in Pittsburgh.

1934: His all-stars play Dizzy Dean's in what becomes long-running rivalry.

1937: Plays for President Trujillo's Dragones team in the Dominican Republic.

1937: Back in the United States, he forms the Trujillo All-Stars, which become the Satchel Paige All-Stars.

1938: Pitches for Agrario team in Mexico City, where he injures shoulder.

1939: Joins the Kansas City Monarchs' traveling team, one of a dozen seasons associated with the Monarchs.

1939: Pitches first of two winters in Puerto Rico, for the Guayama Witches.

1940: Marries Lucy Figueroa in Guayama, winter of 1940–41.

1943: Divorces Janet Howard.

1946: His all-stars play big barnstorming series against Bob Feller's.

1947: Marries Lahoma Brown in Hays, Kansas.

MID-1940s: Forges twenty-year tie to Harlem Globetrotters, playing against and for their baseball team, serving as player-manager, then doing PR for basketball team.

1948: Signed by Bill Veeck to pitch for the Cleveland Indians, his first season in white Majors.

1948: His and Lahoma's first child, Pamela Jean, is born.

1951: Signs with the St. Louis Browns for first of three seasons.

1956: Joins the Miami Marlins and stays three seasons.

1965: Pitches three innings for the Kansas City A's, his last stint in Majors.

1960s: Plays for the Indianapolis Clowns, Portland Beavers, Peninsula Pilots, and other teams.

1968: Begins two-year association with the Atlanta Braves.

1971: Inducted into Baseball Hall of Fame.

JUNE 8, 1982: Dies in Kansas City.

AUTHOR'S NOTE

I made a tactical decision on terminology after consulting with aging African American baseball players: I use the terms *Negro* and *colored* when writing about the eras when that was what they called themselves. I switch to *black* when that expression began to be used.

I quote people I interviewed in the present tense, and use the past tense with those whose words come from earlier writings and recordings.

SATCHEL

CHAPTER 1

Coming Alive

*"I was no different from any other kid,
only in Mobile I was a nigger kid."*

SATCHEL PAIGE ENTERED THE WORLD as Leroy Robert Page. He was delivered at home into the hands of a midwife, which was more help than most poor families could afford in 1906 in Mobile, Alabama. His mother, Lula, was a washerwoman who already spent her nights worrying how to feed and sustain the four daughters and two sons who had come before. Five more would follow. Leroy's father, John, alternated between the luxuriant lilies in the gardens he tended uptown and the corner stoops on which he liked to loiter, rarely making time to care for his expanding brood. With skin the shade of chestnut and a birthplace in the heartland of the former Confederacy, the newborn's prospects looked woeful. They were about to get worse.

The hurricane that battered Mobile Bay just two months after Leroy's birth started with two days of torrential rains carried in on the back of a driving northeast wind. By the next morning ten-foot-high surges had dispatched oyster and fishing vessels to the bottom of the sea. Tornado-like squalls ripped from their roots southern pines, blew tin roofs off Greek Revival homes, and made it look as if birds were flying backward. At historic Christ Church only the choir

loft was left standing. The lucky escaped by fleeing to third-floor at-
tics or climbing tall trees; 150 others were consigned to watery
graves. One area hit especially hard was the Negro slum known as
Down the Bay, where the Pages lived.

Their home was a four-room shack called a shotgun, because a
shot fired through the front door would exit straight out the back.
That is the path storm waters took when they burst through Down
the Bay's alleys on the way to more fashionable quarters. Rental units
like the Pages' were ramshackle and fragile, with no flood walls to
protect them from the nearby sea and no electricity to ease their recovery. The Page cottage remained standing but the thin mattresses
the children shared and their few furnishings needed airing out.
That cleanup would have to wait: Lula's white employers insisted
she be at their homes early the next morning to mop up the storm
damage. The kids would wait, too, the way they did every day when
Mama headed to work, with the older ones watching over baby Leroy
and the rest of the young ones.

Leroy's world was being reshaped in another way that would mark
him even more profoundly. Mobile historically was a center of the
slave trade and the destination for the last slave ship to America, but
Alabama's oldest city also was home to more than a thousand blacks
who bought or were granted their freedom in the antebellum era.
That paradox was consistent with the coastal city's push toward the
conservative state of which it was part and its pull to a more tolerant
world beyond its shores. For more than two hundred years Mobile
had welcomed outsiders—Irish Catholics fleeing the famine, Jewish
merchants, Yankees and English, along with legions of Creoles, the
free offspring of French or Spanish fathers and chattel mothers—and
they in turn challenged inbred thinking on everything from politics
to race. The result, during the Reconstruction period, was a blurring
of color lines in ways unthinkable in Montgomery, Selma, and most
of the rest of Alabama. Jim Crow—the system of segregation named
after a cowering slave in an 1820s minstrel show—was there in Mobile, but so was Booker T. Washington's gospel of black self-help.
The races were separated on trolleys and in other public settings, but
the separation was done by tradition more than law. Blacks not only
could vote for officeholders, a few even held political office. Paternal-
ism more than meanness defined how whites treated Mobile's 18,000
black citizens.

Unfortunately for Leroy, that live-and-let-live mind-set had begun fraying by the turn of the century and it unraveled entirely the very season of his birth. The reforms of Reconstruction were collapsing across the South, as whites who wielded power in the fallen Confederacy began to reinvent the realm and tear down Negroes' new freedoms. The brief postwar honeymoon of racial coexistence survived longer in Mobile than in most of the South, but the backlash finally came there, too. An ordinance mandated separate seating on streetcars. Blacks were barred from most restaurants, cemeteries, saloons, hotels, and brothels. Whites and blacks were not allowed to attend the same school, marry one another, or live together. And in the wake of the devastating September hurricane, Mobile's most influential newspaper stirred up reader resentment with its account of Negroes looting the homes of dead Caucasians and mutilating their bodies.

The rising tensions turned violent on October 6, 1906, when two black men accused in separate rapes of young white girls were being transported by train back to Mobile from protective custody in Birmingham. Forty-five vigilantes with masks and rifles boarded the train, took custody of the accused, and hanged them from a tree in the community of Plateau, just north of Mobile. As word of the killings spread, three thousand spectators, many arriving by streetcar, paraded by the black men's limp bodies. Some snapped photographs. Others stole bits of the prisoners' garments and cut souvenir segments from their noose. The double lynching ushered in four years of racist mobocracy in Mobile County. In 1907 Moses Dorsett, a Negro accused of raping an elderly white woman, was seized by a white mob and strung up fifty yards from the 1906 gallows. Two years later masked men snatched from the county jail a black inmate charged with killing a sheriff's deputy, hanging the wounded man from an oak tree across from Mobile's oldest church. This lynching stripped away any pretense that mob actions were confined to rural areas or resisted by law enforcers. It happened in the heart of the city, two blocks from the main police station, and investigators later established that the jail had been left unlocked.

Lest anyone doubt their meaning, the lynchers left behind notes. "Negroes must be taught that death will always follow attacks on white women," one warned, while another advised, "There [are] plenty of ropes and trees left." Blacks did not need the reminders.

Many church and lay leaders from the Negro community had already gone, heading north or to larger cities in the South. Between 1910 and 1920, blacks' share of Mobile's population fell from 44 to 39 percent. While most had to stay, increasingly the city seemed less an oasis and more like the rest of Dixie. The Ku Klux Klan operated freely. Negroes disappeared from public offices and from voting rolls. In commerce, blacks were supplicants, whites selective benefactors. Less than two generations after the end of two centuries of slavery, liberation looked less like freedom than serfdom.

Leroy Page was too young to understand those developments but they were reinforced every day he spent in his native city. While record keepers used *Colored* to denote the city's dark-skinned residents, the label used by most whites started with *n*. Those first few years "I was no different from any other kid," Leroy wrote half a century on, "only in Mobile I was a nigger kid. I went around with the back of my shirt torn, a pair of dirty diapers or raggedy pieces of trousers covering me. Shoes? They was someplace else." At a too-young age, he added, "I found out what it was like to be a Negro in Mobile."

Lula and John had always known. John Page was at least a second-generation Mobilian. While he was born fourteen years after what many southern whites called the War of Northern Aggression, and he lived through the more hopeful years of Reconstruction, his ancestors almost certainly were dragooned in Africa and brought to America in shackles. John wed Lula when he was seventeen and began married life as a day laborer, which meant hoping he would be hired by white home owners or contractors for jobs ranging from hauling trash to laying bricks. Later he turned to gardening, although he preferred to be called a landscaper. Unemployed landscaper would have been more accurate. His kids saw less of him than they wanted and needed. Lula loved him but knew not to count on him or to argue with him when he was drinking. Still, she was proud that he never laid a hand on her.

Lula Coleman Page was almost four years older than her husband and would outlive him by more than forty years. As inattentive as John was, Lula was a present and steady figure in Leroy's young life and those of his siblings. She raised and supported them. She taught them when to yield to their harsh surroundings and when to fight.

She gave Leroy the love he seldom felt from his father and the certainty he could count on her. None of that was easy given how many other children she had asking for those same things. And none of it was done explicitly; she showed the way through her own struggle to get by.

Lula was pregnant close to half the time over a twenty-two-year stretch starting in September of 1894, nearly two years before she married John. Ellen was her first child, and like the rest she was delivered at home with no thought of a high-priced doctor or hospital. Three years later came Ruth, and the year after that John Jr. Julia was Lula's first baby in the new century; she celebrated by naming the child after her mother, who was born a slave and was one of their few ancestors whose stories were passed on to Leroy and his siblings. There were two more children—Wilson and Emma Lee—before Leroy Robert made his entry in 1906. He had five younger siblings: the twins, Palestine and Eugene, then Clarence, another Lula, and, in 1917, the twelfth and last, Inez.

That averages out to a baby every twenty-two months, which made it a challenge to keep track of who was who in the family. Leroy himself often failed to include Eugene when he listed his brothers and sisters, either because there were so many of them or because Eugene died at birth. There was confusion every time U.S. Census takers visited the Page household, with ages and other answers not quite dovetailing with the children's birth certificates. Some discrepancies were legitimate, given that Lula could not read or write, add or subtract. Others seemed whimsical. She forgot not just when her acclaimed son Leroy was born but where he fit in the birth order. Discretion might have been the motivation when John and Lula's marriage was described as predating rather than following Ellen's birth. Leroy, who got from Lula more than he acknowledged of his wit and his aphorisms, did credit her for one illuminating maxim: "If you tell a lie, always rehearse it. If it don't sound good to you, it won't sound good to anybody else."

Being full-time mother to her eleven surviving children should have been more than a full-time job, but Lula could not afford the indulgence. John did not earn nearly enough to feed all those babies, so Lula took jobs she variously described as washerwoman, laundress, and domestic. All amounted to the same things: scrubbing spotless the homes of wealthy white families; using blue bleach along with red-hot water to clean their clothes, a smoothing iron to remove wrinkles from blouses and dresses, and starch to firm up shirt collars; and helping with the cooking. Later, when her own children were older, she sometimes took home the washing and ironing, setting up a boiling pot and rubbing board in the front yard.

Domestic labor like that must have reminded Lula of her mother's life during slavery. The plantation was in many ways a simpler society, with clearer rules and relationships. In Lula's day, even work as uncontroversial as a maid's could raise racial hackles. "I don't see why Mobile people shouldn't have three meals a day, as they do in other cities all over the country," a white woman complained to the *Mobile Register* in a 1912 article on the "servant problem." "As it is, we have to beg the cook to give us two meals a day, and at night everybody has to eat scraps. Between meals, we have no servant to answer the door bell and the telephone. I think that all servants should be employed for a full day's work." Black leaders rallied to the white cause, vowing to set up training programs to clarify the duties as well as set the wages of domestics and bring the "best class of servants in touch with the best class of employers."

Lula's wages of fifty cents a day helped feed her brood. Leroy never missed a meal, although it was more likely to be cereal, greens, and water than chicken, beef, or milk. Lula stood at the head of the table ladling out each spoonful to the dozen or so bowls set in front of her. When there was not money enough for store food the boys were sent down to the bay where the fish were always biting. "It was poverty-stricken living," Leroy would say later, "before I knew what that meant."

What he and his siblings did know by the age of six was that they had to pitch in. They also understood where, as young Negroes, they could safely work or play. Bienville Square, Mobile's oldest public park with its gnarled oaks and iron fountain, was off-limits. So were the choicest beaches along the gulf, seats near the front of streetcars, and any public accommodation that was not labeled "Colored." Everyone knew which days of the week the Sisters of Charity dispensary cared for Negroes and which were whites only. It was okay for black boys to walk or play in back alleys or on city streets, especially those south of magnolia-shaded Government Street. Librarians winked at the strictures of segregation; police and judges did not.

Guessing wrong could land a sepia-skinned adolescent in the lockup or even the morgue. Asking whether a racial reform tried elsewhere might work here drew this refrain: "This is Mobile and we don't do that." Before long no one bothered to ask.

Leroy worked the alleyways like a pro, collecting and cashing in empty bottles he found there. A half-pint could fetch a penny; four cents for a quart. Delivering ice, a valued commodity in steamy Mobile, also brought in small change. Leroy was springing up like a weed in a bog, and as he grew so did Lula's and John's expectations of his earning power. The obvious place to look for work was the nearby L&N Station, where five separate railroads provided passenger service. Rail depots were a bonanza for Negroes back then. Black redcaps hoisted trunks onto and off the trains. Black Pullman porters served as chambermaids and shoe shines, nursemaids and valets. Black chefs and waiters offered seatside service of sugar-cured ham, Welsh rarebit, and 131 other culinary delights fit for New York's finest eateries, while black firemen shoveled wood and coal to feed forever-hungry locomotives. And black youths like Leroy jumped when wealthy white travelers snapped their fingers in the air, polishing their boots or carrying bags to hotels like Mobile's luxurious Battle House for as little as a dime or as much as a quarter.

Leroy was the quickest among the pint-size porters, but he soon realized that he could not bring home a real day's pay if he made just ten cents at a time. So he got a pole and some rope and jury-rigged a contraption that let him sling together two, three, or four satchels and cart them all at once. His invention quadrupled his income to forty cents a load. It also drew chuckles from the other baggage boys. "You look like a walking satchel tree," one of them yelled. The description fit him to a tee and it stuck. "LeRoy Paige," he said, "became no more and Satchel Paige took over."

Thus was born the most celebrated sobriquet in sports. Or so Satchel wrote in his 1962 autobiography. Fourteen years earlier, in his first memoir, it was string, not rope, that pulled the bags; his neck, shoulders, and waist rather than a pole that gave him traction; and sixteen satchels he carted instead of a mere four. Over the years he volunteered more versions, including telling a radio interviewer that he was first dubbed Satchel when he hung around the Mobile Bears' ballpark collecting beat-up balls and broken bats. He brought his defective equipment to the schoolyard in a bag and "they started to call me 'Satchel.' " Even his spelling of the moniker shifted, some-times putting a second *l* in Satchel the same casual way he occasion-ally capitalized the *r* in Leroy. Relatives, friends, and sportswriters offered up their own etymologies. His real handle was Satchelfoot and grew out of his suitcase–size 14 feet, reporters insisted, even as Satchel insisted that his shoes were mere 11-AAAs. The tag was pinned on him by his family, said sister Palestine, after he borrowed his daddy's old tote bag—or was it his mama's suitcase?

There is one last explanation of why Satchel was called that since he was a boy—not because he toted suitcases, but because he swiped them. A man whose case he stole chased him, retrieved the bag, and gave young Leroy a hard slap across the face. "That's when I named him Satchel, right on that day," Wilbur Hines, a boyhood friend who said he witnessed the theft, recounted in 1991, two years before his death and nine years after Satchel's. Hines was Leroy's neighbor in Mobile and his story is consistent with Satchel's youthful behavior and with his adult determination to shape his own legend. But Satchel not only owned up to that stealing, it would become a rivet-ing chapter in his saga of rising above his roots. Why would he, as Hines claimed, have been embarrassed by this most gripping of all narratives?

No government record can unravel the mystery over his epithet the way it did over his age, which is just the way Satchel would have wanted it. In the end everyone connected with his life claimed a part in his naming. Each version, no matter how fanciful, adds to our un-derstanding of Leroy and Satchel. Wherever the nickname came from, it caught on. Only Lula, who brought him into the world, and later Bill Veeck, who brought him to the Major Leagues, persisted in calling him Leroy. To everyone else he was Satchel. Or just Satch.

But then why worry about the wellspring or even the spelling of a first name when your family name would be remade—Page to Paige—and the justification for that change would itself change? The modification was made just before Satchel launched his baseball career. "Page looked too much like page in a book," said Lula. Satchel had a more exotic explanation: "My folks started out by spelling their name 'Page' and later stuck in the 'i' to make them-selves sound more high-tone." Whatever the reason, the result would be to make it difficult to track down the records on Satchel's

birth, letting him spin out the mystery over his age and keep prying
reporters at bay.

Lula and John enrolled Satchel in the blacks-only W. H. Council
School at the required age of six, as they had their six older children.
He arrived just as Mobile's black leaders were emerging from a
decade-long debate over the mission for their segregated schools.
Booker T. Washington and his followers argued that industrial training was the only practical way for blacks to better themselves; others
dreamed of a liberal arts education that would equip young Negroes
to attend college and, while they dared not say this aloud, to topple
Jim Crow. The debate proved academic since influential whites already had sided with Washington. The goal of Mobile's all-black
schools, as one Negro leader put it, would be to train "educated
helpers" for white-owned businesses. Such a limited vision, city fathers reasoned, required only limited resources, so they gave black
students broken-down buildings, bare-bones budgets for books and
other supplies, and just twenty teachers for a system with 1,600 students. That meant one instructor for every eighty Negro pupils.

Satchel was at school too seldom to notice the overcrowding.
Sometimes an empty stomach lured him to the waterfront with its
promise of a free fish dinner. The need to bring home money also
trumped the need for an education. All the Page children were
forced to grow up fast, feeling compelled to strike out on their own
and "to get married as soon as they could," says Leon Paige, Satchel's
nephew. Ellen, Satchel's oldest sister, was so eager to wed that she
lied on her marriage license, saying she was the legally required age
of eighteen when she was just sixteen. Wilson and Inez likewise inflated their ages when they married.

Lula herself had been barely twenty on her wedding day and had
never attended school. Yet she saw education as the route for her
children to escape Down the Bay, and she took to heart Sunday ser-
mons at Mount Zion Baptist denouncing truancy and encouraging
parents to take a firm hand with renegade children. Satchel, who attended church even less often than school, remembered one time
when Lula caught him and Wilson playing hooky. No sooner did
they reach the baseball field than someone shouted, "Here comes
your ma." The boys took cover the only place they could: in a huge
pipe. Lula couldn't see them and she was too sore to stoop down and

peer into the conduit, but she sensed they were there and knew how to find out. Collecting papers and rags, she lit a fire at one end of the pipe. Satchel and Wilson dashed out the other end, gagging, and found themselves in her firm grip. "Have you learned your lesson, boys?" she asked as she marched them home. "Yes, Ma," they said in succession.

Another lesson Satchel took away from his school years was the joy of baseball. There were no independent youth leagues then, black or white; America's first Little League game was a generation away, and it would be two generations before black adolescents got their shot. But Mobile was a baseball town whose subtropical climate made it possible to play the game year-round, while its passion for playing made it Alabama's only city to allow Sunday ball. Seven days a week kids like Satchel took to the streets looking for enough space to make a field and enough other kids to cobble together two teams. Temperatures topping 100 and humidity nearly as high may have kept their parents rocking quietly on their porches, sipping sugared tea or hand-squeezed lemonade, but it was not enough to sideline these youthful ballplayers. Many learned to hit and pitch playing "top ball," where a stick replaced the bat they could not afford and soda bottle caps substituted for baseballs. "I can still see him as a little boy," said his sister Palestine, who was five years younger. "He had a sun hat, a ball and bat." Lula had similar memories of baseball becoming Satchel's escape and obsession: "Why, he'd rather play baseball than eat. It was always baseball, baseball."

They played just off Davis Avenue, the main thoroughfare in black Mobile and the namesake of the first president of the Confederacy, Jefferson Davis. Ted Radcliffe, a catcher and pitcher who grew up near the Pages, remembers that even the disappearing daylight did not stop intrepid young baseballers like Satchel and him. "We'd make cotton balls and soak them in oil and play night ball," said Radcliffe. "We'd light them and run like hell."

Satchel got his first taste of how good a ballplayer he could be at the Council School. Most elementary schools had teams in that era, although the youngest kids generally spent more time watching than playing. Not so with Satchel. The coach put him in when he was a mere eight years old, pairing him against boys two or three years his senior. He was gaunt and gangly then in a way that reminded people of an ostrich or a crane. He would later claim that he had played each of the nine positions, sometimes all in the same game. "If I'd pitch the whole game I'd strike out seventeen and eighteen with nothin' but speed," he said. "I was under 10 years old strikin' out everybody." He soon became known around the South Side of Mobile as the best school-age pitcher anyone had ever seen. It was partly how hard he threw and partly how artfully. When kids came to the plate and he surprised them with his slow pitch, he said, "they just wet their pants or cried. That's how scared they were of my speed."

While baseball would become his vocation, another childhood passion—fishing—also lasted a lifetime. A dropline or makeshift pole would do, especially during Mobile Bay Jubilee, that magical moment when blue crabs, shrimp, flounder, stingray, and eels abandoned the bay's thirty-five-foot-deep sea and made shallow waters along the shore boil with life. Firemen and police blared their sirens, a sign that the fish were jumping high as a tree, and Satchel headed for the beach with washtubs and croaker sacks to hold his catch. One challenge was keeping away the gnats: smearing dirt on his face helped. Another problem was remembering the many parts of the bay that were whites-only: shouts of "Get out of here, you no-good nigger!" reminded him.

His fascination with fishing was inspired partly by the joy of eating crabs, catfish, and shrimp. He also loved the serenity of the sea, a getaway from the frenetic city and his squalid slum. On the way there he walked under live oaks covered with Spanish moss and reached up to touch the cast-iron balconies of Spanish-style homes. Moisture made the shorefront air softer and swept away the smells of hemp and tar. By the hour he hung over a bridge and puffed on a cigarette, his brown eyes focused on the ocean. Close in were rows of long, flat piers and beyond that steamships and schooners sailing to what Satchel imagined were exotic ports of call, places where skin color did not count for everything. No need even to fish on afternoons like these.

Hunting offered a different sort of escape. He had no guns then, and no need for them. He could bring down a butterfly with a clamshell, nail a squirrel with a rock using his catching hand rather than his throwing one, or make a lasting impression on an adversary's backside with a brick, stone, or pebble. That precision and power made him special and kept him safe. One time he was ambling down the railroad tracks heading home from his job as a baggage porter. In his fist was a pile of rocks, in the air a pheasant. As it flew by he aimed and fired. Dead bird. Another pheasant, another whiplike release of a stone, a second direct hit. Quietly watching were four white men carrying shotguns. Seeing them too late to retreat, Satchel feared he might become their quarry. "You mean to tell me you killed those birds with rocks?" the first hunter asked, incredulous. "You ought to be a baseball player."

Real enemies were not hard to find for Satchel, especially when he was with his South Siders. Their path took them by a white school where a gang was always waiting. When Satchel and his crew got close the rocks started flying. The whites were older and looked like Goliaths, with Satchel relishing the role of David. "I crippled up a lot of them," he recalled. "Most people need shotguns to do what I did with those rocks. . . . Those fights helped me forget what I didn't have. They made me a big man in the neighborhood instead of just some more trash."

Rock throwing also gave birth to what would become one of the most controversial and deceptive deliveries in baseball: the hesitation pitch. When he aimed a brick at a rival gang member, his adversary would instinctively duck. Knowing that, Satchel stopped mid-delivery, catching his foe stooped over in a posture that made him easy prey. The misleading motion worked equally well when he was armed with a baseball. At the top of a painfully deliberate stretch he paused longer than normal, arms high above his head, then thrust his left foot forward. He paused again—slowing but not stopping—as he whipped his arm and sent the ball flying. The result: batters swung at shadows long before the baseball itself arrived.

The brick and rock throwing may have helped his image in the alley and the ballpark, but it did not fly at home. Lula had a low tolerance for brawling and she hit harder than any of his street adversaries. "I used to think she'd hit me because she didn't know how I felt. She didn't know how it was when they told me I couldn't swim where the white folks did. Then I realized maybe she did," he said. "I guess she learned to live with it."

Sometimes Satchel told himself the fights and other troubles were his ways of not living with it, of battling back—against poverty, against Jim Crow, against being robbed of a real childhood. In later moments of candor he acknowledged that it was a game. He was good at outfoxing or outrunning his white antagonists and the police. Like all boys that age, he felt he was invincible. So why not pick a fight? He always had time for trouble.

At school he was absent so often that the Page home became a regular stop on the truant officers' rounds. At the L&N Station he stopped pulling and started purloining suitcases. He stole bicycles, too, along with anything else that was easy to grab. One night in 1918, walking home after dark, he passed a five-and-dime store with an alluring display of gold-colored bands and red and green stones. In he went and, when he thought no one was looking, he stuffed a fistful of the trinkets into his pocket. "Unless you've gone around with nothing," he would explain afterward, "you don't know how powerful a lure some new, shiny stuff is."

Unluckily for Satchel, a burly security guard saw him pocket the loot, nabbed him, and dragged him to police headquarters. That night the authorities released him to Lula. It would be his last night home for more than five years and would mark the end of his boyhood. The next day there was a hearing before a truant officer he called Mrs. Meanie. She was armed with a long list of infractions Satchel thought had escaped notice, from fistfights to skipping school to stealing to not listening to her repeated warnings. He thought she would never finish. She thought he would never listen and would end up on the trash heap that consumed so many black boys from Mobile. Her last words pronounced his punishment: confinement until the age of eighteen at the state reform school.

"No!" Lula screamed. Satchel was shaking so hard he could not say anything. Just two weeks before he had celebrated his twelfth birthday. Now he was being told he would not see freedom again for six long years. It seemed like a bad dream until they shut the door on him. That is when he knew it was real.

IT WAS A BLEAK ARRANGEMENT of timber and concrete buildings. A dormitory with 120 beds for 240 boys. Two small cemeteries with a handful of gravestones. A dairy barn and silo rose up before hundreds of acres of scrupulously sowed cow beans and corn, sweet potatoes, pumpkins, and pecans. The sign out front said ALABAMA

REFORM SCHOOL FOR JUVENILE NEGRO LAW-BREAKERS. That was the only marker of the callow lives trying to sort themselves out behind the whitewashed walls.

When Satchel was dropped off on a steamy July morning in 1918, he had on his only pair of dungarees. His shirt was frayed, his black shoes scuffed. The rest of his possessions were stuffed into a paper bag cradled under his long arm. He had little notion what lay ahead but he knew enough to be scared.

The reformatory was not what he expected. The public image of the all-black institution in Mount Meigs, just outside Montgomery, was of a pint-size prison with barbed-wire fences, rock-tough wardens, and underage but hard-bitten inmates laboring in the fields from sunrise to sundown. That was what Alabama's adult prisons were like then, especially for segregated Negro convicts, and it is a lot like today's highest-security facility at Mount Meigs. That steely picture surely was in Satchel's head as he heard Mrs. Meanie render her verdict, and she did her best to reinforce it.

In truth, Mount Meigs was as much an orphanage as a prison. While many of its wards did, like Satchel, have run-ins with the law, others were just having tough times at home or had no home. Buildings were without bars. The 380-acre campus had neither walls nor fences. "We was free to go, you could go out, run away, go anywhere you wanted," Satchel recalled. The institution was the invention not of white penal officials who saw young black lawbreakers as subhuman. They were happy to continue sentencing the youths to adult prisons. It was the brainchild of the Alabama Federation of Colored Women's Clubs, which opened the school in 1907 to "reform wayward Negro boys." The reformatory was part of the parallel black universe being erected across the South during that Jim Crow era. Denied entry to the dominant white world, blacks built their own network of funeral parlors and stores, churches, schools, and homes like Mount Meigs for wayward boys. Even after the state took the facility over in 1911, the staff stayed all black and ladies from the Colored Women's Clubs kept serving as trustees and benefactors.

Having grown up deep within Mobile's South Side slum, in a shack shared with his ten brothers and sisters and two parents, Satchel appreciated any comfort. It did not seem a hardship that he had to share his bed with another boy. The reformatory gave him more food than he was used to, with more clothes, warmth, and space. The school also was his only vestige of home. While other parents or grandparents visited often, his did seldom if ever. It is understandable why Lula, who had a brood of children in Mobile and no automobile, would have had a difficult time making the two-hundred-mile trip to Mount Meigs. But try telling that to a twelve-year-old who was feeling abandoned.

Satchel tried out for the choir and had a voice so vibrant and resonant that he rose to be its leader. He made the drum and bugle corps. He did work hard, coaxing milk from cows, picking cotton, and helping construct new buildings, yet for at least half the year his daily routine also included ciphering, reading, and other lessons he would have gotten in elementary school. He did not like the school at Mount Meigs any better than the one in Mobile, but there was no playing hooky this time. In spite of himself, some of the learning was sinking in. While his days were full and tiring, evenings were for singing, band practice, and, starting in 1920, looking for an excuse to talk to Minnie Young, Ida B. Sanderson, and the other girls who had just arrived on campus.

Then there was baseball. More of it than he had seen or played at his school in Mobile or on sandlots. There was a coach, too, Edward Byrd, who for the first time taught Satchel the fundamentals, and for the first time Satchel paid attention. Byrd's young protégé had an anatomy that was all up and down. Rising more than six feet and weighing barely 140 pounds, Satchel joked that if he stood sideways you could not see him. His wiry arms and stiltlike legs were aerodynamically perfect to propel a ball from mound to plate. They gave him motion. Momentum. Strength. And he had the ideal launching pads: hands so huge they made a baseball look like a golf ball, with wrists that snapped with the fury and flash of a catapult. Byrd understood what God had given this manful boy with his outsize appetites, limbs, and talents, and the coach was determined that it not be squandered. He showed Satchel exactly how to exploit his storehouse of kinetic energy. The first thing was to kick his foot so high before unleashing the baseball that it blacked out the sky and befuddled the batter. Then the novice pitcher swung his arm far enough forward that it seemed like his hand was right in the batter's face when he let go of the ball. So was born the Paige pose, the look that over the decades made Satchel stand out from pitchers before and after: left leg held skyward, right arm stretched as far as it would go behind him, the catapult cocked to give the ball maximum power as he whirled forward to release it.

Coach Byrd earned his living first as a janitor, then as a salesman at a drugstore, but he made his mark helping shape young athletes at the reformatory. He was precisely the sort of instructor the Colored Women's Clubs had in mind. Baseball coaches cannot manufacture genius but the best of them, ones like Byrd, know how to nurture, embolden, and salute it when they discover aptitude like he saw in Satchel. His coach showed him that physical gifts were not all it took to win. Satchel had to outwit his opponent. Watch a batter's knees, Byrd advised, the way a bullfighter studies a bull. Detect any weakness in the setup of his feet, his stance, the positioning of his bat. Then put the ball where the slugger can't hit it.

Satchel was better at doing that than anyone who had ever come through the Mount. It was less his accuracy, more his velocity. He threw hard. No curveball or slider, no change of pace or special finesse. Not yet. Oftentimes he almost fell off the mound as he was letting go of the ball. He was as wild as young and untamed pitchers often are. Sometimes his pitches hit a batter, or several. However unconventional his demeanor, he delivered. A baseball weighs just five ounces—it is a mass of cork wound with woolen yarn and bound in cowhide—but flying off of Satchel's fingers it resembled a cannonball. Most who came to the plate failed to connect by what looked like a mile. And he kept getting better, the way Coach Byrd said he could.

Tutelage like Satchel was getting on the ball field was just one aspect of a fantastic social experiment under way at Mount Meigs even if he never knew it, and if the architect of the experiment died three years before Satchel arrived. It started with the Federation of Colored Women's Clubs, which saw the reformatory as a way to "give to the State of Alabama better citizens, and give to our race a better name." The formula for doing that came from America's best-known Negro educator, Booker T. Washington, whose base of operations was the nearby all-black Tuskegee Institute.

At the moment the Mount was founded in 1907, Washington was waging a fierce war with W.E.B. DuBois for the leadership of black

America. Washington preached an economic avenue to advancement, arguing that if Negroes became disciplined and skilled workers they could achieve far more than by working to directly uproot a firmly planted framework of Jim Crow. DuBois said Washington had it backward: securing the vote and other civil rights was the only way for Negroes to prosper and be free. DuBois would test his theories at the NAACP and other organizations he helped launch. Washington tried his out on everyone from Negro businessmen in Mobile to the all-black legion of Pullman porters, but nowhere were his precepts applied more consistently and fervently than with the law-breaking boys at Mount Meigs.

The reform school was started by disciples of Washington. He persuaded Tuskegee trustees to donate money and he dispatched teams of advisers from his institute, which trained teachers. After Washington died in 1915, his wife, Margaret, used her post as president of the Federation of Colored Women's Clubs to open a Girls Rescue Home on the Mount Meigs campus and raise funds for the boys' school. The Washingtons' most lasting influence on the reformatory was spelling out just what it meant to reform wayward youths.

Hard work was the centerpiece. The boys learned to build the bricks and pour the cement they would need to erect dormitories, a dairy barn, a silo, and half a dozen other structures at the school. They became experts in raising livestock and growing vegetables, producing almost everything they ate. Surplus corn, cotton, and hay brought in cash. "Think what it means for these ignorant and degraded negro boys to form the habit of caring for cows and keeping a dairy stable," researchers invited in by Governor Charles Henderson wrote soon after Satchel arrived. The boys knew enough reading and writing that they could prepare reports with titles such as "Every Day Pruning the Farmer Should Know." While such practical training was critical, so too, the Washingtons believed, was catering to the spirit. Religious services were held on Sundays, special occasions, and "in case of serious illness." The boys also did anything Washington and his acolytes thought might curry favor in Alabama's halls of power, including assembling a dozen Christmas wreaths for the wife of the governor.

Satchel was an object lesson for the Washington philosophy of self-reliance. He arrived at the Mount in 1918 with just six years of schooling, most of that sporadic and unfocused. He had come there because neither the authorities nor his parents knew what else to do with him. He left in 1923 secure in his letters, numbers, and know-how on throwing a baseball, which was just the sort of utilitarian training that Booker T. Washington advocated. He was learning to harness his arm, using it to play a game that would become his career. He acquired discipline. His five years as a ward of the state also disentangled him from what he called the bums that he had befriended in Mobile. He spent much less energy now blaming his bad fortune on his skin color, even when discrimination was responsible for holding him back, and he discovered that he loved to sing and tap the drums. While he likely never met the ladies of the Colored Women's Clubs, he took to heart their philosophy of using head, heart, and hands to make it in a world where whites ran everything from toy stores to ball teams. For the first time Satchel thought about the future and for the first time his future did not seem quite so desperate. The reform school was impressed enough with his progress that it paroled him on December 31, 1923, six months before his legally mandated release at age eighteen. "Inmate," Mount Meigs officials wrote in the only surviving document on him, "has an excellent record at this institution."

Satchel walked away such an apostle of the Tuskegee philosophy that he later claimed to have studied at the college, which he did not. "Those five and a half years there did something for me—they made a man out of me. If I'd been left on the streets of Mobile to wander with those kids I'd been running around with, I'd of ended up as a big bum, a crook," he said decades later. "You might say I traded five years of freedom to learn how to pitch."

THE MOBILE SATCHEL returned to in 1923 was full of optimism. The Great War had been good to the city, expanding Alabama's only deepwater port and making Mobile a trading hub for products as varied as lumber, tractors, and blackstrap molasses. Mardi Gras was back after a wartime siesta, as was the city's reputation as the Little Easy. It was less commercial and more free-spirited than its Big Easy neighbor to the west, New Orleans. Mobile joyfully embraced prostitution and intoxication and disdained the old evangelist Sam

Jones, who a generation earlier had declared, "I'd be a stockbroker in hell before I'd be a director of a Mardi Gras . . . [where] men are drunk and carousing on the streets and girls go about in men's clothing." Keep it up, Jones admonished Mobilians, and "your city will be damned eternally."

What damnation there was afflicted Negroes and came in the form of Jim Crow, a black slave played by a white minstrel performer. Crow's name came to embody the amalgam of Southern statutes and customs that grew up during Reconstruction, formalizing separation of the races everywhere from public bathrooms to baseball diamonds. It also became shorthand for a racist way of life. By either definition Jim Crow had gotten more firmly entrenched in Mobile while Satchel was at Mount Meigs. Davis Avenue, the city's black Broadway, was alive with black-owned businesses like Owl Drug and black churches featuring gospel groups like the Dixie Spiritual Singers. But Negroes were as unwelcome as ever in the antebellum mansions lining Government Street and in much of the city's downtown district. Even after fighting for their country in the trenches of France, black men had to endure the indignity of whites addressing them as "uncle." Black children were issued toothbrushes and instructions on basic hygiene as soon as they enrolled in school. No sooner did he return to his birthplace than Satchel was reminded that everything in the South gets back to the Negro.

Lula let him relax and celebrate his release from the reformatory for nearly a month before she reminded him that money was as scarce as ever in the Page household and he had better find work. Satchel knocked on doors, but anyone who knew he had been at the reformatory turned him down flat while others turned him down because they had no work to offer or he lacked the requisite skills. One afternoon he ended up at Eureka Gardens, where his older brother Wilson pitched for the semi-pro, all-black Mobile Tigers. Wilson was not there, but after watching other prospects try out, Satchel was sure he could measure up. A master of the first impression, he whistled in a few fast ones that "popped against the catcher's glove like they was firecrackers." Then he challenged the Tigers' skipper to pick up a bat, blowing ten pitches by him. "Do you throw that fast consistently?" the manager asked. "No, sir," Satchel answered. "I do it all the time."

Satchel was signed on the spot, with a fresh dollar bill sealing the deal. He was eighteen at the time, and this was his first job and first team. He quickly established himself as a standout for the Tigers, to the point where fellow players wanted to buy him drinks and "all the gals just wanted to be around, squealing and hanging on my arms." While he chalked up "a few" no-hitters, playing for a scrub team earned him just a dollar a game when fans turned out and a keg of lemonade when attendance was sparse.

Lemonade did not pay even Satchel's bills, much less Lula's, so he pitched not just for the Tigers but for any local team willing to pay. He also cut the grass and cleaned the grandstands where the all-white Mobile Bears played. One day several Bears challenged him to show what he could do, and, as always, he was delighted to oblige. The first batter swung and missed at three fastballs. All the second generated was a breeze. "We sure could use you," one of the players finally told him. "If only you were white."

The lament was familiar to Wilson "Paddlefoot" Page. With a nickname whose origin was beyond dispute—he had size-12 feet—this older brother was even faster than Satchel and could catch as well as pitch. Everyone in and out of the family agreed that Wilson could have been better than Satchel. "But he liked the girls. He didn't want to play ball," said Palestine. "He wanted to follow them dern girls." The truth is that Wilson loved pitching, catching, and playing ball generally, says his son Wilson Jr., who still lives in Mobile. But he was the more responsible and employable of the brothers, so when the family was in especially dire straits, Wilson gave up baseball and "stayed around to help support his mother . . . he did regret not continuing to play."

Most of Satchel's brothers and sisters managed in those difficult years to find work, none of it easy or lucrative. Ellen was a housekeeper. Ruth worked as a servant and later as a laundress like her mother. John Jr. was a laborer, then a helper, then a shipbuilder. Clarence worked as a clerk at Odom Grocery. Inez was a cook. Wilson did deliveries for a grocer, was a gardener like his father, dug graves at the majestic Magnolia Cemetery, and tried but failed to launch a company to clean up graveyards. Their jobs were not the only things shifting for Lula's family. They moved repeatedly, but always to a ramshackle rental and always within the narrow radius of

Down the Bay. Even the spelling of their surname hinted at instabil-
ity as it went back and forth between Page and Paige, finally settling
on the high-tone version with the *i*.

The new name coincided with the death of Satchel's father, and
may have signaled the family's yearning for a fresh start. John Page,
Sr., was barely forty-seven at the time; Satchel was nineteen. John
perished from what his death certificate called "acute deterioration of
health," a standard way of suggesting that he had abused his body
more than it could stand and that there was no time or money for a
more thorough postmortem. A contributing factor was a strangu-
lated hernia, which can starve the bowels of blood, kill tissue, and
cause intense pain as well as a dangerous infection. He was buried in
city-owned Cemetery 2, Square 2, Row 3, Grave 5. Directly across
the street is Magnolia Cemetery, the statued, meticulously maintained resting place for authors, statesmen, and 1,100 soldiers of the
Confederate States Army. Grounds for admission to John's graveyard
were but two: being a pauper and being black. There is no vault,
headstone, or other marker commemorating his death or his life.
Lula visited the cemetery regularly to pull away weeds and scoop together a pile of dirt where she recalled John's casket having been
lowered. "We'd take a hoe," says their grandson Leon Paige, "to
make a mound to indicate it was a grave."

Satchel said later that he had grown up without a real father, and
even as a child he promised he would never abandon his children
that way. There was one thing for which Satchel was thankful to
John. When the boy began playing baseball his father would ask,
"You want to be a baseball player 'stead of a landscaper?" You bet,
Satchel answered, at which point John would nod his head as if to
say, "That's okay by me."

By the time his father died Satchel was on the way to realizing
that ball-playing dream, building a success story that kept outstrip-
ping itself, especially in his retelling. In 1924, just a year out of
Mount Meigs, he won about thirty games and lost just once. That,
he said, was the start of a string of winning streaks. The next year
every team around wanted him. By midseason the following year,
1926, he strung together twenty-five wins in a row. Going for win
number twenty-six, something snagged: with a 1-0 lead in the
ninth, and two outs, his infield made three straight errors. The bases

were loaded and Satchel was fuming. The crowd began to hiss, which made him madder still. "Somebody was going to have to be showed up for that," he wrote afterward. "I waved in my outfielders. When they got in around me, I said, 'Sit down there on the grass right behind me. I'm pitching this last guy without an outfield.' ". He milked the situation the way he once did cows on the Mount, taking his time, pumping back and forth. Three pitches, three strikes, and a win preserved. It was his twenty-sixth straight victory and the crowd went wild. "You wouldn't think a few hundred could make that much noise. But they did."

That story, like others from those years with the Tigers, is impossible to verify. As far as white newspapers in Mobile were concerned, the city had no blacks, or none worth covering, even though Negroes made up 40 percent of the population. Mobile's black papers had trouble keeping their doors open and presses running. The result was that Satchel's brilliant early history on the baseball diamond was left almost exclusively to him to tell and a few old-timers to embellish. Ted Radcliffe, who caught for Satchel when they both were kids, said he was "wild as a marsh hen." Herb Aaron, Hank's dad, remembered Satchel calling in his fielders. In 1949 *Sports Illustrated* interviewed his old manager from the Tigers and others connected to the team, but one of Satchel's games that the article focused on was called because of darkness with the score tied, while he lost the second in fourteen innings.

One person who did not watch Satchel play, then or ever, was Lula. She had neither the time nor the interest. She "didn't like baseball, nohow. She never did see me pitch and I guess she never will," Satchel wrote in 1948. "She thought baseball was sinnin', always playin' and never workin'." Did that bother him? Absolutely, he maintained. "It's a terrible strain on you when your mama ain't behind you."

But Lula did offer up her support—with caveats—when Satchel was recruited to play in the Negro Southern League. The proposal came from the owner of the Chattanooga White Sox, Alex Herman, a former semi-pro player who eventually returned to Mobile and a successful career wheeling and dealing in politics and running a funeral home, insurance company, and family bakery. "My father was driving down Congress Street and saw this kid throwing oyster shells," recalls Kirk Herman. "He was a raggedy kid, he'd throw from a distance of twenty to thirty feet at the telegram poles. He'd throw fast, and curve it, and it hit the poles every time." Alex Herman was impressed enough that he watched Satchel pitch with the semi-pro Tigers, then tried to draft him for the White Sox, a team of full-time, paid ballplayers.

The timing was perfect. While Satchel had proven his pitching prowess, he still earned too little to move out of Lula's shotgun shack or even buy drinks for the girls who flocked to him as he pitched his way to modest stardom with the Tigers. The only way out for him would be to sign with a professional team, and the only way that could happen was through the word-of-mouth network he would dub the " 'Bama grapevine." It worked, and now the all-black team with the ironic title of White Sox was here asking him to join. But there was a catch: Lula. Satchel was underage and needed parental permission to leave Mobile. So he and Herman sat down to work it out with Mother Paige. "Your pa ain't been dead more'n a year and you're going off and leaving," she complained. "You're just a boy. You'll probably even play on Sundays."

Herman kept pressing. He told Lula that he would look out for the young ballplayer. He said Satchel would be paid $250 a month, of which the pitcher would collect just $50 with his mother getting the rest. He offered her $200 in advance. Lula knew that neither Satchel nor she would ever see money like that if he stayed in Mobile, so she relented. "All right Mr. Herman. He's yours for the season," she said. But "if he comes to any harm you'll account to me. And don't mess up on those payments." Her decision was made easier when Wilson, whom Herman also tried to sign, said he was staying home.

It was settled. Satchel would get his first shot at seeing the world beyond Alabama and playing in a real baseball league. Alex Herman would get a tale to recite for the rest of his life. Driving his children by a weed-infested sandlot on the South Side of Mobile, he would say, "That's where Satchel Paige used to pitch. That's where I discovered him." There was a fire in Satchel's belly even then, to hear Herman tell it, and the manager vowed to stoke it. So he swept the boyish ballplayer away from the city of his birth and brought him to Tennessee. Herman would say that, then stop, knowing his listeners knew that was where Satchel's story takes off.

CHAPTER 2

Blackball

"It got so I could nip frosting off a cake with my fast ball."

HE WAS GREEN AS A BIG LEAGUE INFIELD that April day he arrived
in Chattanooga in 1926. Everything he owned—a couple of shirts,
an extra pair of socks, underwear wrapped in an old pair of pants—
still fit into a brown paper sack, the same as it had eight years before
at Mount Meigs, which was a good thing since he still could not afford a suitcase. He rented a room in a flophouse, his first room all to
himself, at the royal rate of two dollars a week. It would be more
than a month before he had anything to store in the large closet. No
sooner did he collect his first five dollars than he headed to the local
pool hall, where a pair of sharks let him win a few games, then ran
the table when the betting began. "I always figured I was pretty
good at nine-ball and eight-ball," Satchel told an interviewer
decades afterward, "but those sleepy-eyed Chattanooga sharpies
played me like the biggest fish in the Tennessee River."

He looked like a rube on the diamond, too. His new uniform
hung limply over his six-foot-three frame, a mere 140 pounds holding it up. Street shoes with spikes nailed to the soles had to suffice
until the team could come up with regulation cleats large enough to
encase his enlongated feet. He was only beginning to sense where to

position his long, slender arms and legs to optimize his delivery. The one pitch he knew was an overhand fireball, so his catchers could dispense with signs; hitters knew it would be all heaters all the time. They quickly learned that while Satchel was fast, he also was wild. That meant looking out for the kind of beaning that had made him the curse of batters at Mount Meigs. Worst of all, he was swaggering. He resisted offers of coaching and crowed to his receivers, "Hold the mitt where you want it. The ball will come to you."

What saved him was a willingness to work hard and a mentor as hard-boiled as Alex Herman. Lesson one was location, location, location. Getting the ball over the plate not ordinarily but every time. The key to control like that was practice. Herman lined up empty soda pop bottles behind home plate. Satchel worked at knocking them down mornings before other players got to the field and evenings once they left. Another exercise was tossing the ball through a knot in the fence the size of a grapefruit. Like the Mount's Coach Byrd, Herman knew there was something magical about the rookie righthander. He saw, too, that unless they were refined, Satchel's raw gifts would remain mere potential. "I talked with him and he took my advice. He learned the proper delivery," recalled Herman. "[Alex] was always pushing me and I guess he taught me more'n anybody else," Satchel wrote in his memoir. "It got so I could nip frosting off a cake with my fast ball."

Herman also kept watch over Satchel off the field, faithful to his promise to Lula. In Chattanooga, the coach regularly invited his young pitcher to dinner and tried to see that he was in bed by 9:30. On the road it was easier. Everyone ate together on the bus, generally crackers with bologna or peanut butter, then slept there with ragged seat cushions as mattresses and suitcases as pillows. While that meant waking with a stiff back and a mouthful of dust, it eliminated any chance of hell-raising at night. When the gate was high enough to let the White Sox check into a hotel, girls followed the young ace back from the field and left scented notes at the front desk. Herman made sure that was as far as they got. The only way Satchel could escape his hotel room and ever-vigilant manager was to risk a fractured leg by jumping several stories to the street.

His new life was not all work. The coach and his charge sometimes went out dancing. "We'd hunt up a couple of dolls and off we'd go—doing the shuffle, trots, waltzes, anything," remembered Satchel. "It kept my legs in shape. But it didn't do much for my sleeping." Herman thought of it as controlled carousing. He had grown up on the same nowhere streets of Mobile as Satchel and knew what a stretch it was for the not-quite-twenty-year-old to have his first real job and first taste of independence. Watching him on the town as well as the mound, Herman could see that Satchel had more imagination than Hollywood and bigger appetites than Paul Bunyan. The manager's goal: to mold his ward into a man along with a pitcher. So close were the two during those formative years, Herman claimed, that it was he who gave Satchel his lifelong nickname.

The truth was that with each new paycheck Herman handed out, Leroy "Satchel" Paige became a bit more difficult to tutor or temper. He could sense his freedom and his magnetism and wanted to test both. He was learning how to give his chaperone the slip and Herman stopped resisting. Satchel went back to the Chattanooga pool hall and won back his five dollars, plus interest. He got acquainted with local moonshiners. When his next payday came around nobody could hold him down. His closet suddenly filled with slacks and jackets, his first that were neither hand-me-downs nor moth-eaten. He bought a steak dinner and a shotgun. He got a bottle, went looking for a gal, and did not come home for two long days.

Pitching was still the main thing, and what kept Satchel in the money and Herman's good graces. His first game, against New Orleans, was a two-hitter. Two days later he gave up just three hits and struck out fourteen batters. His coach's lessons on locating pitches were paying off and his teammates went from calling him "rookie" to "ace." Chattanooga had not been much of a ball club in 1925, Satchel said looking back, but after he arrived in 1926 it won the first-half championship without losing a single game. "In two years with Chattanooga I only lost two." It was not just himself that Satchel impressed. Herman knew his apprentice hurler had a single pitch, the sizzler, but since he threw it with the speed of a bullet there was no point risking damage to his arm by teaching him a curveball or any other permutation. "Satch," Herman said, "was a great pitcher, even then."

His reputation was already spreading in just his first season, at least within the confines of that riverfront city and the Negro Southern League. The White Sox and its Southern circuit were considered the minor leagues, in contrast with the major Negro Leagues of the North, although the Sox were substantially better than all-black semi-pro teams like the Mobile Tigers. The White Sox had a Caucasian counterpart, the Chattanooga Lookouts, and they, too, had heard about the hard-throwing tenderfoot from Alabama. Sammy Strang Nicklin, the Lookouts' owner, dreamed of having Satchel on the mound when his team took on its archrival, the Crackers from Atlanta.

Satchel would be coveted by white teams throughout his career in blackball. "If only you were white" was a cruel tease he first heard in Mobile and would hear repeatedly for another twenty years. Other black players had passed as white, and one even pretended he was a full-blooded Cherokee named Tokohama, but that took skin fairer than Satchel's. Nicklin had something else in mind to get around his league's ban on Negroes. The white owner "offered me five hundred dollars to pitch against the Atlanta Crackers," Satchel recalled. "I just had to let him paint me white."

The notion was as tempting as it was crazy. Satchel and Nicklin agreed to terms and would have pushed ahead if not for the intervention of Herman. It won't work, the black coach insisted. The paint could wash off during the game and your true color be exposed. What then? Satchel finally agreed to give up the ruse, but he looked back on it the way he would so many of his crucibles in that era when segregation reigned supreme—with a mix of hubris and dry humor, focusing on the majesty of his talents rather than the misery of his situation. "Alex finally talked me out of it," he said, "but I sure hated to pass up that five hundred dollars. And I think I'd have looked good in white-face. But nobody would have been fooled. White, black, green, yellow, orange—it don't make any difference. Only one person can pitch like me. That's Ol' Satch, himself."

BASEBALL'S COLOR LINE had not always been drawn so starkly. There was an era half a century before when blacks played on the same diamonds and clubs as whites. The Civil War had just ended. The sport that took form in 1846 on Hoboken's Elysian Fields had caught on North and South at military bases, prison camps, and even on battlefields. By 1867 baseball was entering its adolescence and more than a hundred teams were playing across the land. In those early days, with postwar racial optimism riding high, a young black man named John W. "Bud" Fowler was playing on white teams in farm towns, mining camps, and cities. The son of a barber, Fowler had grown up not far from baseball's folkloric birthplace of Cooperstown, New York. In 1878, when he took the mound for minor league clubs in Lynn and Worcester, Massachusetts, the twenty-year-old second baseman became the first black to play professional baseball.

The next year a nineteen-year-old college student named William Edward White was recruited to fill in for the injured first baseman on the Providence Grays. Thus a black man named White, from a university named Brown and a team called Gray, was the first of his race to make it to the Major Leagues. White had a personal story as gripping as his baseball one: his father was a Caucasian railroad president, his mother a mulatto servant in the father's household in Milner, Georgia. William got a hit, scored a run, and handled twelve balls without an error during his first game with the Grays on June 21, 1879. But his big-league career began and ended with that historic appearance, which was not unmasked until 2003. Given White's short tenure and late discovery, the title of first black big leaguer was generally bestowed on Moses Fleetwood Walker, who played forty-two games for the American Association's Toledo club in 1884. Whether it was White or Walker, clearly blacks were playing baseball alongside the best white ballplayers in America and quietly claiming a right to respect more than sixty years before Jackie Robinson became an icon for integrating—or, as we now know, re-integrating—the American pastime.

Those early pioneers had it even harder than Jackie would. "The unfortunate son of Africa who makes his living as a member of a team of white professionals has a rocky road to travel," *The Sporting News* wrote in 1889. "He gets the wrong instructions in coaching, and when a field play came up in which he is interested an effort is always made to have an error scored against him." Bud Fowler, who like his father was a barber as well as a ballplayer, was spiked so often playing second base that he finally encased his lower legs in wood. Frank Grant, a career .337 hitter and the best black player in the minor leagues, got harassed from both sides. Though he led the Buffalo Bisons in batting, his teammates refused to be photographed with him and opposing players chased him off second base. "They went down too often trying to break his legs or injure them, [so] that he gave up his infield position the latter part of last season and played right field," according to *The Sporting News*. "One of the International League pitchers pitched for Grant's head all the time. He never put a ball over the plate but sent them straight and true right at Grant." That pitcher never got him but a Toronto player did, running into Grant so hard that the second baseman was sent into the air "as if he had been in a thrashing machine. They took him home on a stretcher, and he didn't recover for three weeks." Grant eventually went the way of Fowler, covering his shins with wooden sheathing. His white opponents were not deterred: they sharpened their spikes to penetrate Grant's armor.

It may have been dangerous and surely was anguishing, but the barrier breakers persevered, shredded shins and all. The games were regular, the money good, and the chance to compete against baseball's best was irresistible. Fowler played for thirteen minor league teams over eighteen years. Grant played six seasons. Walker lasted in the Majors for just sixty-one games, batting a modest .251 and ranking twenty-fifth among catchers in fielding, but he stayed in organized ball another five years, ending his career with the Syracuse Stars of the International League, where he was, again, the only black in a white circuit. And there were others. Welday Walker, Fleetwood's brother, made it to the Majors, although only for five games in 1884. At least thirty-three blacks played in organized baseball in the late 1800s; some historians put the count as high as seventy. Their achievements are largely lost to history, as the focus on racial breakthroughs in the 1940s masked the fact that half a century earlier, America's favorite sport held out the promise of being color-blind.

That early era of uneasy integration on the field ended sooner than it had to. Aggrieved by their wartime defeat and the high taxes imposed to pay for Reconstruction, Southern whites took back as many of the Negroes' new liberties as they could, including their right to learn to read and write. Even in the North, a racial caste system was taking shape in America's schools, train and bus stations, and other settings, private as well as public. The Supreme Court legitimized the double standard in 1896, ruling in the landmark *Plessy v. Ferguson* case that separate accommodations for blacks and whites were acceptable so long as they were roughly equal.

Rather than challenge the nation's racial animus, baseball succumbed to it. Most white fans had embraced the idea of black ballplayers, but the pioneer blacks' white teammates were less obliging. The popular press egged on the haters, referring to black players as "dark objects" and suggesting they be met with "watermelons at home plate." Team owners quickly yielded to the rising prejudice. In 1867 America's first professional league, the National Association of Base Ball Players, called for barring "any club which may be composed of one or more colored persons." While the association did not last long, the pattern was set. The International League opted in 1887 to "approve no more contracts with colored men." That same week the National League's whites-only Chicago White Stockings threatened to boycott an exhibition game against the Newark Little Giants if Newark pitched its ace, the Negro George Stovey, and soon after eight players of the St. Louis Base Ball Club signed a petition saying that they "do not agree to play against negroes tomorrow. We will cheerfully play against white people at any time, and think, by refusing to play, we are only doing what is right." By 1898 the last loopholes of tolerance had been closed even as the last black team playing in a white league, the Acme Colored Giants, was going bankrupt. A new era of apartheid had dawned. Baseball split into white and black worlds.

Unlike earlier overt prohibitions, the ban that ultimately kept blacks out of baseball was not a written one, but a "gentleman's agreement" among owners. "There's nothing in the rules that forbids a club from signing a colored player," *The Washington Post*'s Shirley Povich explained in a 1939 column. "But it's definitely understood that no team will attempt to sign a colored player." The player pioneers were crushed but generally stayed quiet, all but Fleetwood Walker. In 1908 he published a booklet, *Our Home Colony,* calling on blacks to abandon America and seek their freedom in Africa. Anticipating Marcus Garvey's back-to-Africa movement by a decade, Walker demonstrated that black ballplayers not only could field, hit, and pitch, they could think, argue, and act.

The next generation of black ballplayers did what blacks were doing everywhere from college campuses to railroad stations: barred from white institutions, they set up corresponding, self-contained black ones. There was a tradition of segregated sports dating to the plantation, where slave owners used whiskey and coins to get their bondsmen to wrestle or race one another. Colored baseball teams were not new, either. Cities, especially in the South, had had informal, unpaid black teams since just after the Civil War. There were professional black teams, too, the first and best known of which was the Cuban Giants, which began in 1885 when waiters at Long Island's fashionable Argyle Hotel proposed a novel scheme to entertain guests who came from the city by rail or steamer. There already was swimming and boating, orchestras and balls; now well-heeled white patrons could watch the men who served them eggs and bacon play a lively game of hardball. The waiters, it turned out, were good enough ballplayers that when the hotel closed for the season on the first of October, they played—and typically beat—Ivy League, semi-pro, and minor league teams along the Eastern seaboard and through the Midwest. The hotel team was funded by a white businessman from Trenton and recruited the best black athletes around. But the very idea of Negro ballplayers was so repugnant to many white fans and teams that the all-Negro Giants felt compelled to call themselves Cuban and speak a gibberish they hoped sounded Spanish.

As the number of black teams grew, so did interest in a black federation. The League of Colored Base Ball Clubs was launched in 1887 and, in a preview of the volatility ahead, it lasted all of one week. The International League of Independent Professional Base Ball Clubs enlisted white along with black teams and survived a full season in 1906. The true birthright of organized Negro baseball traces to February 1920, when team owners convened at a cultural landmark of black America, the jazz district near 18th and Vine streets in Kansas City. Over two long days and nights at Kansas City's black YMCA, they talked and fought, ate, drank, and occasionally slept. Finally they forged a Negro National League out of two teams from Chicago, one each in Kansas City, Indianapolis, St. Louis, Detroit, and Dayton, and the Cuban Stars. Andrew "Rube" Foster was installed as the league's president, secretary, and sovereign.

Foster was a dominating pitcher and brilliant field steward who had built his Chicago American Giants into the model all-black franchise in the Midwest. His players were baseball's best trained—at hitting and running, copping bases, and bunting so precisely they could steer a ball into a cap. It was a skill they practiced day in, day out, much the way Satchel did knocking down bottles of soda pop. Those who couldn't hit the cap were cut. Foster maintained control to the point of telling pitchers what to throw, where, and with which delivery. The exemplar Foster set for his team and the league would outlast the circuit itself—a standard of strong teams, primarily black owners and exclusively black players, and a brand of baseball closer in quality to the ball game played in the all-white Major Leagues than most white owners or players acknowledged.

What we think of today as a single entity called the Negro Leagues was in fact an evolving pastiche. The black Majors represented the best of the bunch. First to reach that level was Foster's Negro National League, followed in 1923 by an Eastern Colored League of teams from New York, Baltimore, and other states in the Northeast. By the 1930s the group's structure mirrored the white Majors with a new Negro National League taking over in the East and a Negro American League replacing Foster's by-then-moribund circuit in the Midwest. Blackball, like white baseball, also included minor leagues, although they were unaffiliated with the black Majors and concentrated in the South. The highest-quality and longest-lasting was the Negro Southern League, which included Satchel Paige's Chattanooga White Sox. Finally, there were scores of semiprofessional teams like the Mobile Tigers whose players were generally part-time and unpaid; while they saw themselves as Negro Leaguers, they were never considered such by black big leaguers, whose baseball job was their only occupation during the season and who made enough money to call themselves pros.

The black Majors set out a hundred-game calendar, but few teams completed that many and some played fewer than fifty. One difficulty was scheduling around white teams whose stadiums they rented. Money was the other problem. Negro League owners faced an imposing economic imperative: while nearly all big league black teams were based in the Midwest and East, 80 percent of their black fan base lived in the South. Cash-strapped owners often had to cancel league tours at expensive stadiums, opting for exhibition games at makeshift fields. Rich teams dominated their circuits. Over the twenty years of Foster's Negro National League, just St. Louis, Kansas City, and Rube's American Giants won pennants. The Pittsburgh Crawfords and Homestead Grays became equally ascendant in the East. The leagues' lack of money and clout let players change teams at will, managers get away without filing score sheets, umpires pull for the home team that paid their salaries, and players and managers assault umpires when they did not like a call.

Thankfully it was not the structural defects that defined black baseball but its spirited ballplayers. They were graduates of universities and reform schools, preachers and moonshiners, men of substance, men of means, and Harlequins. Most came from the South and played in the North, swept up in the Great Migration that was recharting the map of black America. All of them worked long and hard. *Hard.* Their schedule began in the spring, like white baseball's, but the black leagues continued through the winter, when they followed the sun to California or Cuba, Mexico or Puerto Rico. An easy day meant a single game; a rough one involved three contests in far-flung cities. Some games were played between equally matched Negro teams with stars like the Indian half-breed Smokey Joe Williams and the tough ex-soldier Bullet Joe Rogan. More often it was top-notch black teams facing white players who on weekdays ran a hardware store or auto repair shop and over the weekend suited up for a team organized by their town, church, company, or Masonic Lodge. The Negroes won lopsided victories. Games were sparsely attended. The visitors piled onto the bus and were off to the next burg as soon as the home team got its last at bat.

The names of those black players were not written into our sports lexicon as were that era's great white stars, such as Johannes Peter "Honus" Wagner, Christopher "Christy" Mathewson, and George Herman "Babe" Ruth. But their skills and personalities were equally oversize and, in colored America, they were gods. Josh Gibson was called "the Black Babe," yet it was Gibson, not Ruth, who bashed the longest home run ever at Yankee Stadium. Playing once in Pittsburgh, Josh supposedly hit the ball so deep and high that fans lost sight of it and the confused umpire ruled it a homer. The next day Gibson and his team were in Philadelphia when a ball suddenly fell from the heavens into the opposing center fielder's glove. Gesturing to Gibson, the ump shouted, "Y'er out—yesterday, in Pittsburgh." Legend has it that James "Cool Papa" Bell was fast enough to score from first on a sacrifice bunt and steal two bases on a single pitch. Cuban-born Martín Dihigo was so versatile that his managers had him pitch, catch, and play every spot in the infield and outfield, which was especially useful since Negro teams carried fourteen to sixteen players compared to the Major Leagues' twenty-five. The most complete package was Oscar Charleston, the left-handed center fielder from Indianapolis who, in the words of blackball bard Buck O'Neil, was "Ty Cobb, Babe Ruth and Tris Speaker rolled into one."

Negro League owners were equally compelling characters, although most of them were better suited to a rogue's gallery than a hall of fame. Alex Pompez of the Cuban Stars ran the numbers racket in Harlem, with guidance from his mentor, Dutch Schultz. Abe Manley oversaw the Newark Eagles and numbers betting in that part of New Jersey. In Pittsburgh, the red-haired, cigar-chomping Gus Greenlee did it all—hijacking beer trucks, bootlegging, buying off politicians, masterminding gambling, and assembling a black baseball dynasty called the Crawfords. Greenlee's crosstown rival, Cum Posey, initially resisted such influences, but watching as his money dried up and his players were wooed away, the college-educated Posey relented. His new partner, Rufus "Sonnyman" Jackson, collected all the cash he and Posey needed from his jukebox rentals, pool parlors, nightclubs, and numbers running. While not all black owners were hoodlums, that so many were is no surprise. Amassing a fortune as an auto tycoon, beer baron, or mineral mogul, the way white owners did, was out of the question for even the most entrepreneurial Negro. So was securing loans from banks. Far easier to get nickel or even penny bets from working stiffs, especially if you offered payouts as high as five-hundred-to-one when a client's preselected number matched the last three digits of a pre-agreed standard like that day's U.S. Treasury balance. The numbers game ran like today's lotteries, except it was mobsters rather than the government buying, selling, and skimming. The racketeers overseeing this "nigger pool" were the black community's de facto financiers, and there was no higher-profile, more popular investment they could make than bankrolling a team of Negro ballplayers. It was the gangsters' road to respectability.

Underworld ownership was one of many ways in which black baseball, like other black endeavors, was separate but not equal. Black big leaguers like Gibson and Charleston had skills to match those of the white stars, but not their pay or playing conditions. It was easy for fans to follow the exploits of Major Leaguers day by day in *The New York Times, Chicago Tribune,* and other general circulation papers, but the Negro Leagues were covered sporadically and only by black weeklies such as the *Chicago Defender* and *The Pittsburgh Courier.* White teams wore stylish machine-sewn uniforms, played on meticulously manicured fields in stadiums with comfortable seats, traveled in George Pullman's sumptuous sleeping cars, and received steady paychecks. Their black counterparts settled for uniforms that were home-stitched or handed down from white teams. They might play in modern arenas when Major League teams were out of town; more often it was on sandlots or fields of dreams carved out of rows of corn. Fans improvised makeshift fences with their cars and sat on blankets. Players relied on Coleman stoves to fry up chicken and hoecakes, grits and Campbell's pork and beans, washed down with Orange Crush or Grape Nehi. Managers often doubled as players, and coaches were as rare as rubdowns. Umpires recycled baseballs until they got mushy. Owners passed the hat in hopes of collecting enough silver dollars for gasoline to take the team to the next town and game.

Getting from city to city meant eight full-size men piling into a rusting Buick, balls and bats in a box strapped on the back, clothes stuffed into racks on the side, hoping the car had enough life for one more trip. On bad nights, their bed was a train station floor or a farmer's field. On good ones, they found a hotel or rooming house. As soon as they arrived everyone raced up the stairs without stopping to register, claiming the best room by flopping a hat down on a tired mattress. The fastest players got beds to themselves. Lights stayed on all night to keep the cockroaches and bedbugs in their crevices. Lying on newspapers also helped; the crinkling sent the vermin scampering. It was not the best way to sleep, but it was better than the alternative: spending the night on concrete grandstands or in their cars, knees against their chests, scrunched between teammates.

Race even more than money defined the chasm between blackball and white. Restaurant owners who spent the afternoon watching the game told the black players who stopped for dinner, "We don't serve niggers." White teams rented blacks their ball fields but not their lockers or showers. Navigating the road meant knowing which hotel or eatery would serve coloreds and where there was a Negro family offering room and board. Survival in such a hostile environment came naturally to black players from the South, who had been weaned on Jim Crow, but it took getting used to for Yankees. Until they learned a community's particular patchwork of segregation laws and customs, walking down the street could land them in jail or worse, as Jack Marshall and his Chicago American Giants found when they pulled into Lumberton, Mississippi, in the 1930s. A teammate got off the bus and walked to the confectionery to buy a quart of ice cream. "When he went in he didn't take his baseball cap off his head and the fella back there said, 'Hey nigger, you better take your cap off.' When he reached over to take his cap off, a Coca-Cola bottle hit the ceiling above his head and splattered all over," recalled Marshall. Three whites followed the ballplayer back to the bus. "They thought it was a commercial bus, they didn't know it was a private bus. If they thought it was a private bus they probably would have attacked us."

Monte Irvin, who made it to the Major Leagues and the Hall of Fame, recalls a quieter encounter that still rubs raw after seventy years. He and his all-black Newark Eagles stopped at a café on the way from Birmingham to Montgomery, Alabama. As they approached, the café's owner started shaking her head. "Why are you saying 'no' if you don't know what we want?" Irvin asked. "Whatever it is, we don't have any," she said. "It's awfully hot," he persisted. "Can we just use your well in the back, [we'd] like to get some cold drink of water?" She agreed, so they drank up, then "we thanked her very much and she didn't say anything." When he got to the bus Irvin looked back and saw the owner breaking the drinking gourd in pieces. "How could she hate us?" he wondered. "She didn't even know us."

If Negro baseball brought its players this kind of special torment, it bred exhilaration, too. Hundreds of white fans turned out in farming villages and mining towns in what for many was their first encounter with a black—and what an encounter. A Dixieland band would march down Main Street two hours before the game, with players driving alongside urging the locals to quit their fields or come up early from the coal shaft. What they saw, for half the price of admission to white games, was the most intoxicating baseball on the planet. There were old-fashioned hit-and-runs, where the base runner was off with the pitch and the batter always managed to put the ball into play. Bunts were executed precisely. Players slid face-first to beat the tag. Teammates held "skull sessions" after every game to mull over what went wrong and how to make it right. Today it would be called small ball, or smart baseball. It was what the Majors were before the Babe and his era of long ball; it was wild and free, which was liberating for Negroes whose lives off the field were anything but. Baseball was "as good as sex," explained Buck O'Neil, who said the game rescued him from his father's fate of working on a celery farm. "It is as good as music. It fills you up." It also took a physical toll. Cool Papa Bell remembered sliding so much on rough-hewn fields that "I got strawberries all the time. The knees would be skinned on both sides from sliding. I would get sponges, cut holes out of them, and tape them around my knees to keep the uniform off the sore spots. It bothered me a lot, but like everybody else, I just had to keep goin'."

Negro Leaguers pioneered the widespread use of lights—and night baseball—a full fifteen years before the Majors. Night games meant that fans who worked all day and watched only on weekends could now come on weeknights, too. It let owners squeeze three and even four games between sunrises. The generators sputtered and coughed. Moths flocked around the bulbs. So short were the towers and so dim the lights that catchers held up their mitts rather than fingers to signal the pitcher what to throw. Balls vanished into the jet-black sky and fielders, as one related, "just looked up and prayed, 'Dear Lord, bring it here.'" But no one complained. The motorcade—with players in cars, and the generators and lights carried in trucks—crawled across the countryside, signing up promising young players without benefit of white baseball's network of scouts, farm teams, and spring training sites.

While much of black baseball could have been a model for whites, parts of its game were unworthy of imitation. Spitballs were outlawed in the Major Leagues in 1920, but for another generation Negro League pitchers kept dabbing saliva in a way that made the baseball squirt off their fingers like a melon seed. And it was not just spit. A little dab of hair tonic did just as well. So did sanding down the ball with abrasive emery paper hidden in a belt buckle, or nicking the hide with a buckle, nail, fingernail, wedding ring, or Coca-Cola bottle cap. Even Vaseline smeared on the bill of a cap would work. If a pitcher was being scrutinized by the ump, he could toss to first or third and his teammate would do the adulterating. The intent with each manipulation was the same: to let the ball slip off his fingers without backspin, making it dip or jump, sink or sail, in a way that deceived batters and gave the pitcher enough of an edge to transform a home run into a pop fly. "We had to hit balls doctored up so bad you'd think carpenters worked on them," said Mahlon Duckett, who played for the Philadelphia Stars. If doctoring did not work, there was the freeze-dry method. Putting a baseball on ice overnight before a hard-hitting team came to town took the life out of the ball and batter. The only boundaries for cheating were what second baseman Newt Allen called the Coonsberry Rules: "any kind of play you think you can get by with."

Black players saved their best theater for back home. A Negro League game was time for Negro ladies to break out high heels, white gloves, and fur stoles. Some spent a week frying their hair straight. Men donned straw hats and patent leather shoes. Ministers started church early so no one, themselves included, would be late for Sunday's featured pitching duel. Profit-conscious owners called the Sabbath "getting-even day" because they rented out Major League ballparks and fans turned out in the thousands. Merchants were there, alongside redcaps and maids, musicians and racketeers. Black baseball was black society, bringing together all ages and castes in a way that neither churches nor schools could. They came to date and mate along with watching the game. That was the beauty of baseball: action slow enough to require less than full focus. Real fans savored the nuances; Sunday ones breathed in the fresh-cut grass, cotton candy, and perfumes. For a few hours everyone forgot the world's slights and prejudices. They also disregarded its laws. Bets were taken in the bleachers and liquor was as easy to come by as popcorn. All those people buying peanuts and Cracker Jack along with their tickets meant commerce sufficient to rank Negro baseball alongside hair products, numbers rackets, life insurance, and funeral parlors, as exemplars of black-controlled businesses. By World

War II, blackball was the fastest-growing black enterprise in America.

In the end the Negro Leagues were a story of contradictions. Their thirty-five years exemplified black achievement at its pinnacle and black oppression at its depth. Negro Leaguers earned more money and were held in greater esteem than most black Americans, and less than most white baseball players. Blackball was epic and tragic, a gripping, grassroots version of the national pastime and an insult to the American ethos. Baseball in the first half of the twentieth century was like a plantation where white Major Leaguers owned the manor house and Negro Leaguers subsisted in servants' quarters. Playing in the dark half of that segregated universe meant playing in the shadows.

SATCHEL PAIGE ARRIVED IN CHATTANOOGA and the Negro Southern League in 1926, just as Rube Foster was being hospitalized for a mental illness that would incapacitate him and unsettle his world of organized blackball. Satchel eventually would leave an even greater imprint than Foster did on Negro baseball. For now, he was relishing the separation from his Mobile roots and basking in a relationship with fans and scribes intimate enough that box scores used just his nickname, the way they did Babe Ruth's.

He was a star almost from day one, even with white newspapers that barely knew the Negro Leagues existed. "Satchell, a new hurler obtained by the White Sox, pitched a fair game for the locals" and helped them beat the Atlanta Black Crackers, the *Chattanooga News* reported shortly after he arrived in April. Three days later he was back in the paper, this time minus the second *l* and with words such as "brilliant" used to describe his performance. Several hundred fans, white and colored, watched the young flamethrower strike out nine batters over six innings. The Black Crackers got two hits in the third, putting runners on second and third with no outs. Another rookie might have been undone. Satchel was the essence of unconcern, firing pitches overhand and underhand and scoring nine strikes in a row. Side retired. Crisis averted. Applause deafening.

The *Chattanooga Times,* which was owned by *New York Times* publisher Adolph S. Ochs, was equally informal in references to the youthful Mr. Paige, never using his last name, always using two *l*'s in his first, and writing "Pitcher Satchell" as if that were his rightful moniker. Like their competitors at the *News,* sportswriters at the *Times* knew the unseasoned pitcher was special. Barely a month in, he was the staff stopper—the thrower the team counted on to end a losing streak—and he had a confidence bordering on impertinence. "After breezing through six innings with but one hit marked up against him," the *Times* wrote in August 1926, "Satchell became so well satisfied with himself that he refused to obey his manager, who directed him to give Finner an intentional pass. Two were on base and Finner doubled to right."

Satchel was a fast learner. When the same batter came up in the ninth, Satchel issued a walk. He realized that his buggy-whip arm could make a baseball do just about anything; he was learning that sometimes it was best not to test the limits. What had been a single mantra—smoke it in—now added two touches of nuance: Keep the ball away from the bat. Pitch smart. "All I know for sure," he would say, "is that there's a fellow at that plate with a big stick in his hand. It's him and me, and maybe he'll hurt me. But if he does, he's got to hit that fast ball."

Tennesseans were smitten with their new star, but Satchel was not ready to tie the knot with them. He was too impulsive, too restive. It was barely two years since he had walked out of the reformatory and he was relishing his first taste of autonomy. Near the end of the 1926 season he abandoned the White Sox to play for the rival Black Pelicans in New Orleans, drawn not by money, since the Pelicans paid half as much as Alex Herman, but by the promise of an old jalopy. It was his first set of wheels and the beginning of his love affair with motorcars. He was back with the White Sox a week later but the restlessness would never go away. Already he was a celebrity. He had the means to move to greener grass, and the grass almost always looked greener to him someplace else.

Partway through his second season in Chattanooga the Birmingham Black Barons came calling. They bought him from Herman and gave him a contract for what he said in his first memoir was $450 a month ("400 to Ma and the same $50 to me"), and in his second became a more modest and accurate $275. What counted was that the Barons were the powerhouse of the Southern circuit—and they were moving up to Foster's Negro National League. Now Satchel would be playing in the black Majors.

His first big game with Birmingham involved a hit-and-run, although not the sort baseball fans were accustomed to. It was late June 1927 and the Black Barons were playing the St. Louis Stars. Satchel had racked up two outs and two strikes in the second inning, with the score tied at one. Then he let fly a breakneck pitch that whacked the hand of the batter, St. Louis catcher Mitchell Murray. Wielding his bat, Murray charged the mound as fans warned Satchel, "You have nothing to defend yourself with—run, boy, run!" Others, fearful of what was unfolding, screamed, "Murder! Murder!" Paige raced for the dugout, outrunning Murray but not his bat, which struck him just above the hip. With St. Louis players massing near the Black Barons' bench and fans threatening with knives and rocks, the police were summoned. NEAR RIOT screamed the headline in *The Birmingham Reporter.* The umpire tried to restart play after ejecting Satchel and Murray, but the Black Barons refused to take the field without their pitcher and forfeited the game. The hometown *Reporter* not surprisingly took Satchel's side, writing that Murray "did not display much sportsmanship" and calling Satchel "unarmed" and a mere "young fellow." The story ended with an apt epithet for Satchel's early days in Birmingham—saying he "throws the fastest and hardest ball in the circuit" but, in that game at least, "he was throwing hard, fast and wild."

Satchel put a different spin on his performance. His manager had told him to "dust 'em off," pitching as close as he needed to win a batter's respect. So he did, in the process busting the thumbs of the first three hitters. In a later recounting, he said that he hit the first batter in his side, the second in the arm, and the third—Murray, who was his buddy—in the small of his back. Murray chased him with the bat, he wrote, but "it missed. I picked it up and I did the chasing."

The newspaper version of the game, written so soon after the action, presumably is the right one, as is the reporter's observation of Satchel's recklessness. "It was worth half your life to hit against him when he came up," confirmed Floyd "Jelly" Gardner, who was playing with the Chicago American Giants back then. "One time at you, one time behind you, the next time at your feet. You had to be an acrobat." An old St. Louis Stars player, thinking back to a 1927 face-off with the Black Barons, said that "Satchel was just as fast then as he was now and he was wild! We only had sixteen players on our club and before the end of the seventh inning eight of them had broken fingers or thumbs and the other eight was too scared to go up to bat. And that ended the game." It may have been scary. It surely was exhilarating. In a pitching profession where speed and daring were critical building blocks, Satchel was emerging as a master craftsman. He also was a cyclone, raring to go even as he begged to be tamed.

The maturation happened in stages with each team he joined. Satchel looked, listened, and learned from his managers along with fellow players. His manner projected the poise and certitude of a veteran, but his evolving delivery and expanding repertoire of pitches demonstrated he was a crackerjack student. In Birmingham he shared the mound with two of Negro baseball's best pitchers, the lanky sidearmer Harry Salmon and the chunky left-hander Sam Streeter, both of whom racked up fourteen wins during Satchel's first season there. Salmon was a grizzled veteran who had started working in the Alabama coalfields at the age of eight and was still shoveling in the mines to make a living during the baseball off-season. It was a difficult life Satchel did not want to emulate. Streeter came up from the iron mills and would play ball again with Satchel in Pittsburgh. Seeing in their fellow Alabamian a younger image of themselves, Salmon and Streeter helped Satchel harness and steer his fastball. "See, he'd wind up and wouldn't watch his batter," Streeter said nearly sixty years later. "He'd look around, and when he'd come back, he didn't see *where* he was throwing it. I told him to kind of keep his eye on the plate, not to turn too far, to glance at the plate before he turned his ball loose. He got to the point where he had *good* control." Salmon already had pitched against Satchel when he was in Chattanooga, roomed with him in Birmingham, and watched him make rookie mistakes like balks, an illegal pickoff move where all runners advance one base. Satchel learned his control, Salmon said, by "practice, practice. We used to all go out and throw and see how many strikes could we throw. Well, he was a hard thrower, learned how to pitch afterwards."

Satchel's primary tutor in Birmingham was Big Bill Gatewood, the six-foot-seven player-manager who earned his reputation as the sultan of the emery and spit balls during more than twenty years tossing for fifteen teams. Gatewood was the one who taught Satchel how to brush back a batter who leaned in too close at home plate. He also helped fine-tune the hesitation delivery that Satchel had learned as a rock-throwing boy, and schooled him in throwing out runners who took too big a lead off base. Picking up where Satchel's earlier managers, Byrd and Herman, left off, Gatewood seasoned the neophyte pitcher on the field and in rap sessions that lasted through the night. His mentoring started to pay off during the second half of the 1927 season, a couple of months after the twenty-one-year-old pitcher from Mobile had begun working for him. In an August game against the Kansas City Monarchs, Satchel struck out eleven batters and won with ease. The next month he struck out twelve Cuban Stars, allowing just four hits and no runs while notching his third shutout in a row. In one game that summer he promised to strike out the first six batters, but after he'd whiffed five, "one of the guys on the other team's bench pulled out a white towel then and waved it back and forth. They'd surrendered," Satchel said. "The sixth batter came up and I grinned at him and threw quick. He popped out."

He won at least seven games while losing one that season, his second on the professional mound. Victories and defeats are just one way to measure a pitcher's performance and often reflect the quality of his team as much as his pitching. Strikeouts and bases on balls, by contrast, are entirely within the grasp of the moundsman. Satchel's ratio was impressive: he struck out sixty-nine batters in 89⅓ innings, walking just twenty-six. Another telling statistic is the number of runs a pitcher lets in, on average, for every complete nine-inning game he throws. Today, runs that result from a fielder's or catcher's error are not counted, but back then the measure was total runs—unearned along with earned—and Satchel's 3.32 average was better than most other pitchers' of his era and ours, helping make the lowly Black Barons second-half champions of the Negro National League. It did not hurt that the team played in Rickwood Field, a stadium it shared with the all-white Birmingham Barons that was so expansive it was difficult for a batter to hit the ball out and relatively easy for a pitcher to keep it in.

Satchel gave fans at Rickwood their money's worth with not just his pitching but his supersize persona. Ambling in from the bullpen, he looked like an unjointed turkey. A knot of elbows and shanks, wings and pads, moved on their own. His cap tilted slightly to the right. Three pairs of socks bulked up gams as wispy as exclamation points. Warm-ups meant taking out a stick of Wrigley's gum, folding back the wrapper, and sticking it on home plate, then tossing one ball after another over the thin foil until fans and opposing hitters saw just how pinpoint-fine his control was. "When Satchel got to that ball park it was like the sun just came out," said Jimmy Crutchfield, who played with him in the Steel City of Birmingham and the Iron City of Pittsburgh.

As soon as the umpire shouted "play ball" Satchel got serious, kicking back his foot, twisting his leg like a pretzel, whipping his arm around, and sending the ball plateward like incoming artillery. Norman "Turkey" Stearnes, who back then was hitting thirty-five homers a year for the Detroit Stars and batting in the mid-.300s, was so mesmerized by Satchel's preposterously awkward delivery that he watched the pitcher instead of the ball and repeatedly struck out. Bobby Robinson, who played behind Satchel with the Barons, said the only batters who ever hit his way at third base were left-handed. That was counterintuitive: righties normally pull the ball to the left of the infield when they take a full swing; lefties hit to the right. "Right handed hitters never hit my way" when Satchel pitched, said Robinson. "That was because Satchel threw so fast that they would be swinging late." Doing it that way robbed batters of their natural power and put the pitcher in control, which is just the way Satchel wanted it.

The next year he got even better at shooting bullets and steering batters, thanks to a new catcher. Finally he had a receiver who understood him. William Perkins—aka Bill, George, and Cy—would make a career of catching Satchel, following him from Birmingham to Cleveland, Pittsburgh, and the Dominican Republic. The two shared a sense of swagger and humor, with the catcher supposedly emblazoning THOU SHALT NOT STEAL across his chest protector much as Satchel allegedly wrote FASTBALL on the sole of his elongated left shoe. Perkins knew how to extract the most from the temperamental pitcher, even when that meant sitting back and watching. The Georgia-born catcher "handled a pitcher like nobody's business," said Satchel, recalling that when the two first met,

Perkins asked what signs he preferred. No need for signs, answered Satchel. Just hold the catcher's mitt still and he would hit it. "I could see George didn't believe me. Neither did any of the other Black Barons standing around, so I had one of them hold a couple of bats about six inches apart. I fired my fast ball right through that space. I did it a couple of more times just to show I wasn't getting by on luck alone. From then on we went without signs."

Satchel struck out 112 batters in 134$\frac{1}{3}$ innings that season of 1928 while walking just 21, improving his remarkable 2.65 to 1 strikeout-to-walk ratio of the year before to a sky-high 5.33 to 1. The fledgling fireballer mowed down batters like tenpins at a bowling alley. On average he gave up fewer than three total runs per game, and barely two earned runs. His Black Barons team was fading, finishing the year with a record of 29-51, but even with weak hitters and fielders backing him up Satchel managed to surge, ending up at 12-5. *The Birmingham Reporter* used words like "helpless" to describe his opponents. The *Chicago Defender* called him "invincible," writing after a win in September against Detroit that "the withering fire of Paige mowed the Stars down like wheat."

Fellow Negro Leaguers were even more impressed with Satchel's ability to thread the needle his catcher held sixty feet, six inches from the mound. "The man could throw in a cup, his control was so fine," said William "Sug" Cornelius, who started pitching in the Negro Leagues and watching Satchel in 1928. As for speed, he could "show you fast balls here at your knee all day. They looked just like a white dot on a bright sunshiny day—a white dot." Biz Mackey, the finest all-round catcher in Negro League history, had an even better angle, seeing Satchel from in front of the plate as a hitter and later from behind as his catcher. The Paige fastball, Mackey said, was so hard it could pound steak into hamburger and so fast that it "tends to disappear. Yes, disappear. I've heard about Satchel throwing pitches that wasn't hit but that never showed up in the catcher's mitt nevertheless. They say the catcher, the umpire, and the bat boys looked all over for that ball, but it was gone. Now how do you account for that?" *The Call,* Kansas City's black newspaper, did not go quite that far, but it did cover a 1928 game where Satchel threw fifteen strikes in a row, drawing on a fireball "so infernally fast that two were needed to see it."

As promising as his first two years were in Birmingham, the third was the charm. In 1929 he set records that would never be broken. The transformation from rookie to full-fledged star was complete. He vaulted into the limelight and would not retreat for an improbable thirty years. His won-lost breakdown that season was an unimpressive 10-9 and he let in more runs than normal, but it was his new standing as strikeout king that the record books would remember. On April 29 he fanned seventeen Cuban Stars, one more than any white pitcher had managed in the half-century history of the Major Leagues. After just one day off, the rubber-armed hurler beat the Stars again, this time striking out seven. "This boy Satchel," wrote the *Chicago Defender* as it pondered what he and the Black Barons might do to the paper's hometown American Giants, "is one more pain."

The pain got worse. On May 5, having rested for three days after his second win over the Cubans, Satchel went nine regulation innings and five extra ones against the Nashville Elite Giants, striking out eighteen. In June he erased fifteen Memphis Red Sox. Then on July 14 he once again fanned seventeen, this time Detroit Stars, tying his own regular-game record of three months before. "Satchel was in rare form," the *Chicago Defender* crooned, not just with his seventeen putouts but with only one base on balls. That rarefied form lasted all season as he notched double-digit strikeouts at least five times and nine on three more occasions, for a 1929 total of 176. He would never outdo that year's strikeout performance. Yoyo Diaz, the Cuban right-hander who was the second-place Negro League finisher that year, was 74 strikeouts behind Satchel. It was getting to the point, Satchel joked, that it was hard for him to walk a batter.

Off the field Satchel was turning into a lone wolf. He drove his personal car now instead of packing into the team's roadster with six or seven mates. For the first time he could afford his own transportation, with the Black Barons paying him $1,422 in 1929, more than twice what he had gotten just a year before. He liked the independence of going where he wanted and when, stopping to fish if he passed a promising stream or suffered an attack of fried catfish, arriving at the game late or not at all. Having his own wheels also gave him the freedom to take along a lady friend, generally a fresh one each trip. On one excursion with the Black Barons, the owner of a

Philadelphia clothing shop gave the illustrious pitcher the pick of his shelves: Satchel chose two boxes of ladies' panties. Another treat was seeing how fast he could go, whether it was to games against Negro League clubs or to the endless exhibition contests against small-town teams. "I got tickets for speeding in every state I went through and just about every town," he recalled. "I just always seemed to get started late and then had to hurry." As for sustenance, he got a fish fry bonus every time he won a game and supplemented that with ice cream and cake, which he often ate alone.

Some read his self-reliance as aloofness. There was an element of wanting to escape his teammates as well as his bosses. Privacy is easy to pine for the less of it one has and there was almost none on a club that spent nearly every minute together, practicing and playing, eating and sleeping. Riding between towns was the one opportunity Satchel had to be by himself. Teammates came to expect that he would not be there at the hotel when they checked in and would not get to the ballpark until fifteen minutes before the game. "You'd forgive him for everything because he was like a great big boy," recalled Jimmy Crutchfield, who joined the Black Barons near the end of Satchel's time with the team. "He'd warm up by playing third base or clowning with somebody, and then he'd go out and pitch a shutout. How could you get mad at a guy like that?"

What his teammates did not really grasp was that Satchel Paige was an introvert. There are two places to hide if you are shy: off on your own, or at the center of a crowd. Satchel did both. He was a hypnotic storyteller who drew a dugout full of listeners, but most of them he hardly knew. Performing in the middle of a mob masked the fact that intimate relationships were difficult for him. His preferred one-on-ones were taking a teammate fishing for trout or hunting squirrels. Even better: sparring with one of the amateur or professional boxers he befriended, sometimes getting knocked out cold. Fishing, hunting, and boxing had in common a zenlike focus— and no need to talk. They were his way of adjusting to this new life as a public figure. "A man who's got to stand out in the middle of thousands of people all the time, day after day and year after year, got to get him some alone time now and then," he explained. That social awkwardness—a bashfulness, almost—was there even in his childhood. With all the kids he played with on the baseball team at the

Council School in Mobile, Satchel said, "I guess I should have had a lot of friends. But even when I was a kid, I was pretty much of a loner."

Fans would not let him be alone, especially in Birmingham, not since he had shown how good he was at making batters swing and miss. That, along with hitting home runs, is what baseball lovers love most. "Everybody in the South knew about Satchel Paige, even then," said Crutchfield. "We'd have 8,000 people out—sometimes more—when he was pitching, which was something in Birmingham." Not everyone was an admirer. Some white fans would call him "boy" or "nigger." Others cheered him on the field and avoided him off. They could not be caught talking to him, and certainly not letting him into their restaurant or hotel. Not in Birmingham, not back then. Yet as hard as it got in any of the towns where he played, as he said, "it still was better than Mobile."

His time in Birmingham also gave Satchel his first schooling in entrepreneurship. When he was not throwing for the Black Barons, their owner would rent him to another club, netting both of them a few extra dollars. It was a lesson the novitiate pitcher took to heart and put into practice sooner than his bosses intended. In 1928 he briefly abandoned the Barons, although he came back after talking to the team president and presumably working out more favorable pay and hours. The next year he again was on the verge of leaving and, at the end of the Negro National League season, he headed to Cuba, where the owner of the Santa Clara Leopards "waved plenty of green in my face." The twenty-three-year-old pitcher was learning that the way to earn a real living was to play baseball spring, summer, winter, and fall. When he returned from the Caribbean in 1930 Satchel headed to Baltimore in hopes of further fattening his wallet by pitching for the defending American Negro League champion Black Sox.

It was not the best of times for the Black Sox. The team was recovering from an incident that winter in Cuba in which a collegial card game had turned ugly, with player-manager Frank Warfield chomping off part of the nose of third baseman Ollie Marcelle. Warfield landed in a Cuban jail cell, Marcelle in the hospital. Satchel took his teammates' minds off the melee when the new season began, throwing the ball with enough spark that local papers gave him more ink than longtime ace Laymon Yokely. The Baltimore *Afro-American,* which closely monitored the comings and goings of the Black Sox, called Satchel "Big Boy" and "Slim." Sometimes it spelled his name Page, other times Paige, and it elevated his stature by nine inches to bring him to an even seven feet. Reporters relished his triple windup and how he galloped instead of trotting. They were excited about his performance in April and May, when he played in the outfield when he was not on the mound, and went wild in June when he fanned sixteen in an exhibition game against the Bugle Coat and Apron Supply Company. "The long arm of Paige," wrote the *Afro-American,* "shot fire and smoke over the pan to make even the heaviest of the invading clouters look like shuffleboard players. Sixteen times the Buglers beat the air with their stayes in a vain search for the horsehide-covered pellet. Paige merely took another hitch in his belt and kept on pitching."

Satchel could have taken over for Yokely, who after winning seventeen games the previous year was starting to fade. Instead, the rising star decided to head back to Alabama, where he knew the idiosyncrasies of Jim Crow, fans knew him, and he could be close to Mobile without having to live there. While the Black Sox owner was left wondering where his elongated pitcher had gone, the Black Barons were glad to have him back. He won seven games for Birmingham through the remainder of 1930, losing four, and his runs-per-game average was third best in the league. Four of his Black Barons wins were complete games and in two he gave up just four hits. His most unexpected contribution that year came from swinging at rather than pitching a baseball. While his lifetime average in the Negro Leagues was a measly .218—barely two hits every ten times at bat—in 1930 he batted .357 for Birmingham, with ten hits, four runs scored, and a .393 slugging percentage.

At the end of the season Satchel was again rented out, this time to the Chicago American Giants, who were bidding for the second-half crown even as the Black Barons were settling into last place. It was a last gasp for the Barons, who ran out of money and temporarily disbanded at the end of the 1930 season. Within a year a similar fate would befall the rest of Rube Foster's historic Negro National League.

Transition was the watchword in 1931. The league was desperate for strongmen to replace Foster and offer a vision for rebuilding black baseball. Satchel was trying to make it work with the Nashville Elite Giants even as his new team was packing up and moving to Cleveland, where he would pitch a handful of games and win a pair. He also was trying to sort out his attraction to Bertha Wilson, the statuesque live-in girlfriend and later the wife of team owner Tom Wilson. Satchel was smitten enough to visit and write Bertha for years afterward. But with him away so often and her tied to Wilson, a real relationship was out of the question. Then there was his ongoing longing for a shot at the white big leagues. It was stronger than ever now that he had proven himself a star and was living in a city with a Major League team along with the sportswriters who covered it. "I'd look over at the Cleveland Indians' stadium," Satchel recalled years later. "All season long it burned me, playing there in the shadow of that stadium. It didn't hurt my pitching, but it sure didn't do me any good."

CHAPTER 3

The Glory Trail

"They mobbed me like money'd rub off if they touched me."

EVERYONE NEEDS a lifeline occasionally. Satchel did perpetually, starting in 1931 at the still-evolving age of twenty-five. The Negro Leagues were crumbling around him. Bertha was out of reach and no one had taken her place. He had transformed himself from a raw rookie to a legitimate ace, and had shown flashes of brilliance as he repeatedly switched ball clubs. Now he was stuck. He knew what he needed: a team with enough talent, money, and patience to lift him out of the shadows and onto the glory trail. He did not know where or whether he would find it.

Pittsburgh was the last place he would have looked. In later years it would be known as the City of Champions, but in the early 1900s it was still the Smoky City. Coke-fueled blast furnaces powered glass factories and steel mills. Fresh air was in short supply. So were blacks: at the turn of the century the city had barely 20,000 Negroes among its 320,000 residents, with more of them moving out than in. Playing high-quality black baseball in Pittsburgh seemed like a pipe dream. Only one local team had ever made it to the Negro Leagues, and it lasted just a single season.

Less likely still was envisioning Gus Greenlee as Satchel's savior.

Everyone in black Pittsburgh knew "Gasoline Gus," but as a boot-legger and numbers runner, not a sportsman. Few noticed in 1930 when he purchased the Crawfords, a scrappy sandlot club in the mainly black Hill District. No one imagined the Negro racketeer re-making the team into Negro baseball's version of the mighty St. Louis Cardinals.

William Augustus Greenlee was not easily denied. This son of a successful brick mason from North Carolina had dropped out of col-lege during his second year and hopped a freight train headed north, hoping to escape his strong-willed father and hook up with an uncle in Pittsburgh. He arrived in the middle of winter, wearing patched pants and white canvas shoes. He scraped together a living pushing wheelbarrows of bricks across construction sites, ferrying loads for an undertaker, and driving a taxicab. During World War I he served with colored America's proudest unit, the "Buffaloes" of the 367th Infantry, taking shrapnel in his left leg during the Battle of Saint-Mihiel.

Back home Greenlee showed the same grit peddling whiskey from the trunk of his taxi, earning the moniker "Gasoline." As business picked up Gus started serving his booze from a speakeasy, but he never forgot his street ways or how to hold a machine gun. When Prohibition ended and the Chicago Outfit tried to muscle in on the Hill District, Greenlee formed an alliance with pimps, gamblers, and corrupt politicians to defend their nightclubs and rackets. The locals managed to fend off the Mob and Greenlee established himself as a kingpin in the numbers game, where his take could top $25,000 a day. He used that to set up the only bank that mattered in black Pittsburgh, dispensing grants for everything from groceries to col-lege tuition. He also launched legitimate businesses, including the Workingmen's Pool Hall, the Sunset Café, and the Crawford Grill, Pittsburgh's version of New York's Cotton Club.

Taking up nearly a full city block in the heart of the Negro com-mercial and cultural district, the Grill was even more expansive than its redheaded owner, who stood six-three and weighed in at 210 pounds. Greenlee's Lincoln convertible and chauffeur were fixtures on the curb outside the restaurant. Inside, a half dozen men and women were busy in a back room counting and bagging that day's bets of pennies, nickels, and dimes. This life as Pittsburgh's Mr. Big was more than Gus had let himself dream when he left home, convinced that titles like "doctor" and "lawyer" suited his brothers but not him. Now he was a millionaire. Politicians lined up for his protection money as did an army of numbers runners able to turn out the black vote. He was living up to his new nickname, the Caliph of Little Harlem. The only thing missing was what mattered most: the kind of legitimacy and respect his father had back in Monroe, North Carolina.

Gus sought rectitude on a baseball diamond. He had played ball growing up in the South, and in Pittsburgh he had heard about the ragtag collection of black and white teenagers gathering under the banner of the Crawfords, a name taken from a bathhouse on the Hill. In recent years the team had lost its white players and its hardscrabble feel, and by 1929 it was attracting top Negro athletes from across the city. There was a smart catcher named Wyatt Turner, a great ground-ball man in Harold Tinker, and Josh Gibson, a young steelworker who could hit the ball farther than anyone had ever seen in Pittsburgh and perhaps all of America.

Pittsburgh itself was changing then in ways that boded well for its Negro community, black baseball, and Gus's Crawfords. Southern blacks streamed into the city between 1910 and 1930, filling jobs in the mines and mills and doubling the size of its Negro population. Athletics was a unifying force in black Pittsburgh, with young and old gathering at segregated gyms, swimming pools, and, most popular of all, sandlot baseball diamonds. By the early 1930s Pittsburgh was to America's black sports scene what Harlem was to its literary and arts life. The timing could not have been better for Gus. Fans and the press were drawn to his Crawfords in a way that was unusual for a semi-pro squad, with upwards of six thousand turning out for games. Talented young players rewarded that interest by smashing the ball, tearing around the bases, and winning. All the team lacked was money, a gap that Gus Greenlee gladly filled with the roll of bills he carried in his pocket.

At first it seemed like Christmas to the young men of the Crawfords. A rich owner who not only agreed to their pleas that he purchase the team but insisted on paying players their first salaries. Next he bought two Lincoln Town Cars to ensure they traveled in style, to be followed by a custom-built Mack bus with PITTSBURGH

CRAWFORD BASEBALL CLUB INC. stenciled along the side. And he began building a stadium worthy of the team's talent and potential profitability. His other ambitions for the club were less noble, but no need for anyone to know now. The Crawfords' uniforms had just enough room on the back to carry a pitch for Gus's favorite politician, state senator James Coyne, and the stream of clean cash from fans was ideal for laundering his winnings from the rackets. What neither he nor his players sensed was that before long, the ball club would capture this gangster's heart and pay him back in ways he never imagined.

It helps in sports to have a natural rival. Long before Gus arrived, the Crawfords and their fans had loved to hate the Grays, a team just across the Monongahela River. Homestead, Pennsylvania, was a company town dominated by Andrew Carnegie's steelworks, and the Grays were Carnegie's black steelworkers. Like the Crawfords, the Grays started out on sandlots, and they got better even faster than the Crawfords would. In 1913 the Grays beat other area teams forty-two games in a row. They were democratic in sharing expenses and revenues and Machiavellian in raiding top players, first from teams in Pittsburgh, then nationwide. Six-foot-five pitcher Joseph Williams had a fastball so overpowering he was dubbed "Cyclone Joe"; he remained one of baseball's best when the Grays signed him at age forty-nine, and even at fifty-two, when he threw a no-hitter. Future Hall of Famers Oscar Charleston and William Julius "Judy" Johnson anchored, respectively, the outfield and infield. Cuban-born Martín Dihigo, who would be voted into halls of fame in Cuba and Mexico along with the one in America, could pitch or play any position where he was needed. Behind the plate was Josh Gibson, whom the Grays enticed away from the Crawfords when he was a tender eighteen. By 1930, shortly before Gus took over the Craws, the Grays were the best team not just in Pittsburgh but in all of black America. They took special joy in stealing players from the crosstown Crawfords, who still were unpaid semi-pros when the Grays were paying top dollar. Even better was beating the Craws the way they did in their first face-off of 1930, when they won by a single run, and a year later when the score was a crushing 9-0.

The public face of the Grays, Cumberland "Cum" Willis Posey, Jr., was neither a steel man nor a baseball player. His natural sport was basketball. It is doubtful he ever needed to work since his father owned the Diamond Coke and Coal Company, Pittsburgh's biggest black-owned business. What drew him to baseball, and to making a career out of sports, was that he had already accomplished what he could as a top-rung player and manager in basketball at a time when baseball had fewer barriers to someone with his skill, drive, and skin color. He started playing outfield for the Grays in 1911, became the team's manager in 1917, and owned it by the early 1920s. He quickly changed the club's persona. Gone were most of Carnegie's steelworkers from Homestead, replaced with the best ballplayers Posey could find anywhere. He paid salaries high enough to keep the athletes he recruited, pampered his men to the point of ensuring each got his favorite sandwich after a game, and refused, for all but a couple of formative years, to share the Grays' glory or revenues with the wider Negro Leagues.

The old owner of the Grays and the new one of the Crawfords were polar opposites, which spiced up their competition. The former was a serious college man, the latter a dropout. The hulking Greenlee distanced himself from his family and lived on the city's mean streets. Posey, who was a full six inches shorter and sixty-five pounds lighter, relished the ease and access that came with his inherited place among black Pittsburgh's first families. And while Greenlee was a master self-promoter and sports fan, he looked like a greenhorn next to Posey, a sports impresario and amateur journalist whose father was the first president of *The Pittsburgh Courier,* one of America's top-selling black papers. Yet for all that separated them, Greenlee and Posey both knew that winning was everything and they borrowed each other's tricks to make that happen. Posey would turn to Homestead's biggest numbers racketeer to bail him out of financial troubles just as Greenlee raided other teams, including Posey's, to fill his roster with stars.

Augustus Greenlee started courting Leroy Paige almost as soon as he took control of the Craws in 1930. Gus sent a note saying there was a chance he would acquire the pitcher the next season. Satchel responded that there was a chance he would come. Actually, each wanted and needed the other. For a mere $250 a month the owner landed the player who, more than any, would lift the Crawfords to ascendancy over the Grays and give Gus a share of the spotlight that had been Cum's. The bargain price reflected the facts that the Negro Leagues were in transition from the old era of Rube Foster to a new one where Posey and Greenlee would dominate, and Satchel was stagnating in Cleveland where his team was dying. The pitcher set out for Pittsburgh almost as determined as Gus to make the Crawfords a winner. Greenlee, knowing that Satchel performed best with a familiar supporting cast, went about acquiring friendly faces. From Cleveland he brought Sam Streeter, a former Gray who batted from the right side, pitched from the left, and had been in the rotation with Satchel on the Black Barons as well as the Cleveland Cubs. Other newcomers were Jimmy Crutchfield, Satchel's old teammate from Birmingham, and Cy Perkins, who had cemented his reputation as Paige's personal catcher.

Satchel's first entrance onto the field in Pittsburgh was grand. It came on an August afternoon in 1931 partway through the third clash between the Grays and the Crawfords, a rivalry that was taking on the ferocity of Red Sox–Yankees, with the added dimension that these teams were desperate not just to be best but to be the favorite in their shared hometown. The Grays, like the Yankees, spared no expense to beef up their roster. Rube Foster's half brother Willie, who sixty-five years later would be voted into the Hall of Fame, bolstered the pitching staff, while Ted "Double Duty" Radcliffe could catch and pitch. Posey would later say that this edition of the Grays was its best. They looked that way as they slugged their way back that Saturday in August against the Craws, scoring five runs in the fourth inning to even the score at seven. That is when Satchel came in and the Grays' bats went quiet. The newly arrived slinger did just what Gus was paying him to, striking out six and holding Posey's players scoreless while his teammates rallied. The local paper called him "masterful and sensational." The Reverend Harold "Hooks" Tinker, playing his last game for the Crawfords that day, recalled that "they hardly hit a foul ball off of Satchel. . . . He was mowing those guys down like mad. He was throwing nothing but aspirin tablets—fastballs. He hadn't developed all that fancy stuff then."

Before the game a blend of youth and adrenaline dulled Satchel's nerves. Anxious? Not him. No way. Afterward, he said, "we celebrated like no one ever had. . . . Gus just locked the door on the grill and we went to town. I couldn't get away from anybody there. They mobbed me like money'd rub off if they touched me. All Gus' wait-resses pressed around me, smiling those smiles I'd gotten mighty used to."

One waitress stood out by standing back. " 'Lo. I'm Satch," he said, brushing by the others and up to her. "I know you, all right, Mr. Paige," he recalled her answering. "Everybody knows you now. I'm Janet Howard." Satchel was flattered but leery. Even the most reticent of women eventually got to thinking about rings and attach-ments. Marriage, he imagined, "was like walking in front of a firing squad without anybody making you do it." That was how he remem-bered their first meeting years later, when he knew better. In the mo-ment, wariness yielded to ego and libido as he escorted home this waitress whose eyes were so bright and bulging they called her "Toad." Then he asked her out on a date.

The celebration was still going on when Satchel got back to the Grill, and he capitalized on his hero's status by touching up Gus for "a few bucks" to take Janet out in style. "I'll do better'n that," the owner promised. "Tomorrow you go down and buy yourself a couple of suits and hats on me. And you got a bonus—seven hundred bucks a month now instead of two-fifty. . . . That ought to keep you happy enough to stay with me." Satchel was ecstatic, although the $700 surely was a onetime bounty rather than a new monthly rate. What a day—beating the Grays, meeting Janet, and now more money than had crossed the Page threshold during a full year. The next afternoon he bought five shiny suits, charging two to Gus and paying for three himself. He picked out a handful of ties, too, a rich red, deep green, bright blue, and a yellow that let you see him coming a block away. Janet, as he had planned, was dazzled. "You look like a walking bar-ber pole," she said, giggling, then she grabbed him tight and whis-pered, "You look fine."

The 1931 season was nearly over by the time Satchel arrived in Pittsburgh in August, but there would be more celebrating the next season. The Great Depression was in full fury, with one in four Americans out of work. Ballpark receipts were off so much for Cum Posey that just meeting payroll was onerous. A perfect time, Gus reasoned, to give the Grays a taste of the medicine they had been dis-pensing. Gus's finances had fared better—booze and bets are often the last things people give up in a withering economy, although he swore he was out of the numbers racket. Whatever the source of his winnings, he used them to seduce his rivals' finest players and build the most expensive payroll blackball had seen. From the Detroit Wolves, another team that Cum had controlled, came the speedy double-play man John Henry "Pistol" Russell, to be followed the next season by the world's fastest and most composed base runner, Cool Papa Bell. Judy Johnson, whose nickname belied his manliness, moved over from the Hilldales of Philadelphia. Then Gus went beneath the muscle to the heart of the crosstown Grays, raiding them of Double Duty Radcliffe, Oscar Charleston, and Josh Gibson, the pride of the lineup. The Crawfords now had it all: sluggers, speedballers, an infield that rarely let anything through to the outfield, and outfielders who Satchel said were sure and swift enough to catch raindrops. As good as the 1931 Grays were, the 1932 Crawfords—with five players destined for the Baseball Hall of Fame in Cooperstown—made an even more compelling case as blackball's best ever. Satchel claimed it was the best period, white or Negro.

Gus had decided from the first that his team deserved a high-class stadium, one big enough to earn back the tens of thousands of dollars he was spending to lure high-priced talent. It took six months to construct, cost a whopping $75,000, and used seventy-five tons of steel along with fourteen carloads of cement. Greenlee Field's brick walls and expansive fields made it the finest independent ballpark and preeminent black-owned sports complex in America. It was the kind of grand edifice that would have impressed Gus's father, the construction contractor. Even better was that these bricks were laid by Negro workers, and the park and team were owned by a self-reliant black man. No more indignities of renting a stadium where bias banned them from the locker room, not when they came home to what *The Courier* called the "mecca of the Hill district." The field's grand opening, on April 30, 1932, saw the choicest seats filled by the mayor, Pittsburgh's city councilors, and Allegheny County's commissioners, just the sort of notables who were a staple at Yankee Stadium, League Park in Cleveland, and the rest of the white Majors. A marching band escorted the players to the flagpole in dead center field where the Stars and Stripes was unfurled to the tune of "The Star-Spangled Banner." The master of ceremonies was *Pittsburgh Courier* editor Robert L. Vann, who, in an irony especially sweet to

Gus, had been a protégé of Cum Posey's father. Gus, ushered out in a red convertible wearing a white silk suit, got a standing ovation from the more than four thousand fans as he tossed the ceremonial first pitch. Taking the mound, as he would for every game that mattered for those majestic Crawfords, was Satchel Paige.

The game was a pitchers' duel from the start, with Satchel facing off against the New York Black Yankees' Jesse "Mountain" Hubbard, whose career had begun shortly before Satchel took up residence at Mount Meigs. Both pitchers were known for big-game performances. For the first eight innings, Satchel let just two Black Yankees as far as second while Hubbard held the Craws to three hits. Then the New Yorkers opened with a single in the bottom of the ninth, pushed the runner to third on a throwing error during an attempted steal, and scored on a blooper to right field. With two outs in the bottom of the ninth, the Crawfords had one last chance to pull even with monster home run hitter Josh Gibson at bat. On the way to the plate Josh stopped off to greet his mother in one of the field boxes, collecting a kiss along with advice on how to win the game for Satchel. It seemed to work—Josh smashed the ball to deep center field for what looked to be an extra-base hit—but it was not to be. The Yankees' center fielder caught up with the ball near the fence and Satchel took his first loss of the young season.

Revenge came later that summer, in a form that every pitcher savors: a no-hitter. It happened on July 8 at Greenlee Field, when, as *The Courier* wrote, Satchel had the Gothamites "eating out of his hand." He notched eleven strikeouts on the way to handing the Black Yankees their first shutout of the season. He even managed two of his team's twelve hits as they won by a lopsided 6-0.

The 1932 season was a good one for Satchel, but how good it is impossible to know. That is because while Satchel was on the Crawfords' roster, Gus rented his ace out to throw three or so innings for community teams across the nation, earning the player up to $500 an outing and the owner a healthy payout. While the local nine almost always put up a fight, Satchel's victories are difficult to evaluate given the sorry stature of many opponents and the fact that there were generally no reporters on hand to chronicle the action; the few available accounts are passing references in local papers and sketchy recollections from players on hand. Even when he was pitching for the Crawfords, his early-season games were a mix of first-rate foes like the Kansas City Monarchs and bush-league ones like Wiley College. Still, the Crawfords won ninety-nine games that year, losing just thirty-six. Satchel was the team's biggest drawing card and most fearsome pitcher, finishing with a record of 23-7. That was the most wins of any pitcher on his team or any of its major competitors, with many coming against the Craws' hardest opponents. During the season Satchel also batted a respectable .288 and slugged two home runs.

His numbers notwithstanding, some of Satchel's Pittsburgh teammates resented his absences and antics. His shuffle to the mound was a slow-motion spectacle. His windmill windup made him look like a tin lizzie. He talked trash to batters and pantomimed with fans. He bragged, too, about not just his pitching but prized possessions like the green Packard convertible he said had once belonged to the First Lady of the American Screen, Bette Davis. Shameless behavior like that showed that Satchel and the other "southern boys" on the Crawfords "lived a different life than we did," said Jake Stephens, the quick-tempered, acrobatic shortstop who hailed from Pennsylvania. "They didn't dress the way we dressed, they didn't have the same mannerisms, the same speech. Paige was a big mouth, didn't have any education, saying 'You all' and stuff like that. And you have this other problem with southern boys. They've never been used to making money. Give them $150 a month, first thing you know they go all haywire, living on top of the world, walking around with their jackets on: 'Pittsburgh Crawfords.' The older fellows, we had neckties on when we went to dinner. I mean because that's how you were supposed to do. You're a gentleman, you're a big-timer." It did not help when Satchel failed to run out ground balls, trotting rather than sprinting to first. Or when, playing outfield in a game against the Grays, a fly ball came—and went—his way. "All of us were looking out in right field for Satchel to catch the ball—or try to catch it," said Grays first baseman Walter "Buck" Leonard. "He was over there on the sideline lighting a cigarette from one of the fans."

Others were annoyed by the special treatment Satchel got from both Gus and sportswriters. He was a great pitcher, but "we could not use Satchell as an example of colored baseball players," Cum

Posey complained in a *Courier* column. "Gus exploited Satchel throughout the United States and forgot all about such men as Gibson, Matlock, W. Bell, 'Cool Papa' Bell, Oscar Charleston, Perkins, the men who [made] the Pittsburgh Crawfords." While Posey's assault grew out of his envy of Greenlee along with Paige, in a way he was right. Gus did capitalize on Satchel's prowess as pitchman as well as pitcher, a double-edged act matched by none of his other talented ballplayers. The Crawfords' owner gave the public and press a twofer—Josh and Satch—billing them as the "greatest battery in history" and guaranteeing that Gibson would hit two home runs while Satchel would strike out the first nine men. The dynamic duo delivered everywhere from Pennsylvania coal towns to Midwestern farm country. In return Gus helped make Satchel the highest-paid black baseball player in America, with Josh a distant second.

What Posey and other critics missed was how all the Crawfords cashed in on Satchel's stylizing and his hard work. He filled the stands not just for his rental games but for every game the Crawfords played, home and away, swelling ticket sales to 200,000 a season. Out-of-town reporters came, too, mainly to see Satchel but taking in the whole field and team. White America had Babe Ruth's rags-to-riches story to help it through the Depression; blacks had Satchel Paige. It was Satchel, not Josh, who made fans laugh as well as gasp and kept them coming to Major League stadiums for Negro League games during those hardest of times. He was an economic savior for the Crawfords and other teams in 1932 when, for the first time since 1920, no major Negro League was operating.

Satchel was also good to his teammates. He ran what amounted to a savings and loan, dispensing cash to players in need and turning over his Packard convertible to Cool Papa, who unfortunately did not know how to drive. "There always was a mob around when I tossed," Satchel exulted, another boast he could back up. Before that 1932 season and his nonstop travel, "there was no big money for anybody in the Negro Leagues. Guys were making only about a hundred twenty-five a month. Then they started getting nice, fat checks—and those checks were paid by the fans. I got the fans out and I opened up the major league parks to hold them. That's why they paid me more."

Chester Washington, the *Courier* sports editor who had been covering him for years, sounded a similar verdict. Satchel "has 'that certain thing' that the fans like. Whether it's 'it' or 'that,' or maybe 'that's IT,' we're not sure, but whatever he has, the pasteboard purchasers go for it in a big way," wrote Washington, who dubbed Satchel "the Suitcase Wizard." "He may prove to be the Moses who will help lead Negro baseball into the promised land of economic prosperity. At any rate, when Satchel comes to town watch the turnstyles click."

To Buck O'Neil, it was simpler still: "I always say that Satchel Paige wasn't just one franchise, he was a whole lot of franchises."

THE 1933 SEASON SAW GUS GREENLEE branch out from running a team to running a league. Cum Posey had tried that a year before, hoping to pick up Rube Foster's mantle and the skeletons of Foster's Negro National League. The East-West League lasted from January to June of 1932, falling victim to the Great Depression and Posey's egocentric vision. That Posey had left Gus out of his game plan was yet another goad for Gus to push ahead in 1933. While he, too, was stymied by the economy and ambition, his new Negro National League survived that year and fifteen more. One of his first acts as league president was to threaten to suspend "indefinitely" his tardy headliner, Satchel Paige, if he was not in camp when the season opened.

Gus would wield that club repeatedly, with no effect on his biggest star. Satchel operated according to his own schedule and rules. He had always planned to hook up with the Crawfords in 1933, and so he did, although he was late, did not pitch his best, and stayed only as long as it was convenient. That turned out to be until August, when he hopped a train to play for a month in the wheat belt of North Dakota. He returned home without apology in September, helping the Crawfords battle for the second-half pennant. Satchel's double-barreled delivery was more baffling that season. Gus had brought lights to Greenlee Field a year after it opened, and night games made it even harder to actually make out Satchel's blinding fastball. He also had learned to throw a curve, or as *The Courier* called it, "a baffling rook, which he uses to further bewilder all opposition." Headline writers gave him top billing now even when he lost, and reporters had to turn to their dictionaries for fresh superlatives and metaphors such as this from the June 10, 1933, *Courier:* "Satchell presided on the mound for the Craws' like a learned jurister on the bench."

As inventive as journalists were, they could not match Satchel's own poetry. His philosophy of pitching, he explained, was that "it ain't so much how hard you throw, it's why and where." At times he was a Zen master, at other times a court jester. "Bases on balls," he intoned, "is the curse of the nation." So "throw strikes at all times. Unless you don't want to."

That season of 1933 inaugurated another trend that would become a trademark for Satchel: the clash of the titans. The more he dominated, and the wider his reputation spread, the more likely a young star with visions of immortality or an old one fending off mortality would try to take him down. It was the Wild West and he was Jesse James. The gunslingers' names changed year to year, with only the surefire Leroy "Satchel" Paige, the marksman from Mobile, lasting through the decades.

His would-be successor in 1933 was Willie Foster, the Chicago American Giants' ace in the 1920s and again from 1932 to 1935. Satchel had held the edge the year before, but Foster won their first three face-offs early in 1933. Given that history, *The Courier* wrote, their encounter in July was destined to be the duel of the century. On one side, columnist Chester Washington opined, was Satchel, whose "fastest ball looks as if it could beat a bullet to the plate. Particularly at night this Satchell sensation shoots them across the plate so rapidly that many a batter has swung at the old pill after it had lodged itself in the catcher's mitt." His antagonist, Foster, was "one of the best portside pitchers and one of the brainiest moundsmen in the game today," Washington wrote. "Willie can slow-ball, then fast-ball or 'hook' the best batters to strikeouts in rare rapidity." The buildup was so mind-bending that it seemed the game had already been played by the time it was, and the opposing managers decided to pitch their aces at opposite ends of a doubleheader rather than risk their defeat—a move that backfired, with Paige *and* Foster losing.

In 1934 Satchel was back in Pittsburgh for the best season of his life and perhaps anyone else's. His record in Negro National League games was 14-2, with another four wins in exhibition contests. He was a buzz saw, mowing down 144 batters while issuing bases on balls to just 26. Such control was even more astounding considering that gas had been bubbling up from his stomach since the first game of the season, the revenge of spicy food he ate the previous winter. He let in an average of just 2.16 runs, earned and unearned, for each nine innings he pitched. That was .59 lower than Lefty Gomez of the New York Yankees, the American League's top hurler that season, and .72 lower than the New York Giants' Carl Hubbell, the National League's best pitcher. Think of it: Satchel not only bettered white baseball's best, at a time when the Major Leagues said he was not up to their standards, but he did it by 21 and 25 percent, respectively. Add in his nonleague games in California, Denver, and other spots across the nation and his 1934 record soars to 35-2 while his total run average drops to 1.38. In the Negro Leagues, which is what counted most, the suitcase sensation pitched fifteen complete games, five shutouts, a three-hitter, and a one-hitter. On Independence Day, he threw the second no-hitter of his short young career.

The July 4 jewel had something for everyone, starting with Gus. There still was no one the Crawfords' owner would rather embarrass than Cum Posey, whom he already had stripped of his best players. Satchel offered up the first-ever game where the Grays were held hitless. Only two batters reached first, one by an error and the other on a walk. At least one Gray fanned every inning, with two doing it four times and three twice, for a total of seventeen strikeouts. That tied the Major League record set the year before by Dizzy Dean and Satchel's own record from 1929. Two of the strikeouts came in the ninth, against pinch hitters, in what *Courier* sports editor William G. Nunn, Sr., said was Posey's "last minute desperate effort to stave off the inevitable." By his performance that day, Satchel "not only stamped himself as the greatest showman in the game, but proved conclusively to the close to 10,000 fans assembled that he ranks with the greatest in the country," Nunn wrote. "The 'Peck's Bad Boy' of baseball developed into a 'Big Bad Wolf' as he mowed the opposition down without a hit."

Buck Leonard was the best Grays batsman that year and most others, but not that day. After Satchel blew the first pitch by him in the first inning, Leonard asked that the ball be inspected. "The umpire took a look, threw the ball out," recounted sportswriter Ric

Roberts. "They gave Satch' a new ball. Again it came in like a bolt— disintegrated again in Leonard's face, for an eighth consecutive strike! Again Buck asked the ump to have a look, and, as before, Umpire Young tossed the ball out of the game. 'You're gonna have to toss all [of] 'em out,' warned Paige, 'cause they all gonna jump!' " For his part, Satchel remembered somebody shooting off firecrackers every time he got a batter out. What he did not remember was that, in what surely was a novelty for anyone recording a no-hitter, he pitched again later that day. "The stands went wild," *The Courier* said, when Satchel appeared in the seventh inning of the second game of a doubleheader. More cheers when he unleashed his quadruple windup to strike out the first batter, his eighteenth punchout of the day. Then his rival pitcher, Joseph Tarleton "Babyface" Strong, came to the plate and "a dramatic silence settled over the crowd, but in an instant it was broken with the crack of a bat and Strong had poled out a mighty double. It was the first hit the Grays had made off of Paige in ten innings during the day."

Four days later Satchel was with his team in Chicago, blanking the fearsome American Giants over ten innings, his third shutout so far that season against Chicago. The Crawfords won three games in that four-game series, leading a frustrated *Chicago Defender* to "hope they never come back here, and if so, our plea to Greenlee is please, please leave this string bean pitcher Satchel 'Stepin Fetchit' Paige at home. He has been here three times and when he comes again and we score a single run off his delivery 'twill be the first time one of our boys shall have crossed the plate as a result of socks, errors or bases on balls off the mighty right hander. Now we ask you if that is any way to treat a team that has just finished winning the first half of a flag race?"

The way to treat players having seasons like Satchel's was to name them All-Stars, and Negro League fans gave him more votes than any player that summer of 1934, the second season that Gus and his Negro League colleagues staged the East-West Classic. Satchel had been voted in the first year, although he denied it, perhaps because his margin was so thin or because he neither played nor showed up. This time he was ready. He entered the game in the sixth inning with a runner on second, none out, and twenty thousand screaming fans on the edge of their seats in the double-decked grandstand of

Chicago's Comiskey Park. Satchel stranded that runner where he stood, then pitched three more scoreless innings on the way to his East team notching its first All-Star triumph. "Today's game was more than a masterpiece! It was more than a classic!" wrote Nunn of *The Courier.* "It was really and truly a diamond epic!"

Marvin McCarthy, a white reporter with the *Chicago Daily Times,* was even more impressed by Satchel's performance, and more surprised. "With measured tread an African giant crosses the line and heads for the pitcher's box," McCarthy wrote in a column titled "Black Matty," for Christy Mathewson, the dominating white pitcher who won thirty or more games four times. " 'Its Paige! Its Satchel Paige and goodbye ball game' whisper the stands. And it is. He must stand 6 feet 6 inches in his sox. Gaunt as old Abe Lincoln. He walks with that slow Bert Williams shuffle. Maybe it takes him two minutes to cross the 50 yards to the box. He stoops to toy with the rosin bag—picks up the old apple. He mounts the bag, faces third—turns a sorrowful, but burning eye toward the plate, nods a nod that Hitler would give his eye for—turns his gaze back to the runner on second—raises two bony arms high toward the heaven, lets them sink slowly to his chest. Seconds pass like hours. The batter fidgets in his box. Suddenly that long right arm shoots back and forward like the piston on a Century engine doing 90. All you can see is something like a thin line of pipe smoke. There's an explosion like a gun shot in the catcher's glove. 'Strike wun,' howls the dusky umpire."

Coverage like McCarthy's was barrier-busting for a general circulation newspaper, enough so that the column was reprinted in the black-oriented *Courier.* White writers in cities like Chicago were finally discovering Negro baseball, fourteen years after Rube Foster breathed life back into it. Buried in the stories were two messages: that the world would not end if Caucasians and Negroes sat together in the stands watching baseball, the way they had the last two years during All-Star games at Chicago's Comiskey Park, and that there were first-rate ballplayers among those Negro Leaguers, especially the skyscraping Satchel Paige.

That 1934 season featured another mano a mano showdown for Satchel. His foe was Stuart "Slim" Jones, the twenty-one-year-old leftie from the Philadelphia Stars who in just his third year in baseball was doing so well that he had started ahead of Satchel in the All-Star game. The setting for this battle of black knights was the most storied in whiteball, Yankee Stadium, and interest was so intense that no one complained when it came smack in the middle of the Negro League World Series. Satchel's was the game that mattered. Knowing how big it would be he was determined to make it on time, and drove all night from Pittsburgh. "That didn't leave time to get a room so I just pulled the car of mine alongside the curb at 157th Street and fell right asleep with my radio going," he wrote later. " 'You Mr. Paige?' That woke me up. It was the batboy. The manager told him to find me and the kid was going up to everybody outside the park. I got into my uniform just in time to get that first pitch over the plate."

He surrendered a run in the first inning on a walk, a hit-and-run single, and a sacrifice. As the game moved on, Satchel woke up and found his groove. Jones never lost his, setting down his hard-hitting foes one-two-three through six frames. With the action seesawing between pitchers, the 27,000 fans sensed they were witnessing something special: Satchel pitching his heart out to keep the upstart Philadelphia fireballer from stealing his spurs. Satchel's teammates lent a hand in the seventh, scratching out a single, advancing the runner with an error and a sacrifice, and scoring the tying run with another one-baser. Jones seemed flustered, and his mates tried to give him a lift with one out in the bottom of the ninth, loading the bases with help from Satchel's unplanned walk and an intentional one. That is when Satchel's moneyball persona kicked in. He reached down to the mound for a handful of dirt, caressed the baseball, then slung three strikes across the plate. All were called by the umpire, without the batter getting so much as a swing. The Quakerites, in desperation, summoned Alvin Brooks to pinch-hit. He took three healthy cuts, but the only thing he hit was air. "The House of Satchell had scored another signal triumph," wrote Chester Washington of *The Courier.* "It was one of the most momentous occasions in Satchell's life and fans gave him a real ovation for his never-say-die spirit and the great battle he staged in overcoming a 1-run lead in the initial inning to pitch his team to victory."

Washington could be excused not just for a hometown slant but for surmising that Satchel had won the game. His dramatic holding action in the ninth deserved to be rewarded by freezing the game in place forever—and it was. Thanks to a deepening dusk and the fact that the Yankees had not yet installed lights like those at Greenlee Field, the umpires ended the game after Satchel KO'd Brooks. It was officially a 1-1 tie.

Fans and sportswriters gushed that it was the greatest game they had ever seen, a claim they were still making half a century later. But even in the Philadelphia papers, the focus was on Satchel, not Slim, who was at least as masterful. "Those footsteps that you heard walking up to the doorway of the Hall of Fame Sunday and then turn away dejectedly belong to tall, thin Stewart Jones," wrote Ed R. Harris of *The Tribune.* As for Satchel, Harris fawned that he "by super human work destroyed all the Stars' hopes of scoring a run and taking a win back to Philly with them. . . . Satchel Paige was at his mightiest, and turned in a performance that was little short of marvelous."

As fitting as a stalemate is for writers, it will not do for sportsmen. So a month later the hard-throwing gladiators were back for a rematch, with another 25,000 fans flowing into the Coliseum that Ruth Built. Bill "Bojangles" Robinson, the informal mayor of Harlem, was on hand to present traveling bags to the two pitchers as a thank-you for their earlier face-off. This time Jones pitched well, giving up seven hits and fanning six. Satchel pitched better, with five hits and seven strikeouts. Drawing energy from the crowd and the hype, he put the Stars down in order for four innings. While he eased up after that, he had enough juice to carry him through. There was no debating the outcome this time: the Crawfords came out on top 3-1 and Satchel was crowned king of the high-stakes hurlers.

In New York, the latest Paige-Jones punch-out was the talk of the barbershops. Judy Johnson, the Crawfords' third baseman and captain, dropped by beforehand at a local haircutter where Satchel liked to play pinochle and get his shoes buffed. When Johnson "heard the boys bragging that Slim 'would close Satchel's big mouth,' he duly reported it to Paige," recounted historian John B. Holway. "Satch won the game 3-1, strode over to the Stars' dugout, and snapped, 'Go over to the barber shop and tell them about this.' "

SATCHEL'S UPS AND DOWNS were even bigger news at the Crawford Grill, where he held court whenever he came home to Pittsburgh. The nightclub was headquarters for Gus Greenlee's ball club and such a favorite with ballplayers and wannabes that they called it Third Base, as in the last stop before home.

The public action at the Grill was on the second floor, with its revolving stage and glass-topped bar. A watchful eye would have noticed how, throughout the night, people quietly approached Gus as he held court at the bar, asking for his blessing and his cash. Others softly retreated up the stairs, in pairs, to an area the ladies called Club Crawford and their johns called heaven. Steelworkers just off the evening shift ordered up the Grill's special daiquiri and $1.50 T-bone. So did politicians, prostitutes, and ever-attentive pimps. Teddy Horne dealt the poker cards while his teenage daughter Lena worked the room with her flirting eyes and satin voice. Cab Calloway warmed up offstage with "Minnie the Moocher." No foolishness of black performers being banished to the back door here, the way they were at the Cotton Club, with its black patina and white owners. No need to check the clock, since Pennsylvania's blue laws never held sway at the Grill. The jazz was Pittsburgh's best and the crowds the classiest. But what stood out to first-timers was how the clapping hands came in jet-black, bright white, and honeyed like Gus, a reminder of his maternal grandfather who was a prominent white man back in Monroe, North Carolina. That rainbow of colors made the club what its owner wanted: controversial and cutting-edge.

Well into the 1930s the Grill still had the feel of the Roaring Twenties, and no one embodied that gaiety and excess better than the Pittsburgh Crawfords' minstrel of the mound. Satchel would try anything—gyrating to rumbas and sambas, singing jazz or scat, or strumming the guitar. He drank but seldom got drunk. His bar buddies included the Grill regulars—Pittsburgh Steelers owner Art Rooney; the first black heavyweight champion, Jack Johnson; and Bojangles Robinson, who tap-danced on the dugout roof after he became an owner of the New York Black Yankees. When Satchel visited Harlem, Bojangles was his pilot to the nightspots worth seeing or being seen at, from the Cotton Club to Connie's Inn, Small's Paradise, and the Big Apple.

Even bigger fans of Satchel and baseball were the Mills Brothers, or Four Boys and a Guitar, as the singing siblings from Piqua, Ohio, were known originally. They savored the smell of the fresh-cut grass, the sound of a horsehide ball popping into their leather gloves, and the sense of belonging when they donned their own Crawfords' uniforms and traveled with the club. The feelings were mutual. Satchel loved "Tiger Rag," "Bye Bye Blackbird," and other music the Mills boys took to the top of the pop music charts, making it sound like it was being performed by a Dixieland band when it was their mouths mimicking the trombone and saxophone. Ballplayer and bandsmen both reached out, with him inviting them onto the field for workarounds, and them welcoming him onstage with his guitar and sweet modulation.

Satchel's standard spot at the Grill was on a stool beside Gus Greenlee, who defined the club's center of gravity. Gus had always treated his baseball players well, even doling out off-season jobs as chauffeurs or lookouts for his numbers runners. But none got the largesse Satch did—from the beet-red flivver Gus gave him when he arrived in Pittsburgh, to running-around money, to the fat loaner deals the outsize owner made on his behalf with small-town teams. And none hijacked Gus's spotlight to the extent Satchel did, almost without trying. "Did you hear why I was late to yesterday's game?" the pitcher would ask. Then came the narrative—about hitting a helpless puppy, taking it to the vet, waiting while it wavered between life and death. Nothing happened to Satchel anymore that was not worthy of a story. Yet his tales at the Grill had a different twist now: fewer were about Gus, and those were less flattering.

Gus tolerated the change because he saw the pitcher as his protégé, even if Satchel no longer treated him like a mentor or patron. Gus had taken Satchel in as a raw talent, promoted him with the press and public, and made him into a master showman as well as the nucleus of a baseball dynasty. He made him rich, too. That gave Gus a pride of authorship if not ownership. He liked Satchel's passion for winning and his won-loss record. He saw himself in Satchel: a high-stakes gambler who had cut his roots, reinvented himself in grand fashion, and was forever looking for that next roll of the dice. Most of all he fell under the sidewinder's charm, relishing the suddenly brighter nights when Satchel came into the Grill and indulging the ballplayer like he might have spoiled a son, had he and his wife,

Helen, had one. Gus was besotted. That is what kept Satchel in the seat of honor even when his stories began to run down Gus's reputation, and it is what would keep the pitcher alive when he ran out on contracts he had signed with the gangster.

What Satchel got out of the relationship was more straightforward: a seat next to real power, the kind measured in guns as well as money. In his eyes he was not doing Gus a bad turn when he up and left for a better offer. It was just business. He was not looking for a father, at least not in Gus. A godfather would do.

Josh Gibson, the other man in Satchel's orbit those years, was even more of a behemoth. History binds Josh and Satchel at the hip as the two towering figures of the Negro Leagues, but nature left them as mismatched as yin and yang. Josh was a hitter who mashed pitchers, Satchel a pitcher who undid batters. Josh's power emanated from his huge arms and torso, Satchel's from his string-bean legs. The differences, however, went deeper. Josh steered clear of the limelight. Satchel lived in and monopolized it. Josh was eaten up by the limits of his ravaged knees and his Jim Crow world, consoling himself with booze, which had been legalized, and opiates, which had not. Satchel learned to cope and triumph. Josh was a player's player with a bench full of friends. Satchel played to the crowd, which made his teammates admire more than love him.

Yet Satchel's best friend on the team was Josh. It was not a relationship of equals: Satchel was the senior partner in the minds of everyone from Gus Greenlee to the media and fans. It was not a mutual admiration society, either. Josh was closer to other teammates and oftentimes felt ambivalent about Satchel, who befriended few others. It was not even the special bond often forged between pitcher and catcher, since Cy Perkins, not Josh, was Satchel's preferred battery mate. But Satch and Josh spent endless time together, sometimes as roommates, with the Crawfords, on small-town teams, and in winter ball. They were like Butch Cassidy and the Sundance Kid, opposites who fed off and relied on each other. Their trash talking reflected the puffed-up nature of their relationship, yet also its warmth. "I'm gonna throw smoke at yo' yolk," Satchel would taunt before whipping in a fast one. "If you could cook," Josh would yell back after walloping a long ball, "I'd marry ya." Even when he felt like screaming, Josh, like Gus, chose to laugh. Or sigh. To Satchel, meanwhile, traveling with and getting to know Josh was, he said repeatedly, his fondest memory of Pittsburgh and the Crawfords.

It was harder to remember all the women Satchel got to know at the Crawford Grill. He was a honeypot, luring the queen bees. None stopped long, most just a night. "All the womens like Satchel," testified Cool Papa's bride, Clarabelle. "But any woman who trusted him was a fool." Janet Howard would have agreed, in retrospect. Increasingly, Gus's beguiling waitress was there waiting when Satchel came home from road trips or winter tours. They lived just a dozen blocks from each other on Wylie Avenue, with the Grill halfway between. He could see that she was beautiful and playful, but he never knew the young waitress's venerable roots. One grandfather was the illustrious pastor of Pittsburgh's Central Baptist Church, the other Pittsburgh's pioneer Negro dentist.

Satchel was besotted and Janet was, too, but she knew that showing it would scare away this twenty-five-year-old mannish boy. So she played it easy and cool, letting him court her at his slow pace over three long years. He brought back gifts when he was away, which was often; she stayed faithful. This was the first time Satchel had ever had a real girlfriend, and while he would not admit it to her or to himself, being with Janet felt good. Every time she watched him play he bore down a bit harder.

They talked about marriage for the first time just after the 1934 All-Star game in Chicago. "We can't just keep running around like you were just my guy and nothing else," Janet said. He wished they had and, looking back, said he should have known from the start that it was a mismatch. She wanted a man with a steady job that brought him home every night for dinner; he insisted that was okay for a shopkeeper but not a baseball player. He was twenty-eight; she was just twenty-one and nearly a foot shorter. He was already keeping secrets, including shaving two years off his age and, when he was on the road, continuing to "cut loose." Coming from a broken home, she was especially determined to rein him in and keep him honest. Others described her as happy-go-lucky as well as beautiful, although he saw less and less of her easygoing nature as her feistiness increasingly ignited to anger.

They pushed ahead anyway, on October 26, 1934, not long after the Craws completed their season. The wedding was an all-night affair at the only setting they had in common: the Grill. Janet picked out a preacher while Satchel picked out a new suit and tie. Gus set out an eight-course spread. Bojangles was the best man. Big bands kept guests fox-trotting, Lindy Hopping, and tap-dancing until dawn. The restaurant door was locked to keep out Satchel's fans and any old girlfriends who might drop by. Just when everyone had quaffed enough daiquiris and champagne to cloud their judgment, Gus quieted the crowd and called Satchel up. With his guests expecting a wedding toast, the Crawfords' owner threw a curve. "Satchel won't be leaving us, don't worry about that," Gus announced, arm around his star. "I got a new contract here for him." Satchel and Gus sat down and signed right there, as they had agreed beforehand. It was for two years, and it meant as little as all the other contracts that Negro League owners were writing in those years and Satchel was signing. The party was still going on when he and Janet sneaked out, bound for a honeymoon in California squeezed around winter baseball.

No sooner were they back in Pittsburgh early in 1935 than Satchel's troubles with money resurfaced. The more he earned, the more he thought about all that he had gone without growing up in Mobile. He would make up for it now, lavishing his new earnings on friends as well as himself. One shotgun might have sufficed, but he had to have fifteen. Casting a line from shore was okay in Mobile's Down the Bay ghetto, but now he needed a boat along with new fishing gear. "It was like being a kid again—being a kid for a guy who never really had a chance to be one," he said. "You can't tell the guy who's got good gravy all over his shirt front that the gravy bowl is going to be empty some day. I didn't realize that until I'd just about sopped up all that gravy." About the only discipline he showed, in his version of the money story, was sending some home each month to Lula. "I always took care of her," he said, not mentioning that he seldom visited her or anyone in Mobile.

Janet and Gus made Satchel's finances even more challenging. She insisted on knowing where his paychecks were coming from and going. "After that honeymoon," Satchel said later, "I started noticing a powerful lightness in my hip pocket. Married life was a mighty expensive thing and those paychecks of mine just weren't going as far as they used to." Gus was the only one Satchel could turn to for money. He demanded a raise more than asked for it, no matter that he had just settled on a new salary and that Gus had underwritten most of his wedding and honeymoon. But there were limits. "I guess Gus was mad or something," Satchel remembered. "He turned me down flat. Ol' Satch didn't get mad too many times back in those days, everything going so good. But I perked over right then and there. Gus wouldn't give in. All he said was something like 'don't forget those games we got coming up next week.' I was so mad I went home and started throwing clothes into a suitcase."

What to do next was easy. Picking up and going was one of the things he loved most about baseball. It had given him a way out of Mobile, and it got into his blood as he went from Chattanooga to New Orleans, Birmingham, Baltimore, Nashville, and Cleveland. Gus had hoped he would make Pittsburgh his home. That was not Satchel. In truth, both knew when he first arrived in Pittsburgh that Satchel would never settle anywhere, not as long as he had his baseball legs and some owner somewhere still wanted him. The Crawfords had given him a lifeline along with the top-drawer club he needed to prove how good he could be. It was a fair trade: he gave them his best baseball years. Gus understood. Janet was beginning to—he had dragged her along to North Dakota the summer before—although she could not yet accept what it would mean for their marriage. "Where're we going?" she asked as her new husband hastily packed his bag. "I don't know," Satchel said. "We're just going."

CHAPTER 4

The Game in Black and White

"They were saying Diz [Dean] and me were about as alike as two tadpoles. We were both fast and slick. But Diz was in the majors and I was bouncing around the peanut circuit."

THIS MOVE MEANT not just a new team and town, but a new way of being black. No more laments "if only you were white." No more offers to blanch his face with paint. In the hinterlands of the Northern Plains it was okay not just to play on the same field as whites, which Satchel had done before, but to team up with them. That was a first for him. It also was why club manager and auto mogul Neil Churchill enticed the pitcher to Bismarck in 1933 and brought him back two years later when he was feuding with Gus Greenlee. It made Satchel a local hero.

Bismarck in the 1930s was an implausible place for a Negro to be a VIP or to be at all. The entire population of North Dakota was .05 percent black then, and the capital of Bismarck had among its twelve thousand residents only a handful of black ones, most named Spriggs. Everyone knew the Spriggs boys were good basketball players and that their father worked for the railroad; no one thought to ask anything else. North Dakota was not free of the racist venom that infused the nation but it was not consumed by it. More important were dust bowls and crop failures, sinking commodity prices and soaring farm foreclosures. There was no TV to take people's minds off the Great Depression, no money for the motion pictures, and little else to do in a city that celebrated its political and cultural isolation. That left baseball.

Neil Churchill was not thinking about toppling racial barriers when he invited Satchel to Bismarck any more than Satchel was thinking about hurtling them. All Churchill wanted was to beat his nemesis, Jamestown, a city a hundred miles down the road whose team had signed black players earlier that season of 1933. What Satchel wanted was an extra paycheck, and Churchill was writing generous ones to ringers from the talent-rich Negro Leagues. "It wasn't until after I signed up with Mr. Churchill that I found out I was going to be playing with some white boys," Satchel said later. "For the first time since I'd started throwing, I was going to have some of them on my side. It seemed real funny."

Another first was what he brought with him to Bismarck. Three stylish suitcases had replaced his customary paper sack, a sign of the extra sports jackets, neckties, fedoras, and wages he had collected in Pittsburgh. He barely had time to unload his bags after the twenty-four-hour train trip from Chicago before Churchill summoned him to the mound for a Sunday face-off against Jamestown's black ace, Barney Brown. Three hundred and fifty fans had come from Jamestown by special railcar, with an equal number arriving in a caravan of motorcars. Jamestown boosters offered a $500 bet on behalf of their team; Churchill raised the ante to $1,000. Extra bleachers were erected at the Bismarck ballpark for the crowd of 2,200, which must have been the most ever to watch a baseball game in North Dakota. What they saw when players took the field was equally historic: a rainbow of skin tones. Satchel's catcher was Quincy Trouppe, another Negro League star, and his bullpen backup was his old Crawfords teammate Roosevelt Davis. Shortstop Red Haley also was black, but had skin light enough for the local paper to claim he was Cuban. Playing alongside them were men whose fair complexion brought to mind the German chancellor for whom Bismarck had been renamed sixty years before in a bid to attract other Germans. The architect of the unorthodox team and color scheme was Neil Orr Churchill, whose three hundred pounds and perpetual good cheer conjured up Santa Claus without the beard.

Creaky though he was after the long train ride, and unfamiliar with his surroundings and most of his diamond mates, Satchel drew on years of big-game experience to deliver for his new owner and fans. Jamestown struck first with two runs in the sixth; Bismarck pulled even in the eighth. "They don't get no mo' runs," Satchel vowed as he retook the mound in the top of the ninth, following through with three successive strikeouts on ten pitches, inspiring his squad to plate the winning run in the bottom of the ninth. "Without question," the Bismarck paper crowed, "he pitches the fastest ball ever exhibited in these parts." That performance, which included an astonishing eighteen strikeouts and a single walk, was exceeded only by his casual certainty handling a baseball hit his way. He fielded it, leaned over to pick up the rosin bag the way he would to dry his hands between pitches, and only then threw the runner out at first base. Bismarck had a win over Jamestown and the capital city had a team and a star to lift its spirits the rest of that hot August and into September.

While Satchel generally appreciated the way he was received in his new town, there were bumps. Finding a landlord willing to rent to blacks was not easy, and the challenge was made more nettlesome with his then-girlfriend Janet tagging along from Pittsburgh. "Most of the folks there were pretty nice, but there were some of those other kind, like you run into everyplace," he recalled. "They didn't want us living by them." While he and Janet were looking for more permanent quarters, they moved into an old train freight car that had been converted into sleeping quarters for railyard crews.

Satchel took out his displeasure at his living conditions and Janet's nagging on his teammates. Once, after he lit into his outfielders for dropping too many flies and getting too few hits, he heard one mutter what sounded to him like "dirty nigger." The next inning the right, center, and left fielders staged a sit-down strike. Fans incorrectly surmised it was preplanned, the kind of stunt for which Satchel was famous, and he reinforced that conviction by striking out the side. But the pitcher knew when to give in: "I apologized and my outfielders did the same. I guess they felt pretty bad about it, too. . . . After that game, I didn't have any troubles in Bismarck."

Churchill, meanwhile, was making money off his new star. The bleachers filled every time Satchel pitched, which was just about every game the team played the rest of the 1933 season and into a three-game playoff against Jamestown that crowned Bismarck the state champion. It was not just with gate receipts of forty cents a head that Satchel proved a money machine, but with Churchill's wagers. He bet fans that he could pull another player off the field each inning and Bismarck would still win. In the end, old-timers recall, only Satchel and his catcher were left on the diamond. They were enough. Churchill showed his gratitude by loaning Satchel the flashiest cars on his Chrysler lot. He also invited the lanky cannonballer back for the 1934 season, an offer Satchel accepted but did not honor. He did come back in 1935, not long after he married Janet, when Gus Greenlee turned down his bid for more money and he was looking for somewhere to land. This time his living accommodations were first-rate, his salary was fattened to $500 a month, and he had the chance to prove himself for a full season on an integrated baseball team that he led to the national semi-pro championship.

His playing days in Bismarck would constitute not just a defining chapter in a storied baseball career, but a critical link on a chain stretching from Bud Fowler to Jackie Robinson. A half century after Fowler, Satchel and his Bismarck teammates reminded America that blacks and whites could play baseball side by side without the sky falling, fans rioting, or the standard of play being compromised. More than a decade before Branch Rickey signed Jackie Robinson to the Brooklyn Dodgers, the club from North Dakota offered Major League executives proof that integrated baseball could put money in their pockets. That mattered more than all their good intentions. In Bismarck, Satchel summed it up simply, "I'd cracked another little chink in Jim Crow."

SATCHEL ACTUALLY HAD BEEN challenging Jim Crow ever since he took his pitching show on the road, and he did that from the beginning. They called freelance play like that barnstorming, to distinguish it from formal league games. Major Leaguers and Negro Leaguers both did it, but for the former it was restricted to the postseason whereas black players squeezed in exhibitions year-round. The contests were set up by players, owners, or independent promoters, most of whom were white. Touring teams played one another or a local club. Admission was seventy-five cents, and five hundred spectators was a decent turnout. Players earned as much as $150 a day or as little as $15. Barnstormers dubbed themselves "All-Stars" although typically only two or three qualified as such. A more accurate description was "Hungry Ball," since ballplayers needed the extra income to carry them through the year. Barnstorming brought baseball's icons to jerkwater towns with no stoplights but lots of barns, and it gave hamlet heroes at least the fantasy that they might someday be discovered. In the East, games were fitted in between the end of the World Series and the onset of winter; in the Midwest they were scheduled around the harvest; in California, Florida, and the Caribbean they continued until spring.

Black players had been barnstorming since the 1880s, generally in the no-budget, ragtag fashion that characterized the rest of their play, but sometimes in style. Bud Fowler's All-American Black Tourists rented their own railroad car, and each game was kicked off with a parade led by players decked out in swallowtail coats and opera hats and brandishing silk umbrellas. The New York Black Yankees made annual treks to the elegant resorts of the Poconos and Catskills; the American Giants entertained guests at Palm Beach's Royal Poinciana Hotel. More typical, Giants infielder Jack Marshall said, were monotonous road trips where he ate sardines out of a Bell Fruit jar, bathed from a big black kettle fired up in someone's backyard, and was told by a shopkeeper he could not buy milk because it was white. Babe Ruth barnstormed, as did Dizzy Dean, Josh Gibson, Bob Feller, Cool Papa Bell, and most of the greats, white and black, with that wayfaring way of playing continuing into the early 1960s.

No player barnstormed as wide or far, for as long, as Leroy "Satchel" Paige. It suited his disposition: He was eager to follow the sun and money wherever they took him. No need to be pinned down by owners or lovers. Barnstorming let him live each day as it came, and days as a vagabond ballplayer offered boundless adventure and variety. He was the nation's ringer, generating more offers than anyone and picking up as much as $500 for as few as three innings. He learned to pitch not by the week but by the hour. Promoters knew he could fill the stands as well as mow down batters, so they booked him despite knowing he might not show. All of which makes feasible his fantastic claim to have pitched for as many as 250 teams over the course of his career.

His time on the road let him taste America at its least rehearsed. He watched ranchers lubricated with beer fight in the stands after wagering on him. He sat on the porch and sang into the evening with a black family that gave him a bed and meal in Dayton, Ohio, and ate ham and pumpkin pie with white ones in Iowa farm country. He thawed his hands over a fire next to the dugout in chilly Des Moines, rubbed his distended ankles after an all-night drive to Minnesota, and learned to spot a pool shark anywhere by the chalk in his breast pocket. In Harlem he relished the Renaissance. In New Orleans he savored the swing. He was what he called "a travelin' man," logging thirty thousand miles a year and visiting "every state in the United States except Maine and Boston." Among Negroes, only the Pullman porter saw more of America. To Satchel, that freedom and movement were more delicious than the sweetest chocolate.

That does not mean barnstorming was easy. As rough as conditions were in the Negro Leagues, that looked like luxury next to Satchel's early years on the road. He was away from home and family for months at a time. Driving all night and playing all day became his life. He learned to eat out of paper sacks and sleep three times a week. When he and his teammates could find and afford a hotel, it might be five to a bed, and "sometimes the whole club'd be in one room." He got to be an accomplished catnapper. Bunny Downs, who drove the bus for a team Satchel barnstormed with, got a front-seat view of the strains and stresses: "Shucking corn, hoeing potatoes, picking cotton, ain't no tougher than this business. No, sir. For a real, hard-working business, day in and day out, you gotta take this here whatchacallit, tourist baseball."

A nationwide network of Negroes opened their homes to Satchel and other itinerant ballplayers. No need to post "Vacancy" signs; word spread quietly, much as it had for runaway slaves in the days of the Underground Railroad, and as it would in the civil rights era. As for food, "we had to go in the colored neighborhood if we wanted anything hot at all," said Satchel. "If there was no colored in the town or no colored restaurant, then we went to the grocery store again for baloney sausage." Testing whether an eatery would serve them could carry its own curse. Stanley Glenn, a strong-armed catcher with the Philadelphia Stars, remembers taking his teammates into a hotel restaurant in Indianapolis where a policeman asked what they were up to. " 'Well,' we said, 'We're a baseball team, and we're here for the night and waiting for dinner.' He didn't like that, and for no reason at all locked up the entire ballclub in jail. He didn't even bother to tell us why or trump up some charges like disorderly conduct. He did it because he could."

The more roadblocks they encountered, the more the gypsy ballplayers improvised. Having a lighter-skinned teammate like Wilmer Fields, the Homestead Grays pitcher, presented one such opportunity. Fields could order takeout or even rent a hotel room, with darker-hued teammates climbing through the window afterward. Yet the ruse sometimes backfired, the way it did when Fields was in a whites-only café ordering sandwiches for a busload of Grays parked just out of sight. A chocolate-skinned teammate came in, intending to tease the pitcher. The restaurant owner was not amused, yelling at Fields, "Get the hell outta here."

Spending so much time dueling with second-rate white teams and dodging the minefields of Jim Crow made Satchel and his teammates pros at using charm and humor to deflect tension. Batters hit one-handed or on their knees. Satchel took his warm-up throws sitting down, with his catcher stationed behind the plate in a rocking chair. Best of all was a riff called "shadow ball," perfected by a traveling team Satchel later played for called the Indianapolis Clowns. The hitter swung so hard, fielders reacted so convincingly, and the runner tore down the line so fast that fans could hardly tell that it was pantomime. It was baseball so brilliant it could be played without the ball.

Negro players knew it was best not to win by too many runs if they wanted to be invited back the next year. Oftentimes they did not record the score, which would have embarrassed the locals. They learned to tune out when the ballpark announcer told fans that "Nigger Satchel will be doing the pitching today," or when "Bye Bye Blackbird" was broadcast as he exited the game. They tried not to let racial animosities eat away at their humanity. Their stage might be shabby but their performance remained regal. In the early thirties Satchel was hired to pitch for a black high school team in San Diego that was challenging its white rival. Partway through the contest he felt sorry enough for the white kids who were swinging without coming close that he let two of them get on base. Then he bore back down, striking out the San Diego players the way he always did when a game's outcome was in doubt.

Did clowning and cutting corners undermine their dignity? That was a touchy subject for Satchel and other Negro ballplayers. While their tolerances varied on many topics, there was a consensus when it came to "Tomming": it was taboo. It was okay to put on a great display of baseball for white fans. Okay, too, to make them laugh between pitches or innings. Even to ignore the ignominy of being addressed as "boy" or "nigger." But it was not okay to behave like that old slave in Harriet Beecher Stowe's 1852 novel *Uncle Tom's Cabin,* who forever after symbolized subservience. So they calibrated their performances to ensure that the kidding never got in the way of their playing. They would do a lot to support their wives and kids, which was not easy for Negro men in that era, but never to the point of compromising their manhood. When opposing players got cocky, the black barnstormers challenged them to a wager, then showed how dominating they could be with cash on the line. In rare cases where the crowd turned nasty, said Satchel's occasional catcher Connie Johnson, he and his teammates would "run twenty, twenty-five runs on 'em, so they'd leave the park whispering."

Another way Negro players coped with their wayfaring life in racist surroundings was to dream up their own lexicon. Most outsiders never knew because players never used it with them, and even if they overheard they would not have understood. Which was the point. It let players talk about fans, foes, and anything else without worrying about being overheard, the way immigrant parents used Yiddish, Polish, or Italian to keep things from their English-speaking children. For the baseball men, their language was about more than secrecy. It fostered intimacy. It was a shorthand for making their world make sense.

So "walking the bases drunk" became another way of saying loading them up with runners. "Scuffling" meant barnstorming with a black team, where the battle was constant. Young pitchers who were sacrificed in games that were beyond reach or did not matter were, for reasons no one could explain, called "sockamayocks." Old-time Negro Leaguers preferred "Negro" to "colored," and later to "black," much the way they favored "lady" over "woman." Count on a "100-proof guy" and check out a "pretty brownskin with a shape on her hittin' ninety-nine." Beware of "nasty types" or anyone slick enough to have "oil on his bottom"; both were "as unwelcome as an undertaker at a marriage breakfast."

Players got to practice their in-house idiom while they were playing bid whist and shooting dice, or relaxing at favorite watering holes like the Crawford Grill in Pittsburgh and the Blue Room nightclub at Street's Hotel in Kansas City. If giving words new meaning gave the guys a sense of belonging, being baptized with a nickname showed you had really arrived. Some epithets were bestowed by the press, like when Damon Runyon dubbed Ted Radcliffe "Double Duty" for his stellar play as pitcher and catcher. Sometimes it fit their looks, like when Norman Thomas Stearnes flapped his elbows like a "Turkey" as he ran. "Rube" Foster earned his in 1902 by vanquishing the great white strikeout ace "Rube" Waddell. Willie Mays traded in "Buck" for the "Say Hey Kid" when he moved from blackball to white.

No one was better than Satchel at inventing handles for players, white ones as well as black. Dorrel Norman Elvert Herzog already had one, "Whitey," but that did not stop Satchel from calling him "Wild Child," which he was and is. Chet Brewer became "Dooflackem" because that is what the pitcher chanted as he tossed dice. It was natural for Satchel to brand fireballer Bob Feller "Bob Rapid," less obvious why he chose "Old Homer Bean" for Dizzy Dean. Many of his new names were simple cases of not remembering the old ones—as in "Tom Lemons" for Cleveland Indians sinkerballer Bob Lemon, "Mark Griffin" for Washington Senators boss Clark Griffith, "Catch" for all of his receivers, and "Bo" for just about everybody. Pity the teammate Satchel pigeonholed as a "Hawgcutter," another way of saying bonehead. All his nicknames had a common theme: they were a way for this bashful man to reach out to fellow ballplayers.

THE CARNIVAL-LIKE FLAVOR of cross-country barnstorming dissolved when Satchel headed west to play in the California Winter League, which he did for nine winters starting in 1931. The league offered America's only ongoing competition between elite black and white baseball players during the first half of the twentieth century. Interracial engagement like that was ruled out by custom in the

Major Leagues, and by a lack of talent in barnstorming games where Negro Leaguers like Satchel played third-rate, all-white local teams. The few serious tours and tournaments pitting whites against blacks were high-energy but short-term. Negro League teams began wintering in California in 1910, facing off for a relatively full season against all-white teams of Major and minor leaguers. At last, blackball's best had a meaningful yardstick against which to measure their hitting, pitching, and fielding.

The Negro Leaguers beat the big leaguers more than 60 percent of the time and, between 1924 and 1939, they won thirteen of sixteen championships. Those results come with caveats. Negro League teams in the Golden State had players used to competing year-round and playing with one another. They generally included only the hardest-hitting black batters like George "Mule" Suttles and Turkey Stearnes, along with the hardest-throwing black pitchers like Wilbur "Bullet Joe" Rogan, Jim "Cannonball" Willis, and Satchel. The white teams, by contrast, were a mix of top-notch Major League talent like slugger Babe Herman and smoke thrower Bob Feller, along with journeymen from the minors who offered less competition. The white players were also less used to staying in shape year-round, were less likely to be playing with familiar teammates, and played fewer games in California, due in part to limits imposed by Major League Commissioner Kenesaw Mountain Landis, who frowned on interracial matchups.

So what verdict does the California experience offer on the relative talents of Negro Leaguers? The black teams at times were as good as the best of the Major Leaguers, although more often they were on par with the white minors. But when it came to one-on-one face-offs between the most skilled and seasoned players of both races, the black heroes proved they could star in any circuit.

That was no surprise to California baseball fans. Mixed-race games there drew audiences two to three times bigger than same-race ones. To anyone eager for integration, the black-versus-white encounters offered a preview of how it might work a generation before the Major Leagues deigned to experiment. To those skeptical about racial mixing, the California leagues offered a battle between the races. The games were equally heartfelt for the players, giving them a chance to argue for—or against—racial equity. "I'll never go up to the big leagues until I can beat these niggers," said South Carolina–born pitcher Louis Norman "Buck" Newsom, to which Cool Papa Bell reportedly replied, "Let's make him stay out here about two years." Whatever drove players and fans, the interracial contests were such a hit that the single black team in the league played each weekend while most white ones were limited to every third or fourth week, which is when they could get a date against the black team.

The biggest crowds of all turned out to see Satchel, whose presence on the field was good for an extra two thousand fans. They got their money's worth. He tore through white lineups, tossing seventeen shutouts and striking out an average of twelve batters a game during the 569 innings he pitched in the California Winter League. A dozen strikeouts is a great game for any pitcher; to do it every outing is a singular accomplishment. He notched fifty-six wins against just seven losses in California, and lost not a single game over a two-year stretch from 1931 to 1933. The winter of 1933–34 he was even more otherworldly, pitching all nine innings in eighteen of his twenty games, and dishing up seven shutouts, a 16-2 record, and an average of just 1.63 total runs allowed per game. He struck out a league-leading 244 batters while yielding a mere 47 bases on balls. And with Satchel, there was no question about the level of competition: white teams saved their aces for him, the same way Negro ones did, but few could better him. We won, he said, "like we invented the game."

Johnny Pesky, who is such a legend at Fenway Park that a foul pole is named after him and he is called "Mr. Red Sox," remembers seeing Satchel pitch on the West Coast when Pesky was ten and Satchel was in his prime. "He had the best control of anybody I ever saw," Pesky recalled as he was celebrating his eightieth year in baseball. There were no radar guns back then to measure a pitcher's speed, but Pesky swears that Satchel's fastball was at least a hundred miles per hour.

Reporters drew on metaphors from the front lines to capture the Paige glory. One said he shot balls across the plate "like a specially-built Big Bertha." Another crowned him "hero of the battle." The California League showed its gratitude in 1933 by declaring a Satchel Paige Day on November 11, which was Armistice Day and now is called Veterans Day. The only one surrendering that day was the other team, Pirrone's All-Stars, which Satchel shut out 5-0 on a three-hitter. Satchel was having so much fun that, late in 1934, he took time between the games of a doubleheader to serenade fans over the loudspeaker and took time from his honeymoon to pitch game after game. Looking at his contributions over all nine years, baseball historian William F. McNeil concluded that "Satchel Paige stood astride the California Winter League like the celebrated Colossus of Rhodes."

As good as the regular season rivalry was in California, baseball players from peewees through pros have always looked to tournaments to test their skills and try to topple the colossus. Sometimes that took the shape of a single contest like the All-Star games the Major and Negro leagues began staging in 1933. Other times it drew together further-flung teams the way a newspaper in Denver had been doing since 1915. The Denver Post Tournament started as a statewide contest and eventually attracted teams from across the Midwest and West and as far south as Florida. In 1934 the tournament reached another milestone, allowing in the first blacks for what became the highest-profile interracial face-off ever. Most were part of the powerful Kansas City Monarchs, an all-black team that Satchel would eventually join. Two other Negroes—Satchel and his favorite catcher, Cy Perkins—were rented for the occasion by another club, a collection of bearded ballplayers from Benton Harbor, Michigan, called the House of David.

The Israelite House of David was a religious community founded in 1903 by a roving preacher named Benjamin Purnell and his wife, Mary. Purnell declared himself the Messiah and seventh messenger of the Book of Revelation. While waiting for Christ's second coming, he assembled 1,200 followers to help him run an amusement park, hotels, a craft shop, a printing press, a jam and jelly factory, vegetarian restaurants, gold and coal mines, a foundry, and a vast farm that boasted the world's largest cold-storage facility. They were an entrepreneurial lot, claiming to have dreamed up the automatic pinsetter that became a staple in bowling alleys, the waffle ice cream cone, and baseball's pepper game, in which a player hit to three teammates who flipped the ball over their backs and between their legs with such speed that it seemed to disappear. An even better-known contribution was the five House of David baseball teams that barnstormed across North America in the 1930s, each playing more than one hundred games a year. They were a strange sight, with braided hair often reaching their shoulder blades, bushy whiskers, and a community member working the bleachers before each game, handing out religious literature and selling pictures of the players.

The scene became queerer still with the addition of two whisker-less dark-skinned men named Paige and Perkins. No matter that Benjamin Purnell and his successors would not admit blacks to their colony or their team; a breakaway group formed by Judge Harry Dew-hirst had no such color bars. The manager of Dewhirst's premier ballclub, white Hall of Fame hurler Grover Cleveland Alexander, knew that the Negro pitcher and catcher were just what his bearded sportsmen needed to best their seventeen competitors at the Denver Post Tournament, and especially the Monarchs, their regular barn-storming foe. From his first game Satchel justified that faith. The Davids won over the Italian Bakery of Denver 16-0, a tally so lop-sided that, when Satchel came in as a reliever in the ninth inning, the outfielders abandoned their posts and stationed themselves at the outer edge of the infield. After the first batter got on with a single, Satchel bore down with balls so fast and hard they seemed to knock the stuffing out of catcher Cy Perkins's thick mitt. Following a putout, strikeout, and putout, *Denver Post* sportswriter Leonard Cahn predicted that "Satchel is going to be a mighty popular man around these parts before the Little World Series is over or I miss my guess."

Cahn guessed right. In Satchel's first start in the series, he sum-moned a "magic fireball" and a "bagful of mound shenanigans" to fan fourteen and win 6-1. He was even better two nights later, when he struck out seventeen, extended to sixteen his string of scoreless in-nings, and subdued the Texas-based Humble Oilers with a 4-0 shutout. Cahn dubbed him "the Chocolate Whizbang" and said he "meted out a dose of his famous black magic to the hitherto unde-feated Texans." His third and final start was an encore performance, pitting the greatest Negro pitcher in the world against the greatest Negro ballclub. The pitcher prevailed, with Satchel beating Chet Brewer and his Monarchs 2-1 before a record-breaking audience of 11,120 at Merchants Park in Denver. The cavernous wooden sta-dium gave batters nightmares, with a center field fence so far away—457 feet—that only three home runs were hit there in the park's twenty-six-year history, including one by Babe Ruth. It was any pitcher's dream, especially Satchel's. An error spoiled what would have been his shutout against the Monarchs and ended his streak of scoreless innings at twenty-three, but he came away with his third victory in five days, a tournament record, and struck out twelve batters, boosting his total to forty-four in twenty-eight innings. "The Bearded Beauties banked everything on Satchel," Cahn wrote, "and the colored Whizbang did not disappoint." The Davids went on to capture the title and a $6,400 first-place purse. Satchel was voted the tournament's top pitcher. He would return to Denver in 1936 and 1937 on all-Negro All-Star teams that also captured titles, but it was in 1934 that white reporters got their first prolonged look at black baseball's best-kept secret.

THE MORE OF A HEADLINER he became, the more Satchel seemed to be defined by clashes with other oversize characters. It had happened in the Negro Leagues, where his feuds with fire-wielding slingers like Slim Jones took on the drama of a heavyweight title bout. Eighteen players took the field, but the press focused on two: the star pitchers. It was happening again in the California leagues and other barnstorming venues, where there was the added dimension of racial rivalry.

The best of the matchups pitted Satchel against Jay Hanna "Dizzy" Dean. Dizzy earned his nickname in the army, when a sergeant caught him flinging newly peeled potatoes at garbage can lids. "You dizzy son of a bitch," the sergeant yelled in a voice loud enough for the rest of the regiment to hear and agree. From 1930 to 1937 Dean anchored the St. Louis Cardinals' pitching staff, capturing four consecutive strikeout titles and winning the magic twenty games four seasons in a row. Yet, like Satchel, it was Dizzy's persona that lifted him from star to legend. His brand of baseball was raw-boned and hell-bent, as he showed in game four of the '34 World Series, when, inserting himself as a pinch runner, he broke up a double play by leaping forehead-first into the path of the ball. He crumpled to the ground like a broken doll and was carried off the field, but was back to pitch the next game. While he denied having intentionally sacrificed himself, gritty play like that was especially endearing to a nation weary of breadlines and an economy that kept hitting new bottoms. In the same way that Depression America would rally around a crooked-legged racehorse named Seabiscuit, so it took to Dizzy and his Cardinals. Their baiting of rivals, brawling with umpires, and sliding into bases on their bellies and faces earned them the moniker "Gas House Gang." Syndicated columnist Arthur Brisbane wrote that after Dizzy went down in game four, "of 123,000,000 people in this country, 99 percent are more interested in Dizzy Dean than the president of the United States."

Dizzy and Satchel were alter egos. The black pitcher and the white one both were underfed, loose-jointed boys from Dixie whose down-home demeanor belied the sagacity of a Rhodes scholar and the cunning of a corporate titan. Each preferred his nickname to his real one, and his own rules to his team's, league's, or society's. Neither was the kind of guy to whom one would introduce his sister, although fathers and brothers were aching to meet them. Ol' Diz pitched six of the Cardinals' final nine games during the stretch drive in 1934, a work ethic only Ol' Satch could match. Dean went Paige two better regarding his beginnings, equivocating not just about when he was born (was it January 16, February 22, or August 22?), but where (Lucas, Arkansas; Bond, Mississippi; or Holdenville, Oklahoma). Even his God-given name was a mystery (Jay Hanna or Jerome Herman). Their fractured aphorisms were so alike it seemed that Satchel and Dizzy were writing each other's lines, or perhaps stealing them. "It ain't braggin' if you can back it up" was one of Dean's most-quoted folk philosophies. Satchel's was "if you can do it, it ain't bragging." Both were master boasters. Both delivered often enough to earn election to the Baseball Hall of Fame.

That Hall of Fame form was especially apparent on an October afternoon in Cleveland in 1934, when twelve thousand fans saw Satchel's fluid form and lightning motion approach perfection. Most had come to watch Dizzy and his hard-throwing brother, Paul "Daffy" Dean, who also had won two World Series games that fall for the champion St. Louis Cardinals. On this Sunday the Deans had rented themselves out to the Rosenblums, Cleveland's top minor league team, for an exhibition game against Satchel and his Pittsburgh Crawfords. Dizzy was sharp for the three innings he tossed, allowing a single run on four hits before joining Daffy in the outfield.

Satchel was transcendent. For six innings the Dean brothers sat in the dugout watching Paige have his way with Rosenblum sluggers. Eighteen times they came to the plate, the bare minimum, and eighteen times they sat back down not just frustrated but flummoxed. Thirteen were strikeout victims. SATCHELL OUTHURLS DIZZY blared a headline in Pittsburgh. SATCHEL PAIGE DOMINATES GAME agreed a Cleveland paper. Chicago answered with a doubleheader: SATCHEL PAIGE HANDS BEATING TO DIZZY DEAN followed by SO SATCHEL PAIGE SHOWS DIZZY DEAN HOW TO PITCH. The sole fault anyone could find was that the Crawfords' manager took Satchel out after six innings instead of giving him a shot at a perfect game, where all twenty-seven batters are retired in succession—an achievement that happens on average in the Major Leagues once every 11,300 games.

How had Satchel become so dominant? His skills were the same ones he had learned at Mount Meigs and perfected in Chattanooga and Birmingham. Only now he was stronger, smarter, and markedly more patient. He was evolving the way incredible athletes do, making good on his youthful promise and showing no signs of aging. It was like Babe Ruth during his trophy years, when fans were convinced he would hit a home run every at bat, or Sam Snead, whose followers came to expect a hole in one. Satchel was in the zone and looked like he would stay there forever.

His laserlike focus that afternoon in Cleveland was more extraordinary considering that in just five days he was due to marry Janet. But the chance to face off against Dizzy Dean, white baseball's ace of aces, was Satchel's preoccupation all autumn and he made the most of each game. Sometimes Dean's teammates were merely the best local players he could muster. Occasionally they were top-of-the-line Major Leaguers like Wally Berger, a lifetime .300 hitter who mashed thirty-four homers that year for the Boston Braves. Berger remembers one day when he got the only hits off Satchel, a double and triple, and Satchel "followed me around for a second, looked at me and said, 'How'd you hit that one?' I got a kick out of that. Satchel went back to the mound and struck out the next three batters in order."

Talking to base runners became part of Satchel's routine. Normally he shouted from the mound but when he really wanted to make a point or stir up fans, he walked his message to the base. He did that once in Dayton, Ohio, when Dizzy tripled off him with a blooper over first and nobody out. "The fans were yellin' their head off for me," Dean told a radio audience, "when ol' Satch walks over and says to me, 'I hope all your friends brought plenty to eat, Diz, because if they wait for you to score, they're gonna be here past dark. You ain't goin' no further.' Then he fanned the next three." Satchel came back with a story of his own set out west, where he had heard Dizzy on the radio before the game arguing that Satch had no clue how to throw a curve. The truth was that Satchel had been quietly perfecting that pitch and others to go along with his trademark fastball. When Dean came up to bat that afternoon, Satchel yelled, "Hear say you're goin' around tellin' people I ain't got a curve. . . . Well, then, you tell me what this is." He threw three curves, with Dizzy swinging at air each time. "How's that," Satchel screeched, "for a guy who ain't got a curve ball?"

His shrieking often began before runners reached base. He simply loved to talk, and to taunt. "Look for a smoker at your knees," he would say, which to any savvy hitter meant preparing for anything but. But there it was: a knee-high fastball. While batters might not have believed him, his infielders did, knowing the cagey Paige was signaling them at the same time he was teasing the batter. "He told the truth, most of the time," said second baseman Bonnie "the Vacuum Cleaner" Serrell, who would team up with Satchel in Kansas City. "So I usually knew what pitch was coming." Talking had another purpose: unhinging the batter. Satchel was best at that when Josh Gibson was his battery mate and trash-talking confederate. "They'd get you nervous by talking," recalls James "Red" Moore, a masterful first baseman. "Sure it worked, it worked against me."

There was no joking the afternoon in 1934 when Satchel and Dizzy traded scoreless innings at Wrigley Field in Hollywood, California. The art deco stadium, a replica of its famous namesake in Chicago, had compact dimensions that made it a home run hitter's heaven. But not that day. The battle was epic and it lasted thirteen frames, with Satchel's squad eking out a win, 1-0. That accounting comes not from newspapers, where there were no articles on the game, but from one of baseball's best storytellers and Satchel's biggest booster. William Louis Veeck, Jr., says he was in the stands that afternoon, a twenty-year-old college dropout from Chicago watching what he calls "the greatest pitchers' battle I have ever seen." By the time he made that claim, Bill Veeck had seen thousands of games as owner of the Cleveland Indians, St. Louis Browns, and Chicago White Sox. "Even in those early days," the Hall of Fame owner wrote in his memoir, Satchel "had all kinds of different deliveries. He'd hesitate before he'd throw. He'd wiggle the fingers of his glove. He'd wind up three times. Satch was always a practicing psychologist. He'd get the hitters overanxious, then he'd get them mad, and by the time the ball was there at the plate to be swung at, he'd have them way off balance."

The Dean-Paige barnstorming continued into 1945, long past Dizzy's prime. Satchel won most matchups then, as he had from the first, in part because the batters backing him up were more likely to be first-stringers. To the end, the games were about money as much as anything, which is why Satchel and Dizzy generally pitched three innings, the minimum needed to satisfy fans and earn their paychecks of $1,000 or more. Major Leaguers like the Dean brothers could make more money barnstorming than winning the World Series. But there was passion, too, enough that the police were needed to quell a melee at Pittsburgh's Forbes Field after Dizzy talked an umpire into reversing a baserunning call for the Crawfords. "Players swung fists," a United Press International reporter wrote. "Some gripped bats menacingly and fans jumped over the railing onto the field. The police riot squad rushed in and restored order."

Baseball, not skin color, sparked that riot, yet race did help draw fans and it is what marks the Dizzy-Satchel contests as landmarks in American sociology as well as sports. The color-coded pairing of stars gave a human face to the battles between white and black baseball teams that had been playing out in California for twenty-five years. Dizzy was America's darling, hero of the just-completed 1934 World Series and dizziest of the brawling, cursing Gas House Gang. He was also a bigot, or at least that is what a casual observer would have concluded from his roots in segregationist Arkansas and his liberal use of slurs like *coon* and *nigger*. It was precisely that redneck image that gave resonance to a racial rivalry with Satchel that really was a rapprochement. On their barnstorming tour, ballparks that normally walled off blacks let them sit where they wanted. It brought in white reporters along with white fans. And when good ol' boy Dizzy Dean praised blackball legend Satchel Paige, followers of all hues pricked up their ears.

"A bunch of the fellows gets in a barber session the other day and they start to arguefy about whose the best pitcher they ever see, and some says Lefty Grove and Lefty Gomez and Walter Johnson and old Pete Alexander and Dazzy Vance," Dizzy wrote in a newspaper column in 1938. "I know whose the best pitcher I ever see and it's old Satchel Page, the big lanky colored boy. Say, old Diz is pretty fast back in 1933 and 1934, and you know my fast ball looks like a change of pace alongside that little pistol bullet old Satchel shoots up to the plate. . . . It's too bad those colored boys don't play in the big leagues, because they sure got some great players." This was no social reformer weeping over missed opportunities. It was the most convincing endorsement Satchel had from a white player, not to mention one with Dizzy's élan. It was also news, and was reprinted in papers across the country, sparking new rumors that Satchel might be signed by a Major League club. And it was not the first time that Dean had sung Paige's praises: "If Old Satchel and I played together," Dizzy said in 1934, "we'd clinch the pennant mathematically by the Fourth of July and go fishin' until the World Series. Between us we'd win sixty games."

If not being allowed to play together was a frustration for white ballplayers like Dizzy, it was torture for blacks like Satchel Paige. "They were saying Diz and me were about as alike as two tadpoles," said Satchel, "but Diz was in the majors and I was bouncing around the peanut circuit." His barnstorming games against Dean's All-Stars helped make the case that the best of the Negro Leaguers were the equals of their white big-league counterparts. But in so doing— in raising the curtain of segregation for those few games—it reinforced what Satchel and his black teammates were being denied the rest of the year. Once the real season started, Dizzy and his troupe went back to Broadway. Satchel and his returned to the chitlin' circuit.

FOR MANY WHITE BALLPLAYERS during the mid-1900s, crossing swords with Satchel was their most memorable experience on the barnstorming circuit. For up-and-comers it also was an acid test of whether they would make it to the Majors. Ted Williams was just seventeen when he first saw Paige pitch, in San Diego. Two things stuck with him—Satchel was so skinny that "he had trouble keeping his pants up," and he threw so hard that only a young catcher connected and only because Satchel "just let him hit it." Ralph Kiner, a dominant power hitter from the mid-1940s to the early '50s, was also seventeen and a high schooler when he got his shot at Satchel. It was a home run, his first, and Satchel asked teammate Buck O'Neil to tell him when the kid came up again. "So I came up again," Kiner recalled, "and he struck me out. I mean, you know, I wasn't going to [homer] twice." Rogers Hornsby, whose career average of .358 was second-highest in history behind the mighty Ty Cobb, likely never forgot or forgave the time Satchel struck him out three times in one game. That, along with the bigotry that allegedly drew him to join the Ku Klux Klan, probably explains why Hornsby rode Satchel like a drill sergeant when he became his manager sixteen years later.

No one got as much mileage, or joy, out of standing in against Satchel as Giuseppe Paolo DiMaggio. Their first encounter came on February 7, 1936, in Oakland, California. The twenty-one-year-old DiMaggio had Americanized his name to Joseph Paul and followed his older brother Vincent to the San Francisco Seals of the Pacific Coast Baseball League. Joe was invited to join the barnstorming big leaguers by virtue of an MVP season with the Seals that saw him hit .398, slug thirty-four homers, and steal twenty-four bases in twenty-five attempts. Satchel had been enjoying winter ball in Southern California when he got a call from the New York Yankees. Can you come north, the Yankees scouts asked, to help us see what this DiMaggio kid is made of?

Now here they were, DiMaggio facing Paige in the tenth inning, with a man on third, two outs, and the score deadlocked at 1. Backed by a crew of semi-pros and high schoolers, Satchel had single-handedly carried his team against one of the hardest-slugging collections of Major Leaguers he had ever faced. He struck out fourteen, setting down cleanup hitter Gus Suhr of the Pittsburgh Pirates and the Philadelphia Phillies' Johnny Vergez three times each. Batters were baffled as he seemed to be looking at third when he threw to the plate, his sidearm heaters rising, then sinking. Satchel came up big on offense, too, driving in his team's only run and smacking two hits, which was two more than DiMaggio managed in his first three at bats. But this was the one that counted as Joe stepped in with a setting sun casting shadows on the infield and four thousand fans on their feet. He bounced a hard hopper to the right of the mound that Satchel deflected to the second baseman, who tossed to first an instant too late to catch DiMaggio and stop the runner on third from scoring.

DIMAGGIO ALL WE HOPED HE'D BE, a Yankee scout telegraphed his bosses in the Bronx. HIT SATCH ONE FOR FOUR.

Satchel saw the matchup through a different lens. He would face all the great white hopes of baseball on their way up or down, from Jimmy Foxx and Pepper Martin to Charlie Gehringer and Stan Musial. The challenge for him was not to get left behind and lost as they marched to grandeur. Even as he pronounced Satchel the real star that day in Oakland against DiMaggio, *Chicago Defender* sportswriter Eddie Murphy worried that "the greatest baseball pitching attraction in the world is being passed up by scouts, club owners and managers only because the doors of organized ball are closed to him." Satchel was frustrated that in Oakland, like everywhere else, he had to prove his prowess yet again. "When you weren't in the major leagues you had to keep proving it," he said, "because nobody goes around keeping tab of barnstorming and Negro league records like they do the major league's." As for his role in helping DiMaggio make it to the Yankees, Satchel noted that "I got more notice for losing that game than I did winning most of my other games."

One person he never had to prove himself to again was Joe DiMaggio. Over the years the Yankee Clipper repeatedly called Satchel the best pitcher he ever faced. Shortly after the Oakland game, with his memory even fresher, he testified that "Satch has a curve with so many bends it looks like a wiggle in a cyclone: it gave me optical indigestion. And his fast ball? Say, when he fires it the catcher gets nothing but ashes!"

The ultimate clash of white and black titans would have pitted Satchel against Babe Ruth, the strikeout king against the home run king. Satchel said he did meet up with a barnstorming team assembled by Babe on a warm night in Los Angles in 1930 or thereabouts, and struck out an inconceivable twenty-two of them, two more than today's Major League record. "Everybody in that whole place was mobbing me. I almost lost an arm getting it pumped so many times," he wrote in his 1962 memoir, but "I never counted those twenty-two strikeouts as my one-game record. I always said it was eighteen even though I hit twenty-two in other games, lots of times. But when I talk about records, I'm talking about league games and those twenty-two strikeouts always came in exhibition games. . . . I know some of the boys ain't in shape when I whiff them in those games." As for Babe himself, Satchel wrote in his 1948 and 1962 books that he did not play against him in the contest in Los Angeles or anywhere else. "When I was pitchin' he wasn't playin' and when he was playin' I wasn't pitchin'. A keen regret I have is I never pitched to Mr. Ruth."

Others tell a different story. "I saw Satchel play in an exhibition game with daddy and daddy commented on the fact that he's quite a pitcher," Julia Ruth Stevens recalled from her home in Conway, New Hampshire, in 2007. Stevens, who was ninety-one then, had sharp recall of events from her father's playing days although she was not sure how he fared in the exhibition appearance against Satchel. That game was in New York, she added, but "they may have had more than one game together. This was a long, long time back, in the 1930s."

Two more versions come from Satchel himself. He said he played against Babe but offered no details in a 1943 story carrying his by-line in *The Pittsburgh Courier*. Five years later he told writer and publisher Bennett Cerf that during an exhibition game in Phoenix he intentionally walked three men to get to Babe, then struck him out on four pitches. Bob Feller, who one day would replace Dizzy Dean as Satchel's barnstorming sidekick, said he heard and believed similar stories about Satchel striking out Babe, as did Cool Papa Bell.

The last Babe-Satchel account is the least flattering to the pitcher, which may be why he chose not to recall it. Baseball's most powerful hitter matched skills with its most overpowering pitcher in 1938 or thereabouts in a battle of barnstormers on the South Side of Chicago. Ruth would have been about forty-three then, and officially retired for three years. "Babe comes up and the first pitch Satchel throws he hits over some trees, five hundred feet," Buck O'Neil remembered in an interview in 2006, repeating a story he told eleven years earlier during a seminar at Hofstra University. "You know who greets him at home plate? Satchel. He held up the ball game for ten minutes while a kid got the ball and brought it back for Babe to autograph. That's the only time Satchel faced him."

BISMARCK WAS AN OASIS. After his endless barnstorming against white and black stars, and his constant feuding with Gus Greenlee over money, North Dakota seemed the perfect blend of faraway and laid-back. That is why Satchel had gone there to play baseball near the end of the 1933 season, and why he came back two years later for a full season.

Equally telling is what kept him away in 1934. Team owner Neil Churchill had Satchel's word he would return and, based on that, Churchill had added three thousand grandstand seats, built bleachers for the kids, and expanded the parking lot on the far side of the outfield to let still more people watch from their cars. *The Bismarck Tribune* reported in January that Satchel was "expected in Bismarck next week." In May the paper was still hopeful, noting in big print that Satchel and another black pitcher "have not arrived," then explaining that "they might reach here during the day." By September the city was losing faith, with *The Tribune* writing, "the local baseball management are not making any rash promises about Paige's being here. The trouble encountered earlier this year when he promised to report while under contract with the Pittsburgh Crawfords warned them that he is not always dependable." Yet even into October the club kept its fingers crossed that the enigmatic pitcher might yet lead Bismarck against a barnstorming team of big leaguers led by Earle Mack.

The mystery over his whereabouts was easily solved. He was in Pittsburgh, California, and Denver, pitching the best ball of his life. It was classic Satchel: making more commitments than he could keep, then keeping those that offered the most exposure and most cash. He was following the money, same as always. He would walk out on more signed contracts than any player in history. When he came back it was generally on even richer terms than before.

Once Churchill realized he had been jilted, the *Chicago Defender* reported, he "sent sheriffs looking for the lost pitcher with instructions to lock him up unless he agreed to play for their team." The Baltimore *Afro-American* saw things differently, writing that "Paige is being detained on orders from the Pittsburgh police department. . . . Paige is a member of the Pittsburgh Crawfords' baseball team, but was reported on his way to Bismarck, N.D. It has not been revealed under what charges the elongated hurler is being held, but since it is known that he has received money for services not yet rendered it is likely that charges will be based along these lines." While Neil Churchill and Gus Greenlee were both frustrated enough with Satchel's unreliability to want him locked up, it is unlikely that either would have wanted the police involved. Gus steered clear of the law because of his illicit businesses, Churchill on account of his illicit wagering.

The Bismarck owner, like his Crawfords' counterpart, could relate to Satchel's eccentricities and to his Horatio Alger roots. Churchill and Satchel were both raised by widowed mothers who took in laundry to pay the bills and pushed their adolescent sons to find work. "If there was another side of the tracks, that is where I was born," Churchill once said. Serendipity took the Wisconsin native to Bismarck in 1919; ptomaine poisoning convinced him to stay. He liked how people in Bismarck nursed him back to health when he contracted a disabling case of the food-borne illness. He started selling cars, then moved into management, and in 1924 he became one of the original distributors of automobiles made by the new Chrysler Corporation. The Prince Hotel was his, too. He was a stalwart in Bismarck's Elks, Rotary, Shriners, and Masons, and served as mayor for seven years, from 1939 to 1946. While peddling cars and placing bets are not prescriptions for popularity, few in Bismarck then or now have anything but acclaim for their big-as-an-icebox auto magnate.

One wellspring of that esteem was what Churchill did for local sports. He had been a semi-pro baseball standout in Wisconsin, where he caught future Hall of Famer Burleigh Grimes, and continued playing and starring in Bismarck. He managed the capital city team, then bought it in 1933. He also ran the Bismarck Phantoms, a semi-pro basketball team whose opponents included the Harlem Globetrotters. The Trotters were owned, managed, coached, and promoted by Abe Saperstein, a white booking agent who helped find lucrative deals for Satchel and other Negro Leaguers. When Churchill came looking for black baseball ringers to help him beat archenemy Jamestown, Saperstein said he could land Paige.

Recruiting Negroes for a white baseball team was novel enough, but bringing them to the lily-white Northern Plains seemed outlandish, at least to outsiders. Locals knew it was a great match. In 1899 caramel-skinned Walter Ball, known for his finely tailored suits and meticulous control, won twenty-five games and led an otherwise all-white team in Grand Forks to the North Dakota title. The next year an all-black team from Nashville toured Montana and North Dakota, to a surprisingly warm reception. In 1925 a white team from Plentywood, Montana, signed the great Negro League slinger John Donaldson, referred to by local columnists as "that cul'd gentleman, Mr. Donaldson." North Dakota also had a history of circumnavigating what it considered wrongheaded rules of Major League baseball, signing players who had been banned by the pros, had drinking problems, or were kept from working by their pigmentation.

So with Saperstein's encouragement and Churchill's money, Satchel came to Bismarck near the end of the season in 1933. "I wasn't exactly sure that North Dakota belonged to [Uncle] Sam," he said, although he had in fact played there five years before with a famous black barnstorming team, Gilkerson's Union Giants, and the famous cul'd pitcher Donaldson. It did not take Satchel long to reacclimate. As always, he tried to erase his teammates' doubts by dazzling them. Placing matchboxes on a stick beside home plate, he stepped back to the mound and proceeded to knock them off with thirteen of twenty pitches. Okay for control. To demonstrate his speed he fired in a series of fast ones to his catcher, who reached for his chest protector and mask but still felt like he was a sitting duck.

Satchel won six of his seven starts in 1933, including a shutout. He averaged nearly fifteen strikeouts a game, with an astounding eleven-to-one ratio of strikeouts to walks, and let in just 1.25 runs per nine-inning outing. In an end-of-season series versus Jamestown, with the state championship at stake, Satchel pitched a six-hitter, whiffing fifteen and singling in the winning run in the tenth. Two days later, having turned down an invitation to play in the first Negro League All-Star game, he led an underdog Bismarck against a squad of minor league All-Stars, all of whom had signed with Major League teams. It was a blowout, with Satchel's team on the slaughtering end of a 15-2 score. He yielded just four hits, struck out fourteen, and would have had a shutout but for his two errors in the eighth, one on a rushed double play, the other a pop-up he tried to grab with one hand.

Remembering performances like those made Churchill forget the way Satchel had spurned him in 1934 and, as the 1935 season approached, he courted Satchel the way only a lifelong car salesman could. He dangled more money than Gus Greenlee, who had just said no to a raise, and sweetened the deal by offering Satchel the use of a spanking-new automobile, which he knew was Satchel's favorite toy. Yet Churchill was a realist: he made sure the deal locked in his pitcher tight as a drum. Satchel was soon heading to Bismarck for a second time, with his new bride, Janet, in tow. As for Gus, he was not used to being one-upped and he threatened to slice Churchill end to end.

The auto man did not stop with Satchel. He loaded his club with black talent like knuckleballer Barney Morris, who had a fastball to match, and whites like left fielder Vernon "Moose" Johnson, who drank hard but hit baseballs even harder. As the season went on, two stars from the 1934 Jamestown team signed up, Double Duty Radcliffe and infielder Danny Oberholzer. Chet Brewer brought to Bismarck his curve, sinker, screwball, cutball, and a determination to do whatever it took to own home plate, including beaning batsmen. Hilton Smith was master of the curveball and, in the minds of many, the best black pitcher of his age. All those gifts paid off as Bismarck batters pounded out nearly three hundred more runs than their foes while Churchill's top five starters compiled a cumulative record of fifty-five wins and six losses.

The ace, as expected, was Satchel. He won twenty-nine games and lost just two, one of the best records for any pitcher ever. While his 1933 ratio of eleven strikeouts for every walk had been inspired, in 1935 he nearly doubled that, with 321 strikeouts and a mere sixteen bases on balls. During one stretch in July, Bismarck played thirty games in twenty-seven days, with Satchel pitching at least an inning in each. Fielders expect to play every day; pitchers, even relievers who throw just an inning a game, need time off. Satchel beat the

Twin City Colored Giants 21-6 in Bismarck's last home game of the season. That was the team's twelfth win in a row, which raised its record to 66-14-4 and established a mark of 175,000 paying customers over the course of fifty home contests. It also led to antics likely never seen before on a baseball field. Bismarck batters felt so sorry for the Colored Giants that, in their last inning, righties batted left-handed and lefties hit from the right side. Infielders and outfielders, meanwhile, abandoned their positions early so that, at the end, only two of Churchill's crew were left on the field: Barney Morris behind the plate and slim Satchel Paige on the mound.

As much as Satchel was enjoying himself on the diamond in Bismarck, he was having more fun off it. He went rabbit hunting with his baseball buddies Trouppe and Haley. Softball was a distraction when the weather was nice; when it wasn't the trio ate hot dogs washed down with strawberry pop and played card games like coon-can, a poor man's rummy. Satchel also had an understanding with Churchill, who was an avid gambler. The owner counted on Satchel winning to back up bets Churchill placed on Bismarck, which became an increasingly vital source of support for the ball club when sales of cars tumbled during the Depression. Churchill showed his appreciation by giving Satchel gifts like a rearview mirror with a clock and a sleek .22-caliber rifle. Counting his salary, car, and other perquisites, Satchel's earnings that summer reached a cool $8,600, which today would add up to more than $130,000. "Satchel walked into my father's showroom and said he wanted the red convertible," says Neil Churchill, Jr., the auto dealer's son. "Dad said, 'If you win tonight, it's yours.'" That was all the incentive needed for the pitcher, who was soon driving around in an open-top, ruby-colored automobile. Not that anyone in Bismarck needed flashy wheels to recognize the elegant black man with leatherlike arms that reached below his knees.

Janet was less recognizable, and she had no fun being one of the few Negro women in that city, state, or region. The fact that Satchel was around so seldom, and was inattentive when he was, persuaded her to wait for him back in Pittsburgh. With Janet away Satchel looked for the company of local women, which meant white ones, a dangerous proposition even in a relatively tolerant place like Bismarck. The one rule he heard his dad communicate to Negro recruits was "make sure they don't mess with the [white] women," says Randy Churchill, Neil Jr.'s younger brother. Trouppe said the Bismarck owner approached him as an intermediary: "Quincy, I don't know how to put what I'm going to say to you, but it's about Satchel. You know the fans are really wild about his performance, and so am I, but there is one thing I'd like for you to talk to him about on my behalf. I understand a man has to go out with a woman, but there is a way to do it in any walk of life. Just tell him to be careful about riding white girls around in broad daylight."

Satchel got the message, cutting back on his carousing and becoming more discreet. Even so, he "was foolin' around with some girl and got gonorrhea," said Double Duty Radcliffe, who loved to spin tales about his time with Satchel. "He couldn't throw the ball to the plate. I told Churchill to send him to the Mayo Clinic to get him some shots. 10 days later he was throwing hard as hell."

North Dakota was Indian country then as now, and on his off days Satchel hung around the reservation often enough that the tribe gave him the honorary title "Long Rifle." "They took a real liking to me, too, and those Indians watched me good. They even gave me some snake oil," he said in his memoir. "When they gave me the oil, they said, 'That's hot stuff. Don't use it on anything but snake bites.'" Warning him off got Satchel to thinking: if the salve was as potent as the Indians said, it might keep his arm loose. He rubbed some in and it worked, so he started using it after every game. "Since then," he wrote, "I always keep some of it in a jar and it kept my arm nice and young. It's real fine oil, the best. The formula is a secret. I promised those Indians I wouldn't tell it, but I guess I'll put it in my will so folks will have it when I got no more need for it." He never did put it in his will, although he repeated and embellished the story as he got older and the world wondered how his ancient limbs could keep flinging a baseball as fast as a shooting star.

Trouppe, who sparred with Satchel as they warmed up before games, said he learned the real key to Satchel's longevity while the two were clowning. "I grabbed him," said the catcher, who was Satchel's height and fifteen pounds heavier. The pitcher, he discovered, "was mighty powerful. That day I realized why Satchel's fast ball was so deceptive. He had long, wiry arms. His stride was long also, and with his long, strong fingers he could put such tremendous back spin on his fast ball that it would rise two to four inches while traveling from his hand to the batter. That is why his fast ball looked like a marble to the batter." Their time together in Bismarck also taught Trouppe how complicated Satchel was: "He could clown one moment and become deadly serious the next. His complex personality made him immensely interesting."

Interesting is not the word Gus Greenlee was using to describe his ex-ace. He preferred *AWOL.* Or *ingrate.* Gus was outraged enough at Satchel's abandoning his two-year deal with the Crawfords and playing in Bismarck that he tried unsuccessfully to turn over his contract to the House of David and had him banned from the Negro National League for the 1935 season. None of this slowed down Satchel. He knew he mattered more to black fans than the weak-kneed league. What did hurt was that so-called race papers like *The Pittsburgh Courier* and the *Chicago Defender* offered little coverage of his doings in faraway North Dakota, which meant his legions of black fans in the East did not know how alive and well he was. Some might have believed *Courier* sports editor Chester Washington when he wrote baseball's equivalent of an obituary in April 1935. "The champ of today may be the 'chump' of tomorrow," argued Washington, who like other *Courier* writers often acted as Gus's mouthpiece. "So it may be with Paige. The League helped to make him and now the League may be the medium to break him. Satchel apparently made the mistake of regarding his contract as a 'scrap of paper' and now he must pay the penalty."

To Churchill, sour grapes by Eastern owners and writers were inconsequential. Having proven that his team could dominate the regional competition, he wanted to know how it stacked up nationally. The perfect test was at hand in Wichita, Kansas. Raymond "Hap" Dumont was a newspaperman-turned-sports-promoter who was audacious enough to believe that he could pull off a national baseball tournament in the middle of the Depression, with neither the money to finance it nor a completed stadium. What he did have was a commitment that, for $1,000, Satchel Paige would come and bring his Bismarck teammates. Dumont invited thirty-two semi-pro teams, including state champions and other bests-of from the near coast to the far. There was an American Indian club from Oklahoma, a club from California of Japanese Americans, a team of the ten Stanzak brothers from Waukegan, Illinois, and four all-Negro squads. Denver had been hosting a semi-pro tournament for more than a dozen years, but this one in Wichita in 1935, with entries from twenty-four states, would be the first truly national tug-of-war. Satchel's club, the only one in which blacks played alongside whites, assured that the test would be of racial mixing as well as baseball talent.

Neil Churchill loved wagering on sports so much that, in his later years, all it took to bring him to life was the whiff of manure he would catch driving by a racetrack. Yet with $7,000 in purse money at stake in Wichita along with national bragging rights, the Bismarck owner did not rely on chance. The batsmen and fielders who piled into a Plymouth and a Chrysler bound for the tournament were impressive, but it was his pitchers who ranked with the best ever, Major League or not. Satchel led the staff with a record of 29-2, followed by Barney Morris at 12-3-1, Hilton Smith at 6-1, and Double Duty Radcliffe at 4-0. The fifth starter, picked up on the way to the tournament, was Chet Brewer, the Kansas City Monarchs' ace who the year before won sixteen straight. Smith would join Satchel in the Hall of Fame; the other three could have and may still.

The Bismarck team delivered just the way it was built to, sweeping the competition in seven straight games. Fans from the capital city who could not afford the trip to Kansas gathered in the lobby of Churchill's Prince Hotel to hear the good news streaming off the telegraph. They learned how stalwart third baseman Joe Desiderato made a throwing error that let in two runs in the first game and almost cost Bismarck a victory, and how the often-inebriated left fielder Moose Johnson was a no-show for the last game. Most of all, they heard about Satchel.

He won the four games he started, whiffed seven batters in two and two-thirds innings of relief in a fifth contest, and let in a total of just seven earned runs. An earned run average of 3.00 or less is considered top-notch; Satchel's average for the series was 1.62, which is about as stingy as it gets. He ended with just six walks and sixty strikeouts—the latter a record that still stands seventy-four years on. He contributed with his bat, too, driving in two runs in the third game, two in the seventh, and ending with his team's fourth-highest batting average at .308. Satchel was an easy choice as the tournament's outstanding pitcher and most valuable player.

Anything Bismarck fans missed in real-time reports they could fill in from breathless newspaper dispatches. One columnist, noting that Satchel had a queasy stomach the first game, said, "If Paige was sick when he struck out 16, I'd like to see him when he was in A-1 condition." A headline in *The Bismarck Tribune* after Game 5 asked the question on the minds of his opponents: HOW CAN THEY HIT SAFELY WHEN THEY CAN'T SEE 'EM? After the dust settled, George Barton of *The Minneapolis Tribune* wrote a tribute that the Bismarck paper reprinted. Satchel, he said, had everything: speed, intelligence, courage, and control. A white pitcher with those skills would command $100,000 on the open market. "Were he Caucasian instead of Ethiopian," Barton concluded, "Paige would take his place alongside of the Dean brothers, Carl Hubbell, Lingle van Mungo and other pitching greats of the major leagues."

He was not Caucasian, of course, and his dark skin almost kept him from ever appearing in Wichita. "Some of them baseball managers was talking about keeping me out," Satchel wrote years later, a charge made believable by the fact that the next year neither integrated nor all-black teams were allowed. Were he white, Satchel, a virtual quotation machine, surely would have been cited regularly or at least occasionally by white journalists in Bismarck, Denver, Wichita, and other cities where he barnstormed. As it was he was quoted almost never. Bismarck's six black players also ran into trouble finding a place to stay in Wichita, with the team hotel refusing them rooms. That was nothing new for them; they found black-run rooming houses glad to take their money. Dumont was pleased that things worked out for the Bismarcks and especially for Satchel, who proved the money magnet the promoter had counted on. The new Lawrence Stadium was ready in time, fifty thousand fans turned out for the games, and the tournament made money even after paying off Satchel and his teammates.

It also made history. Satchel had appeared on the same baseball field as Dizzy and Paul Dean as well as scores of other white diamond demigods, but never on the same lineup card. Now here he was at a national tournament, on a roster split almost fifty-fifty between Negroes and Caucasians, playing spectacularly enough to grab the attention of even the most entrenched bigot. "They said at the tournament in Wichita, 'Double Duty and Satchel are niggers,' " recalled Double Duty Radcliffe, " 'but they're big league niggers and we can't beat them.' "

CHAPTER 5

South of the Border

*"It was like I was a shot-putter. The ball'd bloop up a little
and then drop, not going anywhere."*

THE CARIBBEAN WAS FAT CITY for Negro ballplayers in the 1930s
and '40s. It had constant sun and soft white sand, emerald seas with
rich reefs of coral, and a Latin landscape where baseball not soccer
reigned supreme. African Americans could pitch and hit on the same
field and team with players who were white or brown, then accompany them to the best restaurants, theaters, or hotels without fear of
being stopped by hostile proprietors or the local *policía*. If there was
prejudice it was a matter of economics, not race. The freedom was so
breathtaking—and such a contrast to the segregated world from
which they had come—that many Negro Leaguers talked about
staying and some did.

That is what had drawn Satchel Paige in 1929 to Cuba, the first
island nation to welcome U.S. ballplayers, and in 1933 to Venezuela,
where he helped lift baseball in the former Spanish colony from amateur status to Latin power. What drew him back four years later to
the Dominican Republic was a suitcase full of cash and the chance to
be the headliner when the brightest baseball stars from across the
hemisphere came together for one exhilarating, explosive season.

Satchel's Dominican story is set in 1937, but its seeds were

planted seven years earlier when a former telegraph operator ran for
president of the republic. Rafael Leónidas Trujillo Molina was a cat-
tle rustler, blackmailer, forger, and exploiter of demurring women of
all pedigrees and maturities. After the U.S. Marines took over the island in 1916, Trujillo joined the constabulary, rising quickly to
major, lieutenant colonel, and colonel. When the Americans left he
became commander of the National Police, then chief of the Dominican army. He kept his troops in their bunkers as the elected
president was toppled on the eve of the 1930 elections, then ran as
the sole candidate and won more votes than there were registered
voters. His soldiers enforced the results, launching what parliament
proclaimed as Year One of the Era of Trujillo. By Year Eight his secret police were quietly disposing of opponents who complained
about the president. Other innovations by "the Benefactor of the Fatherland": anointing his son a colonel at age four and brigadier general at nine; renaming Santo Domingo, the oldest city in the New
World, Ciudad Trujillo; and erecting an electric sign in the capital
that proclaimed DIOS EN CIELO, TRUJILLO EN TIERRA ("God in
Heaven, Trujillo on Earth"). A more fitting sign was the one on the
door of a mental hospital outside the capital that translated to, "We
Owe It All to Trujillo."

The dictator did not give a whit about baseball. His brother, sisters, and son were the fans in the family; Rafael preferred the more
patrician pastimes of polo and sailing. Yet he knew his people were
mad about baseball and he saw an opportunity to exploit that passion in 1937, a year before a presidential election and a year after a
club from San Pedro embarrassed the two teams from Trujillo's capital city. Those clubs, Licey and Escogido, were merged into one
called Dragones de Ciudad Trujillo. After agreeing to the alliance,
the directors of the new team—"in an act of respectful sympathy"—
unanimously elected Trujillo as honorary president and protecting
partner. Then they set about remaking the Dragones in their patron's
image, which is to say *número uno* no matter the cost.

The way to do that, as Gus Greenlee and Cum Posey had demonstrated, was to raid talent from other teams. The best available was
American and black. Greenlee himself had laid the road map by having his publicity department distribute worldwide an annual account of his team and its star pitcher, Satchel Paige, who in 1936 had

returned like a prodigal son to the Crawfords. One avid reader of those reports was Dr. José Enrique Aybar, a dentist, dean of the University of Santo Domingo, and a deputy in the Dominican congress. Aybar was the kind of chameleon that crawls out of the quiet in every totalitarian society. He began his political life as a Trujillo foe but once it became clear the generalissimo would prevail, Aybar prostrated himself. To show his devotion, he offered to take the reins of the capital city's baseball club.

It was a calculated choice. Aybar knew Trujillo was ambivalent about his namesake team. He also knew the president hated to lose. That meant Aybar could act on Trujillo's behalf without worrying about his meddling. The scholarly tooth doctor took control at an apt moment: his team was struggling, with up the only place to go. He set his sights on Satchel as the one player who could vault the club into the stratosphere and bring Aybar into Trujillo's good graces. So in the spring of 1937 the Dragones boss set off for New Orleans, where the Crawfords were training.

Aybar was persistent but he was not alone. His league had just three teams, and the others—Estrellas Orientales of San Pedro de Macorís and Águilas Cibaeñas of Santiago—were making recruiting trips of their own. Everywhere Satchel went in New Orleans he ran into agents whose Panama hats and cream-colored suits betrayed them as Latin even if he mistook them for Haitian. Finally Aybar cornered him, blocking Satchel's car with his black limousine and by one account pulling a pistol to focus the pitcher's attention. "We will give you thirty thousand American dollars for you and eight teammates," Satchel remembered Aybar telling him, "and you may take what you feel is your share." That was more money for a month's work than even Satchel made for a year of backbreaking barnstorming, and in today's dollars would be $444,000. So, after figuring that his share for rounding up teammates as well as playing was worth twice everyone else's, Satchel said sure.

Finding others who would go was no small thing. There was less money for them and more loyalty to owners like Gus Greenlee. But steep payouts and police raids had roiled Gus's numbers rackets to the point where, early in 1937, he could no longer meet his baseball payroll. So Cool Papa Bell reluctantly abandoned the Crawfords, which made it easier to land Leroy Matlock, Sam Bankhead, and a dozen other Negro Leaguers. Cy Perkins, Satchel's habitual battery mate, was already on board but Josh Gibson initially balked. He was playing winter ball in Puerto Rico and it took a sweetened offer to team Josh up one last time with Satch.

Gus and his fellow owners did not take it lightly when their top stars headed south. First the Negro League chieftains lashed out, having several Dominican agents arrested for fraud. When the charges did not stick, Gus, as president of the Negro National League, barred Satchel and the other Latin-bound players from organized blackball. Rather than dissuading the players, the arrests and bans let them know they were in demand and how much the raiders were offering. Half the desertions came from the Crawfords, and within two years Gus would have to give up his ownership.

The Dominican-bound Negro Leaguers got a sense of what was in store for them as soon as they landed on the island. Aybar called a press conference to show them off and send a message on how things ran in this exotic land where mountains, provinces, streets, bridges, and buildings were all named Trujillo. The ballplayers he recruited were expensive, the Dragones manager explained, but their salaries came from fan donations rather than government funds. "Baseball is spiritual in every aspect, as indulged in by Latin races," he went on. "This has been the biggest year in baseball ever seen here, because of peace, unity and goodwill brought to the republic by President Trujillo."

Aybar got it partly right. Baseball was spiritual in the Dominican Republic and fans historically had underwritten their teams. But this season of 1937 was different. Salaries of the American recruits were too high, forcing owners of the Santiago and San Pedro teams to dig deeper into their pockets and those of their friends. Coming up with money was easier for the Dragones. Trujillo's corporate friends like the American Sugar Company were eager to kick in cash as well as passage on its ships, which moved in and out of port without the inconvenience of passport checks. The president had brought unity to the Dominican Republic but at a price: the reporters at Aybar's press briefing knew it could cost them their jobs or more to question his pro-Trujillo propaganda.

What unnerved Satchel was when a journalist confided to him that "Trujillo runs the whole show down here, and he wants a team so good it will win the championship. That'd be a real feather in his cap. You see, his chief rival is a strong man down in one of the provinces and that boy got a ball club, too. Trujillo won't like it if his club goes around losing to that other club." Cool Papa heard similar whispers. The Negro Leaguers' anxieties were fanned by the armed guards who were their constant shadows—at the beach, their hotel, and every ball game. The night before the big game, when Satchel's friend Chet Brewer came looking for him, he was told by a street urchin that the Dragones ace was *"en la carcel"*—locked in jail.

The players' fears were as implausible as they were unsettling. Trujillo had no overt opposition, among baseball owners or anyone else who knew the score. Satchel's journalist was right: the strong-man did run the whole show. Baseball was a distraction from that show more than a subplot in it. The mission of the ballplayers' escorts was protection not intimidation. As for Satchel's lockup, it was a house arrest to ensure the high-priced athlete slept peacefully, ate well, and stayed sober.

The American Dragones actually lived like princes. Stories of Satchel's *travesuras,* or mischief, are retold to this day. He occasionally arrived at the stadium with a hangover, although not as often as Josh and Sam Bankhead did. He and his teammates were regulars at the cabaret, where women with flowing hair tried to teach them to dance the merengue. The menu at Café Lindbergh featured a *plato de jonrón: Pavo relleno Joshua* (home-run plate: stuffed turkey á la Joshua) and a Satchel Paige filet mignon. The local paper complained about the U.S. ballplayers' lack of discipline, calling them "children" and "pikininis." When they were not eating and carousing, the Negro Leaguers were bodysurfing and fishing. "It was just real relaxing, something we weren't used to," said Cool Papa.

President Trujillo himself barely noticed the ballplayers parading around his capital that spring and summer. He was too busy plotting a campaign of carnage against Haiti, the Dominican Republic's French-speaking, soccer-crazed neighbor on the island of Hispaniola. By fall, Trujillo would order what Dominicans refer to as *El Corte* (the cutting) and the rest of the world calls the Parsley Massacre. Trujillo's troops confronted dark-skinned farmers who were living on the Dominican side of the border and were suspected of having Haitian roots. The soldiers held up a sprig of parsley and asked,

"*Como se llama esto* (What is this called)?" If the answer came out *pe'sil* instead of *perejil*—Haitians have a difficult time pronouncing the trilled *r*—the subject was slaughtered with a machete, bayonet, or club. The death toll exceeded fifteen thousand.

Satchel and his fellow players had little inkling of the ruthlessness of the ruler under whose banner they were playing. They did see the sign that was painted on the wall over left field and read NATIONAL BASEBALL CHAMPIONSHIP 'REELECCIÓN PRESIDENTE TRUJILLO 1938–1942.' LONG LIVE THE BENEFACTOR OF OUR FATHERLAND. The tournament, forty-four games over three and a half months, was officially devoted to the president's election campaign. But the only ones who paid attention to the banner or the election were Trujillo bootlickers like Aybar.

Games were played exclusively on weekend mornings or afternoons, and they were hot as well as wild. Arguments sizzled to the point where the police had to be summoned, with the preponderance of problems coming in contests involving the Dragones. Umpires made bad calls, out of incompetence and bias. Fans made their own bets on who should and would win, backing them up with cash. And Satchel was in his familiar role of star, although not at the beginning and not always. The Dragones won the first game he pitched, in April, but another pitcher got the credit and for Satchel it was a "poor debut," according to *Listín Diario,* the nation's oldest newspaper. His first win came the following month in a performance the paper rated as good but not great. Next time out *Listín Diario* was pleased to see Satchel "without a hangover" and pronounced him "somewhat more serious." After that reporters called his curveball "enigmatic" and "indecipherable," his fastball "terrifying," and his intelligence "highly developed." "He is above all a winning pitcher," the Dominican paper concluded, "inspiring confidence in his players."

Satchel was not the only luminary and the Dragones were not the only great team. All three clubs had standouts from across South and North America. The *norteamericanos* generally dominated the action along with the press coverage. Satchel went 8-2, tops in the league. Sometimes he won back-to-back starts, other times he came in as a reliever. Sportswriters for years had labeled his artistry black magic, but this time they might have been right: a voodoo priest from Haiti

had given him a wanga, or magic charm, that he thought was good
luck but later learned was to make him lose.

As the season wound down the action switched to the rooms
where the league's governing board met. The question at hand was
simple: should all three teams keep competing? The board ruled that
San Pedro had no chance of winning, so it was out. It is true that
Ciudad Trujillo and Santiago were well ahead, and nearly tied with
each other. But whether there were enough games left for San Pedro
to catch up is impossible to know. Records of what the remaining
schedule would have been for each team are long gone, as is an understanding of how ties would have been factored in. San Pedro's dis-
qualification probably was the product of squishy math, as the club's
supporters claimed, but that is how numbers were tallied in the Era
of Trujillo. What was left were eight decisive games, Águilas versus
Dragones.

The Dragones won the first four games, with Satchel pitching two
of them. That was not enough to clinch it; the Águilas could have
squeaked in as champion by 0.2 percent if it won all four that were
left. An 0-4 record was enough to dishearten the Santiago club, four
of whose Cuban stars, including Luis Tiant, Sr., headed home. Even
without them, Águilas rallied to win the next two games. That
led to a critical seventh face-off between the two teams, on Sunday,
July 11.

In his autobiography, Satchel set up the action like a scriptwriter.
Every one of the stadium's several thousand uncomfortable seats was
filled, with scores more standing. Soldiers were on hand with long
knives in their belts and guns at the ready. Many fans were armed,
too. "Boy, my mouth was dry that day!" Satchel wrote. " 'Satchel, old
boy,' I say to myself, 'If you ever pitched, it's now.' " He was used to
the starting assignment in games that mattered but none would
matter more than this. And nowhere were the odds stacked against a
pitcher like they were at the capital city's postage stamp–size ballpark, which was tailor-made for home runs.

By the seventh inning Satchel's team was behind by one run and
spectators were warning, "You'd better win." The more they yelled
the harder he threw. His fastball was never better. In the seventh the
Dragones cobbled together a pair of runs and Satchel managed to
shut down the Águilas over the last two frames. "We win," he de-

clared, "6-5." Each time he looked back, the stakes of that triumph grew. "I had it fixed with Mr. Trujillo's polices. If we win, their whole army is gonna run out and escort us from the place," he told *Collier's* magazine in 1953. "If we lose, there is nothin' to do but consider myself and my boys as passed over Jordan." In 1962 he recalled that when he was behind in the seventh inning, "you could see Trujillo lining up his army. They began to look like a firing squad." By 1965 he had ratcheted it up another notch, confiding to *Pittsburgh Courier* columnist Wendell Smith that Trujillo "was re-elected a day or two after we won that game for him. . . . We left by boat and the people came down to the dock by the thousands to cheer us and give us big bouquets of flowers. I often thought afterward that those flowers could have been on my grave if we hadn't won that game."

His electrifying story line was picked up by scores of journalists and authors over the years, most of whom commented on his inventiveness even as they accepted his rendering of the facts. He learned well the lesson: retell a story often enough and it becomes fact, especially when most eyewitnesses are long gone and the rest understand only Spanish. South of the border, he told an interviewer, "I could say anything because they couldn't speak English." The truth is that the Dragones did win that last game, but by a score of 8-6, and Satchel did not appear until there was one out in the ninth inning. With men on first and second and his team leading 8-3, Satchel gave up three hits and three runs before a terrific throw by Sam Bankhead helped him get the game-ending third out. He did preserve the victory, barely. The stakes of that game were also not quite what Satchel said. Had the Águilas won, there would have been an eighth game, although the Dragones were delighted to clinch early. The presidential election was not for another year and Trujillo, facing international pressure over his massacre of Haitians, ended up pulling out in favor of a candidate he could manipulate.

And while it made for a compelling scene for Satchel to leave the island to the cheers of grateful fans, the means and timing of his departure became additional points of contention. In his 1948 memoir Satchel said, "The American consul heard what a worrisome situation we was in and they flew us out in a bird that same night." In 1962 he wrote, "I hustled back to our hotel and the next morning we blowed out of there in a hurry. We never did see Trujillo again. I ain't sorry." Yet *Listín Diario* reported that Josh, Cool Papa, and most of the others left three days after the clinching game, by steamer. In 1937, days after he led the Dragones to the title, Satchel himself painted a decidedly different picture of any peril he faced. In a July 31 story for the Baltimore *Afro-American,* datelined Trujillo City and carrying his byline, Satchel made clear that he had stayed on in the Dominican Republic after "all the boys have left for the States." He later told the U.S. State Department that he was still living in Trujillo City as of September 1937, although he likely left in early August. His teammates might be "running away like the world was on fire," as he wrote in his newspaper column, but he knew better, at least back then.

The pitcher also could not resist having the last word relative to his critics at home. Egged on by Gus Greenlee, reporters had been lashing out at Satchel for abandoning the Crawfords, the Negro National League, and America. Chester Washington of *The Courier* branded him "as undependable as a pair of second-hand suspenders." Satchel shot back in his July *Afro-American* article, which ran under the headline PAIGE SAYS HE PREFERS JUNGLES TO N.N.L. PLAY. "I would be willing to go to South America and live in the jungles rather than go back to the league and play ball like I did for ten years," he wrote. "The opportunities of a colored baseball player on these islands are the same or almost the same as those enjoyed by the white major league players in the States. That's something to think about."

Something else to think about is the legacy of that 1937 season. Recruiting players from Cuba, Puerto Rico, and especially the United States was so financially and emotionally draining for the Dominican teams, in the middle of a depression, that professional baseball there went into a fourteen-year hiatus. But Satchel likely never knew about those ripples. He was too busy plotting his next move to ever look back.

SATCHEL WAS GLAD TO GET HOME and was anxious to reconstruct his baseball life in the U.S.A., but to the poobahs of blackball he returned less the conquering hero than an incorrigible ingrate. Facing a Negro League ban for jumping ship to play in the Dominican Republic, Satchel and his fellow desperados formed a team of their own. Drawing players from the Santiago and San Pedro teams as well as the Dragones, the blacklistees were what the *Chicago Defender* called "perhaps the most sensational team in the history of Race baseball." At first they called themselves the Trujillo All-Stars, even wearing old Ciudad Trujillo uniforms, then they switched to the more American-sounding Satchel Paige All-Stars. The club captured the title at the Denver Post Tournament in August 1937, then it took to the road.

One face-off Satchel would never forget or get over was on September 19 at the Polo Grounds, against a team of Negro League All-Stars led by Johnny "Schoolboy" Taylor. Satchel struck out eight, three more than Taylor, but he gave up eight hits and two runs while Taylor hurled a no-hitter. The *Defender* was ready to dethrone Satchel, writing that he was "until today at least, America's number one pitcher" but had "met his Waterloo" against Taylor, a young buckshooter who newspapers said was between twenty and twenty-six years old. The Baltimore *Afro-American* wrote that by beating Paige, Taylor had joined "the select circle of baseball's immortals." Satchel was even harder on himself: "You've never seen an old man if you didn't see me after the game. I ran back to the hotel and locked myself in my room. 'Maybe I'm over the hill?' I kept asking myself. It's a mighty bad feeling when a young punk comes along and does better than you and you know it." It was easy for Satchel to think of himself as old, having pitched for more than a decade and facing perpetual challenges from upstarts. But at thirty-one he was in his pitching prime, and after a couple of days moping he did what he always did: he shuffled back to the mound and outpitched his *nouveau* opponent, winning 9-5 before more than twenty-five thousand fans at Yankee Stadium. The *Afro-American* wrote that Taylor "was shelled from the mound after five innings of furious slugging on the part of the San Dominicans." The *Defender* called it "sweet revenge."

Gus Greenlee and the other owners were lustfully tracking the success of Satchel's band of outlaws, and in 1938 the Negro League bosses did an about-face—lifting their ban, lowering their fines, and bringing back into the fold any who would come. Gus tried to reconcile with Satchel. He offered more money than his tattered finances allowed—$350 to $450 a month—with the caveat that

Satchel would be docked $15 for each game he was a no-show. The pitcher scoffed that he would not throw ice cubes for such a pittance. He had grown accustomed to fatter paychecks with no strings. He would quit baseball rather than accept Gus's offer, he told a *Courier* reporter who tracked him down in New York, where he was learning the boogie-woogie and hobnobbing with old barnstorming buddies. "I'm holding out because Joe DiMaggio advised me to."

Broadway Joe was a fitting role model given the way Satchel had, in his words, gone uptown. He had tasted success, fame, and money, and wanted more of each. It was a heady experience to be treated like a prince in Cuba, Venezuela, and the Dominican Republic, exotic spots that he had daydreamed about as a boy sitting astride the bridge in Mobile, gazing south. One night after he got back from Ciudad Trujillo he was at a posh nightclub when the waiter told him friends from Mobile were in the lobby asking for him. "Tell them I left already and you didn't know it," he told the server. Then he tried ducking out the back door, but the Alabamians spotted him. Satchel apologized, saying he was late for a meeting but would track them down later. He never did "and never thought anymore about it. It took me a lot of years before I found out it was a mighty little man who did things that way."

Satchel had taken to treating Gus the same way, and the Crawfords' owner had had enough. He let it be known that Satchel was on the auction block and jumped when Abe and Effa Manley, owners of the Newark Eagles, offered more than $5,000 for the temperamental star. It was more money than anyone had paid for a black ballplayer, and it set off a two-year chase that cost them thousands more in legal fees, hobbled their team, and resulted in endless embarrassment as they learned that it was Satchel himself who controlled his fate, not his presumed owner. The Manleys could not reel in Paige despite getting the New York Supreme Court to issue a restraining order preventing him from leaving the country. They could not even unravel where the renegade pitcher was.

He had become a world traveler by then, or at least was in demand worldwide. A club in Argentina was making a high-priced bid for him. He would later claim that he had pitched in Panama and Hawaii, Japan, Brazil, Trinidad, Colombia, and the West Indies. *The Chicago Tribune,* in a promotion for Satchel's upcoming interview on

its sister radio station, WGN, promised that he "will tell of his baseball experiences in 17 countries."

The *New Jersey Herald News* was one in a series of newspapers that
searched the planet looking for him over the years. In September
1938 it reported that "the mystery of Satchel Paige is solved. The
Unpredictable One has skipped the United States again, the *News*
learned late Tuesday. Satchel and several other players are reported to
have hied off to Mexico where they will play baseball this summer."
When Greenlee and the Manleys learned that he had deserted them
again, they convened an emergency meeting of the Negro National
League and banned him "for life." To show they were serious, or at
least better at bluffing, the owners vowed to boycott any team connected to Satchel and his fellow desperados and to keep them out of
league parks. Cum Posey was more philosophical, writing in his
Courier column that "to punish him severely by baseball law or by
civic law is like chastening a child who has been brought up wrong."

Jorge Pasquel was amused by the huffing and hand-wringing. He
and his family had assembled an eclectic empire in Mexico that included a cigar factory and a network of newspapers. Now they were
building a baseball league. The model was firmly rooted in Latin
soil: the best players available in the world were black Americans,
and the best way to lure them was to hook the flashiest among them,
Leroy "Satchel" Paige. Pasquel offered a salary five times higher than
Gus had. Satchel accepted, and U.S. newspapers spread the word of
Pasquel's banditry just the way he hoped they would. Mexico in
1938 was ground zero for Negro Leaguers in Latin America much as
the Dominican Republic had been a year earlier and Cuba before
that. Once they arrived, the black ballplayers learned that their new
home offered more than money. They could embrace or avoid the
same spicy food that white tourists did, get by on the same pidgin
Spanish, drool over the same overpriced yachts, and be viewed by
Mexicans as ballplayers, not black men. "I've found freedom and
democracy here, something I never found in the United States. I was
branded a Negro in the States and had to act accordingly. Every
thing I did, including playing ball, was regulated by my color,"
shortstop Willie Wells explained later. "Here in Mexico I am a
man."

Satchel, too, relished the liberties he discovered during his Latin journeys, with whites and blacks, Latinos and gringos, playing with and against one another in a way that was inconceivable if not illegal in most of the United States. He adjusted to his teammates' speaking Spanish when he did not (" 'Speak English, boys,' I yelled. 'I is with you.' "). He got used to the gamblers, and to suspicions that he was in their tank if he lost a game (fans showed their displeasure by pulling out machetes). And while he seldom stayed away from America for long, he was more in demand than Willie Wells or anyone else, back home and across the world. That was a good thing since he had more wanderlust, ego, and addiction to the piles of pesos waiting for him in places like Mexico City. As he wrote later, "When a guy down there put a few bucks in my pocket—a few more than Gus Greenlee'd give me—I walked down to Mexico."

His Mexico adventure would be derailed by his first major malady in a dozen years of professional pitching. It started in Venezuela, when he felt a sharp pain in his right shoulder after tossing his standard sidearm fastball. When he got to Mexico City he was trying to perfect his curve, which required unleashing the ball with more force, motion, and spin. That meant more strain on his arm. He heard the snapping of his shoulder joint before he felt it. The pain was so sharp he slumped to the mound.

In the past the key to keeping his spindly limb limber had been to keep his stomach trim, his back and legs strong, and to go on pitching. So that is what he did now, even though his right arm felt like somebody had pinched off the blood. He pitched in a handful of games, winning one, losing one, and watching his season compressed to 19⅓ innings as his earned run average soared to 5.21. Fans who had come expecting to witness his dominance left admiring his grit, especially in two games against Cuban jack-of-all-trades Martín Dihigo. To go head-to-head with Dihigo and his imposing team from Veracruz was why Mexico City's Agrario club had hired Satchel. In the first matchup in early September he did what he was paid to do, giving up a single run in eight innings. Two weeks later he could barely hold up his arm but he took to the mound again. Patrons were impressed by how long he had lasted (six-plus innings), but reporters focused on the final score (Veracruz 10, Mexico City 3). He looked, one sportswriter said, like a "squeezed lemon."

Finally Satchel retreated to his hotel, hoping tequila and rest would heal him. "The sun was way up when I woke up in the morning," he said. "It was going to be a good day, I thought, and sat up real quick. My stomach got sick with the pain that shot up my right arm." He tried lifting the arm but couldn't. He sat on his bed sweating, the pain so sharp he wanted to cry. He was scared. Really scared. Again, the thirty-two-year-old pitcher felt ancient. "Have you ever seen an old man, a real old one, one who hurts so he can hardly move and what he can move is so stiff it don't work very good?" Satchel asked afterward. "That was me." He managed to pull on his clothes and head for the ballpark, determined to give his wing a test. He cocked his arm but could not lift it as far as his shoulder. It was less than sidearm. It hurt like nothing he had ever experienced. He tried again. "It was like I was a shot-putter. The ball'd bloop up a little and then drop, not going anywhere."

He was examined by physicians—"about every doctor they had in Mexico City"—but none could find what was wrong. That night he packed up and moved back to the United States, where he once more went from doctor to doctor in city after city. Again, nothing. Finally he heard about a specialist who was supposed to be the best at treating injuries like his. "I remember him," Satchel said, "because after he was done poking me, and lifting my arm, and checking my back, he studied and thought for what seemed like an hour. Then he turned and looked long at me. 'Satchel, I don't think you'll ever pitch again.' "

His reminiscences were always dramatic and often embellished, but this time he was alarmed in a way he had not been since Mrs. Meanie sentenced him to Mount Meigs. The fear was fitting. His arm, after all, is what had carried him out of Mount Meigs and Mobile. Thanks to it, he had gone from eating catfish to steak. It had endured twelve years of travel over tens of thousands of miles, pitching every day without complaint. His default pitch, the one he threw more often and with more velocity than anyone, was the fastball, which puts greater strain on the shoulder than anything else a pitcher can throw. Just cocking his arm back as far as he did was the equivalent of pressing a forty-pound weight against his upper arm and lower neck. The moment he let go of the ball another 180 pounds were pulling at his socket and the tendons in his arm were releasing three horsepower of energy. The faster he threw, the greater the press, the pull, and the power. Repeating that night after night, top-notch doctors were telling him now, had so impaired his arm and shoulder that he was through. Such pronouncements were usually gospel in the 1930s. Sports medicine was not yet a recognized specialty. Orthopedics relied on manipulation, stabilization, and rest to treat breaks, rips, tears, pulls, and other common athletic injuries. Damage to ligaments and tendons that today would be surgically repaired in hours and rehabbed in weeks was career-ending back then. There were no medical miracles, or precious few.

Satchel had been depressed before, but it was only transitory. Now it would not let up. For a week he sat in his hotel room, imagining a life without a vocation or income. It had been a long time since he had thought about what it was like having nothing—no money, no job, no hope—the way he did growing up in Mobile. Now he remembered. He tried finding work as a coach or manager; there were no jobs nor even sympathy for the former high-rider. "I didn't want to go nowhere," he said. "I didn't want to see nobody. I could see the end. Ten years of gravy and then nothing but an aching arm and aching stomach." The one place he did visit was the pawnshop. First it was a shotgun, then a silk suit. Anything to pay the hotel bills and buy a meal or two. Tenderloin was off his menu, replaced by that old mystery meat, Spam. He sometimes thought of Janet, which is something he had stopped doing when he was healthy. "I knew if I couldn't keep her when I was a big man, I sure wasn't going to be able to keep her when I was a broken bum just wandering around looking for a piece of bread."

Redemption came in an unexpected guise. J. L. Wilkinson, the white owner of an all-black team from Kansas City, picked him up from the scrap heap. Wilkinson would become close to Satchel in a way that Gus Greenlee never managed, and the pitcher would show him a fealty he gave to few others as they cemented their relationship over the next decade. For now, it was a job the owner was offering and a modest one. Satchel would pitch when he could and otherwise play first base, not on Wilkinson's first-class Kansas City Monarchs, but on a second-string barnstorming team that its owners named the Travelers and players called the Baby Monarchs. It was now rechristened with the familiar title of the Satchel Paige All-Stars. The squad was a blend of young players on their way up and oldsters ready to retire. The shortstop quit midseason to go back to teaching school and the first baseman kept threatening to leave. No one complained when the manager shot rabbits out of the window of their moving bus. For Wilkinson, adding Satchel to the mix was a chance to trade on the Paige name to draw fans, pay back other broken-down players who in their prime had helped the Monarchs, and, as a risk taker and man of faith, to hope against hope that Satchel would regain his grace and skill. For Satchel, Wilkinson's offer was a godsend.

Working for the Baby Monarchs took getting used to. Sometimes he played first base or coached there. More often he pitched an inning or two, which he had done every night for years for fans who came especially to see him. This time he could barely manage despite plenty of rest. "I was throwing Alley Oops and bloopers and underhand and sidearm and any way I could to get the ball up to the plate and get it over, maybe even for a strike," he recalled. Even that made his arm ache. He knew the pitches he was throwing would never fool anybody in the real Negro Leagues, not without a fastball to go with them. They did not fool his barnstorming foes either, but Wilkinson had fixed it so few batters embarrassed the fallen ace, whose drawing power was paying their salaries, too. Those games took Satchel across the Midwest and Northwest and into California, and after every one he soaked his right arm in boiling water. "How'd he ever get anybody out?" he heard a boy ask his dad. Talk like that wounded him but he kept going because he had to. He traveled and tossed and hurt.

News of his injury was slow to spread. Black reporters did not tag along with the roving team the way they did with the real Monarchs, and it was not in Satchel's or Wilkinson's interest to include word of his wound in their game summaries. The *New Jersey Herald News,* which never stopped digging into why the pitcher had bailed out on the Newark Eagles, scooped the Mexico injury story the same way it had his fleeing there. "Baseball circles have been humming with the report that the great pitching arm of Satchel Paige has gone dead. Several players who were with 'Satch' in South America last summer reluctantly verified this report," the paper wrote in December 1938. That news, the article added, "comes as a shock to baseball fans throughout the country." John I. Johnson, the sports editor of the black-oriented Kansas City *Call,* weighed in afterward with a less timely but more poetic version of Satchel's plight: "The great one, who had been an astonishment to batters in every important diamond center in this country and a revelation to baseball fans in the Caribbean Islands, owned a wing that was as dead as a new bride's biscuits."

It was that bad or worse according to players who teamed up with the crippled pitcher in 1939. "He couldn't even wipe the back of his neck," said second baseman Newt Allen. Frazier "Slow" Robinson, whose perch behind the plate let him see Satchel's arm troubles from the same distance and angle that batters did, pronounced the inveterate ace "washed up. His arm hurt real bad, and everybody knew it. Even though he was trying to get back in shape, nobody really believed that his arm would ever get right again. I was in my late twenties and on my way up, and Satchel was in his early thirties and sinking fast." All that was left in the repertoire of the once-overpowering pitcher was off-speed junk.

Then it turned, just like that. It was a warm Sunday and the Paige All-Stars were playing one of the House of David teams. Satchel approached his friend Robinson and said, "You better be ready because I'm ready today." The catcher was dumbfounded and skeptical, telling him, "I can catch what you been throwing in a work glove." His doubts were confirmed when he warmed up the pitcher: it was like catching marshmallows. Satchel lobbed the ball—underhanded. When the leadoff hitter stepped in, Robinson called for a fastball but expected more lobs. Satchel "threw that baseball so hard that he knocked the mitt off my hand. I walked out to the mound, handed the ball back to him, and said, 'I'll be ready from now on.' " The Baby Monarchs won that day, decisively. And the soreness was gone, just like that.

Satchel called it a miracle, and he called all that came after a second childhood. He was never a religious man and spent little time in church back then, but over the years the tale of his comeback took on a born-again dimension. By the time he sat down for an interview with *Collier's* fifteen years later, he could pinpoint the very moment it happened. He stooped to pick up a wild throw by a teammate and tossed it back—pain-free. All his teammates saw it, the magazine reported, and stood stock-still. Satchel took to the mound, throwing harder and harder. Nobody moved, the stands went quiet, the game waited. His catcher cried, "Easy, Satchel, easy!" But Satchel leaned into his tosses until the ball seemed to vanish in space, the way it used to. Suddenly aware of what was happening to him, he stopped to look around. "Well," he said, "I'm back."

What he was back from is unclear, although today's sports medicine specialists speculate that he had a partially torn rotator cuff in his shoulder caused by the repetitive stress of throwing so hard for so long. Satchel's own diagnosis shifted each time he told the story, growing more colorful in a way that was becoming a pattern with his reminiscences. When he was in Venezuela years before, eating nothing but liver, his gurgling stomach had sapped the strength from his arm, he explained, so in Mexico City he decided to save his speed and pitch curves instead. But the city is 7,400 feet high, and in that thin air it is difficult to get the atmospheric lift needed for a ball to bend. "I worked harder 'n harder tryin' to angry up the air," he said, "but my arm got mad instead." Other times he traced the troubles to staying in the ocean too long, then not covering up in the cool evening air. Or drinking poisoned water in the tropics. Or his bad teeth, which he later fingered as the source of his stomach miseries and all else that ailed him.

Even more mysterious is what healed him, or who. Everyone had a theory. Johnson, the Kansas City *Call* journalist, says it happened one afternoon when Satchel threw and threw and threw in the bullpen until the perspiration was dripping down his face and his shirt was wringing wet. "From that day on," Johnson said, "Satchel had his stuff back." Not quite, said Paige teammate Bonnie Serrell. Satchel's return to form came on a rainy day in Washington State when he was playfully sparring with outfielder Leandro Young. Young punched the pitcher as hard as he could in the small of the back, sending Satchel crumpling to the floor with a crack. The room went quiet but Satchel slowly got to his feet and announced that he wanted to go outside in the rain and try throwing. "You're either going to catch a fastball or catch my arm," he told his battery mate while other players looked on. The eighty-mile-an-hour pitches he had thrown the day before were now traveling at a hundred, Serrell recalled, and Satchel once again could put the ball wherever he wanted.

A more likely sorcerer was Frank "Jewbaby" Floyd, the Monarchs' longtime trainer, who brought ballplayers back from the brink with the magic of his healing hands complemented by training in massage and chiropractics. Jewbaby soaked Satchel's arm first in water that was scalding, then in an ice bath. He alternated cold towel wraps with red-hot ones. He reached into his bottomless black bag for thick ointments and smooth ones, clear gels and a liniment he called "Yellow Juice" that was so ripe it scared away the mosquitoes. He had Satchel rest his arm by pitching fewer innings and playing other positions. All of which, with the possible exception of Yellow Juice, are precisely the treatments today's high-tech healers prescribe for tendon tears in the rotator cuff.

SATCHEL NEEDED A GETAWAY that winter of 1939–40. He had spent too much of the previous year watching in horror as his young arm suddenly aged and shredded, then slowly nursing it back to pitching form. For the first time ever he had felt mortal. Now the question was whether his broken body really was fixed.

Puerto Rico was the place to find out. It had sparkling beaches, passionate baseball fans, and Latin stars like batting champion Pedro "the Bull" Cepeda, whose son Orlando would team up with Satchel a generation later in the Major Leagues. The island was far enough away to let Satchel escape the inquiring eyes of skeptical U.S. reporters and the pitcher's own sense of fragility. And Puerto Rico's political, economic, and cultural ties to the United States gave residents more access than anyone in the Caribbean to news from America, including news about baseball. They knew how good Satchel Paige had been, heard how he had been banished to the Baby Monarchs, and would quickly recognize if the pitcher was damaged goods.

He proved himself from the start with his new team, the Guayama Witches. In early November he shut out the team from Santurce, a barrio of San Juan, by a one-sided 23-0. It was Santurce's worst defeat in its sixty-year history. So flustered were his rivals that Josh Gibson, Santurce's catcher-manager, pitched a third of an inning. The next month there was one for the Puerto Rican record books when Satchel fanned seventeen Mayagüez batters, the most ever at that time. "Paige threw aspirin tablets that morning," recalled Marco Comas, the opposing catcher. Satchel used the same medicine all season long, burning the ball over the plate just the way he had before his arm flamed out. Opposing players called in sick rather than face him. "It took special eyes to see his pitches," Ramón "Nica" Bayron, a pitcher for Mayagüez, said as he sat on his porch recalling the games from sixty-seven years before. Satchel also did a respectable job at first base, where he would play the game he was not pitching in a doubleheader, although he was not the hitter he thought he was despite lugging from home a thirty-six-inch bat. Luis Olmo, a hard-slugging outfielder who later played with the Brooklyn Dodgers, says that that winter Satchel was "the best I've ever seen."

Satchel's powers had returned, and back with them surged all the old swagger. Facing Bus Clarkson, the Negro Leaguer who was leading the Puerto Rican League in homers, Satchel was classic Paige. He had arrived on the island on a Pan Am Clipper just a week or so before, and now he was pitching to Clarkson in the first inning with the bases loaded. His strategy: issue an intentional walk and give up a sure run. The manager came running out of the dugout and said, "No, no, don't walk him," recalled Buck Leonard, Clarkson's teammate, who had a bird's-eye view as the runner on first. "I'd rather walk one run home," said Satchel, "than to have that so-and-so hit all three of them home and score himself." Then he issued his trademark vow: that would be the last run the other team would get all day. It was, with Guayama winning 8-1.

By season's end he had won nineteen games—the most before or since for a single season in Puerto Rico—and lost only three. The Witches were already a championship team, and with Satchel's help they took a second consecutive title. Even though he showed up four weeks into the 1939 season, his 208 strikeouts were the most ever and came in just 205 innings. Puerto Rico's baseball season was 56 games, compared to the 151 that Major Leaguers played in 1939. Assuming he could have kept up the pace for a full big league–style season, Satchel would have ended with a breathtaking 51 wins and 561 strikeouts. As it was, he was overpowering enough to win the island league's most valuable player award.

Satchel was used to being toasted in towns where he pitched. It had happened in Chattanooga and even more so in Birmingham and Bismarck. None of that prepared him for Guayama. Ball games were generally played on Sundays, when there were two, morning and afternoon. Townspeople tried to find time for church before or after the game. If not, God would understand. Baseball was what fishermen thought about when they cast their lines and farmers when they harvested the sugarcane. Theirs was a community remote enough not to matter except when the local club vanquished rivals from bigger cities like Mayagüez, San Juan, and archrival Ponce. Games were announced on metal placards and by cars with roof-mounted speakers blaring, "Come see the incomparable Satchel Paige." Buses and taxis ferried fans across the island. Today, seventy years on, when baseball is less central to Puerto Rico's sense of itself, old men still gather at the makeshift museum in Guayama to replay the years of glory. "Remember Cy Perkins," one will offer, "and how he would sober up just enough to catch the great Satchel?" "Yes," another adds, "but when Perkins couldn't, remember how Cefo Conde padded his mitt with five sponges before daring to receive Satchel's fast one?"

Things went so well that first season of 1939–40 that Satchel came back the following winter. He had less to prove the second go-around and more to distract him, starting with Luz María Figueroa.

Lucy, as she liked to be called, was not unattractive but she was not pretty. She stood five-feet-eight, weighed 140 pounds, and was the kind of girl people described as statuesque and solid. Her clothes were dated and untailored, an easy fit in a town where most everyone dressed that way. But she had a confidence and composure that, if you noticed her, made you look again. She was the sort of upbeat, engaged student who made teachers glad to be teaching. Other kids took to her, especially on weekend afternoons when they gathered to play records, drink sodas, and listen to Lucy sing songs such as "Babalú" by Cuban pop idol Miguelito Valdez.

When she was a child her raven hair hugged her shoulders in ringlets so curly her mother called her "the Spanish Shirley Temple." Her five brothers and two sisters called her "Cotorra," or Parrot, a tribute to her constant chatter. They all loved running free around Guayama, a city on the southern coast so compact and familiar that parents never worried. Even better was curling up on the wicker couch in their living room, the radio tuned to soap operas or baseball. There were enough of them for the Figueroas to make their own team, a decided advantage on an island where everyone was Catholic and a bat, ball, and glove were everything.

It is unclear what made Satchel notice Lucy. Not her looks, which had none of the sleekness or steaminess that generally reeled him in. It might have been her sauciness, and hearing her say *"váyase al carajo,"* words she did not find in the catechism her mother made her memorize. She knew enough English to ensure that Satchel knew just where she was telling him to go, which was more than the other girls could or would say and helped since he spoke but a word or two of Spanish. He tipped his hat that first time he passed her house on the way to the stadium. She said, "Hello, mister." Satchel saw his own overpopulated, dirt-poor family in Lucy's. And he was flattered that a girl fresh from high school and half his age was infatuated with him. Looking back in his memoir he called Lucy a "fine woman," although when he met her she was years away from womanhood.

Lucy could not help but notice Satchel. It was not just his dominance on the baseball diamond. He was tall enough to tower over any crowd, sported a distinctive felt fedora, and had both a tooth and a watch made of gold. Between games Satchel received his admirers in a manner befitting the Indian sovereign from which the city took its name. Sitting on the terrace of his stuccoed Hotel Paris, his liver-flat feet stretched over the railing, he greeted fans passing below in the Plaza de Recreo. At the movie theater he again took to the balcony, tossing candy and peanuts to squealing children. Leaders of old had carriages and chariots. He went one better: a gold Cadillac brought by ship from the United States, one of just a dozen cars in Guayama. One place he drove was the church school, whose students saw him as the Pied Piper for getting them in free to ball games and handing out pesos or dollars. He was Goliath, too. "He was so big that the children looked at him and thought he was in the sky," recalls Desiderio de León, who was a child himself then and batboy for Satchel's team. "He talked about baseball and about discipline. He told them, 'Don't you smoke. Don't drink.' " He might have added, "Do I what I say, not what I do."

Older Guayamans were equally enamored of their baseball hero. After his morning workout at the ballpark and an afternoon siesta, he held court in the town plaza, with its rows of laurel trees. Every shoe shine wanted to buff his wingtips, every fan was eager to talk baseball. A master roller made him a special blend of handmade cigars. His fat salary gave him money to burn, and he used it to buy flan for everyone and wager with the rich man in the big chair on how many Santurce Crabbers he would strike out the following Sunday. Lucy's brother Julio, who was thirteen then, saw his status soar when he lugged Satchel's duffel bag to the hotel or ballpark. The pitcher gave the urchin a dollar for the movies, knowing that admission was just a quarter. "Go have fun," Satchel would say.

Satchel and Lucy met one day when she was sitting on her front porch. They became acquainted between team practices. She loved watching him show off by tossing the ball over matchboxes or even matchsticks, sometimes standing on the pitcher's mound and other times throwing from farther away. He loved waving to her during the game. On the way home Satchel would stop by Lucy's house, which looked like Lula's shotgun shack in Mobile. There was a series of small rooms off a hall and an outhouse in the yard. Lucy slept with her mother, whom they called Doña Genoveva. Julio and his brother Borges shared the marriage bed, whose legs had been cut shorter so the kids could climb in. Papi used the "little bed." When Satchel visited "it was yakkety, yakkety with my sister," Julio recalls. "That's Satchel Paige. He was very friendly. He don't have to announce he's coming, he just walks into the house. He had to bend to walk in because he's so tall. He came to the house to take a bath. It was a shower really, concrete and wood, and the water goes into the street. We had a lot of bats burrowed up beneath the roof. He'd say, 'What's going on here, there are birds?'"

Lucy's family was never rich, but her father, Blas Figueroa Castro, had made a decent living as a brakeman with the railroad until four years before Satchel arrived in Guayama. Early one morning someone accidentally backed up a train and Blas got wedged between two cars, crushing both legs and an arm. His injuries were bad; the infection that set in at the local hospital was worse. After eighteen months at a clinic in Ponce, he came home but could not work and got no compensation from the railroad. María Mercedes, the oldest girl, took a job as a teacher and helped at home, but the pressure to pitch in was intense for Lucy, Julio, José, Félix, Borges, Sonny, and

Hilda. Julio had a gnawing hunger even when the family could afford lunch. Long walks helped. On good days his mother gave him five cents for scraps the butcher saved for dogs. It was mostly fat and gristle, but Doña Genoveva used it to make a soup with noodles and potatoes that Julio pronounced delicious.

Things got better when Satchel landed in the Figueroas' orbit. There was more fun and more money, which Satchel gave to Lucy and she passed on to Doña Genoveva. Blas Figueroa was especially happy having a celebrity visit his home, drink his coffee, relax with a cigarette, and court his daughter. Lucy translated between her suitor and her family. But when Satchel talked about taking her back to America after the season, Papi set conditions: she could go *if* they were married and she was happy. He was a Catholic, after all, and a loving father.

It seemed like a fair bargain to Satchel. By that winter of 1940–41 the middle-aged pitcher was feeling more like his young self on the mound, and who better to reinforce that than a girl half as old who thought he was everything? He showed Lucy off to his Negro League friends, especially Monte Irvin, the powerful and cherubic Newark Eagles infielder who also was playing in Puerto Rico that winter. "One of the nicest persons you'll ever meet," Satchel told Irvin as they neared the Figueroa home. It was built on wooden stilts, with enough room underneath for suckling pigs, chickens, and goats. Irvin remembers seeing one of the goats sitting on a chair on the porch, rocking back and forth. "Look there. Have you ever seen anything like that?" Satchel asked. "Anytime you can train a goat to do that, you know these must be pretty nice people. And as pretty as she is, I'm going to marry that girl."

Marry her he did, that very season. Desiderio de León was an altar boy at the wedding, which was at the Church of San Antonio on the plaza. There were more than a hundred guests, with a horse and carriage to transport bride and groom to a reception at a nearby inn. Satchel wanted a big place for the party, de León says, so it could hold the scores of poor people who were eager to attend. And he wanted everyone to dance the bamba. Lucy's sister-in-law was a witness at the wedding, which was appropriate since she watched the couple meet and fall in love. Julio is sure they were married but recalls just a civil ceremony.

What no one remembers hearing, until later, was that Satchel already had a wife: Janet Howard Paige. The Spanish word for what he did is nearly identical to the English: *bigamia.* He had discouraged Janet from coming to Puerto Rico, saying, "they ain't letting us take wives." In his mind his marriage to Janet had been over for years, no matter that there was no divorce or formal separation. Formalities like that were as malleable as the baseball contracts he ignored and the Jim Crow rules he flaunted. He had grown up believing in de facto, not de jure, and the facts here were that he and Lucy were in love while Janet was a mistake from the past. He also relished the idea of being an outlaw, which is why, once he brought Lucy home with him to Kansas City, he never hid their relationship. Newspapers referred to her as his fiancée, and in 1941 *Life* magazine ran a photo spread identifying her as his wife. Having long ago established his track record for fibbing about his age, Satchel knew neither press nor public would take seriously his claims on marriage. The best place to hide his transgression was in plain sight.

By the time he wrote his autobiography twenty years later, he thought better of laying out his bigamy for all to see. He probably also forgot how deeply he had fallen for Lucy and how impetuous they had been. While he was no stranger to flings and infidelities, he would never have married her and taken her home if it had been anything short of love. But now he had a reputation to think about, and a legend. So as he did often in his memoir, he rescripted his history. The reason Lucy came back with him was that she "had a hankering to get into the United States," he wrote. "Lots of folks tried to spread around the word that we were married and later on when they'd see her at the ball park when I was pitching, they wrote she was my wife. Janet even said Lucy and me were married when we got into divorce court later on, but there wasn't any truth to it. Lucy was a fine woman and we were good friends for a while in the States and that was it. Then I went my own way."

Julio questions Satchel's rewrite of his history with Lucy, but he does not doubt the pitcher's motivation in marrying her. While none of the Figueroas knew about Janet, they were not surprised when they found out. Satchel was thirty-four when he met Lucy, and he was used to people flocking around him. Julio and the others "assumed there were other relationships or involvements." Looking back nearly seventy years later, was Julio angry at Satchel for deceiving Lucy and the rest of the family? "Never," he says, explaining that Satchel always treated his sister well and she never spoke ill of him.

This was not Satchel's first amorous affair on an island in paradise. One hot night during the 1929 Cuban baseball season he was sitting in a park in Santa Clara, munching on peanuts, when he noticed a girl with arresting eyes and almost no English. "She dropped some Sen-Sen in my hand," he told an interviewer. "That was the signal." The first time he called at her mud-walled home he was not allowed in. He persisted, only to find that being admitted meant he and the young woman were officially engaged. "I quit callin' immediately, but pretty soon the owner of the ball club comes to my hotel and says the polices is lookin' for me. So I started goin' back to her house." That is when his performance on the mound started to suffer, and the owner started losing faith. "One night he phones my hotel and says it's all fixed," Satchel said. "He's gonna get me out in a car to the mountains. Then I'll get on a horse and go on over the top and get another car. This car will take me to a place where I can catch a motorboat and go on out to a ship to take me back to the U.S.A. That's how it was gonna be." But there was another problem: the hotel operator, who was listening in, was the young woman's cousin. "Them polices was after me when I was in the car, and on a jackass runnin' up the mountain, and on foot runnin' down the mountain, and right on out to the motorboat. Man, when I finally come flyin' up that gangplank, I was through with love."

Others offer less flattering versions of Satchel's exploits that season in Cuba, when he was single and freely sowing his oats. One dustup involved "a young lady from the provincial mulatto bourgeoisie" and it "resulted in charges being brought against the pitcher," said Roberto González Echevarría, a professor at Yale and author of *The Pride of Havana: A History of Cuban Baseball.* "He quit the island in haste, and remained ever wary of returning, even when the case was dropped," adds Echevarría, who says his story came from the old general manager of Satchel's Santa Clara Leopards.

As for Lucy, she was not Satchel's only distraction the winter of 1940 in Guayama. He ate his first fried green bananas there, and his first papayas and avocados. He fished off the pier and off a deep-sea boat, hooking dolphins as well as sharks. Fans gambled in the stands the same as they did in Bismarck, but in Puerto Rico they had a singular way of showing their gratitude: handing players coins and cash—sometimes $100 or more—through the chicken wire. Satchel had less luck with movies, because they were in Spanish and he thought every theater was playing the same film lit up in letters on the marquee: *Hoy,* which he later learned means "today." Time moved more slowly in the tropics, which put the days in sync with Satchel. One Sunday, between games of a doubleheader, he and Monte Irvin went to a hotel for lunch. It was getting late, Irvin remembered, but Satchel was unconcerned. "I'm pitching the second game," the pitcher explained, "and if I'm pitching, nothing can happen until I get there. Right?" So the pair finished their sandwiches and the contest was held up nearly twenty minutes until they arrived. "I wasn't worried," Irvin said, "because I was with Satchel."

Satchel tried to apply that same tortoise's pace on the field. In one game the weather was so hot that he took as long as five minutes between pitches. Another report said he deliberately threw the ball over an outfielder's head as a delaying tactic. The president of the Puerto Rican League was not amused, fining him $25 and suspending him for a year. Yet in a sign of how valuable Satchel was, the suspension was timed to take effect after the season was over—and three months after they were imposed, the league lifted its fine and ban. Half a century later Satchel was inducted into Puerto Rico's Baseball Hall of Fame.

The pitcher also took time to tutor promising young stars like Irvin, who fanned three times the first time he faced Paige that winter. It was less the strikeouts he remembered than the advice Satchel offered afterward over beers at a local bar. "Notice how high you hold your bat," said Satchel. "By the time you get your bat down and around I'm gone by you. You've got to drop that damn bat down a bit." The next time he faced Satchel in Puerto Rico, Irvin struck out just twice and Satchel complimented him on the improvement. Later that year the two squared off in Yankee Stadium and Irvin doubled. Satchel called time out and walked over to second base. "I congratulate you," the pitcher said, handing Irvin the ball. "You're now a full-fledged hitter."

His new carefree attitude made him more of a man-about-town during that second visit to Guayama, but less of a force or even a presence on the field. He compiled a disappointing record of four wins against five losses. His earned run average of 3.89 was more than double his 1.93 of the previous winter, and he notched just seventy strikeouts. The Witches, after successive years of finishing first, fell to second place. Fans, however, forgave him, so spectacular was his previous season.

Cocky as he was the winter of 1940–41, Satchel knew that his arm was not the rubber band it had been. Mexico had taught him that. He had to take care and he did. He was the first player at the stadium every morning for workouts. He ran more than was his custom. The sun was scorching, even in the morning, and for ventilation he cut the sleeve off his left arm—but not the sleeve on his pitching arm, which he wanted as warm as possible. A trainer massaged that limb using an especially balmy oil that he collected while milking a cow. If it softened the nipples of a cow, the trainer figured it would soften Satchel's elbow and shoulder. The pitcher's arm never felt sore that season in Puerto Rico, which made it two in a row. The resurrection was complete.

CHAPTER 6

Kansas City, Here I Come

"I fascinates them with my arms and
they forget a ball is gonna be throwed."

SATCHEL HAD NEVER HAD MUCH of a home. He fled Mobile, a reminder of his segregated and impoverished lineage, as soon as he was able. He barely unpacked in Chattanooga and Birmingham, Baltimore and Cleveland. Pittsburgh was somewhere to deposit his clothes, his car, and his wife. Ciudad Trujillo, Guayama, and Bismarck were vitalizing while they lasted and spawned tales that lasted him forever, but they were not cities he could or would return to. He had always been a nomad but now he was looking for a safe place to linger.

Kansas City was his refuge. Monarchs owner J. Leslie Wilkinson had signed Satchel when his pitching arm was as lifeless as his marriage to Janet. Wilkinson was more of a baseball man than anyone Satchel had played for, and he became the father figure that Gus Greenlee, Alex Herman, and John Page had tried and failed to be. Wilkinson was also white, which made him an unlikely mentor to the Negro League icon. Satchel loved the fact that Wilkinson did whatever it took for his players and team, choreographing games, recruiting promising rookies, providing grubstakes along with counsel, and maneuvering around Jim Crow everywhere the Monarchs went. The owner knew his ace's vices and loved him anyway. Satchel had traveled the continent for two seasons with Wilkinson's Baby Monarchs. Now that he had scratched his way back to Kansas City and the parent organization in 1941, he felt a loyalty that he had never known before to an owner, team, and city.

This was a city that was happening, a city that burned its candles at both ends. Liquor had always been easy to get, even during Prohibition. There was music—oh, was there music! Count Basie was the opener most evenings, while Charlie "Bird" Parker kept the lights on late into the night with his blistering bebop. Even the barbecue— pig, possum, and raccoon slow-cooked over a hickory pit, slathered with a peppery molasses sauce, then wrapped in newspaper like British fish and chips—had a kick that was legendary. The sprawling Pratt & Whitney factories hummed late into the evening, fueled by America's impending entry into World War II. An elaborate network of train tracks had made the city a hub of commerce by the time Satchel stepped off the platform. *The Kansas City Star* and *The Kansas City Times* were read every morning in the White House— especially when it was home to Missouri's Harry Truman—signaling the community's standing as a major metropolis. Yet it still had its Arcadian flavor, with glass-and-tile drugstores and big backyards, orange-juice stands and a skyline that seemed to sprout out of the wheat fields. Kansas City's forty thousand Negro residents were more than an afterthought although they were just 10 percent of its total population. They orchestrated the jazz, belted out the blues, seared the barbecue, and supplied much of the sweat that fed the economic boom. Jim Crow did limit where they lived, worked, and played, but not nearly as rigidly as where Satchel came from. A lover of ribs, riffs, and reporters, he found Kansas City irresistible.

It was a love instantly requited. For if Satchel adored Kansas City, Kansas City loved him right back, even if he was slightly broken- down when he first showed up. There was no Major League team there then, just a New York Yankees farm club called the Blues, which, despite stars like Yogi Berra and Mickey Mantle, never drew as many fans as the all-black Monarchs. Wilkinson's players were, as the local black paper pronounced, "Monarchs of All They Survey." They defined Negro culture and commerce even more than the Crawfords and Grays did in Pittsburgh. "It was the ambition of every black boy to be a Monarch, just as it was for every white boy to become a Yankee," explained the team's shortstop. It was not just any Monarch they fantasized about, but the one who got the biggest billing, most lavish paychecks, and a starring role in every game that mattered for a decade. From the instant he arrived in Kansas City, Leroy "Satchel" Paige was the king of kings.

This was not the boyish flamethrower earlier fans had known. He was in his thirties now, the stage of life when, George Bernard Shaw said, communists with brains become capitalists, and when baseball pitchers look less like rising stars than sinking ones. His shoulder injury had forced him to face his mortality; the comeback made him appreciate his second chance. He continued to savor the life of a barnstorming gypsy, but now he relished having a home to come back to. Most days he still lived in buses and cars, most nights in rooming houses and hotels. But he bought a house for the first time, and began filling it with Chippendale chairs and roomfuls of trophies and guns. No need to run away this time. Satchel was growing up and settling down, or at least he was trying.

J. L. WILKINSON MADE RUBE FOSTER squirm. It was not merely that Wilkinson, the only white among the Negro League founding fathers, was an affront to Foster's conviction that blacks should own as well as fill the rosters of teams in the segregated league. The team Wilkinson put together in 1912, All Nations, was just like its name—with whites along with blacks, Cubans taking their positions next to players with ties to Mexico, Japan, Hawaii, France, Germany, the Philippines, and the Cherokee Nation. Today it would be a model for diversity; back then it was a provocation to the Foster–Booker T. Washington school of black advancement. Baseball was the center of the All Nations act, but there were sideshows: a marching band that drummed up interest in the game, a wrestler who challenged locals to a bout, and a community dance with music courtesy of the team troupe. The second baseman was a woman, "Carrie Nation," a whimsical reference to the ball club as well as to the era's hatchet-wielding battler for temperance. Yet Foster and the other owners gathering in 1920 in Kansas City had little choice as they sought to recruit clubs from strategic settings across Middle

America. Their first pick as an owner from the important city where they were meeting, a Negro hospital superintendent, lacked the requisite baseball know-how, ballpark, and cash. Wilkinson had all three, along with a newly minted team named the Kansas City Monarchs with the proper racial pedigree.

Wilkinson was not just the only choice but the right one. His passion for baseball began when he was growing up in Des Moines, the son of a real estate developer who was so determined that his boy establish his own identity that he gave him an initial—*J*—instead of a first name, instructing him to fill it in himself. The son, whose life and career would exceed even his father's exalted hopes, saw his birthright as sufficient and would come to be known as J. L. (his preference), J. Leslie (his real middle name), James or John (inventions of writers and ballplayers), or Wilkie (a nickname used by his many protégés and friends). He made his name in baseball as a pitcher for college, semi-pro, and professional teams. An injury in the summer of 1900 ended his days as a power hurler, but he kept playing for years with a club sponsored by Hopkins Brothers Sporting Goods. When its manager absconded with its money, Wilkie added that title as well as captain, helping make Hopkins Brothers the best semi-pro team in Des Moines and one of the strongest in the Midwest.

His next venture blended baseball and big top. At the turn of the century women nationwide were banding together to form Bloomer Girls barnstorming ball clubs, inspired by Amelia Bloomer's loose-fitting trousers that made it easier for ladies to indulge in sports. With his father's eye for selling, Wilkie launched the Hopkins Brothers Champion Lady Baseball Club in 1909. It had the best female players around along with a sprinkling of men, a Pullman sleeping car with six staterooms and a kitchen, a two-thousand-seat canopy-covered grandstand that traveled with the team, and a catcher known as the Rocky Mountain Wrestler. Wrestling matches were one of many sideshows Wilkinson dreamed up to bring in fans, and they were successful enough that he repeated them three years later with his All Nations club. The All Nations team had the added draw of its international roster, which was good enough in 1913 to win 119 games and lose just 17. It was not just ballyhoo that its owner-manager was mastering, but how to recognize and grow baseball stars.

Those skills served Wilkie well in 1920 when he launched the
Monarchs, filling it with the best of black ballplayers. John Donaldson had barnstormed across the lily-white Plains states, averaging an
inconceivable twenty strikeouts a game, and he earned his stripes
on the old All Nations team, pitching an unprecedented three no-
hitters in a row. Wilbur "Bullet Joe" Rogan was one of the few pitchers in history skilled enough with the bat to hit in the fourth or
cleanup spot, where driving in runs is especially critical, and probably the only one who for a full decade started thirty games a year and
was never pulled for a reliever. No one was as fast on the base path as
Cool Papa Bell, as slick at second base as Newt Allen, or embodied
the glory and talents of blackball as much as Buck O'Neil and Jackie
Robinson. The Monarchs were one of the leading teams in Foster's
original Negro National League, winning pennants in 1923, 1924,
1925, and 1929, and the Black World Series in 1924. They soared
even higher in the new Negro American League, capturing seven
league titles and one championship series between 1937 and 1950.
No Negro League club would take home more flags, graduate more
players to the Major Leagues, or see more of its stars exalted in Cooperstown's Hall of Fame than the Kansas City Monarchs. They were
the New York Yankees of the Negro Leagues and America's team in
black America.

Wilkinson's eye for talent impressed his fellow owners, but not as
much as his nose for money. It was he who resurrected a fifty-year-old
idea of bringing lights to the ballpark to allow night games. He put
the lightbulbs on poles, loaded the poles, motors, and generator onto
trucks and buses, and rented out the system—with his brother and
nephew as mechanics—to other teams. That is what kept his team
afloat during the Depression. He made money by booking games
for the House of David clubs, and booked the Monarchs in eighteen states and two foreign countries. His team packed 150 games,
as many as Major League teams played from spring through fall, into
a summer. He scheduled series against Dizzy Dean's all-white All-
Stars and got the Monarchs admitted as the first all-black team in the
Denver Post Tournament. While they lost in the finals to Satchel and
his mainly white House of Davids, what Wilkinson wrought was, in
the words of *The Pittsburgh Courier*'s Chester Washington, "the most
significant announcement in a decade, insofar as Negro baseball is

concerned." It and moves like it helped ensure that the Monarchs were still standing after Gus Greenlee had run out of money for his Crawfords and Cum Posey had to bid adieu to the Grays.

If his fellow owners in the Negro Leagues, all of them black, grudgingly came to accept and admire this white man in their midst, his players adored him from the first to the last of his twenty-eight years with the Monarchs. That was a feat in a business where players often despised their owner more than they did the opposing team. Wilkinson managed it through good deeds. When a league-imposed payroll cap pushed other owners to cut salary, he cut roster spots instead. Where other teams traveled in broken-down cars and buses, the Monarchs rented a Pullman sleeping car, bought parlor buses with reclining seats, and by 1935 were using a pair of special-order Roycraft trailers with bunks, showers, and a kitchen the players stocked with cold cuts and firewater. First thing after a man signed with the Kansas City Monarchs he was ushered to a tailor for a pair of custom-made suits, courtesy of J. L. The owner made sure there were restaurants and hotels that would serve Negroes everywhere the team went. And he gave his players two things white teams took for granted and black ones seldom saw: a farm club in the form of the Baby Monarchs and a trainer in the person of Jewbaby Floyd. Like everyone connected with the club, Jewbaby had another job in the off-season, in his case running a massage parlor at the Belleview Hotel. He wore several hats during the baseball season— handing out posters advertising the team, overseeing the locker room, running the office when the traveling secretary was traveling, and, most important, using his hands and liniments to soothe players' aching muscles and throbbing joints.

Wilkinson paid for Jewbaby and the rest not with an inherited fortune or earnings from a lucrative business, neither of which he had. The team was his main business. When he ran out of money, as he did several times, he took out a loan on his home. "Every year he'd mortgage the house before the season, then come home that fall and pay it off," remembers J. L.'s son Dick. "He never missed a season or a payroll but, boy, he came close a lot of times."

His players knew that and were grateful. "He was the swellest guy in the world. You could go to him in the winter and borrow against your summer salary," said second baseman Newt Allen. "Your face could be as black as tar; he treated everyone alike." So universal was such sentiment that his players composed an ode to Wilkie published in the Kansas City *Call*. "The best club owner in the world to work for," it began. "Who believes in us at all times. Who stands for a fair and square deal to all. Who gives the best and expects the best in return. Who loves and is loved by his players. Who believes that charity begins at home. Who knows and appreciates real ability."

What he probably did not know was that his co-owner of the Monarchs wore the robes of the Ku Klux Klan. Thomas Y. Baird, a white former semi-pro player, was there from the start with Wilkie and bought him out in 1948 to become sole proprietor. Few were familiar with Baird because he handled the business aspects of the club while Wilkinson dealt with the players and public; Satchel was an exception because Baird handled most of his bookings with other teams. Convincing evidence of Baird's ties to the KKK was published in 2007 by Tim Rives, a baseball historian who is the supervisory archivist at the Eisenhower Presidential Library. It was disturbing enough that an owner of blackball's best-known ball club was affiliated with America's best-known organization of racists, anti-Semites, anti-Catholics, and anti-immigrants. As bad is a letter from Baird referring to one of his players as "above the average in intelligence for a Negro." Another missive, trying to reassure a Boston Braves executive worried about having a team "top heavy" with "colored boys," advised that African American Lefty LaMarque "is an inteligent [*sic*] looking Negro, in fact he might pass for an Indian."

What drew Baird to the Klan is unclear, although Rives suggests it was a combination of factors: he embraced mass movements as the way to solve political and social woes, saw the powerful Klan as an ally in his bid for professional as well as political clout, and feared that, unless he joined, his pool halls could be closed by officials with KKK ties. Baird also apparently believed in white supremacy the way so many did in that era and place. The Monarchs' link to the Klan is one in a stream of contradictions from the Jim Crow era, when an ugly color line spawned the brilliant world of black baseball. Baird was not as hard-bitten a hater as many fellow Klansmen. He also was not close to Wilkinson socially and did not parade his KKK ties, which makes it plausible that J. L. never knew.* Had he, it would have broken the heart of the man regularly referred to as the most esteemed white in black America.

The reasons for that respect were clear in Wilkie's generosity to Satchel. The owner had followed the pitcher for years, the way everyone in Negro baseball had, and had rented his services once before—in 1935—for what *The Bismarck Tribune* branded a "winter tour of the south" but amounted to just a handful of games. Satchel had pitched that fall for Neil Churchill's Bismarck team alongside the Monarchs' right-hander Chet Brewer. When Brewer returned to the Monarchs, Satchel came along.

It was a calculated move by Wilkinson. His Monarchs were battling the Chicago American Giants for bragging rights as the best of the West in black baseball, and it was worth $500 to land Satchel for the showdown. Newspapers in Chicago began hyping the contest a week in advance even as papers in New York were bemoaning Satchel's failure to show up at Yankee Stadium for an equally momentous game for his Pittsburgh Crawfords. The Monarchs ended up losing 7-1, but Satchel struck out eight and held the Giants scoreless until Brewer came in to relieve him after the fifth inning. *Chicago Defender* sportswriter Dan Burley paid less attention to the outcome than to Satchel's outing, writing that he "smoked the ball across the platter so fast that the friction thus achieved almost caused the bats of Mister Cole's men to catch afire when by some unforeseen accident the wood became connected with the horsehide."

In 1938 Satchel was back in Kansas City, this time with the Baby Monarchs. He had a wounded arm now and a broken spirit. Wilkie offered him a job he desperately needed and Satchel instantly ac-

---

* J. L.'s son Dick says Baird was a "silent partner" who "never had anything to do with the club." The former is true, although Baird did play a big role on the commercial side of the Monarchs and he and Wilkie were partners in a pool hall and other ventures. Baird's heirs, not surprisingly, saw things differently, with his grandson Tom Wickstrom calling J. L. Wilkinson the "front man who was dealing with the public" while Baird ran the business. "Somebody had to," explained Wickstrom, who was just eight years old when Baird sold the Monarchs and in high school when his grandfather died. As for the suggestion that Baird was a Klansman, Wickstrom said, "Absolutely not. He never was affiliated with anything like that. That would have been so foreign to his personality that it's something somebody made up somewhere. He was a member of the Shriners, a Mason, that type of [KKK] thing just was not in his personality."

cepted. The owner knew he was taking not one chance but two by signing him. It was a gamble that he would ever regain his former form and was a certainty that bringing him aboard would be read as a declaration of war by racketeer Abe Manley, who had purchased Satchel from Gus Greenlee for an unprecedented $5,000. If Gus was annoyed enough at Satchel to sell his contract to Abe, Abe was annoyed when Wilkie snatched the star. Abe's wife, Effa, was enraged. Effa Manley was so striking that *Time* magazine dubbed her a "hula-hipped Harlem beauty." She also was renowned across blackball for her willingness to battle on behalf of both the Newark Eagles and civil rights, her pioneering role as the sole woman of consequence in the fraternity of the Negro Leagues, and her flirtations and more with her husband's ballplayers. Forty years later Effa revealed another secret: she was 100 percent Caucasian, the offspring not of a white mother and black father, the way her half sisters and half brothers were, but of a liaison between her mother and a wealthy white financier. Whatever her birthright, the olive-skinned Effa lived her life as a proud black woman. One of her prides was not to be taken for a fool.

For two full years, Satchel tantalized and taunted Effa and Abe, making them think he would play for the Eagles then not turning up. His wavering not only drove the Manleys mad and drew rebukes from black sportwriters, it put Wilkinson on the spot. The Manleys knew Wilkie had hired Satchel to pitch for his traveling team, and they threatened tit for tat. They would not only raid signed players from Wilkinson's Negro American League, if necessary they would blow up the Negro National League. "I expect each of you to order Wilkinson to send Paige to Newark immediately," Effa wrote the chairmen of the American and National leagues in June 1940. "If organized baseball is not strong enough to do this, it is not strong enough to call itself organized and anything may happen. Whatever decision you reach remember there is a big race issue involved, 'Negro Baseball.' It is probably at the crossroads, and its future may depend upon your handling of this present situation. I pray you will have devine [sic] guidance at this time."

Satchel loved being in the eye of the storm and being fought over by black baseball's best teams and richest owners. He also loved Effa Manley, or so she said forty years later. "I don't know whether I ought to tell you this or not," she gleefully confided to an interviewer in 1977. "Satchel wrote me and told me he'd come to the team if I'd be his girlfriend. . . . I didn't even answer his letter." What Satchel actually wrote, in a letter from Guayama, was more ambiguous: "I am yours for the asking if it can be possible for me to get there . . . listen Mrs. Manly dont Beat around the Bush. I am a man tell me just wheat you want me to know. and please answer the things I ask you." Satchel and Effa did share a flair for dramatics and romantics, although they never shared a bed or even a baseball diamond. She wanted him, but only to help the Eagles soar to the top of the standings. He wanted out.

J. L. Wilkinson was not a passive bystander. While Satchel was making eyes at Effa, the Monarchs' owner was wooing the prized pitcher. He gave Satchel fat paychecks when all he could deliver was fat pitches. Sensing that Satchel's fastball and confidence were returning after his brilliant winter in Puerto Rico in 1939–40, Wilkinson welcomed him home that spring with a new contract and a factory-fresh car. Wilkie used psychology, too, a weapon less familiar to street fighters like Gus and Effa. J. L. knew Satchel was getting older and that his health troubles had unnerved him. He understood that the key to Satchel's loyalty was getting him to see Kansas City as home and to think about the future as well as the moment. He took the pitcher under his wing the way he did his own children. Wilkinson "knew that as long as Satchel lived out of his suitcase, there was still the risk that Satchel could vanish at any time. So in the mid-1940s he got Satchel this house in Kansas City and that's the first time Satchel had any home to go back to," said Slow Robinson, the catcher who was friend to both the pitcher and the owner. "Wilkinson made Satchel see that what he had been doing was wrong—that if he wanted to make something out of himself, he'd have to change his way of living."

The Monarchs' owner knew how to wield a stick along with his carrot. He let Satchel know that a contract was a contract, not a mere piece of paper. "He told Satchel, 'If you think about jumping, I'll put you out of baseball. You won't play anymore in the United States,' " said Robinson. "This got to Satchel; that this man could put him out for good. Wilkinson made Satchel see that it was in Satchel's best interest not to jump." As for the Manleys, they were allowed to keep two American League players they had bought in violation of inter-league rules. It was not what Effa or Abe wanted, and not adequate to compensate them for Wilkie's stealing Satchel, but it was all they would get so they took it.

SATCHEL'S YEARS REHABBING HIS ARM and working on the road had him raring to go. He had already recovered his speed, or enough of it to deceive fans as well as hitters. Connie Johnson, who would later team with Satchel on the Monarchs' pitching staff, was in the stands one night as a teenager in Toledo when the Baby Monarchs came to town. He could see Satchel wind up and deliver the pitch, but could not make out the ball itself. "I thought he was playing shadow ball—where you're pretending you're throwing the ball, but you wasn't," Johnson recalled. The catcher tossed a baseball back, but Johnson presumed it was one he had hidden beforehand in his glove. Moving to the railing to get a better view, Johnson realized the ball was real and Satchel was simply performing the magic he was famous for. One more sign that he was back.

Wilkinson was convinced enough that he signed Satchel to pitch the 1941 season for his Negro League Monarchs. He also was savvy enough to know that Satchel's two years of toiling in the wilderness with the traveling team had kept him out of sight and mind of Negro sportswriters and their hundreds of thousands of readers. So he enlisted New York playwrights Moss Hart and George S. Kaufman to help script the pitcher's return. The trio determined that the only stage big enough was the Big Apple, and Wilkie arranged for Satchel to throw the season opener for the New York Black Yankees. The rejuvenated pitcher "popped in town," as one paper reported, "driving a long car, squiring a pretty girl and 'thinking about' sign-ing a Black Yankee contract." Mayor Fiorello La Guardia threw out the first ball at Yankee Stadium in front of twenty thousand deliri-ous fans, the biggest opening-day crowd in Negro League history. Satchel did not disappoint, striking out eight, winning 5-3, and, in a development that probably pleased Wilkie even more, lasting all nine innings. The coming-out contest was covered everywhere from black newspapers and magazines to *The New York Times*. "When Leroy (Satchel) Paige stretched his hands above his head here Sunday, cupped the ball in his glove and then reared back like a gigantic crane, you felt sorry for the [man] at bat," wrote Dan Burley of New York's *Amsterdam News.* "It was the Great One's first appearance on a local lot since he jumped Gus Greenlee's Pittsburgh Crawfords back in 1937."

While he seemed the spitting image of Gus's ace of the '30s, the 1940s edition of Satchel Paige was an upgrade in everything from his attitude to his pitch selection. He harbored no thoughts of jumping to a new team now, be it the Black Yankees or anyone else, as he made clear a week after his Yankee Stadium debut when he returned to the Monarchs, pitching them to a 2-1 win in their opening game. That performance also let fans see that, to go along with his fastball, he had a newly refined curve. It was not the sharp-bending breaker that Slim Jones had trademarked, more like a wrinkle. It started with the same snap of the wrist and rolling of palm and fingers over the top of the baseball to give it a downward spin, but once he let it go the ball dropped and veered more slowly.

That was one in a series of adjustments Satchel was making to his age, his injury, and a fastball that he admitted had slowed from "blindin' speed" to "just blazin' speed." Cool Papa Bell taught him to throw a knuckleball, which meant gripping the horsehide with the tips, nails, and knuckles of his middle fingers. The ball floated through the air with so little speed or rotation that the slightest breeze sent it bobbing and breaking in a way that even Satchel could not predict. It was difficult for his catcher to hold on to and, when he delivered it right, impossible for the hitter to connect with. He perfected a slow sinker, too, grasping the ball with his middle and index fingers and rolling his wrist downward and in. As it neared the plate the ball suddenly dropped from its horizontal trajectory, deceiving the batter even when Satchel threw it as unhurriedly as he did his knuckleball. His favorite pitch was the hesitation—it seemed to stop mid-delivery—which he had dreamed up hurling rocks as a boy and fine-tuned under Big Bill Gatewood's tutelage in Birmingham.

The changes helped in three ways. His new pitches were slower than his old ones, which meant less force was needed to throw them and there was less strain on his elbow, his wrist, and his recently recovered shoulder. Variety also was a plus, with each pitch requiring a slightly different motion and shifting the stress to a different set of muscles and joints. A third way of relieving the explosive pressure on his injury-prone rotator cuff was to throw more pitches sidearm, with his arm arching forward parallel to the ground, or even underhanded like in softball. His understanding of his body and how to keep it going was as sophisticated as today's avant-garde exercise physiologists and more farsighted than the doctors of his day. "When you stay around as long as Ol' Satch, you got to change your style of pitching," Satchel explained. "I thought that'd save my arm for my old age. I didn't try a fast curve. I never broke it off sharp. I might have cracked a bone in my wrist if I did. Just slow curves, that's all I threw. Slow ones to fool the batters."

It worked. Thomas "Pee Wee" Butts, known as the best shortstop in the East during the 1940s, only played against Satchel one time. "I was leading off. I used to be quite a lead-off hitter, but when they said 'Satchel Paige,' I kind of got a little shaky," recalled Butts. With two strikes on him Butts's confidence rebounded, and he prepared for the fastball he knew he would get. He got a curve instead. "After the game [Satchel] said to me, 'They told you I didn't have a curve ball, didn't they?' I said, 'Yes, Snow told me. I see you've got one now.' He said, 'Yeah, I was just saving it for all you young ones who come up there and think I don't have a curve ball.' "

It was not just batters who were fooled. Bob Motley remembers when he was a rookie umpire and first called balls and strikes on Satchel. "The pitch zigzagged across the plate in a way I had never seen a baseball move. It all happened so fast; I was stunned, and so was the batter. For a split second I was caught off guard, then realized I had yet to make the call. I bellowed, 'S-T-T-T-R-R-R-I-I-I-K-E,' " said Motley. "The moment he released the ball from his hand, it sounded as if a swarm of killer bees was coming down the pike, humming all the way. . . . After striking out, most guys simply laughed and shook their heads in disbelief, shrugging off their poor at-bat almost as if being mowed down by the great one was a badge of honor." John "Mule" Miles did not wait for the strikeout call. Satchel threw his first pitch and the umpire bellowed, "Strike one." The Chicago American Giants outfielder dug in again but never got the bat off his shoulder as the umpire said, "Strike two." With the count 0-2, Miles walked slowly back to the dugout. "My manager asked, 'What the heck are you doing?' " Miles remembers. "I said, 'I didn't see the first two. What makes you think I'm going to hit a third one?' "

Getting the batter to think—or overthink—was one key to the more seasoned Satchel. He would waste the first pitch by throwing it high, watching the hitter lunge and sizing up "where he wants it and what he can't do." He studied scouting reports when he had them and tapped into his own memory bank, which was as dependable as any elephant's. He knew his opponents' weaknesses, from low-and-inside to slow-and-away, and pitched there often enough that when he played to their strengths they were caught ham-handed. Normally a batter gains an edge with each outing; with Satchel, it was the pitcher who was learning and mastering. The art of throwing had come naturally. Now he made it a science, too. Retiring the first batter was especially critical because that "gives the rest of 'em the idea." He threw sidearm, overhand, and underhand—with his trademark windmill windup or none at all. It all had the same effect: to put a batter off his stride. "I seen the time had come for me to be cute," Satchel said. "I fascinates them with my arms and they forget a ball is gonna be throwed."

Control was always his thing, but as his power ebbed, spotting the ball where he wanted it was even more essential. He relied on the X-ray eyes that had helped him fell birds and rival gang members in Mobile. He relaxed more on the mound, taking full advantage of his elongated stride, arms and legs as pliable as elastic bands, and the strong, spidery fingers of a violinist. He depended less on brawn, more on brains. His newfound finesse made it nearly as tough to catch up with his fastball at ninety miles an hour as it had been at a hundred. Batters heard his pitch before they saw it and swung more out of faith than conviction. Three reflex reactions like that made an automatic out.

Art "Superman" Pennington found that out when he was a seventeen-year-old hitting sensation. It was the early 1940s and his American Giants were facing off against Satchel's Monarchs at Briggs Stadium in Detroit, an arena big enough to seat 54,500 fans. "Satchel said, 'Come on up, little boy, don't be afraid,' " says Pennington. "That made me mad. I used to tell pitchers, 'Throw 'em and duck.' I didn't care about no pitcher then. He cocked his foot in front of my face—he wore about a 15 shoe—and the next thing I knew the ball was by me. He struck me out three times—in front of my mother, my sister, and my granddaddy, who I hadn't seen in fifteen years."

Willie "Curley" Williams was thinking about his grandchild, not yet born, when he stood in against Satchel. The Newark Eagles infielder was leading the Negro National League in most batting categories and faced Satchel sixteen times in one week in the late 1940s. " 'Lord,' I said, 'let me get just one hit so I can tell my grandchild about it.' " It was not to be. "I learned later you don't try to outguess him. The ball didn't just come straight, it came in with tricks. At the end of that week I just shook his hand and told him he's a great pitcher."

If Satchel had an Achilles' heel it was the bunt. His full-tilt windup worked as designed to distract batters and may have given him a little extra velocity, but it left him in an awkward position to field a ball. "Bunt and run," managers advised as hitters left the dugout determined to find a way on against the ageless moundsman. Satchel practiced his fielding until he became one of the best around, but he never understood why more batters did not play to his weakness by bunting. Another vulnerability grew out of his reluctance to throw at batters, letting them dig in the way they would not dare against a pitcher who might punish them by aiming for their elbow or head. Satchel worried that if he tried that, with his shotgun delivery, the ball would break bones and even take lives.

He ended the 1941 season with a 5-0 record in Negro League games, pitching a modest sixty-four innings and striking out fifty. The next year with the Monarchs he nearly doubled his innings, to ninety-five, and his strikeouts swelled to seventy-nine. He continued pitching for them through 1947, never winning more than six games in a season yet seldom having the opportunity since he generally pitched fewer than five innings. Fans wanted him out there every night and Wilkinson obliged, not just with the Monarchs but with teams to whom he and Baird rented Satchel. Just when writers concluded that the pitcher could no longer go the distance, he did. He threw as many as twelve innings if the score was tied, usually coming out on top. Such was his efficiency that his pitch count over nine innings was lower than that of most hurlers over five frames. He sometimes led the league in losses but often finished first in strikeouts. He was not the dominant fireballer of his twenties, but he was still better than just about anyone then or ever as he approached, then passed, the milestone of forty.

The best opportunities to strut his stuff during his years with the Monarchs came not during the season, when he was often on the road, but at All-Star and World Series games. The All-Star classic was the biggest Negro sporting event of the year, and Satchel pitched in three of them during the 1940s. He won one (1943), lost one (1942), and had no role in the decision for the third (1941). Win, lose, or draw, Satchel was blackball's most marketable commodity, and his presence at those East-West games helps explain why they drew crowds larger than the Major League All-Star Game seven times between 1938 and 1948. "We want Satch," fans would yell until the manager sent him to the mound. After one such contest, a black scribe credited Paige with turning out "more Negroes . . . than Lincoln freed." As impressive as his pitching was in the five games and fifteen innings he appeared, his All-Star hitting statistics were more surprising: two for six, for an average of .333.

The World Series offers an even better look at a pitcher's performance, since it lets him throw as many innings over as many games as his arm can endure. Satchel's endured forever in the 1942 series. He pitched for the Monarchs in all four games that counted, and in a fifth that did not because their opponent, the Homestead Grays, signed up four players at the last minute. Those appearances set a World Series record for the Negro Leagues and the Majors, but it was a mark he almost missed by almost missing the last game.

That final contest was in Philadelphia, but Satchel spent the prior night three hundred miles away in Pittsburgh because "there was a mighty nice gal over there that I just had to see." He was in Lancaster the next morning on his way to Philly when a policeman arrested him for speeding. "But I got to pitch a ball game over in Philadelphia—the World Series," he protested. "All you got to do is see a justice of the peace," the officer replied, taking him to the local barbershop where the magistrate was busy with his main trade, cutting hair. "I could tell there wasn't any use arguing anymore so I just sat and waited until he finished snipping." The barber-jurist asked Satchel how he would plead. "Guilty," the pitcher said, and the justice fined him three dollars. "I threw that money at him and got out of there quick."

The game was in the fourth inning when he arrived at Shibe Park, with fifteen thousand fans all wondering the same thing: Where is Satchel? He answered emphatically by jumping into his uniform and dashing onto the field to relieve Jack Matchett, who had dug the Monarchs into a 5-4 hole. Satchel warmed up by tossing ten or so balls to first base in a feigned attempt to pick off one of two runners he inherited. That was all he needed as he pitched five and a third innings of no-hit, no-run ball, fanning seven while issuing a pair of walks. "He had plenty of speed and his fast breaking curve added to the misery of the Gray batters," wrote the *Chicago Defender.* "He mixed these with a baffling slow ball." *The Philadelphia Tribune*'s Eustace Gay called it "a case of 'too much Paige.' " His teammates battled back for five runs. Game and series, Monarchs and Satchel.

SATCHEL PAMPERED HIMSELF MORE now that he was with the Monarchs, and he was mollycoddled by J. L. Wilkinson. The instrument for both was Jewbaby Floyd, the tall and scrawny masseur who looked ancient enough to have given rubdowns to Abner Doubleday. While he was trainer to all the Monarchs, his long healing fingers were at work most often on the star pitcher's shoulder and arm. Jewbaby worked out the kinks in the morning and again at night. When Satchel's stomach gurgled, his trainer sauntered to the mound with a mysterious-looking potion of baking soda and water, inducing a burp that echoed in the farthest bleachers. Jewbaby drew the red-hot baths Satchel took after every game, counseled him on his diet, and saw that he got the rest he needed. When the pitcher wanted company on a long drive or needed his suits tended to at the cleaners, Jewbaby stepped in as companion and valet.

Chet Brewer, Satchel's past and present bullpen mate, also drove with him but not because he wanted to. "Satchel was always late getting to games, or he wouldn't get there at all. So Wilkinson put us to riding together. He figured I'd help Satchel," remembered Brewer. "One time in Three Rivers, Michigan, 200 miles to go, game starts at three o'clock; it's one now. Satchel in the middle of the floor shooting dice with some woman for pennies. . . . I said, 'Come on, Satchel, we're going to be late.' " The pair piled into the pitcher's Chrysler Airflow, with Satchel saying, "If the red lights are going to make us late, I won't stop at any more." And he didn't. Another time they were running late and Satchel took the most direct route, which was the wrong way down a one-way street. A motorcycle cop pulled them over, asking, "Doggone, don't you see that's a one-way street?" Satchel looked up innocently and replied, "I'm only going one way." That was the end for Brewer. "I told J. L.: 'Now, instead of one pitcher being later, you got two late. I don't want to ride with Satchel any more. He's going to get both of us killed.' "

Brewer could have saved himself the heartache if he had asked any of the other players anointed as Satchel's babysitter by Wilkie, Gus, and other owners he worked for. All were given the same charge: see that the pitcher gets to the game on time and in one piece. All thought it would be easy. All quit, generally within weeks. Byron Johnson lasted parts of two seasons when he and Satchel were with the Baby Monarchs. "You stay with him. Don't let him out of your sight," Wilkinson told Johnson. That meant holding on as Satchel cut across the highway divider to follow a deer, aiming his rifle out the window or giving chase on foot. Byron learned to love fish fries, with Satchel doing the catching and cooking using a rod, pan, and stove stashed in the trunk. He watched Satchel chase one woman after another, "especially the white women." Johnson loved the camaraderie he found with the daredevil Paige, but not the speed and recklessness. "I figured I wasn't goin' to live through it," he said, "so I stopped riding with him."

Singing helped Slow Robinson and his brother Norman take their minds off the red lights Satchel was running. It was "about the only thing we could do to keep from worrying about getting killed by Satchel's driving," Slow said. They sang "little old love songs," a cappella. "Blue skies smiling at me, nothing but blue skies do I see," began one that Satchel cherished because it focused on life's adventure rather than its drudgery. Another, with a theme more realistic for a barnstormer, went "I know that you and I will never meet again." Four of the teammates formed a quartet, one in a series built around Satchel during his baseball years. Anyone driving alongside could also hear gospels and spirituals, which let Satchel feel close to his church lady mother without having to step inside a church. Music had been utter pleasure for him ever since that first freeing experience of singing with the choir at Mount Meigs.

An airplane would have been a quicker way to get to and from his back-to-back barnstorming engagements, although few players, black or white, flew anywhere then. But Wilkinson was nothing if not a pioneer, and Satchel loved to push conventions. So in 1946 the Monarchs' owner bought a twin-seat Cessna, one of the first built after World War II, with SATCHEL PAIGE hand-painted across both sides of the fuselage. The aviator was Wilkie's son Dick, an Air Force fighter pilot. "We had somewhere in the Midwest booked for a game and I went down, got him, and we flew over," Dick remembers. "A week later I called again and said, 'I have another booking for you.' He said, 'I think I'll drive my Cadillac over there.' I got the idea he was scared a little bit." Stories spread over the years about Satchel flying back and forth across the country with his young pilot, and eventually learning to pilot himself. The truth, Dick says, is that "I never asked him to fly again. I just took the plane and sold it and forgot it. Having Satchel fly was my idea and it didn't work."

His teammates saw the special treatment Satchel got, but they were used to it and to him. He did the same quirky things he always had, only more so now that he was an elder statesman as well as the main attraction. Before each game he visited the other team's dugout, warning the pitcher, "You ain't going to take out nothing," and taunting batters with "I'm going to get you three times today." He was seldom around long enough to face them more than once. After he tossed his three innings it was straight to the showers. He spent the rest of the contest not in the dugout but in the bleachers, signing autographs and visiting with fans, preferably ones with shapely legs and no plans after the game. "Paige thought he was the greatest, that there was nobody like Satch. I wasn't turned off by his egotism because I thought it was well-founded," said Max Manning, who barnstormed with Satchel in the 1940s. "But it made him somewhat unapproachable. He was not easy to get close to. I knew that he had a high opinion of me as a ballplayer or I wouldn't have been on his team, but I felt that if I'd put a hand on his shoulder, buddy-buddy, and said, 'Hey, Satch, how's it going?' he'd resent it. So I stayed away."

Herbert Barnhill was pushed away. It happened in 1943, when Barnhill was a rookie catcher with the Monarchs. An attractive female sportswriter interviewed him along with Satchel before a big game against the Grays, then invited Barnhill to dinner. That apparently upset Satchel, who refused to throw the pitches Barnhill was signaling, then told Wilkinson the young receiver had to go. Wilkinson did what Satchel said, firing Barnhill. When the two players met again, after Barnhill had signed with the Chicago American Giants, Barnhill said Satchel tried to kick him after being tagged out between third base and home plate. "I said, 'What's wrong with you, man? I never did anything to you,' " the catcher recalled half a century later. "I found out he got mad because the [reporter] liked me and didn't like him."

Satchel could be small-minded and vindictive, but more often he was generous and magnetic. He loaned money to players and never asked for repayment. His home became a crash pad for teammates, current and ex. The Monarchs' dugout was transformed into a choral chamber, with Satchel conducting in a way that evaporated other players' pregame jitters. Some of his bad habits hardened but more of them mellowed during his Kansas City years. "Satchel called himself into conference and went over the books," W. Rollo Wilson, a sportswriter-savant for *The Philadelphia Tribune* and *The Pittsburgh Courier* who had followed him for decades, wrote in 1945. "He found out what was wrong in his business and took steps to remedy the condition. Some of the frills and furbelows were dropped from his attire, figuratively speaking, and for several years, we have had a vastly different Satchel Paige. . . . He retained the on-duty color and sloughed off the off-duty trimmings. Now, he travels with his fellows, in uniform every day and is on the field for all pre-game activities. The snob is now a regular fellow."

Younger teammates had always had an easier time with Satchel. Every season he picked one or two he thought listened most closely to his stories, showed the most promise, or happened to be there when he came out of his shell. Ross "Satch" Davis was that fledgling in 1938, when Satchel was assembling a Negro club to play a strong white team in Belleville, Illinois. "They picked me and another boy to relieve Satchel," says Davis. "After Satchel had done his thing he came down to the bullpen to see who would be relieving him. He said, 'Gee whiz, who is this young kid throwing these peas?' Batters knew they weren't going to hit Satchel and they knew an amateur would be coming in behind him, so they were teeing off in the batting circle. When I took the mound Satchel told the hitter, 'No need to dig in, this guy throws the ball harder than me. That's my son out there.' The newspapers picked it up and I became 'Young Satchel,' then 'Satchel Paige Davis,' and finally 'Satchel Davis.' Today they just cut it down to 'Satch Davis.' " The veteran and rookie became friends, with Paige passing on advice on everything from where to stay in Kansas City (generally the Paige home) to how to pick out the winners among the groupies who flock around ballplayers ("wait until Sundays, that's when you see the nicer ladies").

Bill "Youngblood" McCrary was Satchel's favorite Monarch nearly ten years later. McCrary was only seventeen years old, and he stayed at Street's Hotel when the team was in Kansas City. Satchel would swing by in the morning and take him to breakfast, then to the billiards club. "That's how I learned to shoot pool," recalls McCrary, now seventy-seven. "He would tell me on certain shots how to shoot it, what type of English to use, top or bottom. I was the youngest player there and he just took me under his arm." Satchel's counsel was categorical: Keep away from liquor. Don't smoke. Eat healthy. Stay a virgin. It was delivered with the conviction of a reformed addict, or one who was trying to be. Louis Clarizio needed a different sort of mentoring when he joined the Negro Leagues. The eighteen-year-old was white, one of three signed by the American Giants in 1950. Having a friend mattered and one as important as Satchel Paige was a godsend. "He was the best guy you'd ever want to have on your team," Clarizio recalls. "One day he said, 'Want me to pitch to you?' I said, 'Sure, I can use it.' He threw me some knuckleballs and I can tell you it looked like they were going from one side of the plate to the other. I didn't swing until the ball was in the catcher's mitt."

Teaming up with Satchel was harder for Hilton Smith. The tall Texas native was the Monarchs' ace before Satchel came and after he arrived, winning 161 games while losing just 22 during his twelve years with the team. But after Paige got there, Smith was often relegated to finishing off the last six innings of games where Satchel threw the first three. "Satchel's caddy," they called him. The media-savvy, flashy Paige supplanted Smith in the headlines the same way he had Josh Gibson. The contrast was even starker with Hilton, who shared with Satchel not just a team but a pitching mound. Smith resented what he felt was the snub he got from baseball fans and writers, black and white. He watched as less talented teammates and foes were celebrated and ultimately ushered into the Hall of Fame, but he never lived to see his name added to the list. He also had issues with Satchel, telling one interviewer that being overshadowed by Paige "really hurt me" and calling Satchel's miraculous recovery from arm troubles "the worst break I got." Yet Smith's son, DeMorris, says that Satchel and his dad remained fishing buddies and friends. The elder Smith knew that Satchel felt badly about robbing his battery mate of the limelight and he tried to turn the tables at least once. "You're always saving games for me," Satchel told Hilton during the 1942 World Series. "Tonight let me relieve you."

	CHAPTER 7

Master of the Manor

"That poor little colored boy in Mobile had grown up
to be a big money-maker."

SATCHEL FIGURED THE TWO MEN were looking for his autograph as he left the mound that sticky July Sunday in 1943. It was, after all, Paige Day at Wrigley Field, and most of the twenty-two thousand howling fans would have loved his John Hancock after watching him pitch five innings of no-run, no-hit baseball. He had already been showered with luggage and other gifts from admirers at home plate and a fistful of cash as his share of the box-office receipts. So he reached for a pencil and grabbed the piece of paper the two men thrust at him.

But this duo had been dispatched by Janet Howard Paige and they were no fans of Satchel's. " 'I don't want your autograph. This is a summons for a divorce court appearance,' " he recalled one deputy telling him. "I took the paper and just stood there. . . . You just don't expect to have everything going your way like they do on a special day and then have it cut right off by a divorce summons. Finally the fans were gone. So was the summons. I looked around me. There were plenty of pieces of paper, but no summons. I guess somewhere today there's some guy with my autograph on my divorce summons."

Janet's complaint laid out a marriage that had started with hope and ended in ruin. Satchel and Janet "lived and cohabited together as husband and wife" for four and a half years after their wedding in 1934, the petition said, although there "was no child or children borned to them." Starting in the spring of 1939, "without any reasonable or just cause," Satchel "willfully deserted and absented himself from" Janet. He would not take her to the Caribbean when he played ball there, she said, or bring her to Kansas City when he moved there. Up to then the complaint read like any divorce document, conveying its venom in the restrained lexicon of the law. Then it took a turn, accusing Satchel of the crime of bigamy and saying he had abandoned Janet. While in Puerto Rico, Satchel "met one Lucy, to whom he is purported to have married and who now lives with him in Kansas City, Missouri and poses as his wife." He "carried [Lucy] around in open and notorious exhibition as his wife, all to the embarrassment and injury and damage to the feelings of [Janet]." All this, the petition added, while Janet was treating Satchel "in a manner well becoming a good, true and virtuous wife." And she was broke even as he had amassed a small fortune consisting of "a large building" in Kansas City worth $25,000, antiques and curios valued at $30,000, and annual earnings of $40,000 as "a baseball pitcher and known as a star."

Satchel never formally responded to Janet's complaints, and he never showed up in court to answer questions. No need, since his lawyers were in touch with hers and working out a deal. Responding in writing or testifying in person would have meant swearing to matters he did not want to air, or risking perjury. Much better to avoid the reporters following the case and save his side of the story for his memoir, published nineteen years later. In it he wrote that "there wasn't any truth to that business of my marrying Lucy, and Janet was just trying to make things look bad, I figured. Janet also said how I was making about forty thousand in Kansas City, and that my china and antiques were worth thirty thousand. I only wished that was so."

Two weeks after Janet filed her petition she and Satchel were divorced. He paid $1,500 to her and $300 to her attorneys. She agreed not to ask for anything else, ever. The judge found Satchel guilty of desertion but nothing more. The pitching star got off easy financially and easier still legally since Janet was right about his marriage to Lucy, although the wording of her petition suggests she did not fully believe it. The judge apparently did not, either; if he had he could have sent Satchel to prison.

The truth was that Satchel married Lucy in Puerto Rico when he was playing baseball there during the winter of 1940–41, then took her to his new home in Kansas City. They bought a dog. She watched his games, the way she had in Guayama, with the press occasionally taking notice. At the East-West game in 1941, the *Chicago Defender* said Lucy "was there to watch her husband's enthusiastic fans cheer him." *Life* magazine ran a picture of the couple earlier that year, with a caption saying that "Satchel's wife, Lucy, is from Puerto Rico. They met while he was playing ball down there. She can't speak English well and Satchel doesn't know many words in Spanish." Neither account mentioned that Satchel had another wife named Janet.

His Negro League buddy Monte Irvin recalled that Satchel and Lucy stayed together four or five years. But with him away playing ball all the time, she tired of being by herself and went home to Puerto Rico. "I don't know what she did after that," Irvin said. Few others did either, including Satchel. But Lucy's story did not end there, although it did end precipitously. She stayed for a few years with her sister-in-law in Guayama, then returned to the United States, where her brothers Julio, José, and Félix were living and Papi would soon move. Her hair was straight now. No Shirley Temple curls or happy-go-lucky airs. She worked as a nurse at a New York hospital, where she met a doctor from the Philippines. They married and had a daughter, Doreen. The couple worked hard, the family lived in a nice condominium, and Doreen attended a Catholic school on Park Avenue.

One Sunday when Doreen was about eight, Lucy swallowed half a bottle of sleeping pills and fed the rest to Doreen. Lucy survived; Doreen did not. There was a trial, and Lucy was judged mentally ill. No jail time, just careful observation and sixteen months' probation. She seemed to recover her bearings, returned to work, and spent endless hours at Doreen's graveside. Lucy stayed in New York until the late 1970s, when she again went back to Puerto Rico. A few years later her brother Julio got a call saying there had been a fire at Lucy's home and she was dead. She was barely sixty. "It was suicide," says

Julio. Among the items destroyed in the blaze was a picture of Satchel that she had kept on display since the two split.

Janet also dropped out of public view after her divorce from Satchel. She was thirty at the time and working as a waitress at Chicago's Brass Rail, but she never seemed to get her life fully back on track. She worked at the Grand Hotel and Minnie's Midway Inn in Chicago, visited Pittsburgh as often as she could, and kept the name Paige. *The Pittsburgh Courier*'s gossip columnists carried regular items about her over the years, including one in 1945 noting that she "intends to get married again as soon as she finds someone to escort her to the altar." Another, in 1965, mentioned a club called the Chesterfield Girls whose roster "contained the names of some of the most sophisticated, most glamorous and foxiest girls of that era." It named three, including Janet, "all of whom are deceased."

Satchel treated the aftermath of his divorce from Janet briefly and lightly in his memoir. "I'd won a lot of decisions in the past, but this was one I lost bad," he wrote. "When it was all over, I didn't feel anything. Janet and I'd busted up so long before, there just wasn't anything left to feel." It was the same tone he used in describing his relationship with Lucy—"good friends for a while." The reality was that both wives had inflicted as well as received wounds, although theirs were easier for anyone to see and for them to acknowledge. Admitting emotional pain was not part of Satchel's makeup and after the divorce he was eager to move on.

THE WAY HE MOVED ON was to zero in on the "nice-looking gal" he had met the year before at Crown Drugs in Kansas City. "I could tell right off that she didn't know who I was," Satchel said, thinking back to the night in 1942 he went in to buy film for his camera. "That kind of bothered me. Everybody knew Ol' Satch around Kansas City, especially the girls." Not caring, or pretending not to, is what had first made Janet Howard attractive to Satchel. Eleven years later, it was what drew him to Lahoma Brown. He asked for some 120 film; she said they were all out and wondered if he could use another kind. "No," he snapped. "Don't act so smart," she shot back, raising his dander higher. "There have been some that have seen Ol Satch mad," he wrote afterward, "but nothing like that. I guess when you're playing the peacock and somebody pulls a feather, you get a lot madder than when you ain't playing. I yelled for the manager. He knew who I was all right."

Her boss took his side, saying, "Mr. Paige, if she insulted you we'll fire her right now. You just say the word." That was not what he wanted—not for "a gal who was as fine a looker as that Miss Brown." So he told the drugstore manager, "You don't have to fire anyone. But maybe she'll have some manners after this." Satchel was hooked. The next day he rushed back to the store and asked, in a voice he knew she would hear, for "that half-smart girl." He asked the same thing every couple of days for the next week or so, figuring that "maybe by kidding her like that she wouldn't be mad at me for what happened that first night." It worked, just as it had with Janet. Give him the time and Satchel could charm a dead tree. He invited Lahoma on a date, she went, and "we had plenty more. . . . I spent money squiring her around like I'd invented it."

His new love was not the party girl that Janet was, nor as exotic as Lucy from Puerto Rico. Lahoma Jean Brown had just turned twenty-one when Satchel met her, making her sixteen years his junior. She had moved to Kansas City from Stillwater, Oklahoma, which was the home of Oklahoma State University, Lahoma and her four sisters, and not much else. Lahoma had a two-year-old daughter, Shirley Long, and a divorce from Shirley's dad. She was as attractive as Satchel said and as serious as a single young mother had to be. This was not someone to trifle with, the way he did with girls who flocked around him at the Blue Room, the Monarchs' haunt in the heart of Kansas City's jazz district. Everything about Lahoma—short, neatly curled hair, an open face with large eyes, clothes tailored to reveal little—spoke to her maturity. So did her religious fervor, which had her attending church regularly and eventually joining the restorationist Jehovah's Witnesses. She sang hymns at home, loudly, and was an effective enough evangelist that even Satchel started sharing credit for his achievements with "the Man Upstairs." If his new girlfriend was like anyone he had known before, it was his mother, Lula Paige.

Lahoma was the yin to Satchel's yang even more than Josh Gibson had been. She cherished her privacy as much as he did publicity. She was strong-willed and grounded while he yielded to whims and conceits. All she was seeing of the world was Oklahoma and Kansas City while he was barnstorming across the Americas. And like J. L.

Wilkinson, Lahoma was not naïve about who Satchel was but loved him anyway and knew how to manage him. It is unclear whether she knew that he was a married man, twice over, when he first squired her around town; if so, she did not object. She had to know it a year later, when the newspapers treated his divorce from Janet as a major news event.

As soon as he got back to Kansas City after the split-up "I raced that buggy of mine over to Lahoma's," Satchel said. "I'm a free man," he told her. She seemed pleased and the two "started seeing the town like nobody ever'd done before. I could tell she was the gal for me. I'd never met anybody like her and that slowed me down like no gal'd ever slowed me down before." There were lots of things he wanted to tell her, but it took forever before he got up the nerve just to say he liked her. "Finally, one night I got her out for dinner and after we were done I gulped down a drink quick. I figured that might help me ask her what I wanted to ask," he recalled. " 'If you'll be my best girl, I'll be your best boy,' I finally blurted out. That wasn't what I wanted to say, but I'd said at least that much. 'You know I will, Satchel,' she told me."

That was not the question she had expected or hoped for. They had been seeing each other for a year already, and his divorce from Janet freed him to marry again. Satchel, at thirty-seven, was too old to have a best girl but was wary of another wife. Lahoma wanted a father for her daughter and a husband for herself, but she took what she could get, which was a boyish man learning, baby step by baby step, how to make lasting commitments to a city, a team, a woman, and a little girl. It would be four years before he would pop the next question. She was patient.

Step one was making sense of his finances. Satchel was like Uncle Sam: adept at bringing in money, but spending everything he had and then some. He started with a base salary from the Monarchs that was substantially higher than the wages paid the other stars there or anywhere in blackball, and was more than he had gotten in Pittsburgh, Bismarck, or from the dictator Trujillo. Then the team helped him book appearances with small-town clubs or other Negro League ones at rates ranging from a third of gross receipts to a straight payout of between $250 and $2,000 a game, plus expenses. The Monarchs' owners could insist on more money in road games where they pitched Satchel, knowing that the gate would be bigger, and his share of the booty could reach as high as $4,000. Opposing teams made out because with Satchel on the program, Major League owners were willing to lease their expansive stadiums, pulling in more money for everyone. Like Babe Ruth in the Major Leagues, Satchel single-handedly moved team ledgers from red to black. Homestead Grays' owner Cum Posey understood that better than most, which is why he had this clause inserted in a 1944 contract between the Monarchs and Grays: "[Satchel] will pitch at least 3 innings unless sick or injured or from any cause beyond our control or unless he is removed from game for cause."

Satchel was the embodiment of the athlete-entrepreneur, and his steadfastness and success in demanding top dollar added up to earnings in the early 1940s of $40,000 a year. That was nearly four times what the average player made on the pennant-winning New York Yankees, and was almost identical to what the Bombers were paying star center fielder Jumpin' Joe DiMaggio. Ted Williams earned half that from the Red Sox and Stan Musial made even less with the Cardinals. But there was a difference: Satchel had to work year-round to earn his keep while most white stars took the winter off. In 1944, *Washington Post* sports guru Shirley Povich proclaimed Paige "the highest-paid player in the game, white or colored." In the *Los Angeles Times* Al Wolf went one better, crowning him "the 'earningest' baseballer of all time." For years journalists had called Satchel a string bean. Now he was the "Million Dollar String Bean." Satchel, who was generally the source for stories on his stratospheric earnings, said that in those years money "was rolling in free and easy all over the country."

It was rolling out freer still. He had coveted anything on wheels ever since he owned his first car, a Model T Ford. By the late 1940s his collection included a black Lincoln, a blue Caddie, a Jeep, and an army-style Chevy truck with seats built in. There also were two trailers, which made it easy to cart around his teakwood dining room set; Queen Anne sidepieces; three rugs, each costing $1,110; a $300 Meissen drinking stein; complete sets of Wedgwood and Sèvres china; and Royal Vienna dishes. J. L. Wilkinson's wife owned an antiques store and advised Satchel on what to get and where, which made it easy and fun. Even better was defying the expectation of what a ghetto-born ballplayer would want to do with his money.

"It was a sign," he said, "that that poor little colored boy in Mobile had grown up to be a big money-maker. It proved how high I'd climbed—how I'd gone from a place where sometimes we didn't have money even to buy a little piece of meat to go with the greens to a place where I could buy the best stuff or the oldest and most expensive stuff if I just took a liking to it. . . . Every time I look at that collection of mine, I got something to remind me of how far I'd come, something to prove that pitching day after day all year round was worth something."

There were other reminders. His collection of cameras had grown to four and of shotguns to fifteen. He had a four-string tenor guitar to go with his harmonica and ukulele, a stack of calypso records, and all the fishing gear he could get his hands on. In Chattanooga he had had a single closet that was almost empty. Now he had one filled with shoes, another with just hats, and "four closets fulla suits. Just ordered seven suits from Ben the Tailor in Philadelphia. Nothin' less than $75. Most near $150." All had neckties to go with them, along with silk shirts and cuff links adorned with a baseball crest. If he wasn't the best-dressed man in Kansas City he was surely the most dressed.

So much money was coming in and going out that a professional accountant would have had a difficult time keeping track. And, as Dick Wilkinson remembered, "Satchel wasn't a financial man." Dick's dad was, thankfully, and he was as trustworthy as he was concerned about Satchel's well-being. "He relied 100 percent on my dad as far as money was concerned. We gave him a good hunk of the money on everything he did. Satchel spent his money. During the winter I remember my father stopping by his house, giving him some money. Dad always took care of him." One way he did that was by taking a little out of Satchel's salary each month to buy war bonds. The problem, the pitcher said, was that every time he got a bond from Wilkie "it seemed like I was a little short then and I'd cash it in that same day."

The only way Satchel ever saved was by buying real estate. Wilkie pushed him into it, knowing a home would give him more comfort and hold its value better than an automobile or rifle. Lahoma reinforced the decision. It took until his thirty-fifth birthday for Satchel to see the point in owning property, given his life on the move, but once he got into real estate he did it full tilt, the way he did with everything. He bought his first home around the time he and Lucy moved back from Puerto Rico. It was high on a terrace and had fourteen rooms. There was space for his cars and antiques, along with a backyard big enough for hundreds of chickens, a dozen dogs, and a cow. Not only did his neighbors never complain about his urban farmyard, they got used to sharing in the bountiful eggs. But one day a man from the city zoning board knocked on the door. "That was the end of my chickens and cow," Satchel said. "They let me keep my dogs. I was mighty glad of that. They were the finest hunting dogs around."

Home ownership had precisely the effect on Satchel that Wilkinson had hoped: it settled him down. He would remain a devoted Monarch for as long as he remained in the Negro Leagues and a devotee of J. L. Wilkinson for as long as he lived. "I did a great deal of contract jumping," Satchel confessed in a 1943 article carrying his byline in *The Courier* in Pittsburgh, a city that knew all about his lack of loyalty. "Any club that offered me a little more dough, I was Johnny-on-the-spot. However, those days are gone forever. I am going to play with the Kansas City Monarchs as long as the owner and manager want me."

This new master of the manor loved puttering around, a hobby that would sustain him during his retirement and that had him welding, drilling, sawing, and trying to take care of anything that went wrong in the sprawling house. The place had rooms left to rent, and Satchel tried. He even printed TOURIST HOME on his stationery, between his name and address. It was classic Paige humor, wry and understated. "Course, there wasn't too much rent," he explained. "I always seemed to be running into some old buddies who needed a room but didn't have money to pay for it. 'I'll send it to you later when I make a buck,' they'd all tell me. I'm still waiting." Lahoma helped make sense of his finances with the house and everything else, although she says she did not move in until years after he bought it, when they were married. "She was a real businesswoman," Satchel recalled. "I guess that's when I decided for sure I'd better marry up with her before too long. You don't find good business managers that look as good as Lahoma too often."

Satchel's real estate transactions before and after he met Lahoma suggest that he was getting better at orchestrating his investments, although not at holding on to his earnings. He bought three properties over fifteen years and lived in two of them. He made two of those purchases in the name of his mother, Lula, who never lived in Kansas City and likely never saw the homes she nominally owned. Bringing her into the transactions, real estate specialists say, probably offered tax advantages or protection from debtors. It is impossible to know how good a price he got on the homes because the property records contain phrases like "one dollar and other valuable consideration," legalese for "we do not have to tell you and are not going to." What is clear from Satchel's purchases and sales of homes is that, despite his fame and his record-setting salaries, he never had extra money. He admits as much in his memoir, talking about having to sell his first house when he bought his last: "Those two houses would have been mighty good investments if I could of kept both of them. But I just couldn't slow down that spending and when the money got a little short again, I had to sell that first house on Twelfth Street. Stocking away money for when you get old was something I still hadn't learned. It just seemed like I never was going to get too old to pitch."

His mother was not just a foil in Satchel's home buying but a beneficiary. In his memoir he proudly recites the story of buying her a home, and it is retold in a film about his life. It happened, he wrote, while he was visiting Mobile in the late 1930s during his estrangement from Janet. Everyone but Lula greeted him like the star he was. She wanted to know whether he had been playing ball on Sundays, warning, "The Lord'll punish you." Other things on the Lord's and Lula's don't-do list: gambling, late nights, wild women, and missing church. Satchel knew he would never live up to those expectations so he tried to set new ones. After he was home a couple of days he got an idea: "That old shotgun house was the next thing to a shack now. So I decided to buy Mom a new house." She resisted, saying, "You all were born here and this is where we stay." He bought it anyway, taking her to see it without telling her it was hers, and asking how she liked it. "Now that's too big a house," Lula said. "Houses are way too high now. But I've been thinking it over and I guess we could use a new house. But don't you go spending more'n four or five thousand, you hear. That'll buy a fine house." Then Satchel told her he'd already bought the house they were looking at. "How much did you pay for it?" she asked. "Oh," he said, "ten or fifteen thousand."

His story was true in spirit if not in the particulars. It actually took another decade, until 1949, for Satchel to buy Lula that home on Cedar Street. The purchase price was precisely what she suggested—$4,500—not the five figures he boasted. He could have inflated the cost and pushed up the date because of a memory lapse, since he was recollecting more than a dozen years later in his second autobiography. Yet all he had to do to refresh his memory was to reread his first one, published in 1948, when he said that Lula was still living in the home where she was born. "When this season is over," Satchel wrote, "I'm goin' down there and buy her a new home."

A more likely reason he recast the story is guilt. He did not visit Lula as often as he felt he should during his early years in Kansas City. His life was a blur of ball games and road tours. She, in turn, did not put much stock in her son's celebrity. She was too down-to-earth and too busy raising his brothers and sisters, all of whom turned to her even into their adulthood when they ran out of money, needed a home, or faced other demons common to the Paige clan. "You would think that to have a famous son she would be boisterous about it, but she didn't mention Satchel unless someone asked about him," recalls Satchel's nephew Leon Paige, who back then lived with and looked after Lula, his grandmother, and could not help but begrudge his rich, famous uncle. "He never wrote her. Once in a while she'd get me to write and ask him for money when we needed it. We'd write a letter and sometimes he'd get it and send $300 or $500. Satchel didn't come to Mobile too often." Others, especially Satchel's children, describe a warmer bond between Lula and her celebrated son. And Leon was grateful that Satchel bought the Cedar Street house because Leon got to move there with Lula. "It was a big house, a large house, a great house," says Leon, although it was in the same Down the Bay neighborhood of mainly shotgun shacks. While Satchel purchased the home for Lula, he remained the owner and had a difficult time keeping up with the property taxes. "Nobody paid the taxes," Leon remembers, adding that when he got out of the military he paid them. "I stayed in the house and paid the taxes until I got married."

If Satchel did entertain guilt, he might have felt it not just with Lula but with all the women in his life, including the newest one. He tried harder to be true to her than to any of them. But he was away too often, with too many temptingly pretty faces. One time, as Buck O'Neil tells it, the Monarchs were playing a game on an Indian reservation in North Dakota and Satchel met a magnificent woman named Nancy. He invited her to meet him in Chicago; she accepted. Buck was sitting in the coffee shop of the Evans Hotel when Nancy pulled up in a taxi, and he steered her to Satchel's room. A few minutes later another taxi arrived with Lahoma, who by then was Satchel's fiancée and was there to surprise him. Quick thinking by Buck got her to join him for coffee while the bellman warned Satchel to move Nancy to the adjacent room. The day was saved, but not the night. "After we had turned in, I heard Satchel's door open and close," Buck said. "Then I heard him knock on Nancy's door. I think he wanted to give her some money and apologize, but while he's whispering kind of loud, 'Nancy! Nancy!' I hear *his* door open again, and I knew it was Lahoma coming out to see what was going on. I jumped out of my bed, opened my door, and said, 'Yeah, Satch. What do you want?' And he said, 'Why, Nancy. There you are. I was looking for you. What time is the game tomorrow?' And from that night on, until his dying day, Satchel called me Nancy."

Buck told that story repeatedly over the next half century, with his longest and sweetest version lasting a full four minutes. That night at the Evans Hotel a parade of Negro notables from Olympic gold medalist Jesse Owens to boxing champ Joe Louis stopped by to pay tribute to Satchel. His being somewhere guaranteed a crowd, be it in a city or hamlet, with bartenders pouring drinks for free and ladies flocking to the front. Satchel, Buck said, "might have been the most famous black man in America then." Joe Louis was better known among white folks, but no one—not Harlem Renaissance bard Langston Hughes, big band maestro Count Basie, or the majestic jazzman Edward Kennedy "Duke" Ellington—was quite the hero for blacks that Satchel was. It was easy to see why: all the African American luminaries had climbed to the top of their fields, but none did it with Satchel's over-the-top style and charm, which is what had drawn the real Nancy to him. And none of the others had been seen up close by as many blacks in as many places as the itinerant Leroy "Satchel" Paige.

Each time Buck told the Nancy story, and had extracted every last drop, everyone who heard it had the same question: Did Lahoma find out? "Of course she did," Buck explained. "She *knew* Satchel. She loved the story. I never would have told it if she hadn't heard it from him first."

SATCHEL'S BARNSTORMING, TOO, WAS DIFFERENT during those more settled years in the mid-1940s. It was less ragtag and random than when he was starting out. Games were scheduled further in advance. No brass bands enticing farmers from their fields. No sandlots masquerading as baseball diamonds. No easy wins against weekend warriors. The competition now was first-rate, the money big-time.

Bob Feller saw to that. The Heater from Van Meter was Iowa's favorite son then and always. He was the real-life Roy Hobbs, the farm boy baseball prodigy played by Robert Redford in *The Natural*. Feller's dream was to be the most overpowering pitcher the Majors had ever produced, and he may have been. He was the winningest pitcher in the history of the Cleveland Indians. He pitched three no-hitters and led the league in strikeouts for seven seasons and in wins for six. At age seventeen he fanned seventeen Philadelphia Athletics, an American League record that he would break two years later. Feller also wanted to be the richest player ever and came even closer there, in part by organizing a series of barnstorming tours that played to enormous crowds. The biggest and best came in 1946.

Feller dreamed up the idea during his long days and nights manning antiaircraft guns on the USS *Alabama* during World War II. He knew that getting other Major Leaguers to join him would be easy, given how desperate most were to supplement their meager salaries, and he signed up the best. There were two batting champs: Stan "the Man" Musial (.365) from the National League and Mickey Vernon (.353) from the American. Spud Chandler and Johnny Sain were both twenty-game winners, while Feller had won twenty-six for Cleveland that season and set a Major League record with 348 strikeouts. Phil Rizzuto was a great double-play man and his fellow New York Yankee Charlie Keller smashed thirty home runs in 1946.

The next hurdle was finding a way around a limit set by Commissioner of Baseball Kenesaw Mountain Landis, who ruled that Major Leaguers could barnstorm only during the ten days following the World Series. But Landis had died in 1944 and Feller convinced the new commissioner, Albert Benjamin "Happy" Chandler, to extend the cutoff to thirty days. Feller chartered DC-3 planes to ferry his players to the thirty-four games he set up. He hired a doctor, a trainer, a lawyer, a secretary, a publicity man, and an advance man, then booked ballparks and hotels. He bought insurance in case the planes crashed and the players died. Feller was a meticulous man and personally saw to everything that mattered, including transforming himself into a corporation—Ro-Fel—and checking receipts at each stop. The only thing missing was the right opponent, one talented enough to give Feller's big leaguers true competition and gritty enough to give fans their money's worth.

Only one man could deliver on that tall order. Feller had been an immature seventeen, and Satchel a ripe twenty-nine, when the two faced off for the first time a decade earlier in an exhibition game in Des Moines. The teenager took mental notes. He also saw how successful the first round of interracial barnstorming was in the 1930s, when Dizzy Dean captained the whites and Satchel was majordomo of the black crew. By the time Feller was contemplating his own barnstorming tour in the mid-1940s, Dizzy was past his prime but Satchel, four years Dean's junior, could still pack a stadium and pitch with impact. He proved both when Feller faced him in Oakland in 1945, and he showed how affable he was when the lanky Midwesterner invited him over afterward to listen to the World Series. Feller knew the Negro Leagues were the only source of players on a par with his Major League stars. He turned to Satchel as the sole Negro Leaguer with the savvy and showmanship to match his.

Feller and Paige were an unlikely twosome. Rapid Robert was as stiff and awkward as Ol' Satchel was playful and charming. Feller came of age in the Iowa cornfields, Satchel in an Alabama ghetto. One was the feel-great story of an American hero making good on a Major League diamond, then enlisting in the navy and earning six battle citations. The other was an American tragedy of an athlete who served his country in ways it would acknowledge only belatedly and had played his baseball in the shadows of the Negro Leagues. Yet both were motivated by money, in pursuit of which they formed an improbable alliance and even a friendship. And while both were racial moderates at best, the games they organized substantially advanced the integration of America's pastime and America itself.

With help from J. L. Wilkinson and Tom Baird, Satchel assembled a team that was the black analog to Feller's. The pitching staff included Monarchs' ace Hilton Smith and Dan Bankhead of the Memphis Red Sox, who would become the first black to pitch in the Majors. Batting titlist Buck O'Neil was at first, and playing third was Howard Easterling, who batted .321 for the season despite entering it late after returning from three years of war duty in the Pacific. It was, as Feller's press release claimed, a "Who's Who in Negro Baseball." As for Satchel, the release called him "the old wizard of colored baseball . . . whose name is legendary on two continents," while Feller's souvenir program labeled him "a credit to the race he represents and a model for clean sportsmanship."

Black or white, most players signed up for the greenbacks—$3,500 for a month's work, which was twice what most black players earned for a whole season and about half the annual salary for the average Major Leaguer. Both teams also had something to prove. For Feller's players, many of whom had grown up in the segregated South, it was a matter of demonstrating their hardball and racial supremacy. Satchel's mates had even more at stake: affirming their equality, the way they had in integrated leagues in California and the Caribbean. What made this series different was the national spotlight. Never had so many fans or journalists been on hand to weigh the barnstormers' relative merits. "The whole trip was because of racial rivalry," says Feller. "We knew that was what would happen and we knew that would draw very well."

Draw they did, with the tour attracting 250,000 fans. Satchel's team got off to a strong start, taking the first game 3-1 in Pittsburgh. Feller's club came back in a doubleheader the next day, with an 11-2 shellacking of the Paige All-Stars in Youngstown and a 5-0 shutout in Cleveland. Games bounced back and forth from there as the teams moved around the country, from Pennsylvania to Ohio and Illinois, Missouri to Colorado and California. Seventeen states in all. Along the way there were brilliant touches of showmanship, as in Council Bluffs, Iowa, where Chicago White Sox catcher Frankie Hayes drew a walk off Satchel. Hayes took a three-foot lead off the bag, then fell asleep. Literally. "Old Sachmo' disdained the orthodox procedure of snapping a throw to First Baseman Buck O'Neil," the Council Bluffs paper reported. "Instead he ran over in person and was standing squarely on the sack with the ball when Hayes finally woke up. The Sox catcher was an easy victim."

The racial rivalry was less of one than the Negro Leaguers antici- pated, as they finished with five wins and fifteen losses. There are a series of possible explanations for the blacks' weaker-than-hoped-for performance. The white stars had more players and teams to choose from, and those teams had better facilities, bigger coaching staffs, and larger salaries. The white Majors also had a bigger base to recruit from, with Caucasian Americans outnumbering Negroes ten to one. Still, winning a quarter of the games was respectable if not convinc- ing for the Negro Leaguers, and scoring sixty-three runs compared to the big leaguers' ninety-one was not bad for a bunch that white owners felt did not belong on the same field as their white players.

The Paige-Feller pitch-off is more difficult to weigh since neither threw more than five innings a game and they generally went just two or three. But in fifty-four frames against Satchel's team, Feller gave up fifteen runs, for an average of 2.50 per game. Satchel pitched forty-two innings, allowing eighteen runs, or 3.86 per game. Feller recorded slightly more strikeouts and fewer walks per nine innings. The verdict was clear: Satchel pitched well, Feller pitched better. The bad cold Satchel suffered for part of the tour might have played a role. The Major League batters he faced were, as a group, better than his Negro League teammates, and, as Feller said, "they all bore down to see what they could do against such a fabled figure as Satchel Paige." Yet in the end the gap was mainly a matter of age: Feller, at twenty-eight, was in his prime, having just completed the strongest of the eighteen seasons he would pitch in the Majors. Satchel, at forty, was trying to prove he was as good as ever but in- stead confirmed he was not quite. His games against Feller looked more like a father-son rivalry than an encounter between peers.

In his memoirs, Satchel preferred to focus on his competition with Feller the following year, 1947, when there were fewer games and he fared much better. Feller over the years bared both sides of his personality—the prickly and the charming—in evaluating Satchel and his black All-Stars. He took the low road to start, when *The Sporting News* in 1946 asked whether any of his colored opponents were big-league material. "Haven't seen one—not one," said Feller. "Maybe Paige when he was young. When you name him you're done. Some are good hitters. Some can field pretty good. Most of them are fast. But I have seen none who combine the qualities of a big league ball player . . . Not even Jackie Robinson."

After being slammed then and later for alleged racism, Feller changed his tone, at least with Satchel. He went from equivocal to gung ho. In 1962 he made a persuasive pitch in *Sports Illustrated* for Satchel's admission to the Hall of Fame. In *Bob Feller's Little Black Book of Baseball Wisdom,* published in 2001, he was more effusive, saying Satchel had "perfect control" and "could spot a hitter's weaknesses very quickly, quicker than anyone I ever knew. . . . Satchel Paige was one of the top five or ten pitchers in the entire history of baseball." In a 2006 interview Feller raised his rating, calling Satchel "one of the top five in history" and saying, "I had a great relationship with Satchel."

The truth is that Feller did not have a great relationship with many players, white or black. He had few social skills and no humility. Satchel felt he was not getting the money he was due for the 1946 tour and he sued Feller for $3,800. Feller retaliated at the end of the tour by replacing the Paige All-Stars with a team led by Jackie Robinson. The next year there was another disagreement; again Satchel demanded his money. He was not the only one. Jackie Robinson said Feller had paid him and his teammates less than they were owed and Ray Doan, Feller's old agent, sued him for alleged irregularities during a 1945 barnstorming tour. Feller saw things differently, saying he was the one who took the risk in setting up the tours and bore the expenses, so he deserved the fattest paychecks. He got them, earning $80,000 from the 1946 tour alone. That, along with his $50,000 salary from the Cleveland Indians and thousands more in endorsements, made for what *The Sporting News* called "the most profitable playing season enjoyed by any player in the history of the game. Bob's earnings for 1946 far exceed the largest take ever drawn down by Babe Ruth."

Feller never pretended to be a social activist. He did not worry about where his Negro League opponents stayed or ate or where they were banished from. "That was their problem," he said. "They had their own traveling secretary. . . . We had nothing to do with each other away from the ballpark." The point was to make money. And in doing so the tour gave many of the black players their first chance to ride in a plane and play to sellout crowds of whites as well as blacks. They got to match their skills against a team not just of Major Leaguers but the very best of whiteball. That is what mattered

The Great Satchell Paige

Satchel demonstrates the classic Paige pitching pose: Just before unleashing the baseball, he kicked his foot high enough to black out the sky and befuddle batters. *National Baseball Hall of Fame Library, Cooperstown, New York*

No one had a greater lifelong influence over Satchel than his mother, Lula Paige, a washerwoman who gave birth to twelve children and continued to mother them until she died in 1966 at age ninety. *Image by Jacqlyn Kirkland from Leon Paige Collection*

Lula Paige as a young woman. *Image by Jacqlyn Kirkland from Leon Paige Collection*

Satchel was twenty-three when he signed on to pitch winter ball for Cuba's Santa Clara Leopards in 1929. *Negro Leagues Baseball Museum, Kansas City*

1935

SMITH   HALEY   MORRIS   PAIGE   JOHNSON   TROUPE   RADCLIFFE
    DESIDERATO   LEARY   CHURCHILL, MGR.   OBERHOLZER   HENDEE

Satchel on his 1935 championship team in Bismarck, North Dakota, one of the first times blacks and whites played not just on the same field but on the same team. *State Historical Society of North Dakota*

Satchel with Cecil Travis (left) and Dizzy Dean, two of the white stars he faced off against during interracial barnstorming tours in the 1930s and 1940s. *National Baseball Hall of Fame Library, Cooperstown, New York*

Satchel wore the uniform of the Guayama Witches when he pitched in Puerto Rico during the winters of 1939 and 1940. In the first season, he was almost unhittable. In the second, his performance fell off, but not his popularity. *Jay Sanford Collection*

Satchel with Lucy Figueroa, whom he met and married while playing winter ball in Guayama, Puerto Rico. *Photo by George Strock/Time Life Pictures/Getty Images*

Holding their weapons of choice, old friends Satchel Paige and Josh Gibson share a few words before a face-off in Kansas City in 1941. *Photo by Mark Rucker/Transcendental Graphics/Getty Images*

Satchel drew a crowd of kids everywhere he went, and he loved it. *Photo by George Strock/Time Life Pictures/Getty Images*

Kansas City Monarchs trainer Frank "Jewbaby" Floyd works his magic on Satchel's rubberlike pitching arm. *Negro Leagues Baseball Museum, Kansas City*

Satchel loved music, whether it was singing, plucking a guitar, or, as seen here, trying his hand at the piano. *Photo by George Strock/Time Life Pictures/Getty Images*

Satchel and his Negro Leagues pal Jesse Williams check out the merchandise at a sporting goods store. *Negro Leagues Baseball Museum, Kansas City*

Satchel gets the full treatment: manicure, haircut, shave, and shoe shine. *Photo by George Strock/Time Life Pictures/Getty Images*

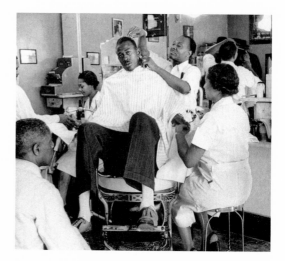

Satchel (top right, in door of plane) and his barnstorming teammates, among them Hilton Smith (far left), Buck O'Neil (fourth from right), and Quincy Trouppe (far right). *Jay Sanford Collection*

With the possible exception of fishing, there was nothing Satchel liked better than leashing up his dogs and loading his rifle for a day of hunting. *Negro Leagues Baseball Museum, Kansas City*

Cleveland Indians owner Bill Veeck watches Satchel work out a day after Veeck signed the forty-two-year-old pitcher to his first contract in the Major Leagues. *Cleveland Public Library*

Satchel shows his Cleveland Indians teammates how to relax, strumming a guitar in the dressing room after an afternoon practice. *Photo by George Silk/Time Life Pictures/Getty Images*

Satchel, who in his years with the Cleveland Indians usually was surrounded by reporters as well as fans, enjoys a moment of solitude. *Photo by George Silk/Time Life Pictures/Getty Images*

In the latter half of his career, teams installed a rocking chair in the bullpen for Satchel, a tribute to his age and his agelessness. *Cleveland Public Library*

In the late 1950s, Satchel suited up for the minor league Miami Marlins. *National Baseball Hall of Fame Library, Cooperstown, New York*

Satchel shows off his pitching technique during a break in the action while filming *The Wonderful Country*, a Western in which he played a U.S. Army sergeant. *Pictorial Parade/Getty Images*

In 1965, Kansas City Athletics owner Charlie Finley signed Satchel for what turned out to be his last three innings in the Majors. Satchel delivered, pitching shutout baseball and setting a record for oldest major-league pitcher that likely will never be broken. He also took time to offer tips to rising stars like Athletics rookie Jim "Catfish" Hunter. *Jay Sanford Collection*

In the 1960s, Satchel barnstormed with the Indianapolis Clowns, where he and his teammates blended breathtakingly skillful baseball with belly-laugh antics. *Bill Heward Collection*

Ed Hamman, the Indianapolis Clowns owner and general manager, signed Satchel to what he said was a four-word contract: "No show, no dough." *Bill Heward Collection*

Satchel finally started to look his age in his fifties and sixties. *University of South Alabama Archives*

Baseball commissioner Bowie
Kuhn congratulates Satchel
after his induction into the
Baseball Hall of Fame in
1971. *National Baseball Hall
of Fame Library, Cooperstown,
New York*

Satchel offers tips on how to play him to actor Louis Gossett, Jr.
(right), and helps Ernie Barnes with his portrayal of catcher Josh Gibson during production of the 1981 made-for-TV movie *Don't Look
Back: The Story of Leroy "Satchel" Paige. Dean Williams Collection*

in the end to most of the Negro Leaguers who barnstormed with Feller, including Satchel. By showcasing their skills and those of their teammates, these two traditionalists did as much to advance the racial cause as anyone in baseball. Satchel said as much when he was inducted to the Hall of Fame, by which time he had repaired his breach with Feller and had played with him again on the barnstorming circuit and on the Cleveland Indians. Feller was proud that "the case for Satchel Paige had been made in part by what baseball people saw in his outstanding performances against my barnstorming team." The world, the unlikely emancipator added, saw "that good black players could succeed against good white players."

BLACK AMERICA HAD ALREADY FALLEN for Leroy Robert Paige by the time he hooked up with J. L. Wilkinson and his Monarchs baseball teams. Redcaps competed for the privilege of toting his bags. Sable-skinned farmhands and factory workers traded and embroidered tales of his pitching conquests. The Italians had "Joltin' Joe" DiMaggio. The Jews worshiped "Hammerin' Hank" Greenberg. The Negroes had Satchel.

The challenge now for black baseball and for Satchel was getting his story out to the white world. Wilkie helped, as would Feller. But the master word spreader was Ted Shane, a magazine writer known for ginning up controversy along with his copy. His articles carried titles like "Ballplayers Are Sissies Now," "Why Managers Hate Wives," and "I Hate the Dodgers." In the summer of 1940 he wrote one called "Chocolate Rube Waddell" that introduced Satchel and blackball to ten million readers of *The Saturday Evening Post.*

Shane gave them a Satchel who was transcendent. He "flung a ball over as fast as a bullet" and was "one of the greatest pitchers of all time." So skilled was he that "he can turn on the heat whenever he pleases, [and] pin back the flapping ears of any great batter, be he white, black or green." His throw was hard enough to carry the ball "through a catcher's glove." He was a "one-man melee." While his fastball had slowed a bit, he "has developed into a finished pitcher. He knows his hooks and plate corners. . . . His strikeouts are Fellerian."

The Negro Leagues shared the spotlight in the *Saturday Evening*

Post piece. Shane took his readers through the history of black baseball, from its earliest days in the hands of entertaining waiters at the Argyle Hotel, to the excitement of the American and National Negro Leagues. "Negro baseball is much more showmanlike than white baseball," Shane wrote. "Negroes never play deadpan ball— their baseball is to white baseball as the Harlem stomp is to the sedate ballroom waltz. They whip the ball around without looking where it lands, and woe to the receiver if he isn't there instinctively. They play faster, seem to enjoy it more than white players. . . . Some are positive magicians at bunting, being able to English it so that it either stops dead as a fielder reaches for it, or corkscrews back around a catcher as he tries to pounce on it."

Yet the writer slipped into caricature in depicting Satchel and his setting. He quoted what he called "Harlem," as if the neighborhood spoke with a single voice, and used expressions like "nobody can say nuffin'." Satchel ate a whole watermelon, cranked his "apelike" arms, and showed a "Stepinfetchit disingenuousness." Negro Leaguer Oscar Charleston "tore his kinky hair" while blacks who tested their luck south of the border were paid in "Mex dollars unless the player is wary, which Negroes usually are not." Shane also played fast with his facts. Satchel, he said, was born around Birmingham not Mobile, disappeared for four years when he actually was playing high-profile ball, and was sold to Abe Manley for $900, a fraction of the $5,000 the Newark Eagles owner actually shelled out.

Today we would brand such journalism sloppy if not racist. Then it was par for the course and a brilliant beginning. "For the first time, a white magazine had burned incense at the foot of a black man outside the prize ring," said Ric Roberts of *The Pittsburgh Courier.* "*The Saturday Evening Post* made him ten times more famous than the black press had." Buck O'Neil was equally elated, in spite of Shane's stereotyping. White America discovered Satchel Paige, Buck said, "in the same way that Columbus discovered America. We knew he'd been there all along, but most of the country had to 'find' him." While some worried that the *Saturday Evening Post* story made black ballplayers look like clowns, O'Neil said that "we knew it was no circus, and we figured that now people would come to see us and that they would find out whether it was a circus or not. It was more important to us that this was the first time a magazine like *The Satur-*

day Evening Post had ever written about black baseball. We weren't resentful that Satchel was getting all the publicity, either, because it meant that we were getting publicity, too."

Taking up four pages in America's most popular magazine, Shane's piece was Satchel's most important introduction to the U.S. mainstream. But it was not the only one. *The New York Times,* the *Los Angeles Times,* and the *Chicago Tribune* had started writing about more of his games. He made great copy. White sports fans for the first time heard the legends that had been on the Negro grapevine for a generation. Six weeks before the *Saturday Evening Post* story ran, *Time* published a half-page lead item in its "Sport" section called "Satchelfoots." The *Time* piece was as triumphant as Shane's, marveling at Satchel's "blinding speed" and "marvelous control" and calling him "one of the greatest pitchers of any hue in baseball history." It dipped into hyperbole by crediting his strength to carrying two-hundred-pound blocks of ice as a child, and into racial convention by referring to him as "large, dark Leroy." It ended by noting that "many a shepherd of a limping major club has made no secret of his yearning to trade more than a couple of buttsprung outfielders for colored players of the calibre of Satchelfoots Paige." While it got his birthplace right, the magazine said he was thirty-one when he was about to turn thirty-four, invented the nickname "Foots" to go along with Satchel, accepted as fact his fatuous claim to be a "prodigious hitter" with a lifetime batting average of .362, and had him "snatched up" by the Homestead Grays, who may have wanted to but landed him for just one game.

Satchel had always drawn a mixed-race crowd, but this wave of coverage in the white press swelled his audience and transformed it. Blacks kept coming but there were many more whites now. The more they came, the crazier white America became about this fantastic African American player. To some it felt like slumming, the same as when they headed in droves to Harlem's Cotton Club to feast on black music. For others it was simply a chance to see for themselves the fastest, sharpest pitcher in the universe.

That attention by press and public was partly an outgrowth of the era. An America mired in the Depression and drawn into a two-front war desperately needed a distraction, and no one needed it more than black America. More than a million of its young men were taking up arms for a nation that denied them equal rights at home. Yet World War II meant opportunities, too, including opening high-paying jobs at war plants that had been racially segregated and filling them with thousands of Negroes recently arrived from the South. More money in their pockets meant more to spend on entertainment. What better way to keep up morale, President Roosevelt asked, than with a visit to the ballpark? The war years were a gilded age for the Negro Leagues, which grew into a $2-million-a-year enterprise. Throughout that period, the top-drawing team was the Kansas City Monarchs. An average game meant six or seven thousand fans; thirty to forty thousand turned out to see Satchel.

The war increased Satchel's appeal. Fourteen of his teammates were called off to fight, along with scores of other Negro Leaguers, forcing Wilkie and his fellow owners to fill their rosters with players who were over- or underseasoned. That made stars like Satchel shine even brighter. He wrapped himself in the war cause, auctioning off his autographs to raise money, selling bonds, and visiting army camps and military hospitals. "Those wounded boys'd lay on their stretchers and say, 'I heard tell of you when I was a baby.' They'd reach out their hands and feel my right arm and'd ask how it hung on there after all those years pitching," Satchel said. "You always feel kind of quiet after you leave those boys."

Satchel's support for the troops was sincere but he was not above using it as a foil for his other causes, especially enlarging his bank account. In 1943 he told Negro National League chiefs he would not play in their All-Star game unless he got what he said was an extra $200 and the press put closer to $800. He got it. In 1944 he set a new condition for playing: that team owners donate $10,000 to a war relief fund. Satchel said the demand grew out of watching a bunch of wounded soldiers being unloaded from a train. "They were just pieces of men." Fay Young, sports editor of the *Chicago Defender,* said it grew out of self-interest and self-promotion. "Who," Young asked in print, "is Paige trying to fool and when did he suddenly become so patriotic?" Whatever the motivation, the fans lost out by Satchel holding out. "He was missed," Kansas City *Call* sports editor Willie Bea Harmon wrote after the game. "Not a single player on either team has the color or should we say glamour which envelops Paige. He is, as they would say in Hollywood, a 'star.' "

All the hoopla around Satchel and the war raised the more personal issue of why he was never drafted. His Selective Service records
show he had an evolving set of classifications—from 1-A, which
meant he was available for service, to 2-A, which meant he was "deferred in support of national health, safety, or interest," to the final
and likely dispositive 4-A, which meant he was too old. "You got to
help out in the war some way or other," he wrote in his memoir. "I'd
registered for the draft like everyone else and'd even moved my birth
date up to September 1908, instead of July 1906, but they still never
called me." His draft record does indicate 1908 as his birth date,
making clear that he again fudged his age but this time for the noble
cause of defending his country.

Rejection was an old story for Satchel, and he stopped searching
for or caring about the reasons why he was never called up to the military or the Majors. He had grown up in the segregated world of
blackball in the 1920s. In the '30s he played on the same field with
whites and even teamed up with them, which offered a painful peek
at a color-blind future. Now, in the 1940s, the white press had finally discovered him and tens of thousands of white fans were turning out at his games. But while they could see him in his world, he
was still not allowed in theirs. There were more rumors about white
owners scouting black players, with Satchel at the top of their list.
But it remained just that, talk. His home now was Missouri, the
Show-Me State, and by the summer of 1945 he was impatient for
proof. "With all of them reporters coming around to ask me about it,
I got that old bug real bad again," he wrote looking back. "It wasn't
too long before I heard for sure what was starting all those rumors.
Branch Rickey of the Brooklyn Dodgers'd been scouting some
Negro league players. Even with Branch Rickey out scouting, I
wasn't believing that any colored boys were going to be signed.

"I'd been hearing about the white boys scouting colored ballplayers for twenty years but I didn't see any of them playing in the major
leagues. I was thinking there might never be any."

CHAPTER 8

Baseball's Great Experiment

*"I'd been the guy who'd started all that big talk
about letting us in the big time."*

SATCHEL WAS BARNSTORMING IN CALIFORNIA when he got the news he had been anticipating for two decades. Brooklyn Dodgers president Branch Rickey had just signed a Negro to a big-league contract. The *first* Negro in modern times. Word was tearing through America's clubhouses and grandstands that October afternoon in 1945. A black man was going to be in the minors, then the Major Leagues. Jackie Robinson would topple baseball's color bar. And Satchel Paige would not.

Earthshaking—almost like the emancipation of the slaves, integration supporters proclaimed. It was fitting "that the end of baseball's Jim Crow law should follow the conclusion of a great war to preserve liberty, equality and decency," wrote Lee Dunbar of *The Oakland Tribune.* A desecration of the natural order, segregationists shot back. "We live happier with segregation in athletics as well as all other activities," argued Bud Seifert of South Carolina's *Spartanburg Journal.* Bob Feller, the flamethrower with a golden arm and tin ear, told reporters that if Jackie "were a white man, I doubt if they would consider him as big league material."

The public listened to the cacophony of voices, but the one it wanted to hear most of all was Satchel's. What did America's best-loved black ballplayer—the man everyone had assumed would be first—make of the Dodgers' historic move? "They didn't make a mistake by signing Robinson," Satchel said. "They couldn't have picked a better man." The words ate at him even as he uttered them. Not only was he being bumped but by his teammate in Kansas City, an untested rookie who could not hit a curve, gun a throw to first, or land the job as the Monarchs' second baseman until an injury forced out the incumbent. Satchel had little use for Jackie and he was not alone.

Other seasoned Negro Leaguers were resentful that the young slugger had never served his time in the sandlots and barnyards, eating dust and fending off slurs. He had not proven himself against the best of white baseball the way Satchel would do again that next night in San Diego against Feller's All-Stars. Rather than show deference to the old hands who had, Jackie showed disdain. He complained about the seedy hotels. He objected to puny paychecks and uneven umpiring. It was like spitting on Satchel's baby.

Satchel tried to be philosophical. He understood that he was aging and old-school, while the twenty-six-year-old Robinson was a college boy and army veteran who Rickey felt could bear the ruthless scrutiny of being first. Jackie did not balk at Rickey's plan to start him in the minors, in faraway Montreal. Satchel never could have abided the affront. Jackie had the table manners whites liked, Satchel was rough-hewn and ungovernable. Satchel realized he was a specter from the past rather than the harbinger the Dodgers wanted of a more racially tolerant future.

Still, it hurt. It was Satchel who had proved that white fans as well as black would come to see great black ballplayers, and that proof was what pushed Rickey to rip down baseball's racial barricades. Satchel was so dominating, especially when his teams were beating the best of the white big leaguers, that even good ol' boys like Dizzy Dean could not help but be impressed. Major League owners noticed, too. One of them—flamboyant Bill Veeck of the Cleveland Indians—said he had tried to sign Paige and other blacks in 1944, a year before Rickey's deal with Robinson, but was blocked by the baseball commissioner. It was Satchel who brought a limelight to the Negro Leagues, the amazing Kansas City Monarchs, and their first-year second baseman Jackie Robinson. Satchel Paige had led blackball to the promised land of big-time baseball. But like Moses, Satchel was not allowed to enter, not at first.

He was savvy enough to know that Americans have room for just one hero at a time. If Jackie became the knight who slew Jim Crow, the roles of the real pioneers would be lost. Satchel felt sorry for Fleetwood Walker, Rube Foster, and Josh Gibson—and sorrier still for himself. He worried that he would be remembered as a Stepin Fetchit, or worse, an Uncle Tom. Satchel had not gone to war over every racial slight, but he had stood up. He refused to play in a town unless it supplied lodging and food to him and his teammates, a defiance for which young civil rights workers would get arrested and lionized a generation later. Only a player of his stature and grace could manage that without getting his skull cracked open. It was painful, after all those years of hearing "if only you were white," to be told now "if only you were younger."

"I'd been the guy who'd started all that big talk about letting us in the big time," Satchel wrote in his memoir. "I'd been the one who everybody'd said should be in the majors." To be denied that chance hurt as badly as "when somebody you loves dies or something dies inside you."

When the pain ran that deep only one person could ease it: his girlfriend and confidante, Lahoma Brown. So cherished was her advice that Satchel recalled it word for word seventeen years afterward. "They took that kid off our team and didn't even look at me," Satchel told her.

"He's young, Satchel," Lahoma answered. "Maybe that's why."

"He's no Satchel Paige."

"Everybody knows that, Satchel. . . . If they let one colored player into their leagues, they'll be letting others. Maybe the major leaguers'll come to you."

"They'll have to come real pretty-like. They've been puttin' me off too long to just wiggle their fingers at me now."

"Don't you go sounding like you're sour. When they come for you, you know you'll go. You've been wanting it real bad for too long not to."

"Well, it still was me that ought to have been first."

That sense of having been wronged never left him. Satchel had etched his legend as a ballplayer and performer, but he was right about people's memories. When it comes to integrating baseball there is only one name that today's children or even their grandparents know: Jackie. This time Satchel was not interested in rewriting history. He just wanted to be remembered. If Jackie Robinson was the father of equal opportunity in baseball, surely Satchel Paige was the grandfather.

THE PUSH TO LIFT BASEBALL'S COLOR BAR had never let up since the barrier was imposed at the end of the nineteenth century. Even as the Negro Leagues were thriving and apartheid had become embedded in the architecture of America, one or another black player was always asking the all-white Majors, "Why not me?" Renegade white managers answered by trying to sneak in black recruits by disguising them as Spanish, stamping them American Indian, or whitening them with cornstarch.

The inclination to integrate America's favorite sport became a crusade thanks to one source most of all: sports columnists. They were unlikely agitators. The typical sports journalist is and was apolitical if not apathetic. Yet he was the one watching Negro Leaguers face off against whites in California, the Caribbean, Denver, Wichita, and in cities big and small where Satchel was making a case for racial parity by matching Dizzy pitch for pitch. The verdict was unavoidable: the best of the blacks were equal to their Caucasian opponents, and the baseball was better when both were on the field. It was a matter not of ideology but of box scores and common sense.

The Sporting News reached that conclusion earlier than most and even before the interracial barnstorming. While a generation later the influential journal would become a lightning rod for its tepid reception of integration, in 1923 it condemned racial exclusion as a "hideous monster" and an "ivory-headed obsession." Few others in the white media joined the chorus that early. By 1931, however, Westbrook Pegler of the *Chicago Tribune* was asking what seemed like a subversive question: How could baseball be "the national game" if blacks were kept out? Their exclusion, he wrote, "has never had any logical or practical justification." Worse still, Major League owners "haven't the gall to put on paper" the ban they put into practice. This was not just any scribe venting his feelings. Pegler had been a war correspondent and would go on to win a Pulitzer Prize, be dubbed America's most respected columnist, and, by the early 1940s, be syndicated to 174 newspapers and ten million subscribers.

Other sportswriters picked up the cudgel. In the white press there were Jimmy Powers of the New York *Daily News,* Dave Egan of the *Boston Record,* Shirley Povich of *The Washington Post,* and Heywood Broun, a columnist for the Scripps Howard chain and founder of the American Newspaper Guild. Black papers were pushing harder still, led by Sam Lacy, Joe Bostic, Chester Washington, Rollo Wilson, Ed Harris, and Dan Burley. No newspaper was more relentless than *The Pittsburgh Courier,* which orchestrated a twelve-year campaign to open the big leagues to blacks, and no reporter was more intrepid than *The Courier's* Wendell Smith. Within a year of arriving at the paper, Smith, who had experienced integration up close as the only black student at his high school in Detroit, was awarded a sports column that he used as a bully pulpit. "Major league baseball does not want us. It never has," Smith wrote in his first essay on the topic in 1938. "Still, we continue to help support this institution that places a bold 'Not Welcome' sign over its thriving portal." The solution? "Quit spending our money and time in their ball parks."

One more wing of the Third Estate would weigh in. It was not a welcome ally to many in the integration movement, but none could deny the attention-getting power of the hot-blooded paper published by the Communist Party USA. The *Daily Worker* had always had Jim Crow in its crosshairs, but never the sports scene. It was not until the Seventh World Congress of the Communist International, in 1935, that Joseph Stalin and his minions decided that each national party should appeal to its masses through local traditions. In America that meant baseball. The *Daily Worker* hired as its first sports editor twenty-five-year-old Lester Rodney, a New York University night student from Brooklyn who knew as little about socialism as he did about journalism. Yet Rodney loved baseball and, like Smith, he made ending its color exclusion his passion for more than a decade. His opening salvo set a tone that was part Karl Marx, part Rube Foster. "Tell the big league magnates that you're sick of the poor pitching in the American League. You want to see Satchel Paige out there on the mound," Rodney wrote in an unsigned editorial in

1936. "Demand better ball. Demand Americanism in baseball, equal opportunities for Negro and white. Demand the end of Jim Crow baseball."

Tactics differed depending on the writer and the publication. Most joined the wider struggle if not each particular skirmish, covering as many barnstorming or Negro League games as their editors allowed, and dropping in lines whenever they could pointing out the skill of black players and the stupidity of keeping them out of the Majors. A few, like Smith and Rodney, took on segregation point-blank. They put big-league players and managers on the record on race, getting Leo Durocher of the Brooklyn Dodgers in trouble for saying he would have no problem signing a black if it boosted his team. They linked their campaign to World War II—asking how blacks who were dying overseas to defend freedom could be denied it back home on the baseball diamond, and proposing that Negro Leaguers fill the glaring holes left by white stars serving in the army and navy. They even swapped stories, with Smith's and Rodney's bylines appearing in each other's publications, although Smith later claimed that the Communists damaged the desegregation cause more than they helped it.

The journalists had allies. There was an incestuous relationship between crusading sportswriters and stars they covered like Dean and Paige, the way there always is, only this time the stars were entrepreneurs who drew more fans when writers played up the racial angle of their tours. Organizers of tournaments that invited black and white players formed similar partnerships with the press, as did interracial leagues like California's. Also lining up behind equal rights for Negro athletes was a parade of prominent Negroes, led by Paul Robeson, the singer, actor, and college athlete who lettered in football, basketball, track and field, and baseball.

Liberal politicians got into the act, too. In Boston, city councilor Isadore Harry Yaver Muchnick knew about discrimination from having grown up Jewish in an era when "no niggers, no Jews, no dogs" was a familiar refrain. Muchnick was offended by baseball's racial policies and threatened to ban Sunday ball in Boston unless the Red Sox and Braves offered tryouts to blacks. The Sox did, for a trio that included Jackie Robinson, but it was a charade; it would be fourteen long years before the team signed its first black player, ending its status as baseball's last holdout against integration. The tryout with the Braves never happened. In New York the pressure for change was even more intense. Major League Baseball, which was based in Manhattan, named Branch Rickey and his Yankees counterpart, Larry MacPhail, to study the matter of admitting blacks. New York mayor Fiorello La Guardia appointed his own study committee, again including Rickey and MacPhail.

Thick as their skin was, the baseball owners felt the heat. It was no fun to have elected officials breathing down their necks and traditionally friendly sportswriters branding them bigots. If those were the sticks, even more convincing was the carrot: higher profits. White baseball titans knew that black fans were turning out in sizable numbers for their games and in droves for Negro League and exhibition contests, especially during the war years. They knew, too, that black stars like Satchel and Josh Gibson were crowd pleasers of the kind that the Majors longed for in the wake of the retirement of Babe Ruth in 1935—and that, with the exception of Satchel, Negro Leaguers could be had cheap. It was the color green more than black that had Branch Rickey wringing his hands at public hearings and plotting to actually do something about integrating the sport.

Another baseball mogul—Bill Veeck—almost beat him to it, and if he had it might have been Satchel instead of Jackie whose number is raised in tribute in every baseball stadium in America. Veeck said that he tried to buy the Philadelphia Phillies and stock the team with blacks two years before Rickey signed Robinson. "With Satchel Paige, Roy Campanella, Luke Easter, Monte Irvin, and countless others in action and available, I had not the slightest doubt that . . . the Phils would have leaped from seventh place to the pennant," Veeck wrote in his autobiography. He was undone when baseball commissioner Kenesaw Mountain Landis and National League president Ford Frick, alarmed by his scheme, arranged for another bidder to buy the team at half the price. Baseball scholars still argue whether Veeck, a self-described hustler, invented the story to inflate his role in history. He may have, yet given his chutzpah and how he later assembled the most integrated team ever, he might just have done what he boasted. One thing is certain: putting Satchel at the top of his list of lusted-for players gave the plan and the would-be owner immediate credibility.

Veeck was also right in painting the honchos of organized baseball as enemies of equality. Landis was baseball's first commissioner and he had burnished the sport's tarnished image after the Black Sox cheating scandal of 1919. But history will remember him as baseball's version of George Wallace, the Alabama governor who would say or do anything to keep blacks in their "rightful place." For Landis that place was not on the same field as white big leaguers, even if it was only in postseason moneymaking shows. The commissioner took the Dodgers' Leo Durocher to the woodshed for embracing the signing of black players. And he failed to use his near-dictatorial powers to even dent the color bar, all the while insisting there was no bar, "formal or informal . . . subterranean or sub-anything." Landis's successor, Albert "Happy" Chandler, promised enlightenment when he took over in 1945, telling one Negro reporter that "if a black boy can make it on Okinawa and Guadalcanal, hell, he can make it in baseball." Chandler's files tell a different story. Even as the commissioner was endorsing integration, a committee composed of the American and National league presidents as well as influential club owners was arguing that segregation had to be sustained to safeguard the rents Negro League teams paid for Major League ballparks and to protect those parks from being overrun by black fans.

Their defenders say Landis and Chandler were reflecting the attitudes of the times, which, while not an excuse, was true. Reminders of racism were everywhere in America in the mid-1900s. Riding through the South, Negro ballplayers saw a black man hanging from the branch where he was lynched, and they heard about a black child who had been pulled from his bicycle and had an air hose pumped in his rectum. Water fountains and lavatories were labeled "White" and "Colored," and woe to anyone, even a big-time pitcher, who crossed that color line. Up north, players were told they could register in hotels only to be informed when they arrived that the last room had just been rented. Fans still asked, "Which nigger is Satchel?" when the Monarchs took the field. The movement to integrate baseball had enlisted the Communist Party but remained way too controversial for President Franklin D. Roosevelt, despite entreaties from his wife Eleanor and from Wendell Smith.

A jolting sign of how entrenched racial hatreds were came during the summer of 1938, when New York Yankees outfielder Jake Powell told a radio interviewer that he worked as a policeman in the off-season and to keep in shape "I beat niggers over the head with my blackjack." "*L'affaire* Jake Powell," as *The Nation* magazine called it, became a catalyst to rally journalists, activists, and others pushing for racial reform. Commissioner Landis, facing a public outcry, suspended Powell for ten days. The Yankees, worried about a boycott by fans who wanted Powell fired, ordered the outfielder on a mea culpa tour of black newspapers, businesses, and bars. Sportswriters, white and black, portrayed Powell as the personification of Jim Crow. "Powell got his cue from the very men whose hired disciplinarian had benched him," columnist Westbrook Pegler wrote in a swipe at Landis and the rest of the Major League establishment. Looking back at the reaction, it seems logical and appropriate. At the time it was unprecedented.

Powell, not Pegler, reflected mainstream America then, but it was Pegler who increasingly defined the racial boundaries for America's pastime. Baseball did take longer than it should have to lift its color bar. Yet Rickey's hiring of Robinson still came nine years before the Supreme Court acknowledged that racially separate schools were unlikely to be equal, and a full decade before Rosa Parks's refusal to yield her seat on a Montgomery bus to a white passenger launched the civil rights movement. Martin Luther King, Jr., was just sixteen when Jackie was packing his bat and glove for the trip to Montreal. The Robinson signing did not negate baseball's shameful record of racial intolerance, but it marked a new beginning. The Major Leagues had always been a microcosm of America; now they were also a leading indicator.

Baseball's experience advanced the coming changes. No Negroes in the nation so regularly and compellingly impeached the underpinnings of a segregated society as did black baseball players. Jackie showed how good Negro athletes could be, winning the Rookie of the Year award in 1947 and watching other black National Leaguers win it five of the next six years. Fans flocked to see the new black stars, with National League attendance jumping 15 percent that inaugural season. Each white fan who saw a black ballplayer for the first time—and each black who saw a fellow Negro playing big-time baseball—made it easier for America to envision integrating its classrooms and boardrooms. That change in thinking was clear as day to the all-black Philadelphia Stars, who were desperate for a place to sleep one night in 1947. Jackie was just being called up from Montreal to Brooklyn, and the baseball-crazed manager of a hotel in Worcester, Massachusetts, made the Stars a onetime exception to his whites-only policy. Then he dropped the exclusion altogether.

It made sense for America's most popular sport to be at the cutting edge. Reforming racial policies in the armed services or public transport required legal and political as well as social transformation; baseball's fate, by contrast, was in the hands of a cadre of team owners driven almost exclusively by economic self-interest. Once Rickey helped them see that signing blacks meant making money, the rest was straightforward. Negro ballplayers were also perfectly cast as ambassadors of racial reformation. They were big and brash and their bosses were generally black, so they could test race taboos without risk of firing. They were among the very few Negro men to see the country and work up close with whites, which showed them opportunities available and opportunities denied. They had stared down Birmingham's Bull Connor and counseled the young Martin King. These sports stars were role models for grown men and small boys in their segregated world, and would become heroes in the integrated game they were entering. It would not be easy for blacks to win the right to sit where they wanted on buses or at lunch counters, but it was easier than if blacks had not first set a standard for understanding and tolerance in the arena of sports.

"Without the Brooklyn Dodgers you don't have *Brown v. Board of Education*," said Roy Campanella, an outstanding Negro League catcher who was called up by the Dodgers a year after Jackie. "All I know is we were the first ones on the trains, we were the first ones down South not to go around the back of the restaurant, first ones in the hotels. We were like the teachers of the whole integration thing."

SATCHEL LOOKED LESS LIKE A SCHOOLTEACHER than a Stepin Fetchit to many blacks of his era and subsequent ones. But as with the real Step—character actor Lincoln Theodore Monroe Andrew Perry, who happened to be Satchel's friend—the truth is more nuanced.

Yes, the pitcher did conjure up the sadly comic persona of the shiftless Step as he shuffled to the mound. It was an image that grew out of Satchel's loose-limbed anatomy, with legs so long he had to lift his feet high to keep from tripping and arms that nearly touched the ground. Where nature left off the performer took over. He knew whites would love his caricature, the way they did Step's, playing as it did to their stereotype of the happy-go-lucky colored coot. He knew, too, that his slow-motion stroll offered the ideal setup for his supersonic delivery. So Satchel stretched out his entrance, and to anyone who dared wonder why he quipped, "Why rush, they can't start the game without me."

Satchel also was guilty of most charges leveled against him by sportswriters and other critics. Money was his main motivation and he did care more about himself than about his teammates or kinsmen. He knew his value and cashed in. He saw himself as the centerpiece of Negro baseball and wanted others to see him as the greatest pitcher ever. That is what superstars are like. A true team player like Frankie Frisch of the St. Louis Cardinals or Pee Wee Reese of the Dodgers is a rarity today and was back then. No one faulted Babe Ruth for putting himself first.

Yet Satchel's story has a subtext. In his own way he was as important a race trailblazer as any who surfaced in that era of baseball or America. Some of it was just being himself, pitching splendidly and often enough to make believers out of even confirmed white supremacists. He showcased his gifts and those of his dark-skinned mates against white baseball's best. He made fans and friends out of Dizzy Dean, who referred to Negroes as "coons," and of Bob Feller, who had little nice to say about any ballplayer but Bob Feller. Even more telling was the effect Satchel would have on white teammate Clint "Scrap Iron" Courtney of the St. Louis Browns, a segregationist from the backwaters of Louisiana who made it clear he would never warm up the black fireballer, not to mention catch for him in a game. Satchel challenged Courtney to a pregame test of skills. First the pitcher played shortstop, throwing out Courtney on a ground ball. Then Satchel donned the catcher's gear, gunning down Courtney as he tried to steal second. Lastly he trudged to left field, chasing down a fly ball and erasing Courtney, who was twenty-one years younger, as he tried to score from third. The catcher was convinced. "One day I noticed Clint was warming him up," reported Browns

owner Bill Veeck. A week later "I walked into a bar in Detroit called
The Flame. There were Leroy and Clint having dinner together.
Courtney told me, 'My pap's comin' up tomorrow from Lou'siana
and he's gonna be mighty mad when he hears about us being friends.
But Satch and me figure we can whup him together.' "

With players, Satchel made friends one by one. With fans, it was
by the hundreds, then the tens of thousands; in the end ten million
may have watched him pitch. The formula stayed the same: use
humor to disarm those who think they hate you, then dazzle them
with your talent. They cheered and laughed as he ambled in from the
bullpen, but the stadium went silent once he started striking out
batters. Always a showman, he never let himself become a sideshow.
He also managed to transcend the black-white split. White onlook-
ers loved that he was unthreatening and unstoppable, blacks loved
that he could lick the finest that whiteball threw against him. Both
were getting as human an argument as anyone could make for integration.

As for his playing to stereotype, it was his way of bucking the system. Frontal assault was dangerous and often futile, as Jackie Robinson would find out. Easing in, the way Stepin Fetchit did, was safer
and often more successful. Racist whites thought they were seeing a
black man who was lazy as well as stupid when they really were seeing a brilliantly defiant parody. He was mowing down white batsmen, getting rich off white fans, and doing it all to rousing applause.
The last laugh, Satchel and Step knew, was theirs. "The way he
walked, the way he carried himself, Satchel did not want anyone to
know how bright he was," says his friend George "Meadowlark"
Lemon, whose Harlem Globetrotters were masters at seducing white
America through a blend of humor and athleticism. "He'd tell me,
'If they don't know how smart you are, you've got an upper hand on
them.' "

While Satchel believed his best weapons to take on Jim Crow
were his ball, bat, and glove, he had more in his arsenal. From the
late 1930s on, he set clear conditions before his traveling team
agreed to play anywhere: find me and my teammates a place to stay,
and to eat, or we will not come. Generally they were colored hotels,
but not always, and not just any place would do. It had to be, he said,
"the best of the rooms." Word spread that it was a bad idea to refuse

to serve Satchel, which helped open up eateries and other establish-
ments that were typically closed to blacks. Word got around, too,
that it was not just Negroes the pitcher would stand up for. "If anyone gave me a problem, like calling me 'Jew bastard,' he'd kill
them," says Arthur Richman, a baseball executive and former sportswriter. Satchel used his celebrity to navigate the minefields of his
racially separated universe and defuse them when he could, doing it
quietly and, uncharacteristically, leaving it to others to do his bragging.

The press took up that challenge, especially columnists who were
leading the charge against the segregated leagues. In 1942 the
Chicago Defender listed Satchel alongside actor Paul Robeson,
botanist George Washington Carver, and educator Mary McLeod
Bethune as evangelists who were converting white Americans "to
right and fair thinking." Ted Shane ended his 1949 profile of Satchel
in *Reader's Digest* with the story of "an old colored woman" whom he
saw "step up to Paige and, with tears in her eyes, say, 'Thank you,
Satchel; you done a lot for all of us.' " Around the same time, Bill
Gleason, a longtime reporter in Chicago, watched Satchel use his
trademark repartee to handle a sticky question. "These [white] journalists with long hair came into the Milwaukee dressing room after
a game," remembers Gleason. "One of them asked Satchel, 'Would
you let your daughter date a white man?' Satchel said, 'I wouldn't let
her if he looked like you.' "

It took more than God-given talent and mother wit to impress
Lester Rodney of the *Daily Worker.* He wanted Satchel to speak out
on race in a way the pitcher normally did not, to get off his tightrope
and overtly condemn the separate and inequitable baseball structure
that made him a superstar and a rich man. It was asking for something few if any other players were doing, and certainly none with
Satchel's following. This was in 1937, before there was a real civil
rights movement and when there were all-too-real lynchings of
black men. It was asking a lot—and Satchel obliged.

Under a banner headline PAIGE ASKS TEST FOR NEGRO STARS,
Satchel proposed three experiments to determine whether Negro
Leaguers were the equals of Major Leaguers: (1) the winners of the
big-league World Series would play Satchel Paige's All-Stars at Yankee Stadium, with his crew not getting paid unless it won; (2) he

would pitch for any team in the Majors the following year, getting a paycheck only if he proved his worth; (3) big-league fans would vote whether to let in blacks. It was audacious for him to talk to the Communist publication, bolder still to lay down the gauntlet for white baseball. "Before this interview Satchel was considered a great pitcher but sort of a clown," Rodney says looking back after seventy years. "The thought was that Negro stars wanted to play only among their own people, which was patently ridiculous. Here was a guy who knew he was the best pitcher in the game and he wanted to go where the money and notoriety would be best. He wanted to prove his worth. It's like if you're one of the greatest violinists in the world and you lived in Podunk. You want to go to Carnegie Hall, you don't want to stay in Podunk. He understood exactly that somebody of his caliber pitching in the big leagues would lead the way for a new generation of black kids."

Detractors who dismiss Satchel as a self-absorbed cartoon character would never accept Rodney's vision of him as an exemplar, but the Federal Bureau of Investigation did. It understood that the pitcher was congenial but hardly conciliatory, and that quiet dissenters could threaten the status quo more than loudmouthed troublemakers. His Bureau file—Number 100-7002-A, "Leroy 'Satchel' Paige, Cross-References"—includes articles from the *Daily Worker,* resolutions from labor unions, transcripts from court hearings, and reports from FBI special agents. All zero in on what the agency saw as a subversive bid to bring down Jim Crow in baseball. All mention Satchel as a linchpin of the insurrectionists' case.

That does not mean Satchel did not do dumb things that exasperated reporters who wanted to like him and activists who wanted to recruit him. The most embarrassing was his 1942 interview with the Associated Press on whether he and other blacks should and would play in the Majors. The big leagues could not match the $37,000 salary he was making in blackball, he said. "And considering it strictly outside the financial angle, which is all I'd be interested in because of conditions that would exist, it wouldn't appeal to me because of the unharmonious other problems. You might as well be honest about it. There would be plenty of problems, not only in the South where the colored boys wouldn't be able to stay and travel with the teams in spring training, but in the north where they

couldn't stay or eat with them in many places. All the nice state-
ments in the world from both sides aren't going to knock out Jim
Crow." The smarter way to take on segregation, Satchel added in a
lesson he learned from Booker T. Washington, would be for one or
both of the Major Leagues to admit complete teams of Negro stars.
Appearing under headlines like PAIGE NOT IN FAVOR OF NEGRO IN
BIG LEAGUES and PAIGE SAYS NEGROES NOT READY FOR BIG
LEAGUES, the pitcher's words set off a firestorm. The integrationists'
poster child seemed to be siding with Commissioner Landis and
other obstructionists.

Satchel tried to undo the damage two weeks later at the Negro
League All-Star Game in Chicago. He showed up at Comiskey Park
late and was not summoned from the bullpen until the seventh inning. He walked not to the mound but to the dugout, where he
grabbed a waiting microphone and addressed the capacity crowd of
forty-eight thousand. "I want you to know that I did not say anything against the use of Negro players in the big leagues," Satchel
said. "A reporter came and asked me what I thought about Negroes
playing on major league teams. I told him I thought it was all right.
He said, 'Satchel, do you think the white players would play with
the colored?' I told him I thought they would, but that if they
wouldn't it might be a good idea to put a complete Negro team in
the majors." He ended his unprecedented address by insisting he had
been misquoted on his salary and nearly everything else in the AP
story.

Reporters knew too well the echo of his bravado to buy that the
AP had gotten it wrong. Art Carter, sports editor of the Baltimore
Afro-American, reflected the consensus when he called Satchel's
Comiskey speech a "pointless statement" that "few people heard and
fewer were interested in." Among those who did hear was Red Sox
general manager Eddie Collins, a foe of integration who bolstered his
case by parroting back Satchel's argument that Negroes were doing
too well in blackball to care about joining the big leagues.

In fairness to Satchel, he was right about the barriers blacks would
face in the Majors, as Jackie Robinson would later attest. Satchel also
was exasperated over the teases from the Pittsburgh Pirates, Cleveland Indians, and other white teams, who said they might sign Negroes, then didn't. Even if they someday did, the pitcher understood,

it would mean less security and celebrity for someone like him who was already an icon. He had been the subject of integration rumors for a decade and by 1942 he was feeling wounded. So he said what he meant to the AP, regretted it when he witnessed the outcry, and never said it quite that way again. Candor, he was learning, had its price.

What he said in private was something else. One day the Monarchs were visiting Charleston, South Carolina. While the hotel was readying their rooms, Satchel took Buck O'Neil to an old warehouse where slaves brought in chains from Africa had been sold to the highest bidder. "We stood there 30 minutes not saying a word to each other," Buck recalled. "Finally Satchel said to me, 'Nancy, I feel like I been here before.' I said, 'Me, too.' He said, 'My grandmother or grandfather could have been auctioned off here.' "

"*That* was Robert Leroy Paige," Buck added. "A little bit deeper than most people thought."

NO BASEBALL PLAYERS in the 1940s thought of free agency, or knew what the expression meant. If they had, they would have seen that Satchel was the first free agent in the history of the sport.

It took Major Leaguers until 1975 to successfully challenge the imperial control that owners had exercised over ballplayers since the days of Cy Young and Christy Mathewson. Before that challenge, a player was bound to a team for life or until his owner wanted to get rid of him. Afterward, pitchers or fielders with sufficient seniority could sell their services to the highest bidder. An owner willing to spend the money could make his team better overnight by buying superstars. The marketplace became the sport's driving force, giving players unprecedented freedom—and riches. "Mr. October," Reggie Jackson, cashed in big-time in 1976 with a five-year, $2.96 million deal from the New York Yankees. Three decades later the free-spending Yankees again set the standard, agreeing to pay third baseman Alex Rodriguez $275 million over ten years.

Satchel had been auctioning off his services since the 1920s. He freed himself from the shackles of owners' whims, played for the teams that bid the most for his talents, and rattled the foundations of the player-management relationship half a century before those changes came to the big leagues. He was earning record-high pay-checks for a player in blackball or anywhere in baseball. Satchel was the true pioneer, although the nation was paying too little attention to Negro ball to notice. If it had, people might have noted the irony of black ballplayers, whose very existence was defined by the bondage of segregation, pointing the way to freedom.

Even those who did follow the Negro Leagues failed to give Satchel his due. Black reporters called him a "jumper." They branded him disloyal, undependable, out of control, and infantile. They joined the owners' bandwagon, first saying blackball should ban Satchel for a year, then forever. "He won more games than he lost for a number of seasons," Al Monroe of the *Chicago Defender* wrote in 1939, "but his rating suffered from the lack of season-long compilation because he was rarely around at the close even though he opened with his league club that spring." If that annoyed Monroe, it outraged Effa Manley, whose husband, Abe, bought and paid for Satchel but could not get him to suit up for a single game with the Newark Eagles. The whole situation, she said, "makes me ill." Abe was more resigned, saying, "I don't own Paige. He owns himself."

Abe Manley saw what the press could not, even if he did not like it. Owners were called that not just because they had legal title to ball clubs and ballparks but because the players were theirs, too. It was, the Eagles owner knew, a feudal system begging to be challenged. Satchel could not fathom being controlled by Abe or anyone else. He could not articulate the theory behind his discomfort, but he knew his value and knew that the men who managed his teams did, too. He sensed that players deserved more rights and freedoms, more leverage and power. He was not the only player who thought the old system stank, but he was the only one with the credibility, cachet, and audacity to act out his frustrations and get away with it. He was also candid about his motivation: it was less about democracy than capitalism. "When the green's floating around," he said, "make sure you get your share."

While he was thinking mainly about himself, what he did rubbed off on other players and on the Negro Leagues generally. He drew so many fans that blackball owners started renting out Yankee Stadium and other cathedrals of white baseball, which meant more money in their pockets and, over time, fatter paychecks for ballplayers. Satchel took Josh Gibson, Cool Papa Bell, and a boatload of other stars with him to Latin America, walking away with Generalissimo Trujillo's cash and giving the players greater leverage when they came home to their star-starved teams in the Negro Leagues. When Satchel skipped out on contracts, then was welcomed back, it broke the vise in which owners had held players. When he raised the profile of the California League and helped open up tournaments in Wichita and Denver, it gave Negro Leaguers more visibility and year-round opportunities to earn a living. In recalibrating the power structure of the game, he took for himself and others a kind of control players had never exercised before.

"Those other players ate that lean meat because I pulled like that," Satchel said of his power to fill owners' bleachers and wallets. "If it wasn't for me, they'd have been eating side meat, that's what."

Josh Gibson was the clearest beneficiary, because he came closest to Satchel's fan appeal. His salary rose along with Satchel's, although not to the same heights. So did those of other players, most of whom had to work second jobs to keep their families fed and clothed. Satchel was doing in the Negro Leagues what Babe Ruth, Joe DiMaggio, and Hank Greenberg were doing in the Majors: raising the salary roof in a way that gave players closer to the ground the courage and precedent to argue for higher pay. "If it don't be for Satchel I never would have had the nerve to ask my owner for a raise," says Negro League pitcher Raydell Maddix, adding that "he gave me the raise but he didn't say for how much." By the early 1940s blackball had become as prestigious a career as there was in black America, not just because of the glory but because of seasonal wages twice as high as the average black worker's. Some credit goes to World War II and the prosperity it brought; Satchel Paige deserves much of the rest.

Gus Greenlee, the Manleys, and other owners admitted as much when they backed down each time they tried to stand up to Satchel. They knew he was as big as the game, bigger maybe, when it came to the bottom line. Wilkie knew, too, which is why he paid Satchel sky-high salaries along with a cut of the gate, acted as his booking agent, and insisted that, in return, Satchel agree to an ironbound contract. His bosses over the decades saw him not as the country cousin he pretended to be but as the Wall Street raider he behaved like. Satchel did not argue the point.

That economic boost, even more than what he did for integration, earned him the gratitude of diamond mates. "We all wanted to join up with Satchel, because on those barnstorming tours we would go on, when Negro League all-stars played teams headed up by Dizzy Dean or Bob Feller, guys could make more money in thirty days than they made all season," said Buck O'Neil. "When I joined the Monarchs I was making $100 a month, but when Satchel came we'd go into a town and play in front of 10,000 people. That meant the team was making more money and I could get a raise. I started getting $1,000 a month."

"Satchel," Buck added, "was a money tree for all of us, and for our game."

JACKIE ROBINSON WAS TOO YOUNG to have lived that history and too brash to care. He played a single season in the Negro Leagues, which was enough to earn his contempt. "My five short months experience in Negro baseball convinced me that the game needs a housecleaning from top to bottom," he wrote in a 1948 *Ebony* magazine story entitled, "What's Wrong with Negro Baseball." "The bad points range all the way from the low salaries paid players and sloppy umpiring to the questionable business connections of many of the team owners." He might have added that he was not about to kiss the ring of the league's gray eminence, that old minstrel Satchel Paige.

Robinson's confidence, bordering on defiance, was a huge plus when Branch Rickey was sifting through Negro Leaguers for the one he would catapult into history. The Dodgers' president liked Jackie's college education and military training, and the fact that he had lived in integrated settings in the service and the university. Jackie also happened to be one of the greatest natural athletes ever. No one could stop him when he was running the open field in football. He may have been the best broad jumper in America. He was a prolific scorer and elbow-wielding competitor on the basketball court and a standout in golf and tennis. As for baseball, he could tear around the bases, lay down the perfect bunt, and hit hard and straight enough that he led the Monarchs with a .345 average, tallying ten doubles, four triples, and five home runs in a mere forty-five league games in 1945.

His Kansas City teammates preferred to focus on what he could not do. When he was playing second, and the ball was hit to his right, "he couldn't come up and make that long throw" to first, said Newt Allen, the longtime second baseman assigned by Wilkinson to evaluate the rookie Robinson. "I told them he was a good ballplayer. 'A smart ballplayer,' I said, 'but he can't play short.' " Monarchs ace Hilton Smith called Jackie "an average fielder." Buck Leonard of the Grays said that blackball "had a whole lot better ballplayers than Jackie." At the time of his signing nearly everyone rallied around Jackie, the way Satchel had, but the barbs and swipes flowed freely in later years. It was not just his deficits on the field that ate at the veterans but the way he stayed back at the hotel playing checkers or pinball while everyone else was out on the town. There was one more thing old Negro Leaguers held against Jackie: he never paid homage to the earliest barrier breakers like Fleetwood Walker or to them.

Each of the reigning black stars could make a case for why he, rather than Jackie Robinson, should have been first. Josh Gibson had been teased twice in recent years, by the Pittsburgh Pirates and Washington Senators, but neither came through with an offer. He was still a power in 1945, hitting .375 and leading the league in homers, but age and alcohol ruled him out for Rickey and left him dead a year after Jackie started in Montreal. Monte Irvin was the right age and had the right skill set. He had put in his time in the Negro Leagues and would eventually star in the Majors, but not until two years after Jackie. Bonnie Serrell, whose move to Mexico had opened a place on the Monarchs' roster for Jackie, was another logical choice as trailblazer. Like the rest, his heart was broken when he was not chosen and he stayed on in Mexico for three more years.

No one wanted it more, and had more reason to feel he deserved it, than Satchel Paige. Theories abounded on why Rickey passed him over. His mouth and his morals were too loose for the pro-Prohibition, Bible-quoting Brooklyn boss, who would have liked Lula Paige but had little use for her famous son. He was too volatile, too expensive, and had made public his doubts about the sort of integration Rickey envisioned. He was having a mediocre year in 1945 and, at thirty-nine, it looked like he was at the end of his line. "I had not approached anybody about Paige," said Wendell Smith, the *Courier* journalist who was surreptitiously scouting for Rickey. "I just ruled him out because I thought a Major League club would laugh and say, 'this guy?' " In later years Smith had his regrets, saying that Satchel was, in fact, not too old and "deserved it for all he had done."

At first Satchel accepted the naysayers' logic and took the high road when asked about Jackie, but over the years the bitterness built up and seeped out. Robinson, after all, was in the history books while Satchel was relegated to sports tracts. In an interview a quarter century later he said that had he been first "I might have set my race back 50 or some more years. Because I couldn't of took what Jackie took." Translation: Jackie took too much without fighting back. Would he have been better prepared for the attacks directed at Jackie than Jackie was? the interviewer asked. "Oh, yes, I've had that and more. Jackie didn't have to go through half the back doors as me, nor be insulted by trying to get a sandwich as me, nor be run out of places as me. No, there's no baseball player in America that took as much as me." Every chance he got Satchel pointed out that Jackie had started out on the bench with the Monarchs. Was he good enough to make the first team? "No sirree, Bob." Satchel took glee in the fact that, while he was thirteen years older than Jackie, in the 1960s he still was playing baseball while Jackie looked and acted like an old man. "His hair's white," Satchel told a *New York Times* columnist, "and you'd think he was my grandfather."

Jackie took a similar tack with Satchel, publicly calling him "the greatest Negro pitcher in the history of the game." To normal ears that sounded like a compliment; to Satchel's it raised the possibility that there were white pitchers who were better. Robinson's private verdict on Paige was less equivocal. "Jackie detested Satch, strongly," said Larry Doby, who broke the color barrier in the American League just eleven weeks after Jackie did in the National and shared Jackie's feelings about the aging pitcher. "Satch was competition for Jack. Satch was funny, he was an outstanding athlete, and he was black. He had three things going. Jack and I wouldn't tell jokes. We weren't humorists. We tried to show that we were intelligent, and that's not what most white people expect from blacks. Satch gave whites what they wanted from blacks—joy."

But there was more than Doby saw to the schism between Satchel and Jackie, just as there was more to Satchel. Satchel was caught between generations. When he began, white America was enforcing

Jim Crow with an iron fist in baseball as everywhere. Satchel was still pitching deep into the era of racial reconciliation. He made the transition better than most and helped lay the foundation for the radical change wrought by Rickey and Robinson. Satchel did it by playing to whites' expectations of blacks, as Doby said—then exceeding and defying them. His humor affirmed his intelligence in a way that was difficult to comprehend for the more dour Robinson and Doby. Satchel was not alone. Joe Louis was fighting and winning similar battles in the ring, Louis "Satchmo" Armstrong onstage, and A. Philip Randolph in union halls. All refused to commit spiritual suicide in the face of unbending bigotry. All were New Negroes if not modern militants. All were denounced or dismissed by later generations unschooled in their history.

Robinson and Rickey, by contrast, became the darlings of activists and historians. Neither gave much credit to those who came before, and neither anticipated nor cared about the damage their avant-garde agreement did to the Negro Leagues. The first reaction within blackball was exultation. *Finally,* players sighed. We thought it never would happen. Owners were quicker to grasp the downside. Tom Baird of the Monarchs was outraged not just that Rickey stole Robinson without consultation or compensation, ignoring his contract with Baird's team, but that this would surely be the first of many poachings by Major League owners. "We won't take it lying down," Baird fumed to the Associated Press, adding that he would appeal to Baseball Commissioner Chandler. But Negro League owners faced a Hobson's choice: defending their economic interests looked like they were defending segregation. The bind was doubly bad if, like Baird and his co-owner, J. L. Wilkinson, they were white. No sooner did his AP comments appear in papers like *The New York Times* than Baird was back charging that he had been "misquoted" and "misinterpreted." What he meant to say, Baird explained in a telegram to Rickey, was that the Monarchs "would not do anything to hamper or impede the advancement of any Negro ball player, nor would we do anything to keep any Negro ball player out of white major leagues."

None of it mattered to Rickey. He had already made clear how he felt about blackball and saw no need to justify having raided Robinson. "The Negro organizations in baseball are not leagues, nor, in my opinion, do they have even organization," he told reporters. "As at present administered they are in the nature of a racket." It was left to Clark Griffith, the owner of the Washington Senators and no friend of integration, to stand up for blackball: "While it is true that we have no agreement with Negro leagues—National and American— we still can't act like outlaws in taking their stars. If Brooklyn wanted to buy Robinson from Kansas City, that would be all right, but contracts of Negro teams should be recognized by organized baseball."

While white owners battled over ethics and egos, Negro League owners and aging stars watched their world crumble. First the most promising young players went: Jackie, Doby, Henry Thompson and Willard Brown of the Monarchs, and a dozen others in 1947 alone. Most started in the minors, although some like Doby went directly to the big leagues. Many lasted for a career; Thompson and Brown were back with the Monarchs in a matter of weeks. The defections were enough to make Negro League fans switch allegiances to the newly integrated Majors, but not enough to offer jobs or security for the majority of the two hundred Negro Leaguers left. Most black clubs lost money in 1947. The next year revenues fell further and, at season's end, the New York Black Yankees folded, the Homestead Grays dropped out of the league, and the Manleys watched the Eagles' new owners move the team from Newark to Houston. The Negro National League was dead and the Negro American League was reeling. The only source of revenue for most remaining clubs was to become de facto farm teams for white baseball, selling off any players they could for as high a fee as the market would bear. The holy grail of integration meant far fewer Negroes earning a living from baseball.

Baseball was not the only casualty. Just as the rise of the Negro Leagues had spawned culture and commerce in the Negro community, their fall killed off cultural institutions and traditions. Street's Hotel in Kansas City, the center of the Monarchs' world, closed down. So did the Vincennes in Chicago. Churches no longer had to worry about letting out in time for the Sunday ball game, and congregants had one less occasion to don mink stoles or straw hats. Rather than attending a contest in the neighborhood, fans watched on television, cheering for faraway teams without the company of friends or neighbors. The gladful community of blackball, brought to life by Jim Crow, was disappearing as segregation ebbed. It was an omen of what would happen to the proud if unequal blacks-only schools, to cherished African American occupations such as Pullman porter, and to the Alabama Reform School for Juvenile Negro Law-Breakers that helped rescue wayward boys like Leroy Paige.

Lost, too, would be the story of blackball and all but its biggest legends. Like Jackie, most black Major Leaguers felt little debt to the Negro Leaguers who preceded them. It was left to a few old-timers to keep alive their stories and retell the tales of glory. Almost every time they did, it was Satchel Paige rather than Jackie Robinson on center stage. Certainly they respected Jackie for being first. They adored Satchel for who he was, all he did, and the way he embodied their once-brilliant universe. Jackie opened the door to the new racial reality but, as one veteran Negro Leaguer said, it was Satchel who inserted the key.

CHAPTER 9

An Opening at Last

"We had a lot of Satchel Paiges back then."

SATCHEL'S TELEGRAM TO CLEVELAND INDIANS owner Bill Veeck was point-blank: IS IT TIME FOR ME TO COME? The pitcher had reined in his regrets when Jackie Robinson got his offer. He was kicked in the gut again but kept his mouth shut when, three months after the National League's Brooklyn Dodgers called up Jackie, the Indians toppled the American League's color bar by hiring Larry Doby. Veeck had been saying for years that Satchel was the greatest Negro Leaguer of all, the one who deserved to break barriers. Now, a day after the Doby signing, Satchel simply had to ask.

The owner's reply was a cruel twist of the old tease: ALL THINGS IN DUE TIME.

It was not that Veeck doubted the legend of Satchel Paige. Growing up in a rich suburb of Chicago, he had watched Satchel play in Negro League games there. Paige's thirteen-inning, 1-0 triumph over Dizzy Dean in California in 1934 remained Veeck's benchmark for pitching perfection. The Indians' owner, the premier showman in the history of big-league bosses, loved the whole package that was Satchel, from his carousing to his storytelling to his filling whatever room he was in. Veeck had only two questions when he took over in

Cleveland in the mid-1940s: Did the aging flamethrower have enough fire left to help the Indians? If so, when was the time right?

Abe Saperstein, who for years had helped find bookings for Satchel, assured his friend Veeck that the pitcher could still work his magic. That left timing. Veeck almost signed Paige instead of Doby in the summer of 1947, but he had worried that Satchel's advanced age and roguish reputation would let baseball's old guard muddy the waters by charging that his interest in black players was promotional and mercenary. Now it was the summer of '48 and Cleveland was embroiled in the tightest pennant race in history, along with Ted Williams's Red Sox, Joe DiMaggio's Yankees, and Connie Mack's Philadelphia Athletics. The Indians had the mighty bats they needed to end the team's twenty-eight years without a championship, the longest drought in the league. Bob Lemon was a star on the mound, knuckleballer Gene Bearden's meteoric rise fueled dreams of a title, and Bob Feller was great some nights although not as often as before. What was missing was one more pitcher they could count on, someone who could start, relieve, and carry the young staff through the dog days of summer. So a year after Satchel sent his plaintive telegram, Veeck again contacted Saperstein. The old guard be damned, the Indians owner said. It was time to invite the moth-eaten pitcher in for a tryout.

Satchel got what he called the biggest news of his life while he was barnstorming in Iowa for J. L. Wilkinson. "Dad called me on the phone and said, 'The Majors want Satch to report to Cleveland,' " remembers Dick Wilkinson, who was running J. L.'s traveling team. "I walked over to Satchel and said, 'You're going to the Majors. Dad says get home.' He looked at me with a big grin and said, 'Oh boy!' He jumped into his Cadillac and took off. That's the last time I saw Satchel."

The pitcher had a lot to think about on the drive to Kansas City. He would not be the first Negro to reach the big leagues, nor even the first in Cleveland. But he was looking forward not back as he sped past the cornfields. He was already dreaming of throwing meteoric fastballs by cowering batters, sending the crowd into a frenzy. When Satchel reached Kansas City a letter was waiting from Saperstein asking when he could be in Cleveland. "After twenty-two years of throwing, I was going to get a crack at the major leagues," he recalled. "Lahoma and me danced all over the house. 'You'll do it, Satchel,' Lahoma kept telling me. 'You know you can.' "

He arrived in Cleveland the morning of July 6, 1948, for a tryout that was as clandestine as Jackie Robinson's had been. Bill Veeck was there, along with his player-manager Lou Boudreau. "Bill called me at home and asked, 'How'd you like to get a little extra batting practice?' " recalled Boudreau. "I wasn't much under .400 at the time and I was surprised that the boss thought I needed more batting practice but I said 'Okay,' in a polite way. Not at all enthusiastic, you understand—just polite. 'I've got a new pitcher down here,' Bill went on, by way of clearing up the confusion. 'I'd like to see you catch him and hit against him a little. I think he might be able to help us.' He didn't tell me who the pitcher was."

The secrecy with Jackie Robinson was needed to keep word of the racial breakthrough from leaking out. With Satchel it was to keep Boudreau from balking at the notion of the Indians finding salvation through an over-the-hill hurler. When the manager got to the field he asked, "Where's the kid?" Veeck pointed to Satchel, who was sitting in the opposing dugout. Boudreau kept looking, sure it was a ruse. Satchel explained that he had just gotten off the plane and would like to limber up by running around the park "a few times." He made it barely seventy-five yards. "You know, Mr. Lou, this is an awful big ball park," Satchel huffed. "I guess I just won't run after all."

The tryout was next—throwing to Boudreau for twenty minutes, then having him stand in with a bat. As soon as Boudreau stepped to the plate, Satchel reached back with his patented corkscrew windup and blistered in a pitch that the player-manager hit foul. Then he did it again, overhand, sidearm, and underhand. More foul balls, weak grounders, and infield pop-ups. The surreal scene playing out before seventy-eight thousand empty seats was made more so by Veeck hobbling around on his artificial leg shagging balls. Boudreau might have been vying with Ted Williams for the batting title, but "against Paige, he batted .000," recalled the Indians owner. "Satch threw twenty pitches. Nineteen of them were strikes. Lou swung nineteen times and he had nothing that looked like a base hit. After a final pop fly, Lou dropped his bat, came over to us and said, 'Don't let him get away, Will. We can use him.' "

The Cleveland owner signed Satchel to a contract the next day—

July 7, 1948, the pitcher's forty-second birthday. While few knew for sure his month and day of birth, fewer still his age, he was eight years older than Veeck, fusty enough to have fathered several of his teammates, and the most geriatric rookie in the history of baseball, a record that still stands. His deal with the Indians also made Satchel one of just four blacks in Major League baseball as well as the first African American pitcher in the American League. And it made him and Bill Veeck easy targets for journalists.

"Veeck has gone too far in his quest of publicity," wrote J. G. Taylor Spink, publisher of *The Sporting News*. "To sign a hurler at Paige's age is to demean the standards of baseball in the big circuits. Further complicating the situation is the suspicion that if Satchel were white, he would not have drawn a second thought from Veeck." It was painful to read for a pitcher who had been told so often that his race was all that kept him out of the big leagues. Other writers agreed with Spink, some because they were lukewarm about blacks entering the Majors, while several worried that the grizzled Paige would embarrass the Indians and set back the cause of blacks in baseball.

Tom Meany of the *New York Post* begged to differ. "The signing of Satchel Paige to a Cleveland contract is far more interesting than was the news when Branch Rickey broke baseball's color line by signing Jackie Robinson to a Montreal contract. It was inevitable that the bigotry which kept Negroes out of Organized Ball would be beaten back, but I'd never heard of Robinson at that time. With Paige, it's different. The Satchmo has been a baseball legend for a long time, a Paul Bunyan in technicolor." Ric Roberts of *The Pittsburgh Courier* went further, writing in an open letter to Spink that while "no other ancient, colored or white," would have been signed to a Major League contract at a comparable age, "this happens to be Leroy (Satchell) Paige, the Great! To me, it is a beautiful gesture, chock full of the mellow richness of the American ideology which often prevails in this land. Give Paige his hour of triumph; let the thronging thousands see him in the plush-lined, gold plated backdrop of the majors."

That back-and-forth set the stakes for the timeworn pitcher: Would this be a final burst of glory or a tragic last act? The outcome was in Satchel's massive hands and long ropy right arm.

" 'SATCHEL' LEROY PAIGE, number twenty-nine, now pitching for Cleveland," the announcer at Municipal Stadium intoned as 34,780 fans roared their delight. It was the fifth inning and Bob Lemon had dug the Indians into a 4-1 hole against the St. Louis Browns. Lemon was out and Satchel, just two days after his signing, was summoned from the bullpen. He had spent the previous four innings warming up his arm and the previous twenty-four years fine-tuning his skills. No pitcher was ever readier. Still, he was nervous, or "as close to that feelin' as I could be." He had never felt jitters like these before, but then he had never pitched in the Majors before.

The route from the Indians bullpen seemed especially long that night, although Satchel had walked it before. More than fifteen years earlier, when he was with the Pittsburgh Crawfords, he had been the first Negro Leaguer ever to throw at Cleveland's then-new ballpark. Now he was the first black Major Leaguer to ascend that mound, and when he got there he found a welcoming party. A small army of newspaper photographers had gotten special dispensation from the umpires to record the historic moment. Flashbulbs unleashed a shower of sparks with each warm-up pitch. "Am I playing the fool?" the implausible apprentice asked himself. "I had been in many serious spots before, but this was the MOST serious." Lou Boudreau wandered over from his position at shortstop, advising, "Don't be scared if they hit you. Pitch loose like you always do."

He did, and they did. After watching Satchel's first pitch zip by wide of the plate, Browns first baseman Chuck Stevens lined a fastball to center for a single. First batter, first hit, but not the first time. Stevens had batted against Satchel fifteen or twenty times during interracial barnstorming, and "I always had pretty good luck against him, including one of the longest home runs of my life," he remembered sixty years later. Cleveland fans did not know that, not that it would have mattered. To them, blackball was shadow ball and the ledger that counted was the one he would open that night. "Has the old man lost it?" they whispered to one another. Six pitches later they had their answer, with three outs, one a called strikeout. His second and final inning was nearly identical: one batter reached base followed by three quick outs. Only two balls he threw that evening missed the strike zone.

By the time Satchel was lifted for a pinch hitter, fans had been treated to a single windup, a double windup, a triple windup, and a no-windup. They watched him throw sidearm, overhand, and under-hand, and saw his hesitation pitch, his fastball, and his blooper. The full repertoire, all delivered with no apparent exertion. "Satchel didn't mow 'em down, but he kept 'em swinging," the Cleveland *Plain Dealer* reported. "With a carload of different pitches, he showed 'em how it's done in as grand a coming-out party as any ball player ever had."

His first victory came in another relief role a week later in Philadelphia. Three weeks after that was his first start, a spectacle that drew 72,434 fans. It was the most ever for a night game in Cleveland and double what most arenas of that era could fit. Even Bill Veeck, a master promoter who knew Satchel's fan appeal, was caught by surprise as his stadium ran short on everything from peanuts and Coke to ticket sellers and policemen. Satchel did not have his best stuff but he had enough to last seven innings, beating the Washington Senators, 5-3, and catapulting the Indians into first place. Nearly every breakthrough for him was one for his race, too; that relief appearance in Philadelphia made him the first black pitcher to win a big-league game since the Fleetwood Walker era in the 1880s, just as he would be the first to lose one and the first to spin a shutout.

The rejuvenated Negro Leaguer was the hottest story in baseball that summer and the hottest draw at box offices nationwide, as he proved again ten days later in Chicago. The White Sox packed Comiskey Park with a capacity crowd of 51,013, their first sellout in three years and their most ever after dark. Another 15,000 were turned away. Streets were jammed with cars and pedestrians, making many ticket holders up to three innings late for the game. Once they got there some found their seats occupied by fans who had literally crashed through gates that gave way in the face of the surge. "It was the only time in my life I have ever been frightened by a baseball crowd," Veeck recounted. "There was not a place in the park that was not covered by human, sweating flesh. I am not talking only about the seats and aisles and the standing room in back of the grandstand. There was not even loose standing room *underneath* the stands." Adding to the madcap atmosphere was the fact the umpires' uni-forms had been shipped to the wrong city, forcing them to don street clothes and White Sox caps, although they claimed the *C* stood for Cleveland as much as Chicago. Even the ball-and-strike counters were missing, leaving home plate umpire Art Passarella no choice but to keep track with his fingers.

Veeck was determined to win in light of all it took simply to get into the park. Just before the game he stopped by the bench and told Satchel, "Leroy, this one is very important to me. Really give it to them tonight." In a pregame ceremony the pitcher got another give-'em-hell speech from Joe Louis, the black world heavyweight champion who two months earlier had knocked out German strongman Max Schmeling just 124 seconds into their bout at Yankee Stadium. Satchel delivered almost as lethal a blow with his right hook, shutting out the White Sox, 5-0, and yielding just five singles. His win put the Tribe back into first place in the seesaw race for the pennant and had reporters elevating him to the baseball equivalent of sainthood. Paige "may be destined to fill the shoes of the once great Babe Ruth who died Monday of last week," wrote Doc Young, sports editor of the black-oriented Cleveland *Call and Post.* "Surely no single player, not even Lou Gehrig, Ruth's teammate who passed before the Bambino, has been able to pack 'em in as has Paige."

All that was a warm-up to Satchel's most defining rite of passage, on August 20. His bullpen mates on the Indians had tossed three shutouts in a row and gone thirty innings without allowing a run. If he could pull off a fourth shutout it would tie the American League record and give the team a shot at the mark of forty-one consecutive scoreless innings. A win of any kind would keep Cleveland safely ahead of the A's, Red Sox, and Yankees. It was games like this that Veeck had in mind when he took a chance on the venerable pitcher. It was games like this that Satchel dreamed of during a generation when no white owner would give him a shot.

Fans understood. Two weeks after Satchel set a nighttime attendance record at Cleveland's Municipal Stadium, the lines this night were longer still. The paid attendance of 78,382 smashed big-league baseball's all-time benchmark for evening crowds by 3,535. It was the size crowd one expected at college football games, not late-summer baseball. Ohio governor Thomas J. Herbert was there. So were four hundred Ohio mayors. More than even the Brooklyn Dodgers' historic call-up a year earlier of Jackie Robinson, Satchel's fairy-tale story was capturing the imagination of Americans. It was about endurance as well as race. And he was easier than Jackie to like.

As Satchel watched the fans queue up, the stress building within him went straight to the weakest link: his gut. "The miseries were doing more playing in my stomach than most teams did on the field," he recalled later. Reporters and fans who had seen him pitch in his heyday knew that Satchel was one of the best ever, but others had doubts. They reasoned that the Negro Leagues were not quite up to par and neither was Satchel. A shutout tonight would set everybody straight.

The game was just an hour away as he headed for the showers. The scalding water ran over his pitching limb and helped calm the butterflies in his stomach. He toweled off, suited up, and ambled across the grass toward the mound, milking the cheering crowd until it was all noise. For a full minute he stood and listened. At last he began his delivery, winding up with the arm-cranking motion that went out of fashion with the electric car. He mixed his sizzler and his curve in a way that confounded batters. His teammates managed just a single run, but he made it hold up. Satchel pitched all nine innings and retired the last nine Chicagoans in order. Only three White Sox got hits; none got as far as third. His scoring line was a pitcher's wish list: five strikeouts, one base on balls, no runs. The Indians tied the league mark of four straight shutouts and Satchel notched his second in a row. He extended the team's shutout streak to thirty-nine innings, paving the way for a new American League record the next night. After six weeks in the Majors, Satchel had five wins against one loss. He was doing what he had claimed he could, making believers out of any doubters who remained.

No sooner did Satchel complete his blanking of the White Sox than the Indians owner fired off a cable to Spink, the publisher who had called Paige's signing a publicity stunt: "Paige pitching—no runs, three hits. Definitely in line for *The Sporting News'* Rookie of the Year award. Regards, Bill Veeck." Sportswriters offered their own instant verdict on Satchel's latest performance. Everyone in the press box stood and applauded as the pitcher walked off the field. "Seldom has this writer seen this sort of tribute paid an athlete by the men who have seen many great champions down through the years," wrote one veteran journalist who was there. "It was their way of admitting to themselves that they had seen a remarkable exhibition. It was their way of paying tribute to a championship performance by a great champion." It also was their way of saying they were sorry that it had taken so long.

Owners are supposed to be cheerleaders. Sportswriters often are, too, at least for their hometown teams. But not umpires, whose job demands impartiality if not silence. Yet two veteran umps stepped out of role in this special case. "There are few better pitchers in baseball today. Maybe there aren't any," Bill Summers said a week after Satchel's second shutout of the White Sox. Art Passarella agreed: "Calling balls and strikes for him's a breeze. I was behind the plate for that shut-out he worked in Chicago and I never had an easier game in my life."

As the season wound down Satchel did encounter bumps. The sixth-place St. Louis Browns knocked him out of the box twice in September. The Red Sox continued to give him problems, especially Joe DiMaggio's kid brother, Dom, "the Little Professor," who hit one over the left field wall at Fenway his first time facing Satchel and remembers "glancing over at him. Satchel was scratching his head." While conceding that the aging pitcher was doing better than he had forecast, Spink pointed out that four of his wins were against the feeble White Sox and Senators. "All this raises the question," he wrote, "whether Satchel's early successes are due to his sterling pitching abilities or to the fact that some major clubs still have a considerable distance to go before they attain prewar standards."

Statisticians were positing starkly different questions and answers about how Satchel did his first year in the Majors and the first season where solid statistics were kept on him. His earned run average, a measly 2.47, was second-best in the American League. His performance over the half season he played so impressed the nation's baseball writers that, when the Associated Press polled them, twelve voted for Satchel as Rookie of the Year, enough to place him fourth. (He joked that if he had won the honor he would have declined since "I wasn't sure what year the gentlemen had in mind.") His 6-1 record was neither a joke nor an afterthought; it was the highest winning percentage on the Indians staff and a key factor in the team's capturing the pennant, which it did by a single game over the Red

Sox. Each game he won had fans and writers marveling over what he must have been like in his prime and which other lions of blackball had been lost to Jim Crow.

As always, the most puzzling as well as dazzling of Satchel's stockpile of pitches was the one he had learned as a child throwing stones, where he paused mid-delivery, hands high above his head. Yankees manager Casey Stengel would dub it "that blankety-blank hesitation pitch" and call it "the toughest pitch in baseball to hit." It made Ted Williams and other sluggers look foolish against the mighty Paige, as they swung at shadows long before the ball itself arrived. And in 1948, just weeks after Satchel arrived in the Majors, American League president Will Harridge ruled the pitch illegal if there was a runner on base. There may not have been anything in the rule books specifically banning the delivery, Harridge said, but it gave the pitcher such an advantage that he ordered umpires to call a balk and award runners an extra base when Satchel threw it.

Satchel helped take Cleveland to the World Series that season, but once there he spent all but two-thirds of an inning watching like a fan as the Indians beat the Boston Braves, four games to two. Satchel's abbreviated outing will nonetheless be remembered. Umpire George Barr warned him about wetting his fingers, an indicator of an illegal spitball. Umpire Bill Grieve called him for a balk when he wiggled his fingers before throwing with a man on base. Fans gave him the biggest ovation of the playoffs. He may not have lasted long, but he was the only one of five Cleveland pitchers not scored on in an 11-5 rout by the Braves. And once again he made history. "I'd been in a World Series," he wrote delightedly in his memoir. "It was the first a colored boy'd ever pitched in a World Series."

The best sign of how the Indians felt about Satchel was that they brought him back the next year, with what he said was a bump in pay. The year after a world championship is almost always anticlimactic for a team, and it was for Cleveland, which finished behind its archrivals, the Yankees and the Red Sox. Satchel, meanwhile, suffered the sophomore jinx: his record fell to 4-7, his earned run average rose to 3.04, and he pitched only eleven innings more than the year before even though he was with the team twice as long. For anyone else it was a better-than-average performance—all the more so considering that in 1949, following the retirement of two players born in 1905, Satchel was the oldest player in pro baseball. But it wasn't good enough for him.

Critics said that batters, having seen him once, were no longer fooled by the hoary pitcher. Satchel blamed his gurgling innards. The year before he had well-documented stomach problems that Indians trainer Lefty Weisman would solve by rushing to the mound with a glass of baking soda much like Jewbaby Floyd had with the Monarchs. One day when Weisman was out sick, Bob Lemon wielded the trainer's black bag. Lemon came up with a white pill that Satchel thought was bicarbonate, Boudreau insisted was aspirin, and others said was a cold pill or perhaps a cure for dandruff. But it did the job, convincing Satchel's catcher, Jim Hegan, that the pitcher's troubles originated in his head not his stomach. The gallstones that materialized near the end of the season were real enough, although Satchel dreaded the surgeon's knife and skipped out on his scheduled operation, hoping the trouble would quiet down on its own and the stabbing pain would go away.

In 1949 his self-described miseries worsened to the point where he could not last more than two or three innings. He went to see a doctor, who surprisingly sent him to a dentist, who gave him the bad news: "They'll have to come out—all of them." Satchel balked at first, then relented, taking out four of the infected teeth per visit until he was left with "an old sunken hole for a mouth and nothing to chomp food with." When his mouth finally healed the dentist put in "them store teeth. I felt like somebody'd shoved a baseball bat in my mouth." That discomfort went away, and clearing up the infection in his kisser seemed to help his gut, too. While his stomach was still sensitive, the stabbing pain seemed to be gone for good.

His time with the Indians opened new spheres for Satchel not only in his career but in his relations with white ballplayers. Barnstorming had been a case of pitch-and-run for Negro and Major leaguers. Socializing off the field was not explicitly forbidden, it just was not done. The big leagues were different. Although he still preferred colored hotels, he rode with his fellow Indians on Pullman sleeping cars, flew with them in planes, and spent endless hours listening to or telling stories in the dugout and bullpen. Jackie Robinson and Larry Doby had gotten to the Majors before Satchel, but neither communed with white teammates the way Satchel did or was accepted as fully and naturally. Just seeing a black man sitting next to a white one on a bus, train, or plane was enough to get people talking—and to get the Negro arrested—in 1940s America. What Satchel was doing was an experiment in human and racial interaction, for the pitcher and his teammates, and it was an enormous success.

One indication of how much the rest of the Indians liked him was that they gave Satchel a full share of World Series loot even though he had been with the team just half a season. Another was including him in their barbershop quartet, with Hegan the catcher singing tenor, first baseman Eddie Robinson as baritone, Satchel as bass, and Larry Doby leading the way as they crooned tunes like "Sweet Sue, Just You" and "Old Black Joe." "Satchel was a very humble guy, not braggadocio or overbearing," said Robinson, who like Hegan was white. "He was immediately embraced by the team. That was difficult with Doby but not with Satchel." It was also a measure of how comfortable Satchel was with people, whatever their color, so long as he was the wise old hand and the center of attention. Everyone was on tenterhooks in those early days of integration, and white teammates found it as easy to warm up to Satchel as white fans did.

His matter-of-factness kept the young team loose during its stressful 1948 pennant drive. He became fast friends with rookie pitcher Gene Bearden by showering him with deserved praise. He shot craps in the men's room on long train rides with third baseman Ken Keltner, second baseman John Beradino, and utility man Allie Clark. He also relished the practical jokes that were the social currency of ballplayers, never taking offense but always looking to one-up. Feller got Satchel once by tossing him what he said was an ice cream sandwich; Satchel realized the white layer was soap only after his false teeth were embedded in it. He got even by nailing a mate's shoe to the wall of the clubhouse and gluing shut a fielder's glove. His favorite comeback was with a wit so deadpan no one was sure if he meant it to be funny. It was on display on the flight back from Boston after the final game of the '48 Series, or, as Satchel called it, the World Serious. He gulped down two meals so fast that the stewardess good-naturedly offered a third—which he accepted and ate. She returned with a fourth, which he declined, explaining, "No, miss, I'm not full. I'm just tired from all that eating."

One teammate who never laughed at Satchel's jokes was Larry

Doby. Veeck had hoped Satchel would make things easier for Doby, who felt enormous pressure as the first black in the American League, and it worked for a while. Satchel became Doby's roommate as well as a lightning rod for the press attention Doby hated. But the two were from clashing worlds and eras. Doby grew up in New Jersey, a long way from Satchel's Jim Crow South, and the hard-hitting outfielder was a young twenty-four to Satchel's forty-two. Doby was made uneasy by the gun he saw in Satchel's luggage and made sick by the pungent catfish Satchel fried on a portable cooker in their hotel room. Most of all he was embarrassed—by Satchel's Cadillac and chauffeur, by his refusal to stay in team hotels that welcomed blacks, and by his unperturbed and unbridled approach to baseball and life. When Satch asked Larry why Major Leaguers did not wear hats the way Negro Leaguers did when they went out for the evening, Doby snapped, "Do as we major leaguers do; don't ask questions!" Satchel showed how he felt about his roommate by nicknaming him "Old Lady." Doby called Paige "Roomie" but told anyone who asked, "Supposedly I roomed with Satch while he was in Cleveland, but I roomed with his luggage."

The back-and-forth was also strained with Lou Boudreau, who doubled as the Indians' shortstop and manager. He loved Satchel's competitiveness and his ability to deliver in the games that mattered most. He did not appreciate the pitcher's unwillingness to adhere to curfews, training regimens, or rules of any sort. Boudreau fined Satchel for related infractions weeks after he joined the team. First he failed to show up at Yankee Stadium for a game because his arthritic toes had told him it would rain even before the weatherman knew. That made him miss the early train the team took to Boston. He thought he made up for it by catching a plane; instead of reimbursing him for the air travel, Boudreau hit him with a pair of fifty-dollar penalties and handed him a schedule, warning him to keep it with him at all times.

What did the manager really think of his unmanageable pitcher? Like most of Satchel's bosses over the years, it depended when you asked. Boudreau was bemused by the player who called him "Mister Lou." "Satch never rode the team bus to and from our games. No matter what town we visited there was always a Cadillac waiting for him. Not just an ordinary Cad but a lavender, sky blue, red or cardinal Cadillac," Boudreau told an interviewer years later. "And he never started the engine until after those of us in the bus were on our way. Then he'd drive up alongside, honk the horn and flash those white teeth at us with a big grin." But in private talks with Indians general manager Hank Greenberg, Boudreau vented his frustrations. "Lou Boudreau didn't want him on the team any more. It was as simple as that," Greenberg said, looking back to 1949. "He wouldn't abide by the rules of the rest of the club and he broke up the morale of the team."

Satchel's longest-lasting and most telling relationship on the Indians was with its owner. Bill Veeck was Satchel's kind of guy. His appetites were supersize: four packs of cigarettes a day, two hours of reading while soaking his stump of a leg wrecked during World War II, and an ashtray carved into his wooden leg so he could smoke, read, and soak uninterrupted. He won and lost a succession of teams—the Cleveland Indians, the St. Louis Browns, and, twice, the Chicago White Sox. It was Veeck's idea to greet home runs with fireworks and to stage morning games for wartime swing-shift workers. He bought beers for and traded lies with friends in high society and the underworld and gave sportswriters expensive TV sets for Christmas. His favorite pastime was riling up his staid fellow owners. They expunged from the records any mention of Eddie Gaedel, the midget Veeck brought to bat in St. Louis, ensuring both Gaedel's and Veeck's legends. They raged when the callow Cleveland owner drew more fans than had ever watched a season of any sport to his 1948 team and made the team champions of the baseball world. They seethed when, a year after bringing the first African American to the American League, he signed baseball's equivalent of Ol' Man Mose.

Paige and Veeck got off to the right start because the owner, like the pitcher, appreciated the prerogatives of money and spent his lavishly. Satchel reportedly received a $10,000 signing bonus along with $5,000 a month, for a very grand total of $25,000 for half a season's work. Almost as pleasing to Satchel was that Veeck paid deference to the Negro Leagues by paying J. L. Wilkinson $15,000 for Satchel's contract and giving another $15,000 to Abe Saperstein. The moves were meant in part to one-up the Dodgers' Branch Rickey, who offered Wilkie neither money nor an apology when he stole Jackie Robinson. But master though he was of the rich gesture,

Veeck was sincere in his devotion to integration. His 1949 Indians had three blacks, the most in baseball. He moved the team's spring training camp from Florida to Arizona because Arizona had fewer Jim Crow laws. And, in the spirit of the Monarchs' Wilkinson, he treated Satchel like his friend and son as well as his star and cash cow.

Veeck insisted that his public address announcer introduce Satchel as "Satchel," the name fans knew, but in a sign of respect, the owner addressed him as Leroy. Satchel called Veeck "that curly-haired fellow in the front office" (Satchel had trouble remembering his name), then "Burrhead" (Veeck's blond hair was short and wiry). The owner repeatedly loaned his prized pitcher money, then burned Satchel's IOUs. Veeck characterized Paige as "interracial and universal" and claimed he "can hold forth, with equal ease, on baseball, dictators or mules." Paige insisted that Veeck was one of the finest men he knew, saying, "I'm gonna pitch my arm off for that fellow." He did that and, in a sign of esteem, shaved off his mustache after Veeck told him he could keep it even though no one else in baseball had one.

The owner and pitcher were both born with ballyhoo in their blood, and they formed a partnership more heartfelt than Rickey's with Robinson. Veeck realized the ground he was breaking by signing Satchel, and although he kept manager Lou Boudreau in the dark about who was trying out, key sportswriters knew and at least one was invited to document the momentous event. When Boudreau fined Satchel, Veeck paid, just as when writers like Spink attacked, Veeck rushed to Satchel's defense. While the Indians owner did not give birth to Satchel's riddles on age, he did spin them ever finer, telling the world that the antiquated moundsman must be fifty or even sixty and telling Satchel to walk even slower. That stagecraft was especially apparent when Satchel offered to pay five hundred dollars to anyone who could prove he played professional baseball before 1927. A Cleveland man, Carl Goerz, produced a photostat of a Memphis *Commercial Appeal* article showing that Satchel had pitched for Chattanooga in 1926. Veeck signed the check to Goerz and invited the press in for the payout. "I musta slept out a year. An expensive sleep," Satchel said. Learning that Goerz had paid just two dollars to copy the Memphis article, Satchel told him, "Five hundred for two. Say, maybe I oughta quit pitchin' and start lookin' 'round for suckers like me."

His close relationship to Veeck was an asset so long as Veeck owned the Indians. It became a liability when Veeck sold the team after the 1949 season to pay for his divorce. The Indians offered Satchel a contract for 1950 that was 25 percent below his 1949 pay, which was the biggest cut that baseball allowed. Satchel said no, as the team hoped he would, bringing to an end his career in Cleveland. Clearly the Indians were tired of Satchel's antics and Veeck's egging him on. "[Satchel] didn't keep the rules, he missed a few games and didn't show up and Lou [Boudreau] never knew where he'd be," general manager Hank Greenberg explained years later. But Greenberg, one of baseball's all-time power hitters and first Jewish stars, acknowledged that dumping Satchel might have been shortsighted: "Perhaps the fault was we didn't realize and appreciate enough that here was an unusual and outstanding performer who had pitched great for so many years in the Negro leagues and he wasn't about to be treated like a rookie."

TWO THINGS HAPPENED in the late 1940s that would change Satchel forever: he was called to the Majors and he was called to the altar. The world quickly learned about the first but few knew of the second. That is the way both Satchel and his new bride wanted it, for different reasons.

Lahoma and Satchel had been close ever since he met her at the drugstore in Kansas City in 1942. She was the one he turned to first when there was crushing news like Jackie Robinson's signing, and again when he finally got his offer from the Indians. She helped him sift through conflicting emotions and steered him to the most generous response. When he felt down, she was his antidepressant. When spending sprees left him penniless, she taught him to save and invest. "A man," he said looking back, "just can't let a gal who takes care of him like that get away. And the only way to make sure a gal doesn't get away is to marry her."

He had been saying that for years. He finally did something about it in the fall of 1947, just before he left for a barnstorming tour on the West Coast. "You know what I'm gonna do when I leave?" he asked Lahoma. "No. What?" "I'm gonna take you with me. We're gonna get married." That got him a juicy kiss. "We didn't hardly tell anybody what we were doing," he wrote in his 1962 memoir. "On

October 12, 1947, we ran over to Hays, Kansas, and got married."
Satchel's gravestone lists a different wedding date: March 5, 1946.
Lahoma, in sworn testimony years later, gave a third version: October 13, 1947. Forgetting one's anniversary is understandable—but
not when the mix-up is in an autobiography, at a public hearing, or
on a headstone.

It was also peculiar that two Kansas Citians would pick Hays as a
place to run over to for last-minute nuptials since it was 253 miles
away, they had Lahoma's young daughter, Shirley, to think about,
and all Hays had to offer was rich farmland and underground oil
reserves. Hays has no record of Satchel and Lahoma marrying on the
dates they gave or anytime between 1940 and 1949. Nor does Kansas
City. Given Satchel's penchant for ginning up mystery around big
events in his life, it is possible he was playing a game here, too. He
and Lahoma might have been protecting their privacy by not pin-
pointing the actual where or when of their marriage, especially since
she became pregnant shortly after they said they were wed. Or they
may never have married, officially, although there was no doubt about
the bond that lasted until death parted them.

Lahoma had always been reserved and discreet, feeling that her
business was just that. Having known Satchel for five years, she understood how public a figure he was and how that could encroach on
their life together. So she set ground rules that she would pass on to
their children. Home was the center of the Paige universe and family was what mattered. Satchel, she made clear, might be a legend to
others but to them he was a husband and father, with strengths and
foibles. As for the media attention, it was to be endured like any
other torment the Lord sent their way.

No memoirs for Lahoma or chatty sit-downs with reporters. The
few times she broke her vow of public silence, what emerged was a
woman who was savvy if not sophisticated. She had been there at
Satchel's games on the road as well as at home and understood the
hard life of a barnstorming baseball player. "No place to sleep, you
got to go four hundred miles to the next town. Okay. Then you get
some bologna and crackers. You sing bass? Okay man," she said.
"Then somebody would pretend to blow a horn and down the highway they'd go." She knew the impossible expectations fans had for
her husband: "They didn't even want to let a person foul-tip his ball.

If they tipped his ball they'd say, 'Satchel hasn't got it today.' " She was stalwart but could take only so much: "I would leave the ball park and just go sit in the car because I didn't want to see him lose. I would build up a terrible feeling inside. I didn't want him to make any mistakes because of the pressure of the fans."

Satchel knew her sensitivity and strength, and believed that marrying Lahoma was the best thing he ever did. She was his third wife, but the only one to whom he felt permanently attached. She gave him that "settled-down life I never had before," he wrote. And she gave him a family. He understood and came to share Lahoma's penchant for privacy about his home life, and especially his kids. That is one reason he kept her a secret for so long. He told the press he was wifeless when Bill Veeck signed him in 1948, nine months after he was supposedly married in Hays. The 1949 Indians press guide listed him as single when he was already a father as well as a husband. Even his boss and confidant Veeck was not sure about Satchel's marital status, or at least he pretended not to be, with Satchel sometimes indicating on team questionnaires that he was married and other times that he was not. "It's like this," the Cleveland owner remembered Satchel saying. "I'm not married, but I'm in great demand."

Veeck also recalled Satchel leaving a ticket every day at the box office for Mrs. Paige—"and every day a different woman was picking it up." Baseball buddies tell stories of the pitcher continuing his flirtations and liaisons long after he had a wife and children. Satchel and Ned Garver were in the same train compartment heading to Washington in the early 1950s "and he pulls out three telegrams and has me read them," recalls Garver. "Three women were going to meet him in Washington. I said, 'How in the world are you going to handle that?' He said, 'I'll put each one of them in a different hotel.' " A few years later Satchel introduced Jack Spring "to two different women, both as his wife. I'm not sure which was, but both were quite pretty ladies. Satch seemed to be a bit of a ladies' man but he didn't flaunt it." Around the same time Duane Pillette was in the shower room after a bad pitching performance and Satchel overheard him saying he hoped his luck would change. "He said, 'I don't know what you meant about changing your luck but I've got two of the cutest girlfriends you have ever seen, and you can have one.' "

Satchel never addressed his alleged adultery head-on, but he alluded at several points to wishing he had behaved better about his family. "Don't let anybody tell you I ain't always thinking about them," he wrote in his autobiography, "no matter how I act."

Satchel had always been great with kids. Children from his baseball world remember being mesmerized by him at ages when they were too young to care about his being a star. "He always either picked me up or squatted down to talk to me, so we were eye-to-eye," says Sue Durney, whose dad, Bill, was an executive on two of Satchel's teams. "I do remember clearly those deep, dark, kind eyes and the music in his voice." Bill Veeck's son Mike, who now is co-owner of six minor league teams, says Satchel "had this character he'd keep in his pocket, Tom Thumb, and he said he had to interpret for Tom. Many people as they get older mistakenly imagine how children like to be dealt with. They'll talk baby talk. Then there are people like Mr. Paige who spoke to you as a small person. He wasn't condescending. He was always happy, always laughing. He was the greatest storyteller."

He was that way with his own kids, too, although he admits he had a lot to learn with his first, Pamela Jean, who was born the year Satchel broke into the big leagues. "It really staggered Ol' Satch," he said of himself. "It was just like trying to hit a change of pace after the pitcher'd been throwing nothing but blazers. You're thrown all off stride. There ain't a man alive won't tell you that first baby don't do that." Carolyn Lahoma, their second baby, who was born a year later, was spoiled as Satchel tried to make up for what he said were mistakes with Pamela. After that the rearing came more naturally and the children came in quick succession: Linda Sue in 1951, Robert Leroy in 1952, Lula Ouida in 1958, Rita Jean in 1960, and in 1965 the last, Warren James.

Satchel said he loved all of them the same, but like most parents one child especially carried his hopes. That was Robert, who shared his three names although in a different order. Satchel would have to wait to see if his elder son shared his baseball passion and skill, but he saw himself in Robert from the start. Even as a youth Robert had Satchel's big feet, skinny legs, and spindly but solid frame. The boy loved cars the way his father did, and had a natural wit that made him a standout in a houseful of children. There was one other way,

Satchel said, that Robert was like him: "When things don't go his way, he can get mighty mad."

A wife and seven children heightened the pressure for money, especially after Satchel lost his job with the Cleveland Indians. A logical response would have been to trim what he spent on clothes, jewelry, and other nonessentials. Sensible for anyone but Satchel, who saw such possessions as an affirmation that the scruffy youth from Mount Meigs was a man and a star. Larry Doby remembered the twenty suits his rubber-armed roommate brought with him to Cleveland. Silk was his preference in dress wear, underwear, and especially neckties. Nearly identical ones could be had for fifteen dollars, but Satchel went straight to the thirty-dollar rack. Even when he started going tieless he still wore a clasp of gold engraved with his name and fastened to his shirt. The collection of antiques and shotguns was expanding inside the twelve-room house he had moved to, and that move had transported him from the heart of black Kansas City to a neighborhood with elegant homes and almost exclusively white home owners. Outside the Paige manse were three new cars, one with enormous horns mounted on the fenders, along with a new motorboat and another litter of hunting dogs. Having gotten used to steak, he found it hard to digest the prospect of going back to catfish.

It was easier to track the cash going out than coming in, but Satchel was determined that his kids not share his burden of a father who was better at breeding than sustaining. He worked with sportswriter Hal Lebovitz on a series in the *Cleveland News* that pumped up circulation so much that it was stretched to eighteen installments and was such good publicity for the Indians that Satch could demand, and Veeck obligingly paid, more than his agreed fee. While his syntax and spelling remained atrocious, he started carrying a typewriter on the train and in his car, using the hunt-and-peck technique to generate letters to fans and material his ghostwriters would turn into two memoirs. "His book earnings," says second ghostwriter David Lipman, "certainly were measurable but he could not have retired on what we made." His first book—*Pitchin' Man*—was an expansion of the *Cleveland News* articles, completed not long after the Indians won the World Series. Satchel was getting extra compensation from Veeck, but that did not keep him from touching up

Lebovitz for still more. "You wont know how bad I need the money bad," he wrote. "Looking to hear from you at once your pal."

His primary income still came from baseball, and he played anywhere he got a reasonable offer. He was in his mid-forties now, feeling sore more and taking longer to get warm. The mainly white Mallards of Minot, North Dakota, rented him to get their season off to a stadium-packed start in 1950 (he did fill the seats, and pitched three scoreless innings in each of their first three games). The all-black Philadelphia Stars brought him in that summer for what *The Sporting News* said was the princely rate of two thousand dollars a week. In the fall he signed on with a black all-star team called the Kansas City Royals, joining them in California to throw against his old teammates Bob Lemon and Bob Feller. Next he pitched for the Chicago American Giants. It was like revisiting his past, "going back to barnstorming, back to sleeping in my car, back to playing in little parks, back to playing in small towns, back to pitching more innings than any man around. It was a rough kind of life, but it paid. And I'd been doing it so long I guess it didn't matter." Throughout, there were rumors of Major League clubs that were interested in him—the New York Giants, the Boston Braves—offers Satchel said he turned down but that others said were never firm.

RESURRECTION ONCE AGAIN CAME BY WAY OF Bill Veeck, the new owner of baseball's beloved also-rans, the St. Louis Browns. Veeck bought the team in the middle of 1951 determined to do whatever was necessary to win back its fans and reverse its fortunes. No other owner would have concocted a stunt like Grandstand Managers Day, where fans were given signs reading YES and NO, then polled on everything from whether the batter should bunt to whether the manager should protest an umpire's ruling. No one else would have spit in the eye of the archrival St. Louis Cardinals by hiring its heroes as manager (Rogers Hornsby), radio announcer (Dizzy Dean), and shortstop (Marty Marion). No owner other than Veeck would have dreamed of making his first and costliest hire a forty-five-year-old pitcher whose best days were twenty years earlier.

Second-guessers, the Browns' boss pointed out, made one fatal mistake in evaluating Satchel: "They thought he was human." Paige justified Veeck's faith and money with his legendary fan appeal. The owner did not expect Satchel to pitch much at his advanced age, thinking he would instead contribute by "performing public relations, which he did beautifully," says Buddy Blattner, a former ballplayer who teamed with Dizzy as the radio voice of the Browns. "He went to luncheons. He amused and confused and certainly entertained audiences like Kiwanis or Elks. He talked baseball and told stories about the Negro Leagues. It was just amazing how he could hold an audience." In fact, Satchel did not need to move his mouth or even his arm to draw the interest of fans who had seen him barnstorming across America. At Sportsman's Park they were content to glimpse the ancient athlete sitting by the bullpen in the contoured easy chair Veeck had bought, a canopy engraved with SATCH shielding him from the summer sun and giving him the aura of a king on his throne. Riding by train to a game in New York or Chicago, Satchel would stand on the rear platform, campaign-style, waving to adoring fans as the train whistled through at half speed.

The impact of ballyhoo like that could be measured in turnstile clicks and column inches. Stories on Satchel made their way not just into St. Louis papers but to best-selling magazines like *Collier's,* which published a three-part series on the pitcher by Richard Donovan. In 1951, the year Veeck took over at the halfway mark and signed Satchel, the Browns drew just 293,790 fans, not surprising for a club that would finish forty-six games behind the league-leading Yankees. The following year they again finished way out of the running, but thanks in good measure to Satchel, attendance nearly doubled to 518,796.

More surprising to Veeck and those half million fans was what Satchel did upon returning to the big-league mound after a season and a half away. While his record was an unimpressive 12-10 in 1952, his first full year back, he was mainly a reliever and figured in twenty-two of his team's sixty-four victories. That win quotient was the best in baseball that season and surely the best ever at his age. He finished thirty-five games where he relieved the starting pitcher, a Browns record. He led the American League in innings pitched and relief wins. He racked up ninety-one strikeouts in 138 innings, along with ten saves and a stingy 3.07 earned run average. He did it all with a fastball that had lost some zip but could still nibble at the corner of the strike zone, a changeup that was as misleading as ever, and a "side-arm, cross-fire curve" that looked like it was coming from third base. Sportswriters pronounced him one of the best relievers in the American League. At mid-season Veeck said he would consider trading "anybody and everybody" on his team "except Leroy"; by season's end he crowned Satchel "the best relief pitcher in baseball."

To anyone who saw him on August 6, 1952, Satchel looked more like a starter than a reliever and seemed on his way up rather than a superannuated veteran. He shut out the Detroit Tigers for twelve innings, earning a 1-0 win and outlasting Tigers ace Virgil "Fire" Trucks, who pitched two no-hitters that season. Fans were especially entertained in the tenth when Satchel loaded the bases with no outs, then masterfully extricated himself from the jam. It was the longest shutout of the season by anyone, and at forty-six he was the oldest pitcher to ever throw a complete game. "His slow ball," the *St. Louis Post-Dispatch* wrote, "particularly the ones he fed to an over-eager giant, Walt Dropo, seemed to hang in the air, as though manipulated by wires. In missing a mighty swing at such a pitch Dropo lost his balance and almost fell on his face." Veeck was pleased enough that he bought Satchel a new suit of clothes. Satchel told reporters that "we just had to win. We had orders to take morning practice if we lost—and I'd much rather go fishing than take morning practice."

Fish would figure into another Paige performance with the Browns that was worthy of the legend books. It happened in Washington when Satchel was called in to relieve in the twelfth inning. He was unhittable, but so was the moundsman for the Senators. As the game dragged into frame seventeen, Browns traveling secretary Bill Durney groused that unless someone scored, the team would miss its train to St. Louis. That got the attention of Satchel, who had a midnight date with a catfish the galley chef was frying just for him. The pitcher promptly singled in the go-ahead run, then asked Durney whether they could make their train if he shut down Washington on nine pitches during its last at bat. As the team raced to the railroad station Satchel seemed sullen and the Browns manager asked why. "Because," he explained, "I promised the man I'd do it on only nine pitches and that empire (the ump) had to go miss one."

Even when he was shelled he was the one fans talked about afterward, and not just hometown ones. At Fenway Park the Browns called him in to relieve and Boston scored six runs before the inning was over. "Throughout this disaster," a magazine writer wrote, "the Red Sox stands sat in stony, embarrassed silence. When he finally wobbled off the diamond, the cheers could be heard in Cambridge. Paige has never been booed in the majors."

Veeck never hesitated before re-signing Satchel for the 1953 season, bumping him up to slightly less than thirty thousand dollars; Satchel never bothered to read the contract, such was his trust in the owner. Along with the money came a miniature uniform for Robert, Satchel's four-week-old son, complete with rubber-lined rompers, shirt, cap, socks, and a pint-size bat. The Browns also dusted off the old riddle about Satchel's age. In 1952 they listed his date of birth as "Sept. 11, 1892, 1896, 1900 (or) 1904—take your pick." The following year they streamlined the entry in their press guide to "date unknown—'aged.' "

Satchel had what he called his worst season ever in 1953, with a 3-9 record and a 3.54 earned run average. Part of it was the team: the Browns were back to dead last in the American League, 46½ games behind the New York Yankees. Records aside, Casey Stengel of the Yankees named Satchel to the American League All-Star team. Stengel had been known over the years to point to Satchel warming up in the bullpen and warn his players, "Get the runs now! Father Time is coming!" He had designated Satchel an All-Star in 1952, when he earned it, but the pitcher never made it into that rain-shortened game. So the New York managing wizard had him back the next year, as he said he would. Fans knew they were watching history, with forty-seven-year-old Satchel the oldest ever to pitch in the midsummer classic, and they loved bearing witness even as he yielded three hits and two runs in a single inning.

Taking their cues from Veeck, Browns managers waived their normal rules when it came to the estimable pitcher. When the team traveled he could stay where he wanted, which was generally with friends, and go to bed when it suited him, which was always later than the curfew. A personal valet picked up after him in the locker room. Even sacrosanct strictures on alcohol were ignored. "Satchel would be down there in the bullpen sitting under that sun visor and a couple gals would pass him some kind of liquor in little perfume bottles. He'd just sip on those bottles," remembers Joe DeMaestri, a teammate on the 1952 Browns. Ted Lepcio was with the Red Sox then and recalls Satchel coming out of the visiting tunnel at Fenway carrying a bucket covered by a towel. Lepcio's teammate Lou Boudreau, who had been Satchel's mate and manager with the Indians, "peered in the bucket and saw three bottles of beer. Satchel sauntered out and walked with that pail to the bullpen," says Lepcio. "I'll never forget it. I can't imagine anyone else doing that. We just bust out laughing." Others remember him sitting in the clubhouse whirlpool sipping a glass of Early Times Kentucky Whisky and say he always stocked up on spirits when he played north of the border. Years later a *Boston Globe* columnist described Satchel's lasting lore in Beantown: "They still talk of the black pitcher who appeared at a refreshment stand behind the visiting bull pen at Fenway Park, between innings, and said, 'One beer, please.' "

Satchel was being Satchel fifty years before Manny Ramirez started being Manny and it was a hit with Paige's Browns teammates, most of whom were born just as he was breaking into baseball. Who else but Satchel could toss a bar of soap onto a slippery wall-mounted dish and make it stay? Once might be luck, but he did it twice in a row. No one else hummed when they pitched. When his fellow Brownies doubted he could catch a catfish as big as he bragged, he kept one alive and put it in the whirlpool. "It was four feet long and fat as a hog," recalls J. W. Porter, who at nineteen was the youngest player in Browns' history while Satchel, at forty-six, was the oldest. Porter recalls how a sportswriter convinced the team trainer, Bob "Doc" Bauman, to perform a test. Satchel sat stark naked on the bench next to the equally exposed Porter, who was six-foot-two and 180 pounds. Wearing a blindfold, Bauman felt the two players' muscles and took the measure of their thighs in a bid to differentiate the old warrior from the young stud. He picked Satchel as the teenager. "It broke my heart," says Porter. "That's the type of body Satchel had." That was also the way the pitcher played along as teammates teased him about his age and gauged his limits.

Veeck had an experiment of his own for his pitching star. Photographers snapped shots of twenty-five hitters standing in the batter's box with just their hips showing. "We painted out all possible marks of identifications—socks, and so on—and showed the photographs to our pitching staff," he said. Satchel picked out eighteen from their batting stance alone. The next best guesser got six right. He might not know a young Ted Williams or Joe DiMaggio by face, but Satchel remembered how they stood at the plate and what pitches they typically hit and missed. It paid dividends. He generally stopped DiMaggio cold, a feat few others managed. As for Williams, the Major League's last .400 hitter prided himself on studying pitchers and was sure he had Satchel figured out. If his wrist was straight a fastball was on the way; a cocked wrist signaled a curve. The Splendid Splinter tested his theory while taking two strikes, then dug in confidently for the next pitch—a wrist bent to deliver a fast one. Strike three. The next day Satchel peered into the Sox dugout, eyes sparkling, admonishing the world's purest hitter, "You should know better than to second guess on Ole Satch."

Satchel's trouble placing faces went beyond baseball. One of America's most distinctive mugs appeared before him one day in the Browns' fitness room hoping for an autograph. Satchel obligingly reached out of his whirlpool to sign, but he was taken aback when the strange little man took to his knees, bushy brows twitching and one-liners flying. Who was that? the pitcher asked. Didn't you recognize him from TV? the team trainer said. That was Groucho Marx.

Satchel's stories and jokes were a boon to young players trying not to lose hope on a hopeless team. Satchel kept them listening as well as laughing, taking their minds off the losses that came twice as often as wins. He was a historian along with a morale builder. The latter was not an easy role for a man who believed winning was what counted and had experienced more of it than any other pitcher in history. He was a teacher, too. Don't waste energy throwing the ball to the first baseman to keep a runner from taking a big lead, he chided his protégés, when stepping off the mound does the same thing effortlessly. "He said none of the young pitchers and a lot of the old ones don't move around on the rubber. They start at the right and if they don't have control that day they still pitch from there," remembers Matt Batts, Satchel's catcher in 1951. "He said if you don't have control you should start moving to the left until you find it, then stay right at that spot. I'd never had a pitcher say anything like that. He knew more about pitching than any pitcher I knew, and I'd caught Feller and Virgil Trucks and Ellis Kinder."

The only Brownies not impressed were his managers. Marty Marion knew that Satchel was ungovernable—that he had his own relationship with the owner and his own rules—and Marion went along. After Satchel pitched ten innings of relief, Marion was informed the pitcher would be late the next day. "Let him roll over and snore a couple times," the manager told a reporter. Half a century later Marion complained that "Satchel came and went as he pleased. He didn't obey any orders from the manager." Rogers Hornsby, Marion's predecessor, learned that the hard way. He pushed Satchel to run laps, chase flies, grab grounders, and do other drills. He insisted the pitcher show up on time to games and practices. He was quick to slap on fines when Satchel broke the rules, no matter the reason. When his regimented style failed to turn around the hapless Browns, Hornsby, a two-time Triple Crown winner, was out. Looking back he faulted Veeck for not collecting his hundred-dollar levy against Satchel. "The boss," he said, "should back his manager up."

Hornsby had predicted from the start that bringing blacks into baseball would be a disaster, and he did his best to ensure it was. Satchel, as the only black on the Browns, bore the brunt of that bigotry. When Hornsby fined the pitcher for missing an exhibition game in Corpus Christi, Texas, it was not another case of Satchel living by his own clock. It was Jim Crow flexing his muscle, with the bus driver who transported players from the train station to the hotel barring Satchel from boarding. The pitcher was stuck at the depot until a black mail carrier took him home and fed him, by which time it was too late to make the game. "Hornsby didn't care," says Lou Sleater, Satchel's bullpen mate. Worse, adds another white teammate, Ned Garver, "Hornsby said, 'Next time I'll fine you twice that.' " At the Browns' next stop, San Antonio, there were just three taxis in the whole city that served blacks and Satchel would have been stuck again, says Garver, but thankfully Garver had a car waiting and shuttled Satchel to and from his blacks-only hotel. "One day Satchel wanted to show me the place," recalls Garver. "It had low ceilings. It was dark and dingy, the kind of place you didn't know whether there were rats or what. It just wasn't a place for a big-league ballplayer like Satchel Paige to be spending his time."

A third white teammate, Duane Pillette, got his own look behind the curtain of race when he arrived early at the team's Pullman sleeping car and found Satchel spraying his compartment with air freshener. Pillette asked what he was doing. "Boy, sit down. I want to tell you a story," Pillette remembers Satchel saying. "I know everyone thinks we smell a little different and maybe we do, but you smell different to us. I spray this stuff every time I get in the berth because I don't want you to think of me as being black. I want you to think of me as Satchel." Pillette responded that to him, Satchel Paige was a legend, no matter his race. Satchel was touched, but explained, "Boy, you just don't realize what a black man must go through."

What Satchel went through in the Majors was different from the indignities he had endured before. Many umpires saddled him with a strike zone that was shorter and narrower than for his Caucasian counterparts. White pitchers hit black batters too many times for it to be chance (Pillette says his manager paid him fifty dollars for clipping Jackie Robinson when Jackie was with Montreal). In spring training cities like Phoenix, Satchel could stay at the team hotel but had to have his meals in his room because he was barred from the restaurant. He accepted that as the way things were; his fellow Alabamian and teammate Virgil Trucks did not. Trucks, who is white, was determined that Satchel join him for dinner at Phoenix's elegant Flame Restaurant, which like the one at their hotel was whites-only. Earlier in the day he met with the dining room manager and talked him into seating Satchel that evening, "we presumed in a corner where nobody could see us. Satchel was reluctant to go, he didn't know I had already set it up. There were a couple hundred people in the restaurant. We could hear them buzzing, they didn't know what a black man was doing there. We were seated at center stage. After people found out who he was they wouldn't stay away from our table. They came over to get his autograph. He signed 150 to 200 autographs that night. I never signed one. They never asked for mine.

"We never really discussed it but I could tell Satchel appreciated what I did. I knew that. I liked him that much more after that night."

The Jimmy Piersall story had a less happy ending. It was the ninth inning of a 1952 game at Fenway Park and Satchel was on the mound, protecting a 9-5 lead. The Red Sox outfielder taunted the pitcher, saying he was going to bunt against him, then doing it successfully. On base Piersall went wild, "flapping his arms like Sharkey the trained seal, yelling himself hoarse and imitating every move Satchmo made," *The Boston Globe* reported. Piersall moved to second when his teammate singled, and from there he yelled, "Oink! Oink! Oink! Gosh, but you look funny out there on the mound." He eventually scored on two walks, yelling at each turn and again from the dugout. Satchel was so undone that he yielded a grand slam to rookie Sox catcher Sammy White and lost the game, 11-9.

It later became clear that Piersall had been in the midst of a mental meltdown that would land him on the violent ward of a state psychiatric hospital. But the question that night at Fenway was whether the outfielder's antics had turned racist. Satchel insisted they had, and that Piersall referred to him as a "black so-and-so." Garver said he was close enough to see Piersall imitating a monkey but too far to hear any epithets. *The Globe* missed the race and the mental health angles. Piersall, a half century on, acknowledges that he jumped up and down that evening but says the charge that he made a racial remark is "bullshit . . . I didn't say a word to him." Whatever happened, Piersall got to Satchel in a way that few others had managed despite all the slurs and cuts that came his way. When the two met the next season, Satchel dusted Piersall with a pitch and, according to a *Globe* columnist, "war was nearly declared."

Reflecting back years after he had cooled down, Satchel said he had expected things to be easier in the newly integrated Majors but quickly learned that "old man prejudice hadn't been killed. . . . After that newness wore off, those mean folks started acting up again, started letting that meanness run out again. All those years I'd put in taught me how to handle that kind of trouble real easy, but when it surprised me I could blow up with the best of them."

There was one circumstance where Satchel was especially likely to lose it: when racism singed Lahoma. "One time Satchel and I were barnstorming in Southern Indiana and got into a town that made no provision for black folks to eat," recalls Garver, who never saw any racial tensions or any blacks growing up in the tiny Ohio town of Ney. "Lahoma was with him, and they had to get back on the highway, go in the back door of a truck stop restaurant, and stand up while they were eating. Satchel had endured many, many, many, many things in his life but when Lahoma was with him, that was a different story. It grieved him to beat the devil. At that day's game we were standing along the first baseline facing the field, just visiting a bit, and a person came up to Satchel and wanted him to sign an autograph. He was so aggravated about how they'd mistreated his wife that he refused. In his book he tells something about that, mentioning that I was there with him and didn't understand why he didn't sign. But believe you me, I did understand."

SATCHEL'S CAREER ORBIT IN ST. LOUIS followed a trajectory nearly identical to the one in Cleveland. He arrived defying the odds and shutting down batters with his trademark efficiency. Then his performance slipped to levels that were respectable but no longer otherworldly. Finally he was dumped when his guardian angel, Bill Veeck, sold the team at the end of the 1953 season, in this case to owners who moved the Browns to Baltimore and changed their name to the Orioles. "The new bosses told me they were starting a youth movement and didn't have room for an old man like me," Satchel recalled. Neither did any other American League club; all passed on the chance to pick him up for the bargain-basement waiver price of $10,000.

That left Satchel with four children, meager savings, no job, and an impending date before a Kansas City judge on a charge of drunk driving. He had cracked up his new Cadillac just after midnight on January 1, 1954. The responding officer said he was intoxicated. It was, by Satchel's calculation, his thirtieth arrest in Kansas City for speeding or careless driving. His defense: "I was in the Blue Room at the Street Hotel. I was sittin' there talkin' to the bartender, Kingfish. I had me one bottle of beer." The judge told him he would drop the charge of driving while intoxicated because there was reasonable doubt, but said the pitcher had been driving too fast and been in too many accidents. The verdict: guilty of careless driving, which carried a fine of twenty-five dollars.

It was an inauspicious way to start a new year. Rather than sulking or going on a drinking spree the way his dad might have, Satchel picked up a telephone and a baseball. Old friend Abe Saperstein agreed to sign him for the hardball version of Saperstein's famous Globetrotters basketball team. Satchel would be the general manager as well as a pitcher, a deal that would take him on a tour of small-city America and could earn him up to $30,000. It was a way to make a living, although not an easy one at age forty-eight. "I am still one of the best in the game," Satchel told reporters. "I'll prove it pitching for the 'Trotters."

He said he threw in 148 games in 1954, or one every two and a half days. The next year he was equally nomadic and prolific, this time for his old friends the Monarchs, who paid him $40,000. Tom Baird had bought out his partner, J. L. Wilkinson, in 1948 for more than $50,000, and in 1955 Baird would sell the team for a mere $3,500 to Ted Rasberry, a black businessman in Michigan. The Monarchs' top players were already gone, to the Majors, minors, or retirement, and the team quickly cut its ties to Kansas City. The Negro Leagues were on life support, and the only way Satchel could sustain his family was by having Wilkie book him out to Midwestern teams even as he was scratching out what he could from the barnstorming Monarchs. That once-regal team was so cash-starved that Rasberry sold its bus and players packed into station wagons as they traveled from sandlot to sandlot, the way they had in blackball's impoverished early days.

By 1956 Satchel was weighing retirement, which was not unreasonable for a ballplayer about to turn fifty, when Bill Veeck swept to the rescue yet again. Veeck was helping friends run the Miami Marlins, a minor league franchise in a city more interested in surfing than baseball. What better item to stir up interest, the Marlins PR impresario figured, than a pitching legend who was nearing the half-century mark? Veeck arranged a secretive and breathtaking first act: having Satchel climb out of a bubble-top helicopter flown onto the field on opening night. The prank almost backfired. "We lost contact with the tower and we missed our cues," recalled Marlins business manager Joe Ryan. "We were running out of fuel." Satchel had had his fill of flying years before when the Monarchs bought him a plane. "I was so scared," he said of his landing in Miami, "that pilot and me was like husband and wife until we landed."

Don Osborn, the Marlins' manager, did not object to Veeck's caper but thought it was the beginning and end of Satchel's tenure with his team. "He didn't come down here for a gag," Veeck told Osborn the next day at lunch. "He came down to pitch for us." Then Veeck offered a test to prove Satchel's worth: "You just line up your nine best hitters, and you tell them you're going to give them ten dollars for every base hit they get off him. . . . I'm paying." Satchel struck out nine men in a row and, as Veeck tells it, "Osborn fell in love with him on the spot."

The Marlins parked the pitcher in a large rocking chair in the bullpen, bringing him out to throw more often than even Veeck dreamed possible. On an August night in 1956 he drew 51,713 fans to a charity game against Columbus at the Orange Bowl. Organizers billed it "The Baseball Party to End All Baseball Parties"; record keepers called it the biggest crowd ever to watch a minor league game. Satchel pitched into the eighth inning to collect the win and drove in three runs with a 330-foot double to left-center. A week later he pitched a one-hitter, beating Rochester 4-0 and leaving to a standing ovation. When he was not starting he stayed in the clubhouse until the late innings, then sauntered to the bullpen with towels covering his neck to keep him warm. During three seasons with the Marlins, Satchel compiled a record of 31-22 and an earned run average of 2.73, both impressive for a pitcher of any age.

He also made more friends for life. The Marlins were a blend of promising teenagers on the way up and retiring veterans looking for a soft landing. All appreciated having a relic and character like Satchel along for the ride. Anyone who happened to room near him could hear calypso melodies spinning off the phonograph he carried everywhere. The last one to check out of the team hotel often picked up the beat-up Underwood typewriter Satchel was always forgetting. Railroad porters helped him lug his record player, typewriter, trunk-size suitcase, and the extra case he carried to hold the gifts lavished on him wherever he went—but no one was allowed to touch his medical bag loaded with lotions and potions.

On one plane ride to Rochester, Satchel courageously joined in the word game Ghost, where players take turns adding letters to a growing word fragment. "Q," Satchel began. Teammate Henry "Bo" Mason challenged, doubting the aging hurler knew any words starting with that letter. "Cucumber," shot back Satchel. "Gimme my quarter." From then on club mates called him "Q." He was better at other games, yearning to pick up a stick anytime he walked by a pool hall and wanting to fish in every puddle he passed. Whenever Duke Ellington or Fats Domino was performing he took his fellow players to the show. "He knew both of them and he introduced me," says Bo

Mason, a young black pitcher whom Satch took a special interest in. "He also knew I wasn't making much money and that I liked corned beef hash and poached eggs. He'd call me up to his hotel room and order me breakfast."

He did more than that for bonus baby Tom Qualters. It was early in the season near the end of a nail-biter against Buffalo when the eighteen-year-old rookie got the call to pitch. "I was totally petri-fied, my teeth were chattering," Qualters recalls. "You'd rather jump off a building than let your teammates know you are scared. I some-how managed to throw the ball up there and batters got themselves out, but later that night I was thinking how I could go quit. That's how bad it was. The next night I told Satchel. He laughed out loud and said, 'Those sons of bitches can beat you but they can't eat you.' I was back in the game that night, shaking, but saying to myself, 'You sons of bitches can beat me but you can't eat me.'

"It meant everything to me," adds Qualters, who has passed on the advice to countless young players he has coached. "Satchel meant that it's not a life and death situation. You do the best you can and don't let mental things interfere with the job."

While age gave Satchel perspective, it was also taking its first toll. He sliced the sides out of his shoes to let his bunions breathe and spent half of each day in the whirlpool. His flat-as-a-pancake mitt made him look even more antediluvian, and he took longer to release the baseball than anyone in the game. A pitcher who once set the clock for speed now threw a changeup so slow that his catcher could get a drink of water before the ball reached home plate. Rather than rollicking with women between games, he was playing with his kids, who along with their mother joined him in Miami for the sum-mer. "I almost feel like as big a celebrity as you," Lahoma told Satchel. "I wish it could be this way always."

His honeymoon with the Marlins ended the same way it had with the Indians and Browns. Veeck left. Satchel's pitching stayed strong, but not as strong. Disagreements flared over everything from meal money to salary. In August of 1958 Satchel was suspended for what the team said was his "utter disregard of rules"; he asked for but was denied his unconditional release. He finished out the season but after that both sides called it quits.

All that was left was barnstorming. In 1959 he pitched for the

Havana Cuban Stars, who played a long way from Havana with Satchel the only legitimate star. In 1960 he threw for the Salina, Kansas, Bluejays and the Wichita Weller Indians, which was mainly a route back to the cherished national semi-pro tournament in Wichita. In 1961 he returned to the Monarchs, then signed with the minor league Beavers in Portland, Oregon. He pitched twenty-five innings in Portland and recorded a 2.88 earned run average. "It was obvious he was there to spike the gate and make a few bucks for himself and the team," remembers Dwight Jaynes, the Beavers' batboy. "He earned every dime. He pitched okay and got people out. But it was hard to look at him and not think, 'This is an old guy.' He looked and moved like a fifty-five-year-old guy. He was all stove up."

Stiff, truly, but with enough life in his immortal arm that he kept renting it out. Expectations ran high for his sentimental appeal and were low enough for his pitching performance that he generally exceeded them. In the summer of 1965 he found himself in Alaska, with a welcoming committee that included former vice president Richard M. Nixon. The future president's jet happened to be stopping there on the way to Tokyo and Vietnam just as Satchel's flight was arriving. Seeing the streamers and balloons, Nixon wondered how word had gotten out about his secret mission; when he realized they were not for him, the avid baseball fan said he would love to meet Satchel. "I've always wanted to greet a celebrity," Nixon told the gangling pitcher, adding that he was sorry he could not stay to watch him play that night. Satchel dazzled Anchorage fans with his throwing, then delighted them by announcing that he would run a team being organized there under the name Earthquakers. It was a deal done tongue-in-cheek, at least by Satchel, whose mind was still fixed on one last go-around with a big-league club.

Bill Veeck shared that fantasy and almost managed to pull off one more Cinderella rescue after he took control of the Chicago White Sox in 1959. He sent six scouts out to look over Satchel, none knowing what the others were doing and all reaching what he said was the same conclusion: "There isn't a better reliefer around." Veeck's manager, future Hall of Famer Al Lopez, was harder to please. "Al wants only the players who catch every plane and meet every roll call," the owner explained, "and Satch wasn't a particularly good bet to catch the next streetcar." Other teams scouted him throughout his Miami

years and afterward, yet they shared Lopez's reservations. "Too old,"
Nap Reyes, the former-Major-Leaguer-turned-scout, wrote in 1956.
The next year Reyes weighed in with an even less generous verdict,
saying the pitcher was "slipping (wash-out)," was just a "fair" hustler, and was not a good man to have on a ball club. In 1958 Tony
Pacheco offered this scouting observation on Satchel: "sleep too
much and always late." That same year, Reyes wrote his third and
most optimistic report, calling Satchel "the best control pitcher in
this league" and saying he was a winning player for the Marlins.
Still, he advised against signing him.

Scouts in those days relied more on instinct than today's SABR-
metrics wizards, who mathematically anatomize baseball records,
but the statistics would have confirmed their doubts. He did have
brilliant years in the Majors, but he was not consistent. His performance slipped in Cleveland and again in St. Louis because batters
figured him out the second time around or because he was, after all,
subject to the normal forces of aging. An optimist would zero in on
his .857 winning percentage in year one with the Indians; a scout
whose job depended on delivering winners would fixate on Satchel's
.250 win ratio his last year with the Browns. His glove was a bright
spot: he had cleanly fielded all seventy-nine balls hit to him, for an
errorless Major League record. His bat was a blot: he collected just
twelve hits in 123 at bats in Cleveland and St. Louis, for an anemic
average of .098.

Thankfully for Satchel there was one owner in baseball with as
much whimsy and even more cash than Bill Veeck. Charles O. Finley made a live mule the mascot when he took over the Kansas City
Athletics, naming him Charley O. and parading him into the press
room. The insurance magnate installed a pop-up mechanical rabbit
that gave baseballs to the home plate ump. His team sported a uniform that blended kelly green, Fort Knox gold, and wedding gown
white. He pledged to keep the club in Kansas City, then tried to
shop it to Dallas, Atlanta, Louisville, and Oakland, its eventual
home. Finley was part masterful innovator, part maddening egotist.
He was also as enamored with Satchel as Veeck had been.

As the 1965 season was winding down in Kansas City, Finley star-
tled the baseball world by signing Satchel to a contract and announcing that he would pitch against the Red Sox on September 25,
Satchel Paige Appreciation Night. "I thought they were kidding,"

Satchel told reporters, quickly adding, "I think I can still pitch and help this club." For Paige it was another reprieve and another chance to prove himself. For Finley it was a bold-as-brass publicity stunt to inflate attendance. His team had drawn barely 500,000 fans all season and was in last place, thirty-seven games out of contention. By writing one check for $3,500, he had given a swift kick to his staid fellow owners and drawn the attention of America's sportswriters and fans.

Finley himself choreographed the big night. Satchel sat in a rocker strategically placed next to but not in the A's belowground bullpen. "At my age," the fifty-nine-year-old pitcher explained, "I'm close enough to being below ground level as it is." A nurse in a white uniform rubbed liniment on his right arm as his personal water boy stood by. Among the 9,289 fans at Municipal Stadium were Satchel's six children; Lahoma was home ready to deliver the seventh and last. The press was there in force. In its story that morning, the *Los Angeles Times* captured the tenor of Satchel's return: "A gimmick, yes. A joke, no."

The evening's drama may have been staged by Finley and promoted by the press, but it was Satchel who scripted the closing act. He needed just twenty-eight tosses to get nine outs. He struck out one and walked none over three innings. Batters popped up his pitches and tapped meek grounders. The only base hit was a double by Carl Yastrzemski, an All-Star who led the league in doubles and had seen his father hit against Satchel a generation earlier in a semipro game on Long Island. Tony Conigliaro, the brash Boston right fielder, had boasted that "I'm going to get a hit off this old so-and-so." His was one of the easiest outs. "Satchel had better swings off me than I had off of him," says Bill Monbouquette, the longtime Sox ace and Satchel's last strikeout victim in the Major Leagues. "He was throwing 86 to 88 miles per hour with excellent control and location." Ed Charles, Satchel's teammate on the A's, says that after a twelve-year hiatus from the Majors, the veteran fireballer took just ten warm-up throws. "He proceeded to go out on the mound and shove the ball right up their you know what. Most of the kids on our team were saying, 'What's this old man doing? He should be in a retirement home.' " Yaz, a slugger of few words, paid his respects after the game by wrapping the aged pitcher in a bear hug.

The hometown fans cheered when Satchel came to the plate. They cheered louder when he struck out. The plan was to send a reliever in to start the fourth, but Satchel came out for a few practice pitches so he could leave to a standing ovation, doffing his hat as he slowly walked off the field. In the locker room he had stripped to his long underwear when someone burst in to say, "Satch, they want you back on the field." Minutes later he returned to the darkened ballpark as fans flicked matches and lighters in his honor. "The old gray mare," an appreciative audience sang, "she ain't what she used to be." But on that night, he had been what he used to be. "Now I'll stay in shape," Satchel told reporters after the game, "because now they know what I can do."

Satchel's appearance with the A's—at the age of fifty-nine years, two months, and eight days—set a Major League record for longevity that will never be broken. He was two years older than the runner-up and thirty-three more than his catcher that evening. He seemed as old as baseball itself. His sixth season in the big leagues underscored another milestone that, as the years went by, mattered more to Satchel than the tired question of age. He knew better than any historian that "we had a lot of Satchel Paiges back then." But he had experienced something that eluded Josh Gibson and Cool Papa Bell, Smokey Joe Williams and Bullet Joe Rogan. Satchel was the only Negro League legend who lived to savor life in the Major Leagues.

CHAPTER 10

Crafting a Legend

"I ain't ever had a job. I just always played baseball."

HE CALLED THEM HIS RULES for staying young. No one in America carried more credibility on eternal youth than this ageless ballplayer who appeared destined to pitch forever. All of America seemed captivated by Satchel's blend of the poetic philosophy of Mark Twain and the practical bromides of Dr. Spock. What do you do when your stomach is on fire, the way Satchel's always was? *Lie down and pacify it with cool thoughts.* How do you keep in shape for the long run? *Avoid running at all times.* Was there a secret to defying Father Time, Mother Nature, and Jim Crow? *Don't look back. Something might be gaining on you.*

It was the last one especially that became his calling card as he neared sixty, an age when heroes often revisit old glories. Nothing captured as clearly Satchel's existential eloquence and triumph over tragedy. It would make its way into the columns of *The New York Times* and *Reader's Digest,* the titles of books, and the pages of *Bartlett's Familiar Quotations,* that ultimate arbiter of sayings that matter and sages worth quoting. So closely did Satchel identify with his rules that he printed business cards with the six of them etched on the back. So exalted did his aphorisms become that President

Dwight D. Eisenhower reportedly posted them at the White House. "One cannot help but wonder," a respected internist wrote in *Good Health,* "what Mr. Paige might have achieved if his father had given him a stethoscope instead of a baseball."

Satchel loved the ongoing scrutiny of his precepts, although not of how he put them into practice. The latter posed a problem from the beginning, starting with rule one: *Avoid fried meats which angry up the blood.* There was no questioning the severity of his stomach miseries, which made his gastric juices churn and sometimes implode. The sensible response would have been to swear off the fried food he loved. He swore he did, saying he subsisted on broiled lamb chops, boiled chicken, steamed carrots and peas, and a big bowl of vegetable soup. Other times he told a spicier story: "Here I am on some old sorry-assed gravel road four hundred miles from nowhere, what kind of breakfast can I cook on my Coleman if I can't fry me up something? Maybe them reporters figure I eat some Corn Flakes or some Rice Krispies. . . . I eat fried eggs. And I eat fried bacon. And I eat fried ham and fried sausage and fried everything."

Those dueling versions of the truth mirrored his push and pull over diet and image. Fried generally won out, as attested by the clubhouse boys who regularly replenished his stockpile of bicarbonate of soda. Yet better for the world to see him as a model for clean living, which also explains rule four: *Go very light on the vices, such as carrying on in society. The social ramble ain't restful.* He claimed fidelity to that one only when he was talking to cherubs or had his tongue in his cheek. Carrying on had always been his hallmark. Rambling was a way of life for barnstorming men like him.

The most tenable of his rules was the admonishment against running. Satchel was famously languid. His slow shuffle from the bullpen to the mound was likened to an amiable camel. The only place he ran, he said, was for the showers. He declared himself the "eternal rester" and kept in shape by "rising gently up and down from the [bullpen] bench." Even there, there was a dissenting view. Not only did Satchel train regularly during his years with the Pittsburgh Crawfords, the team's former publicist confided years later, but his workouts included runs of eight to ten miles.

If the rules did not always fit they could be altered. *Don't look back* became *Never look over your shoulder.* What started as Satchel's guidelines for *How to Stay Young* morphed into a guide for *Livin' the Good Life*. Double Duty Radcliffe remembered Satchel offering up a more lyrical set of canons that went like this: "If you want to live a long time don't fool with nothing old but money, nothing big but a bankroll, nothing black but a Cadillac, nothing over twenty-two years, nothing that weighs over 130—if you do you're in trouble." The number of rules shifted, too, with only five sent to the Eisenhower White House in 1955 by the chancellor of the University of Kansas. The president wrote back saying, "Thank you for sending me Satchel Paige's words of wisdom. I agree that we would do well to bear some of his thoughts in mind." Did Ike, a longtime baseball fan, put the ballplayer's musings on his office wall, the way the press claimed? "I found no evidence in our files indicating that President Eisenhower had posted these rules in the White House," says an archivist at the Eisenhower Library, adding that the commander in chief's reply to the chancellor does "not indicate a ringing endorsement."

Then there was the matter of provenance. The rules first turned up in print in 1953, in a three-part profile of Satchel by Richard Donovan in *Collier's*. To make clear that Donovan was merely the transcriber, and Satchel the author, the six maxims were listed in a sidebar signed by Satchel. The story behind the story is that Donovan's editor ordered up a list of Satchelisms. When the reporter did not have enough, he was sent back to his hotel room and told to dream up the rest. They all sounded like the pitcher and were based on his ruminations during hours of interviews. The spirit was Satchel's, the words Donovan's.

No matter. Much that was written over the years about Satchel Paige was engulfed in half-truths and apparitions. The shoestring black press relied on word of mouth, which begged for interpretation and, yes, exaggeration, especially coming out of the mouth of a princely storyteller and self-promoter like Satchel. White reporters did not know how to take a black player seriously or how to write about him. They compensated for decades of ignoring Satchel by constructing fables even more fantastic than his feats. The Satchel Paige they cobbled together in his golden years was part Cy Young, part P. T. Barnum, Stepin Fetchit, Will Rogers, and Frank Merriwell.

That was just the way Satchel liked it. He knew he had accomplished most everything he claimed, in and out of baseball. His rules for healthy living mattered because they reflected his life—a deceptively slow pace, the capacity to keep pitching for an unprecedented five decades, an inspired determination to forge ahead rather than look back. Satchel strayed from such truths only enough to cultivate the mystery, never enough to undermine the essence. He courted reporters but was sufficiently mistrustful that he told his story himself in two autobiographies. Doing that, he knew as instinctively as any modern-day spinmeister, was the way to build a legacy and a legend.

SUPERSIZE FEATS WERE SATCHEL'S LONG SUIT. He was the most proficient pitching machine ever and the most idiosyncratic. The less likely another player was to try something, or even think it possible, the more enticing it was to Satchel the scene stealer. His favorite ploy was calling in his outfielders. He summoned them when the batter was positioning himself at the plate, making it clear that merely lifting the ball out of the infield meant an automatic hit and probably a home run. It was a dare if not an insult. He did it for the first time with the Down the Bay Boys when he was a boy in Mobile. His teammates had committed three straight errors and he was determined to show them up, no matter that the bases were loaded and his lead was just 1-0 with two outs in the ninth. Batter up. Three strikes. Point made.

The crowd ate it up and Satchel did it again. And again. Sometimes it was just his outfielders, other times the infielders, too. They would sit and watch, talk among themselves, and play poker or at least pretend to. He did it when he was angry at his team or his opponents, or felt fans were losing interest in the game. One time it was to show up rivals he heard make a racial slur. He did it in Birmingham and Bismarck, at the 1934 Denver Post Tournament and in Puerto Rico in 1939. Usually it was with the game in the bag, or against a weak semi-pro club, but not always. He tried it more than once with the game on the line against Negro League foes, against big-league bashers like Jimmy Foxx, and against Puerto Rico's most feared batsman, Francisco "Pancho" Coimbre. The caper was not his invention: the eccentric Major Leaguer George Edward "Rube"

Waddell had made it famous back at the turn of the century. But no one did it as often as Satchel or talked about it as much afterward.

No need to take his word for it. Newspapers documented it and witnesses swore to it. "With two down in the third, he signaled his outfielders they were through for the inning, bore down and struck out the next batter," the *Chicago Defender* wrote about a July game in 1941 against the Chicago Giants. The opposition might not have been the greatest but Satchel's performance was when Bob Wymer of Bellville, Ohio, saw him intentionally walk the bases loaded, call in everyone but his catcher, then strike out the side with nine pitches. Wymer might not have remembered it so clearly if it had happened just once, but "I saw him do this three different times." Bob Motley authorized the nap time for fielders when he was an umpire in the Negro Leagues, telling Satchel, "You can call them in. They just have to stand on the field, they can't go to the dugout. The rulebook says you have to have nine guys on the field." Satchel struck out the next batter with three fastballs over the heart of the plate.

Generally the prank ended well, but not always. One night in the 1930s, pitching for Bismarck against Jamestown, Satchel stood on the mound mopping his brow with his pitching hand. His team was ahead by one run with a man on base in the last of the ninth, and he was wiping away perspiration. His outfielders saw something else: their pitcher's well-honed signal for them to take the rest of the inning off. "While my outfield was strollin' off the field behind my back," Satchel recounted to Donovan and *Collier's,* "I fed the cleanup man a little outcurve which I intended him to hit on the fly to right field. He did. It was some time before I again visited the city of Bismarck."

There was less risk involved in the antics that spotlighted his pinpoint control, since most of these came before the game. Satchel's favorite foil was a soft book of matches. Sometimes he laid it on home plate, then threw eight of ten pitches directly over it. Or he set the matchbook atop a stick, then knocked it off. Other targets of choice: a postage stamp, a handkerchief, the knob on top of a base-ball cap, and a gum wrapper, preferably Wrigley's Spearmint. The gum went into his mouth, the silver wrapper on home plate, the ball right over the wrapper. With practice targets so small, home plate looked as big as a mattress.

Teammates were joyful accomplices in the Satchel sideshow. Bonnie Serrell, the Monarchs' second baseman, would stand with his hand on his waist as the pitcher threw a ball through the crook in his arm. "I never worried about being hit," said Serrell. "I never saw Satchel hit a batter." When no batters were available, bats alone would do, with three standing side by side topped by baseball caps. He pitched three balls over each to get his bearings, then used a fourth to knock down the bat. "He didn't miss, he never missed," says Joe Scott, who played alongside Satchel for six years. He also never walked a batter unless he meant to, or almost never.

The tenpenny-nail act went like this: stick four nails in a one-foot-by-two-foot plank behind home plate, march off the pitching distance of sixty feet, six inches, then fire ten baseballs at the nails. Satchel would drive them all deep into the board. Whereas the other routines were about control, this was a twofer: it took on-the-money precision to hit the nails on the head and hard-to-believe horsepower to pound them through the wood.

He made it look effortless, but that was a mirage. No one worked harder than Satchel to fine-tune and maintain his accuracy. He rehearsed at home as well as on the field. In Kansas City he set up a net in his basement with spots marked for the strike zone. Nights he could not sleep he headed to the cellar to practice. When his Harlem Globetrotters buddy Reece "Goose" Tatum visited, he and Satchel sat around talking and, as if it were second nature, tossing quarters into faraway paint cans.

The pitcher was at his best when a wager was on the line, like it was one night in 1957 in Rochester, New York. There was a hole just big enough for a baseball in the outfield fence, and Satchel's Miami Marlins teammate Whitey Herzog had tried nearly two hundred times to throw one through. No go. Tired of hearing Satchel brag that he could do it, Herzog dared him to try. "Wild Child," Satchel asked, "do the ball fit in the hole?" Herzog said it did, barely, whereupon Satchel bet a fifth of Old Forester bourbon that he could do it from sixty feet, six inches if he had three tries. He had, after all, done the same thing day after day for his old coach Alex Herman thirty-one years before in Chattanooga. "The next night Satchel came early to the ballpark and I walked off the distance," said Herzog, who became one of the big league's best managers. "The first ball he threw went brrr and came back out. The second went right through. Holy moley, he could do some of the darnest things."

Equally amazing was the night the Marlins sponsored a distance-throwing contest for outfielders. Herzog, who could play all three outfield spots, managed to peg the ball an impressive 380 feet. "Satchel told me after that contest, 'I can throw farther than that.' The next night he threw damn near to the backstop from home on the fly," or about 400 feet, remembers Herzog. Satchel was over fifty then, Herzog twenty-six. The Marlins outfielder was not around several years earlier when Satchel made a similar bet with catcher Clint Courtney of the St. Louis Browns. Satchel's throw then went an estimated 427 feet—eighteen feet shy of the current Guinness World Record of 445 feet, 10 inches. Depending on just when he made his toss he might have had a claim on an earlier record of 426 feet, 9 inches, which stood from 1910 until 1952.

Nearly everyone Satchel played with or against had a comparable story. He pointed to fielders to designate who would make the next play, then pitched the batter in a way that guaranteed it was hit there. The twitching of fingers that foes presumed was a nervous tic really was a signal to his defense how to position itself for the next batter. He created jams simply to show he could work his way out of them. Then there was his heart-stopper, a move reported by teammates throughout his career much the way Ned Garver saw it when he and Satchel were with the St. Louis Browns in the early '50s. The tying run was on third in the eighth or ninth inning, and the batter hit a one-hopper to Satchel. "Satchel put his glove down, had the ball before the batter left home, and started to walk towards third," recalls Garver, who was watching from the dugout along third base. "There were only two outs and he's just ambling towards us holding on to the ball. I started to rise off the bench and holler. Maybe he thought he caught it on the fly. Without breaking stride Satchel threw that ball across his body, a perfect strike to first, and got the third out. Positively amazing."

What eyewitnesses cannot attest with certainty is how hard Satchel threw. Some teammates say that in his prime he topped 100 miles per hour, or even 105, which would have made him the fastest pitcher under heaven. Satchel's fastball, thrown with his marksman-like control, was unhittable in the mid-90s; anything speedier and it would have been unseeable, too. A pitch that crosses the plate at 100 miles an hour is closer to 108 miles an hour when it leaves the pitcher's hand. It reaches the catcher in four-tenths of a second, giving the batter a mere fifteen-hundredths of a second to react. That is quicker than a normal human can move his eyes, and surely too fast for any hitter to make contact using a bat that is just two and a half inches in diameter. Radar guns were not introduced until 1935, which meant there was no way to prove or disprove the claims about how fast Satchel was in his flame-throwing youth. The most convincing evidence lay in his receivers' paws. "Lord, my hand was so swelled up I had to catch him with two hands," says Art Williams. Leonard "Bo" Walker said he put a two-dollar steak in his palm when he was Satchel's catcher; at the end of the game his hand looked like hamburger. Double Duty Radcliffe, who lived to be 103, ended up with what Bob Motley called "the gnarliest, ugliest, most deformed fingers I have ever seen. His catching hand had been bent and battered from—as he said—'catching Satchel's heat for over 20 years.' Duty once told me, 'Catching Satchel is like trying to catch a freight train barreling at you with the brakes gone bad!' And from what I saw, he was hardly exaggerating."

Satchel's on-field exploits were outlandish enough that half a century later they still astonish and delight perennial baseball men like Motley and Herzog, who have seen it all. Sometimes Satchel did it for fun. Other times it was to make a buck, intimidate opponents, or entertain fans who had come to see him put on a show. Best of all, it was because he could. "Making believers out of doubters was sweeter than winning any ball game," said Satchel's friend Buck O'Neil. "It was as sweet as life itself."

Most doubters did become believers, as Satchel showed he could pull off what he promised. In some cases the conversion went the other way. People accepted as gospel stories passed through the years, by Satchel himself or his acolytes, but that faith wavered as new evidence emerged. That is what happened with tales from the Dominican Republic, which turned out to be dramatic but distorted. It is happening again with two of Satchel's biggest games in a career filled with them.

His 1934 no-hitter for the Pittsburgh Crawfords against the Homestead Grays happened on, of all days, Independence Day. It is true he set off fireworks with his brilliant hurling, but in his memoir he amplified the story into iron-man territory: "I ran out of the park, hopped into my car, and drove all night to Chicago. I got there just in time to beat Jim Trent and the Chicago American Giants one to nothing in twelve innings." He did score a big win in Chicago, but on July 8th not the 5th, against the good William "Sug" Cornelius not the masterful Ted Trent (there was no Jim Trent), in ten innings rather than twelve, and by a score of 3-0 instead of 1-0. His feat that July 4th was impressive—pitching relief in the second game of the Pittsburgh doubleheader after going the distance in the first—but he gave up the winning run in game two, which might explain why there was no mention of that appearance in his book.

The other controversy also involved a game against the Grays, and it, too, is coming under new scrutiny from baseball historians. This time Satchel was pitching for the Monarchs and confronting the most explosive batter in the history of blackball and maybe all of baseball. A decade earlier in Puerto Rico, Josh Gibson had kidded Satchel that someday he would face him in a big contest, with the bases loaded, and would take him deep. Now was his chance. It was the second game of the 1942 Negro League World Series. With two outs in the bottom of the eighth and the Monarchs ahead 6-3, Satch gave up a single, then intentionally walked the next two Grays to set up the showdown with Josh. "Up come Josh Gibson swingin' his big bat," Satch wrote six years later. "I yelled to Josh. 'Remember Puerto Rico? Well the bases is filled. Now you're too smart to fool, so I'm goin' to tell you what's comin'. I'm goin' to throw you two sidearm fast balls down around the knees.' The umpire was John Craig, I remember clear. Josh let the first pitch go. Craig called, 'Strike one.' Josh let the second pitch go. Craig called, 'Strike two.' 'Now,' I said, 'Josh, you're too good for me to waste any pitches so I'm goin' to finish you with a sidearm curve. That's your weakness.' I threw it and Josh stepped back. It broke over and he swung a slow motion strike three. Josh came out to the box and shook my hand. They had to halt play for 'bout an hour to clear the field of straw hats."

The moment was defined. The Negro Leagues' biggest icons had gone face-to-face, talking trash, with the bases filled and the game on the line, playing for the crown. In the end, one was still standing, the spindly flamethrower. The story was a classic, maybe *the* classic.

But the truth was not quite enough. When Satchel first wrote about it a year afterward in a bylined story in *The Pittsburgh Courier,* he mentioned one intentional walk. In his 1948 memoir it was two. By 1962, when he published his second book, the ante was up to three premeditated passes and the lead was down to a single run. The first basemen for the Grays and Monarchs, Buck Leonard and Buck O'Neil, backed up Satchel in their memoirs. Before Josh came to the plate Satchel summoned Jewbaby Floyd to the mound for bicarbonate of soda to settle his stomach, O'Neil wrote. "Satchel drank it down and let out a great big belch. He was playing the crowd like a fiddle." Before Josh swung and missed for the third time, O'Neil added, Satchel taunted him with "I'm not gonna throw smoke at yo' yolk—I'm gonna throw a pea at yo' knee." Then he did. "Boom! Strike three. Josh never even took a swing as the ball smacked Joe Greene's glove like a clap of thunder."

The dramatic showdown did happen and Satchel did prevail, but not like that. Unlike many Negro League games where no reporters were on hand, all the major black papers and white ones, too, covered this story. None showed Satchel issuing a single walk, intentional or otherwise. All missed the theatrics of trash talking, burping, and a stadium enthralled by Satchel's daring gamesmanship. Not that there wasn't drama. As the Baltimore *Afro-American* wrote, the game was "highlighted by Satchel Paige's dramatic feat of striking out Josh Gibson with the bases loaded." But it happened in the seventh inning, not the eighth, with the Monarchs leading 2-0. And instead of three swings into the breeze, the paper reported that "Josh fouled off the first two pitches, then whiffed at the third."

What really happened? The sportswriters on the scene almost surely got it right. Satchel and his teammates probably saw the game with eyes ever more rose-tinted, which is how memory works with our grandest accomplishments. The two Bucks took their leads from Satchel, who wrote his memoirs first and always managed the last and most poetic word.

NUMBERS ARE PART of any athletic epic and are especially resonant in baseball, a game slow enough that its elements can be broken down, old enough to offer a rich history for reference, and so energizing that aficionados argue and reargue the most esoteric issues. But finding and comparing statistics was more problematic in the Negro Leagues, which could not afford the record keepers the Majors had. The black press was similarly cash-strapped, unable to send reporters to many games or to publish complete box scores for some contests it did cover. The upshot is that there are few reliable numbers for the best of black stars and for many second-string players there is no evidence of their even having played. Imagine trying to tell Lou Gehrig's story, or Mickey Mantle's, based primarily on their memories and stories passed down.

Satchel defied that shadowy system by keeping his own records. He carried a notebook listing innings pitched, game scores, opponents, strikeouts, bases on balls, and, according to one sportswriter who said he saw it, "a very important item to [Satchel], his end of the gate." The Paige almanac had him pitching in more than 2,500 games and winning 2,000 or so. He professed to have labored for 250 teams and thrown 250 shutouts. His per-game strikeout record was twenty-two, against Major League barnstormers, which would have been an all-time record for all of baseball. Other claims that would have set marks: fifty no-hitters, twenty-nine starts in a month, twenty-one straight wins, sixty-two consecutive scoreless innings, 153 pitching appearances in a year, and three wins the same day.

The numbers were dizzying, but each required an asterisk explaining that Satchel kept records the way he set them: with flair, grace, and hoopla. The numbers changed as he added to his accomplishments and as yet another reporter wanted to peek at his books. All longed for something new and daring, an exclusive to impress their editors; none asked why the numbers or stories kept shifting. Satchel's tally of no-hitters was as low as twenty, as high as a hundred, and perhaps most accurately, "so many . . . I disremember the number." The picture was equally muddled for shutouts. Press accounts, and Satchel's, offered options: 250, 300, or 330. Sometimes he dished out a figure so outrageous he seemed to be testing whether his reader was paying attention, like when he wrote that "I never batted less than .300 any season." (His career Negro Leagues average was .218; in the Majors he dropped to .097.)

Just when any serious statistician might be tempted to dismiss it all as a ruse, closer scrutiny suggests that much of it is true. Pitching

2,500 games seems inconceivable since the Major League record holder, Jesse Orosco, managed just 1,252. But Orosco's numbers are just for the big leagues, where he pitched twenty-four years starting every April and ending, when he was lucky, in October. Satchel's include games played as a semi-pro and professional, in the Negro Leagues, on barnstorming tours, in Latin America and Canada as well as the United States, and in the Major and minor leagues. He played spring and summer, fall and winter. He often threw just three or four innings a game, but he did it every day or couple of days for forty-one years. By that schedule, pitching 2,500 games amounts to slightly more than sixty games a year, which does not seem high enough.

The same is true for his other assertions. One hundred no-hitters, or even twenty, looks like a stretch considering that Nolan Ryan holds the Major League record with just seven, followed by Sandy Koufax with a mere four. But press accounts detail Satchel doing it against highly touted opponents like the Homestead Grays, and it is easy to imagine him repeating the feat with relative ease and considerable frequency against the sandlot teams he faced in his wayfaring across the Western Hemisphere. His two thousand wins would give him four times as many as Cy Young, whose name is attached to the award signaling pitching excellence. His calculation of career strikeouts would have bested Ryan not by a hair but by several thousand. Some pitchers were brilliant during short runs at glory; others made their names for duration as much as dominance. Satchel excelled at both, to the point where it is difficult to overstate all that he did or to dismiss even his most outrageous boasts.

Does that make him the best ever? It is difficult to say, given the unevenness of his opponents and the scarcity of reliable statistics. Some baseball historians insist he was not even the best in blackball. Smokey Joe Williams threw at least as hard and almost as long. Bullet Joe Rogan fielded, hit, and blended a fastball and curve with exquisite control. John Donaldson had a curveball faster than most pitchers' fastballs. The Foster half brothers, Rube and Willie, could also make claims to the throne, along with Richard "Cannonball Dick" Redding, Hilton Smith, and José Méndez. In the end, however, Satchel was the frame of reference, the one everyone compared themselves to and whom historians perpetually lift up to the pedestal only to swat back down.

Sizing him up against white Major Leaguers is dicier still. Whether or not Satchel had more wins than Cy Young, the two played on different planets. Contrasting his strikeouts to Nolan Ryan's would not just be a matter of apples and oranges but peas and cantaloupes. Yet sports buffs cannot resist. One baseball statistician extrapolated Satchel's Negro and Caribbean league totals to the Majors, concluding that he would have won just over three hundred games. Another imagined a big-league record of 391-246, giving him slightly more wins than Christy Mathewson, slightly fewer than Walter Johnson, and enough to rank number three all-time. The mighty Hank Aaron goes one better, saying that if Satch had been a Major Leaguer from the start "he might have won 300 games with his outfielders sitting down." Historian Bill James ranks Satchel seventeenth on his list of the hundred greatest baseball players of all time, six spots ahead of Cy Young. "Satchel deserves to rank, with Cy Young, Lefty Grove, and Walter Johnson, as the guys that you talk about when you're trying to figure out who was the greatest [pitcher] that ever lived," argues James. Journalists Mark McGuire and Michael Sean Gormley place Satchel at thirty-three in their hundred greatest of the twentieth century, writing, "How good was Satchel Paige since we don't know, at least statistically, how good he was? Better than most, and on many days, all."

IT TAKES MORE than a blazing fastball to elevate an athlete to the mythic status of a Cy Young, Jim Thorpe, or Joe Louis. Intrigue helps. So do whimsy and controversy. Fans love a hero bigger than life in all aspects of his or her life. None was as titanic as Satchel Paige. He was a comic and preacher, a warrior and student of human behavior. He could weave a brilliant tale, then reweave it for a new audience, keeping a straight face and keeping his listeners guessing where fact ended and folklore picked up. The guessing continues.

He loved driving and relished recounting his run-ins with the law. He was pulled over for hauling a trailer without a license, parking illegally, ignoring a police signal, and driving the wrong way on a one-way street. When he carried a license it was said to be as old as he was. His most frequent infraction was speeding, which seemed fitting for a pitcher renowned for his speedball. He never denied it, saying that if he had not been over the limit when the officer pulled him over, "I had been fixin' to." He paid his fines, post factum or pre-emptively. "We were out in Wyomin'," recalled Frank Duncan, Jr., a pitcher with the Monarchs. "The police pulled him over and Satchel told us, 'Don't say nothin'; just keep quiet. Let me talk.' So the guy walked up to the window and says, 'Say, don't you guys know we have old folks and kids in this area, like anywhere else in the country? You're drivin' like maniacs.' So Satchel says, 'I guess we didn't realize.' He says, 'Where you goin'?' Satchel says, 'We're on our way to Phoenix.' 'What you goin' there for?' 'We play baseball.' He said, 'Damn it, I *knew* your face looked familiar. You're Satchel Paige . . . Mr. Paige, it sure is nice meetin' you. It's gonna cost you $25.' He got the book out and started writin' a ticket. So Satchel reached in his pocket and handed him a $50 bill and started the car. He said, 'Wait a minute! Here's your change.' Satchel said, 'Keep it. I'm comin' back through here the same way next week.' "

That would have been story enough. But this tale was about Satchel's charm, too, which few could resist. "Then," Duncan continued, "Satchel got out of the car and was walkin' down the side of the road with the [officer], arm around him. We say, 'Uh-oh, Satchel got him now.' So when Satchel came back to the car, he got in the car and showed us the $50 bill. The guy give it back to him."

Hard-boiled judges also softened in Satchel's presence. When he was with the Marlins in 1958 a Miami magistrate punished his speeding by ordering him to the slammer for twenty days, with two caveats: the sentence would be delayed until after baseball season, and he could get one day less for every win he scored or strikeout he recorded against Negro League rival Luke Easter. In Kansas in 1972 a judge suspended his sentence for a traffic violation and ordered him to sign autographs at the county courthouse in Oskaloosa. "He wasn't here 10 minutes," hizzoner reported, "before every kid in town knew it." And in New Orleans back in 1947, nine highway patrolmen had joined the chase by the time Satchel reached Pelican Stadium. "They followed him into the clubhouse and were talking to him as he was putting on his clothes," remembers Frank Evans, his battery mate. "He pissed off one of the patrolmen who said, 'Tell you what, I heard you pitch no-hitters. I'm going to make a deal with you. If you pitch a no-hitter tonight, we won't give you no ticket.' Satchel went out there and I ain't never seen a man pitch like he did.

Didn't nobody even foul off a ball. They didn't give him no ticket 'cause he pitched a no-hitter."

Those anecdotes, like most passed down in blackball and black America, have a point in addition to a punch line. They show the un-tamed Satchel—taking on cops, jurists, and white America. Yet his defiance remained within the unthreatening domain of traffic law, where whites as well as blacks often test limits and where getting away with it is considered brazen. The final making of the folk hero comes with his thinking that he can, at will, grasp the holy grail of a no-hitter. Then doing it.

Not all his encounters with the law were capricious. Satchel had just struck out six of the nine Homestead Grays he faced one August evening in 1945, and collected his $1,000 paycheck, when he was pulled over by Officer Robert Lewis of Washington's Metropolitan Police Department. Lewis told Satchel he had nearly run over his foot, and then, according to one newspaper account, he called Satchel a "smart black b———." The policeman, who also was black, meted out his punishment then and there: lacerating jabs to the left eye and cheek. Word of the beating quickly spread and the crowd of onlook-ers swelled to a thousand, all of whom worshipped Satchel and were enraged at Officer Lewis. A riot call brought three patrol cars to the scene and calmed the crowd if not the pitcher. "Paige was brooding over the fact that he allowed a man to hit him and get away with it," a second newspaper reported, adding that it was "the first time that it has ever happened to him."

The only long-term damage that time was to Satchel's ego, but not so with an auto incident in Birmingham. "I was ridin' 'round the curve in a Chrysler Imperial I had," the pitcher said. "So was a truck. The other way, y'understand. My face needed eight stitches." The scar on his left cheek never went away.

The same magnetism that won over beefy cops and hard-hearted judges saved the day, and perhaps his life, in the jungles of Venezuela in 1933. His adversaries this time were short, swarthy natives dressed in G-strings who shot poisoned darts at oil workers and liked to watch baseball. "I was on a jackass ridin' around in the jungle sight-seein'," Satchel told *Collier's* twenty years later. "I was wearin' some cream-colored pants, a sport shirt and two-tone shoes, as I rec-ollect. When I come to a clearin' in the forest I thought I'd get off and rest. But the clearin' was jammed with these fans, sittin' around in front of a big grass house and eatin' pig and roots and bugs and all that mess they eat. When they seen me, they grabbed up their blow-guns and aimed right at my new Stetson hat." At first it was a stand-off, him staring at them, them glaring back. Then one dashed into his hut, bringing back a baseball and pointing to it, then to Satchel. Blowguns were lowered. He joined the natives in a meal of pork, bugs, and roots, and gifts were exchanged: his autograph for their blowtube. "I could have been a big man in that outfit if I'd stayed on," he said, "but I had to get on back to the States, where I also had some fans."

Another story line centered around Satchel's longevity on the field, which is fitting for a player who launched his career when Calvin Coolidge was in the White House and ended it when Lyndon Johnson was president. If Randy Johnson was a force of nature when he signed on with the 2009 San Francisco Giants at age forty-five, and Nolan Ryan a medical miracle still pitching in the pros at forty-six, what are we to make of Satchel suiting up for three innings with the Kansas City A's at age fifty-nine? His durability was more as-tounding considering that, for most of his career, he twirled nearly every day on unmanicured fields, without the doctors, trainers, and other pampering enjoyed by Johnson, Ryan, and other Major League pitchers. Journalists likened him to Rip van Winkle, Ol' Man Mose, Grandma Moses, and Moses. Fans and even physicians wanted to know how he did it, which spawned not just a set of rules for staying young but a raft of narratives.

"Methuselah was my first bat boy," Satchel joked. Surveying the excitement over his endurance, he added, "It seems it's as important as the secret of the atomic bomb. . . . The way things are going now pretty soon they'll be givin' wash machines, vacuum cleaners, auto-mobiles and a year's vacation 'round the world for the right answer." Satchel stoked that hoopla by dishing out estimates of his age that were more baffling than his pitches, but *Sports Illustrated* was not de-terred. It published a copy of his birth certificate along with a three-page story in February 1949. "Satch was born in Mobile on July 7, 1906," Arthur P. Glass reported. "So that's that. You can bet on it."

The puzzle did not stay solved for long. Satchel's publicity-conscious owners spun stories making him more ancient and alluring by suggesting he was born no later than 1900. Every few years newspapers or magazines sent a reporter to Mobile to check the records, then trumpeted their unearthing of the birth date that *Sports Illustrated* had already revealed. Satchel, meanwhile, alternatively acknowledged and denied the accuracy of the Mobile certificate, ensuring that the matter of his birth remained as much of an enigma for baseball lovers as whether Babe Ruth pointed beforehand to the spot where he hit a home run in the 1932 World Series. The artifice had become such a part of Satchel's personality that it actually outlived him, with his original gravestone listing the year of his death as 1982 and the year of his birth as "?".

The part of his ageless anatomy that drew the most attention was his velvet arm, and just what it was he rubbed on it before and after games to keep it limber that long. Reporters asked him, then did their own investigations. The secret is chloroform liniment with cologne, announced the *St. Louis Post-Dispatch,* not bothering to explain how the exotic brew could yield more than a sweet smell. *Collier's* begged to differ, although the best it could do was to narrow the formula to kerosene and olive oil, or perhaps wolfbane and wild cherry stems. Too complicated, said *The New York Times.* It's "plain, old-fashioned olive oil." Teammates had their own theories—from whiskey and goose grease, to oil of wintergreen, to rancid water drawn out of an old tree stump. Satchel agreed with everyone. He also offered up multiple choices on where whatever it was came from: the Indians in North Dakota, Big Bill Gatewood in Birmingham, Jewbaby Floyd in Kansas City. So convinced was he of the healing powers of the salve—he called it "cremogesics" or, in lay terms, "foo foo juice"—that he later rubbed it onto his own kids.

The truth about Satchel's arm, like his age, was there to see for anyone not distracted by his storytelling. From collarbone to fingertips, his right limb was the best conditioned on the planet, the product of flinging baseballs every day for forty years. He railed against exercise but did more than anyone by doing his job. It was apparent as soon as he stepped out of the shower: his right arm was half again as big as his left. His wrist, the fulcrum for everything since it had to move nearly as fast as the baseball it released, was Grade A beef. What he rubbed on was subterfuge; what mattered were the muscles and fibers, tendons and tissues. "His pitching arm had a tennis player's forearm," one teammate observed. "When you stood back and saw his two arms it looked like two different guys."

There was no hedging in the debate between fire and ice. He had tried both and was a hot man all the way. He carried a collapsible heat lamp with him on the road (alongside a massage machine). No need for the cold tap when he ran a bath. His showers were so scorching teammates knew not to go near. "He put his arm under there to test it," recalls Yogi Berra, who showered next to him after an All-Star game. "I would have been scalded to death if I put mine under there, but Satchel said, 'That's what keeps me going.' " Dusty Baker, now the manager of the Cincinnati Reds, recalls Satchel's advice half a century ago to "stay out of that training room and don't be putting ice on me." Baker said he has tried both hot and cold, with mixed results. "I don't know if Satchel was right or wrong, but it was right for him."

Satchel was more elusive about what he put into his body. One day he was preaching the wonders of grease and lard, of hot pastrami, hot dogs, and hot tamales. "A man," he said, "needs all the grease he can handle." The next day it was boiled chicken, boiled broccoli, and boiled greens. Friends even told of finding him eating pureed baby food. All those versions hinted at the truth. He ate less fried food in his later years, a concession to ulcers, acid reflux, and other medical terms doctors at the Mayo Clinic attached to the condition he called "stomach miseries." But he never entirely eschewed the skillet and deep fryer. There was nothing better after a game with the Monarchs than a late-night trip to Gates Bar-B-Q and an order of short ends, the tender ribs at the front of a pork slab. At home he relished sizzle-fried chicken. On the road he kept an electric stove in his hotel room to pan fry (in expensive sherry) the catfish he caught or bought. All of it angried up his stomach along with his blood, but that paled next to the fury he displayed when anyone tried to manipulate his diet.

As for washing it down, he liked to portray himself as a teetotaler. The best thing for his balky stomach was goat's milk. When he could not find that he made do with iced milk or hot water with lemon. No tea or coffee, which inflamed his ulcers, and surely no alcohol, or at least not more than a very occasional drink. "Some said he drank heavily," wrote the venerable Negro sportswriter A. S.

"Doc" Young. "But Satch was never drunk, not even during the post-season party when almost everyone on the team got giggly." Roy Walker, who was a boy in Bismarck in the mid-1930s when he got to know the pitcher, remembered differently: "Satchel would often drink too much. So the manager had a guy who would stay with him when he was drinking. After he had a drink or two the night before a ballgame, the man would put him to bed and keep him sober."

Both were right. Satchel drank more when he was younger, spending many a nomadic night with old friends Jack Daniel and Old Taylor. The bottles fit neatly into his suit roll. They were a less neat fit with his later-life determination to clean up his image or with his increasingly sour stomach. He did cut back but never all the way, despite what he said. He also said he did not smoke, which was not true, and on the rare occasion when he admitted he did he said he did not inhale. "I just blow it out my nose." He told those and other stories to the Second International Gerontological Congress when it met in St. Louis in 1951. The doctors were fascinated with the ancient ballplayer and he loved the attention. "Most of you could be between thirty-five and fifty-five," one of the medical men told Satchel, "but your arm doesn't seem to be a day over nineteen." Then Satchel got his say: "I just explained to the gentlemen that the bones running up from my wrist, the fibius, which is the upper bone, and the tiberon, which is the lower bone, was bent out, making more room for my throwin' muscles to move around in there. I attributed most of my long life, and so on and so forth, to them two bones. The gentlemen was amazed to hear about that."

Satchel would have made an even better case study for doctors of heredity and psychology as they waged war over nature versus nurture. Was his pitching prowess a gift of birth? A learned skill? Those were not abstract questions to legions of young pitchers who modeled themselves after him and wanted to know whether they were stuck with the abilities they inherited or could get better. He came down on both sides. "You born with speed, see," Satchel told one interviewer. "You can gather control if you're wild when you come up. . . . I just practiced control. Anything you practice, you begin to become good at." In his memoir he insisted that accuracy as well as speed were there in the womb: "I was born able to throw fast and straight. If you don't believe I came into the world with speed and control stoved in me, look at my brother Wilson. It was stoved up in him, too."

His baseball roommates over the years could have settled the debates over his drinking and other matters of nurture, which is one reason he did not have roommates once he got to be star enough to dictate his terms. Another was so he was free to share his bed when the opportunity arose. He attracted more fawning females, young and old, than Frank Sinatra. He told one gullible teammate that he had sired ninety children over the years and paid $100,000 in maternity bills. But Doc Young says the stories got out of hand. "Gossip-mongers," he wrote, "invented wild tales. . . . One night when Satch was in the company of this writer in his hotel room, someone said he had been seen in a night club with two blondes."

When he had to have a roommate his first choice was his speed-demon friend, Cool Papa Bell. Knowing that Satch loved pulling practical jokes, Cool decided to trick the trickster one night in California in the late 1930s. Cool had gotten to their hotel room early and discovered an electrical short that caused a three-second delay between the time the light was switched off and when it went off. When Satchel arrived, Cool bet that he could shut off the light and make it under the covers before the room went dark. He did, and Satchel was speechless. The pitcher quickly added the tale to his repertoire, showing audiences how fast his buddy Cool Papa was and reminding them how good a storyteller Satchel Paige was. It was almost a half century later, a year before Satchel died, that Cool let him in on the real story and assured him that, however inadvertently, "he's been tellin' the truth all these years."

Other claims made about Satchel, or by him, are more susceptible to yes-or-no analysis. Did he write *FASTBALL* on the sole of his left shoe, forewarning batters? No, although they knew what was coming anyway and were still helpless. Was the batting helmet invented in 1936, when a white team from Borger, Texas, donned them before facing Satchel in the Denver Post Tournament? No, they had been tested in the Majors as early as 1909, although it may have been the first use in the Negro Leagues. Did Satchel try to shake up the opposing team by buzzing them as he was flying in for a barnstorming appearance? "No, unh-unh," says Dick Wilkinson, his pilot for the single flight Satchel lasted. He also never landed in a cornfield, sprung an oil leak, or flew the plane himself. "Someone," testifies Wilkinson, "made it all up and thought they had a good story."

One rumor that was true was that Satchel was even more superstitious than the average ballplayer. Winning meant not just gearing up his windmill delivery but donning the right lucky clothes on the right day. Letting a woman be the first to cross his threshold in the new year could unleash a dozen years of bad luck. He stayed out of sight of cracked mirrors and never let a sweeping broom touch him. Other players might risk tossing their hats on a hotel bed to claim it; Ol' Satchel knew the bum luck that could bring. Tornadoes were scarier still, but there was a remedy: bury an ax in the ground just where the tornado was likely to hit. "The ax," Satchel's son Robert explained, "was supposed to split the tornado in two."

His hunting stories were a mixed bag. He was probably a good enough shot to hit a hawk on the first try with a .45 pistol, the way Monte Irvin said. It is less likely that he and his partner were ambushed by a bear they were tracking on a hunting trip in Alaska. Satchel said he ran back to his hotel while the bear mauled his buddy. A more revealing hunting story was set in the Everglades and told by Buck O'Neil. Heading home after a morning of fishing, Buck, Satchel, and slugger Luke Easter saw their boat encircled by water moccasins. "I grabbed a .22 to shoot the snakes," said Buck, but "Satchel stopped me. 'Put that rifle down, Nancy,' he said. . . . 'If these snakes were hanging around the Sir John Calvert Hotel, sure it'd be okay to kill 'em. But this is *their* domain. We're the intruders. Let's just take our three fish and go home.' "

Buck was the Negro Leagues' most loyal booster, and he savored his anecdotes about Satchel because he knew his friend was blackball writ large. He knew, too, that "the stories about Satchel are legendary, and some of them are even true." Bob Feller was of a similar mind. "Writing a book about Satchel is kind of like writing a book about Cooperstown," says Feller, who has written or cowritten four books. "While it's a great town, Abner Doubleday didn't invent the game of baseball so all of these things they said about it are myths. But I'm glad they have a Hall of Fame in Cooperstown and I'm glad Satchel is in it."

WHAT AN ATHLETE SAYS about what he does helps separate the mere star from the superhero. Josh Gibson did at least as much with the bat as Satchel did with the ball. He hit home runs farther than Babe Ruth and may have slugged more of them. He lived his life large and saw it end even more dramatically and tragically than Satchel's or Babe's. But while Josh resisted touting his glories or telling his story, Satchel relished both. The result: Satchel Paige remains one of the most recognizable personalities in sports while Josh Gibson is largely unknown.

Satchel could hold court on matters ranging from making love to making a boat. He was as agile at verbal sparring as Muhammad Ali and quicker-witted than Yogi Berra. He would begin a road trip sitting alone on the train; by the end the whole team was gathered round to listen, together with Pullman porters and dining car waiters who carried his tales out west and down south. Understanding that sports was part showbiz, part religion, he did more than any player to spread the gospel of baseball and with it the story of Satchel Paige.

Reporters feasted as he twisted stale sayings into artistic aphorisms. What was his philosophy on faith? "Don't pray when it rains if you don't pray when the sun shines." On self-respect? "Ain't no man can avoid being born average, but there ain't no man got to be common." Did he have anything to say about the big three: money, love, and letting loose? "Work like you don't need the money. Love like you've never been hurt. Dance like nobody's watching." As for his love of his sport, "I ain't ever had a job," he said. "I just always played baseball."

Names were another Satchel specialty. Call a fastball a fastball and no one paid attention. Fireball, bullet, and rocket were so hackneyed, even in mid-century, that they seemed flat. Whipsy-dipsy-do was another matter. Satchel loved to riff on his pitches: "I got bloopers, loopers and droopers. I got a jump ball, a be ball, a screw ball, a wobbly ball, a whipsy-dipsy-do, a hurry-up ball, a nothin' ball and a bat dodger. My be ball is a be ball 'cause it 'be' right were I want it, high and inside. It wiggles like a worm. Some I throw with my knuckles, some with two fingers. My whipsy-dipsy-do is a special fork ball I throw underhand and sidearm that slithers and sinks. I keep my thumb off the ball and use three fingers. The middle finger sticks up high, like a bent fork."

Fans loved it, so this bard of baseball gave them more. There was his Barber Pitch, which furnished batters who leaned in too close with a razorlike shave. His Titty Pitch nipped their chest while the Bow Tie snipped their Adam's apple. He stayed up all night dreaming up his Nightmare Pitch. His fastball came in several sizes: Long Tom was the hardest, Little Tom slightly softer. If a batter knew to look, he could tell Tom was on his way when Satchel pursed his lower lip. The Trouble Ball was so slow that hitters thought it might never arrive; the Wobbly Ball was how a knuckleball looked from home plate. The more reaction his names drew, the more creative he got, giving birth to the Four-day Rider, Slow Gin Fizz, Butterfly, Step-n-Pitch-It, Eephus, Thoughtful Stuff, Two-hump Blooper, Midnight Creeper, Submariner, Sidearmer, Alley Oops, Drop Ball, Single Curve, Double Curve, and Triple Curve.

Sportswriters had trouble keeping track of his labels. Catchers did not try. "I don't know what they meant," admitted Joe Greene, Satchel's receiver for eight years with the Monarchs. Slow Robinson also caught him, and said, "He had a way of naming pitches because it made a good story. People loved it. . . . But as far as separate signals for Long Tom and the rest, that was just Satchel talking. He loved to tell stories. To this day, I still don't know which one Long Tom was."

Satchel's own name was a yardstick of his lore. Woody Allen and Mia Farrow were so taken with the pitcher that they named their son Satchel. Spike Lee and his wife, Tonya Lewis, also borrowed Satchel's name, but for their daughter. Tom "Satch" Sanders, a linchpin of Boston Celtics championship teams in the 1960s, took on his handle in middle school. "There weren't that many outstanding black athletes acknowledged then in the media," says Sanders, and Satchel Paige was his favorite. Hitting a homer off Paige was a career maker for anyone skilled enough to manage it; even striking out ensured a story for life. Fans wanted to touch him, like they might Superman or the Lone Ranger, to test if he was real and hope the magic rubbed off. Hank Aaron was not easily impressed, but he was with his fellow Mobile native: "There was something about the man that made me believe in him. He was brilliant. A lot of people might not understand how a man who talked and carried on the way Satchel did could be brilliant, but coming from the same background, I understood him. Believe me, Satchel Paige had life figured out."

Satchel became a standard and namesake for ballplayers and baseball buffs. He laid down his rules and imparted his proverbs. He anthropomorphized his pitches. It all helped define the Paige mystique, but it was not enough. So he bought a typewriter and took time off from pitching to sketch his story in a ninety-six-page memoir titled *Pitchin' Man,* which came out in 1948. Fourteen years later he did it again, in a 295-page version called *Maybe I'll Pitch Forever.* Not bad for a ballplayer who was schooled in a reformatory and spelled the name of his benefactor and boss, J. L. Wilkinson, "Wilkson." Unlettered yes, but not unlearned. The nitty-gritty composing, of course, was done by two ghostwriters, the first a former sportswriter for the *Cleveland News* and the second from the *St. Louis Post-Dispatch.* They corrected his spelling, cleaned up his grammar and diction, and filled in the missing words, phrases, and ideas, much the way Richard Donovan had with his *Collier's* rules for how to stay young.

The autobiographies were like long yarns. They were written in the homespun, colloquial tone that Satchel spoke, only more so. Every phrase had a word ending in an apostrophe, as in "I was a regular travelin' man, followin' that buck wherever it did show, jumpin' to greener pastures whenever they put out that green." Largely missing were expressions that punctuated his oral histories such as "ain't no maybe so about it," "far as that concerned," and "if I'm lying I'm dying." Some passages read like a white man trying to sound like a Negro, which was inevitable, black critics said, when Satchel chose white collaborators for both books. The first—which in later printings had a publisher's note, three forewords, a preface, an introduction, and three appendixes—was impressionistic and cursory. The second attempted a more complete accounting of Satchel's exploits on the field and off, along with his take on everything from his marriages and divorces to his battles with team owners and Jim Crow.

A third book, *Satchel Paige's America,* was a pseudo-memoir. The author, William Price Fox, neither took notes nor turned on a tape recorder even though many of his 142 pages quoted Satchel directly. He also waited nearly thirty years—until 2005—to publish his recollections. "If I taped him he went flat and ordinary and almost uninteresting," wrote Fox, a writer in residence at the University of

South Carolina. "And if I took notes, he'd read what I was writing and start editing himself." After a week of drinking with Satchel, listening to him, and visiting with him and Lahoma, Fox explains, looking back, "I just knew how he sounded." Fox promised Satchel not to mention his smoking, his age, his lady friends, or other touchy topics—"I was determined not to do anything to do him any harm"—and he did keep such references to a minimum.

While the words were not always Satchel's, the three books of reminiscences, like Donovan's rules, did accurately represent the pitcher's thinking. Jack Smith, a *Los Angeles Times* sports columnist who blew the whistle on the rules' true authorship twenty-seven years after *Collier's* published them, imagined that his friend Donovan was "in such psychological and spiritual rapport with Paige that he was somewhat in the position of Moses receiving the Ten Commandments; a mere medium; and that Paige himself was the Source." Fox says that he had internalized Satchel's voice and spirit. David Lipman, the as-told-to writer for Satchel's longest and most thorough memoir—*Maybe I'll Pitch Forever*—says that he, too, tried to be true to his muse. "Much of the memoir was in response to questions I posed," Lipman explains, "and once you got him talking, Satchel was quite a talker. . . . He was articulate, he just wasn't Ivy League articulate." Lipman concedes he did some "dressing up, plugging in a word here or there, obviously literary license was taken." Not much license was needed, he adds, because "over the years Satchel had been interviewed often enough that you could come up with some real gems attributed to him."

Satchel had indeed done endless interviews. He was cited more than seven thousand times in major white and black papers from *The New York Times* and *The Washington Post* to the *Chicago Defender* and *The Pittsburgh Courier.* Generally it was in the sports sections, but what he said spilled onto the business pages and even into editorials. He might be the most quoted athlete in the history of sports. The question is, were the gems he offered up accurate? The answer: sometimes. Stories of his pitching brilliance everywhere from Chattanooga to Birmingham and Bismarck were true blue. Ones about his beginnings in Mobile, early marriages, and other personal matters were a mix of recounting the past and reconfiguring it. Then there were the inventions—inflated margins of victory, conflated dates and circumstances, and tales like the ones about his 1942 face-off against Josh Gibson that were real only in snippets and perhaps in Satchel's mind.

That did not stop reporters from publishing them verbatim. There were too few definitive sources against which to cross-check facts and too little inclination to try. Satchel was a masterful raconteur and a master of indirection. When he told the stories orally, listeners could see the glint in his eye; a wink and a nod were tougher to convey on the printed page. Unraveling the tales today we see that many were handed down like in the children's game of telephone, where a phrase whispered from urchin to urchin to urchin emerges barely recognizable. When the pitcher played the game, it was Satchel to Satchel to Satchel, but the ending still differed each time. Once a sportswriter put to pen one of Satchel's versions, it became mythic. Repeat a myth often enough and it becomes truth. Those crooked renderings found their way into Satchel's memoirs, leaving them as a blend of factual recounting and errors of fact.

Why did Satchel feel the need to inflate? He did it because reshaping history was intoxicating and empowering. It was the same insurgence that saw him defy traffic laws and the laws of nature, lie about his age and his wives, and adopt as his own a ghostwriter's rules for clean living. He did it because his memory faltered over the years, and he had accomplished so much and told his story so often that he believed many of his own adornments. He did it because he had to. White stars like Dizzy Dean and Bob Feller knew the mainstream press would fan their legend. Satchel had to stump for himself. Enlarging his narrative was meant to ensure that America would never forget him.

It worked. That very ambiguity—our not knowing where reality left off and embellishment began—helped catapult Satchel from the realm of hero to the rarefied universe of icon. In that respect he was like Babe Ruth. Both rose above reform school roots. Both were boyish men with oversize appetites in everything from food to women to sports. Both understood Satchel's seventh rule for living: do things so big they invite exaggeration, ballyhoo what you have done, then let the press and the public weave it into lore.

CHAPTER 11

Maybe I'll Pitch Forever

"People think Satch is either rich or dead."

IT WAS HIS MOMENT of majesty. Here he was on the dais at the Baseball Hall of Fame in Cooperstown, New York, ready to be enshrined as a diamond demigod. The White House had telegraphed offering President Nixon's congratulations and saying, "If you still persist in not looking back, your many friends and admirers are pleased to do it for you." Seven white heroes were being honored, too, but it was the black flamethrower with the horn-rimmed glasses almost everyone had come to see this August morning in 1971. When Satchel makes it, newspapers across America trumpeted, so do the Pittsburgh Crawfords, the Birmingham Black Barons, and a lineup of black stars from Moses Fleetwood Walker to Johnny Schoolboy Taylor.

Even as he relished the limelight, familiar voices dueled in Satchel's head. Should he be grateful that the lords of hardball were finally acknowledging that blackball had brilliant players, or should he resent them—and all of America—for making him pitch his best ball in the shadows? Was what counted that he was the first vintage Negro Leaguer to be voted into this most exclusive club and the only pitcher ever to make it with a losing record in the Majors? Or was it that the Hall had tried to banish him to a separate and unequal wing?

Getting here had not been easy. He pitched his heart out during twenty years in the Negro Leagues, then reminded the Majors of all that he could do at an age when most players were feeding beer bellies and watching from the bleachers. Supporters helped force the doors open for him at Cooperstown. Bill Veeck never stopped reminding baseball why its conscience should be guilty, while Bowie Kuhn, the new commissioner, worked from the inside to change people's minds. The staunchly Republican Ted Williams led the push, taking time out during his own 1966 Hall induction to urge "that Satchel Paige and Josh Gibson somehow will be inducted here as symbols of the great Negro players who are not here."

The press beat the drums for Satchel for a full generation, just as it had agitated to lower the color bar. "If you believe Leroy Robert Paige of the St. Louis Browns belongs in Baseball's Hall of Fame, you had better start writing to your favorite sports columnist about it right now," Ed Fitzgerald wrote in *Sport* in 1952. "He won't have a Chinaman's chance of making it if you don't turn on the heat and turn it on good." Twenty years later the Hall relented, sort of. It would let in one black a year based on his record in the old Negro Leagues, starting of course with Satchel, but it would be to a wing separate from other honorees. "This notion of Jim Crow in Baseball's Heaven is appalling," Jim Murray wrote in 1971 in the *Los Angeles Times*. "What is this—1840? Either let him in the front of the Hall—or move the damn thing to Mississippi."

Satchel did not need white scribes to tell him how much it hurt to be exiled to the Hall's black ghetto. Yet having endured a lifetime of being locked out of organized baseball, Satchel saw this opening—even through the back door—as progress. He also needed the world to grant an old man his day in the sun. So he played along, telling the media through tightened lips, "I'm proud to be wherever they put me in the Hall of Fame." It was left to friends to vent the resentment that Satchel would acknowledge later. "Some dark night," confided Veeck, "I'm going to sneak into Cooperstown and find out where Satchmo's plaque is and put it in the front room where it belongs."

Now, six months after they announced his election to the Hall,

Satchel was in Cooperstown for the actual induction. The public had weighed in with outrage at the spectacle of a segregated baseball museum, forcing baseball's rulers to agree to hang his plaque alongside all the rest. He quieted his competing instincts by siding, as he always had, with moderation over militancy. "Thank you, Commissioner and my fans and baseball players from all around as far as Honolulu, Mexico, and I don't know where the rest of 'em come from. I know they're my friends, I know that," Satchel said as he looked out at the mostly white audience of 2,500. "I got the best names called to me since I've been here."

His remarks were touching and funny. He talked about barnstorming across America in cars so tightly packed that his knees were "sticking up in front of me. For five years I didn't know where I was going. I couldn't see." He talked about the enigma of his age, of pitching 165 games in a row, and of never looking back. He was not just in his element, he was in heaven. His seven-minute speech was interrupted thirteen times by laughter. "I was called some bad names back then," Satchel said, recounting the years of segregation and discrimination. But today, his day, he declared himself "the proudest man in the place."

He was more pointed and more political after the formal ceremonies, when his heart took over from his script. This proud black man had been at the forefront of interracial baseball. He had pointed the way toward free agency. Why, he asked now, should blacks like him who had proven their prowess as players not be hired as coaches and managers? "I could manage easy—I've been in baseball 40 years. And I would want to manage," he told reporters. Then he answered his question in a way that unsettled the baseball elite, which had hoped that Satchel's entry into the Hall would divert attention from a history of exclusion to its belated gesture of inclusion. "I don't think the white is ready to listen to the colored yet. That's why they're afraid to get a black manager—they're afraid everybody won't take orders from him."

His critique did not end there. These were years when Satchel was less active, which meant more time to stew on what had gone right in his life and how he had been wronged. When he was invited back to Cooperstown for a luncheon following the induction of other ex-players, he was even less inclined to deflect his hurt with humor.

"They asked me to get up and say a few words. I did," he recalled years later. "I started telling them that I thought too many good young black ball players were being kept down in the minor leagues instead of being brought up to the majors. There was this assistant to the commissioner there. I won't use his name. He interrupted me and said, 'Satch, sit down. This is no place for that kind of talk.' I sat down. They keep asking me to come back but I've never been back to Cooperstown."

MOST HARDBALL LEGENDS had hung up their cleats long before their plaque was posted on the wall at Cooperstown, but not Satchel. He never retired, not really. Baseball was what made him special. It had lifted him out of Mount Meigs and Mobile and was the only way he had ever made a living. Too late now to look for a new career, not with seven young kids at home depending on him, eight counting Shirley, the daughter Lahoma had before she met him.

His pitching these days was not poetry. There was little steam left in his fastball and not much bend on his curve. He could still locate his pitches over a matchbook and fool batters with his hesitation delivery, but he was mixing in more of the soft, slow stuff that sportswriters called junk. The main thing now was showing up, which was a feat for a man of sixty. His thick spectacles made him look more scholarly and less athletic. His dentures sat soaking in a glass in the locker room. On the field he wore a long-sleeved shirt even in sweltering heat. The formula now was an inning or two of pitching, then off to the next stop, with fewer total innings than before and more rest in between. Teams sometimes carried him there in style, in a stretch limousine with a chauffeur; more often he drove his own dirt-caked station wagon.

Occasionally there was a reminder of the old nobility, like the day in the mid-1960s when he blew into Jefferson City, Missouri, in a pink Thunderbird convertible. His black barnstormers were taking on the Jefferson City Redbirds, who had just one black player, a young second baseman named Logan. Satchel's catcher told Logan to expect a half-speed pitch right down the middle of the plate. It was a batter's dream and Logan connected for a single. "Satchel wanted to give him a chance to hit," says Bill Clark, a professional scout who was home plate umpire that day. The next batter was a decidedly different story—a "big old boy who had some power, although his other tools were pretty well disintegrated," recalls Clark. "He said he was going to show Satch how it's done." Instead it was Satchel putting on the show. His first pitch was a no-windup fastball, thrown from a standstill. Wishhhh. He knew he could no longer blow the ball past hitters consistently, but with the occasional pitch he could and did. The next toss was a big, old sweeping curve, for a second strike. Finally he used his standby: the hesitation pitch. "I swear the guy swung three times before the ball got to home plate," says Clark. "The batter stood there hammering the plate with his bat and glaring at Satch. Satchel said, 'Hey, big ole fat white boy. If you'ze as good as you think you was, you wouldn't be here in Jefferson City.' I thought we were going to have a riot. Then Satch grabbed his jacket, got into his car, and I haven't seen him since. That's pretty much the way Satchel lived his life."

He rose to the occasion again during one of his many pilgrimages to Canada. In Kindersley, a small town in western Saskatchewan, Satchel managed to pitch a full nine innings. In the seventh, the manager of the local team inserted as a pinch hitter a four-year-old who stood three feet high. "Everyone thought that Satch would lob the ball, or perhaps walk him," says Bob Joyce, who was calling the balls and strikes. "But he threw three perfect fastballs, knee high, and I had to call the kid out. Imagine the strike zone at 60 feet, 6 inches." In the same game Satchel singled, then took a lead off first. "Kindersley attempted a pick-off," says Joyce. "They had him by three feet. He went into a kind of a stutter-step dance with his foot back and forth. He mesmerized the first baseman who was supposed to tag him, then stepped back on the bag. He said, 'You'all had me boy, but you didn't get me.' The man was a pure delight."

Satchel took special delight in teasing his fans, like when he passed off as his son a pitcher as tall and lanky as him. Sherman Cottingham had played with Satchel on the Monarchs, then joined him during summer barnstorming in Saskatchewan in the 1960s. Cottingham was working on his doctorate, and was just the blend of student-athlete Satchel hoped his own young sons would become. But he knew that his boys, even if they took to baseball, would never get there in time to play with him. So, as Cottingham recalls, "Satchel claimed me as his son. I was on him all the time getting as much information as I could. It didn't dawn on me at the time how valuable and rewarding it would be to have the opportunity to spend time with this man."

In a career full of milestones—some for being first, others for how long he lasted—one that stood out was the June 21, 1966, contest between the Peninsula Pilots and the Greensboro Patriots. Satchel pitched just two innings for Peninsula and gave up two runs on four straight singles. His appearance was a publicity stunt, with only 3,118 fans there to watch at the Pilots' ballpark in Hampton, Virginia. But it was the pitcher's last official game in organized baseball. It also was especially sweet because, eleven years before, Satchel was supposed to play for Greensboro but was barred by Jim Crow edicts.

Two weeks later Jerry McGinn bore witness to what Satchel had left in his geriatric right arm. The UPI reporter abandoned his journalism colleagues, who were battling Satchel in an exhibition game in Spokane, Washington. His assignment was to write a first-person story, and the optimal angle for that was from behind the plate. "The reason this story is three days old," he explained to readers, "is that my hand finally became un-puffed to the point that I could type." McGinn was still talking about his outing as Satchel's catcher forty years later, recalling that the pitcher "had a great smile and beautiful eyes. That smile wasn't just nice or obligatory. It was sincere, caring and complete. He smiled after a good pitch, I assume at not just the perfection of the delivery, but the response at the batting end, too. It was a very self-satisfied and friendly smile. He was enjoying himself. Immensely. He was enjoying the challenge, the communications between two artists, the contest. Each and every pitch, no matter what the outcome."

The smiling and teasing came less often as Satchel approached, then passed, the milepost of sixty. Dave Shury recalls collecting tickets at Abbott Field in North Battleford, Saskatchewan, when two beat-up cars pulled up and a dozen black ballplayers poured out, Satchel in front. "He readily admitted to me that they were out of money and were supposed to be in British Columbia that afternoon," said Shury, an ex-ballplayer and baseball historian. "They did not have gas to get there. The team was absolutely destitute and had not had a decent meal for several days. Keith and I invited them into the ball park and I sat with Satchel during the rest of the game. . . . The North Battleford team put Satchel's team up in a local hotel and saw that they were fed. . . . Enough money was raised to get them back to the States."

Satchel drew the line at clowning, or at least he tried to. "I ain't no clown. I ain't no end man in no Vaudeville show," he wrote in his first memoir in 1948. "I'm a baseball pitcher and winning baseball games is serious business." The truth was, there was always pressure to entertain in the Negro Leagues and even in the Majors. Gus Greenlee promised that Satchel would strike out the first nine batters he faced; Bill Veeck dropped him onto the diamond from a helicopter. Charlie Finley set him up in the bullpen with a rocker and a nurse. As masterful as his owners were at hamming it up, he was better—calling in his fielders, talking trash to Josh Gibson, stretching out his walk to the mound until every fan in the stadium noticed and applauded.

Now any pretense was gone of a distinction between entertainer and end man. He was playing alongside a contortionist, a clown prince, and a thirty-one-inch midget who supposedly saved the team hotel expenses by sleeping in a suitcase. His new club's very name—the Indianapolis Clowns—made clear its mission. They were the Harlem Globetrotters of baseball, combining breathtaking skill with belly-laugh antics. In their heyday the Clowns boasted players of the stature of Hank Aaron, but that was fifteen years earlier. By the mid-1960s the Clowns were all that remained of a blackball world bankrupted by integration. And the only big name left was Satchel Paige.

He had no choice but to join them. The Clowns offered fifty dollars a night for pitching a single inning and Satchel needed steady employment. "How we gonna work it?" he asked Ed Hamman, the team's owner and general manager. "Well, I've got the shortest contract in baseball," Hamman answered. "No show, no dough." Satchel: "You're kinda hard on a guy, aren't you? They sure weren't that hard on me in the big leagues." Hamman: "This is *not* the big leagues. This is the *bus* league. As far as I'm concerned, you're just like any other rookie. You got to make that bus."

In reality, Hamman was more solicitous of his star and crowd pleaser. No sooner did the team show up in a town than Satchel was dropped at the nearest stream with a line and a hook. Once practice was over the angler-pitcher was picked up and inserted into the game—early if the crowd came early, later if fans were late taking their seats. Sometimes he threw for the Clowns, other times for their nightly opponent, the Baltimore Stars. Whoever he was playing for, Satchel was allowed to wear his old Cleveland Indians uniform. "Sixty years old," marveled Hamman, "and he could still get 'em out. He threw them dipsy-doodles."

The spectacle of this icon tossing for a team of clowns was disturbing to some sportswriters. "The Clown infielders wore multi-colored pullovers, a midget batter walked and scored and, in the middle of it all, Satchel Paige made his 10,318th start," the Philadelphia *Sunday Bulletin* wrote in 1966. "There was a sadness watching perhaps the greatest righthanded pitcher in history allowing a run in two innings of the Barnum and Bailey atmosphere. It was like asking Sir Laurence Olivier to play lead in My Mother, The Car." *The Sporting News* was even bleaker in its report the next year: "[Satchel] squinted through bifocals from the mound and it took him longer than usual to read the catcher's signs. The uniform was wrinkled and dusty and he looked rather pathetic. The stuff is gone from his once strong right arm. . . . Minutes after the game, Paige climbed aboard the old bus with his teammates. He was off to Rockford, Ill., for another game. It would be another night in a cheap hotel, a quick meal at a second-class restaurant and probably another ball park with mosquitoes but not a dressing room."

While his young teammates on the Clowns were at times frustrated with his curmudgeonliness, they traded stories about him for decades. James Alderman, who was a teenager when he was Satchel's receiver, recalls how the antique pitcher would "sit all the way in the back of the bus, take his shoes off, and we'd drink Canadian whiskey. He was a comic on the bus." But he also remembers that Satchel "always wanted us to pray. He knew God." "Birmingham Sam" Brison had a less reverent recollection: "One time Satchel and I were in some club in Mobile, and this young woman, you know, she comes up to the Satch and tries to set him up. Tells him it costs him twenty bucks. Satch says, 'Hell, honey, if you can get this ole pole up I'll give ya fifty.' "

Satchel generally took this phase of his baseball life in stride, explaining that returning to the road with these performer-players was sending his kids through school. On occasion, however, the Clowns' coffee-and-cake circuit was more than he could stomach. "I'm just an associate member of this organization," he told reporters during an exhibition game in Beloit, Wisconsin. "It's a real crummy one. I don't even have a place to dress. It's this way in every town. I'm tired of it. I'm going to tell the world soon what I think about this outfit."

The truth was he could not afford to tell anyone how he felt any more than he was doing. He needed the job too much, the same way he needed one with the basketball-playing Globetrotters. He had worked on and off with the Trotters dating back to the 1940s, pitching for or against their baseball team as part of his association with Globetrotter founder, owner, and coach Abe Saperstein. Now, in the mid-1960s, his role with Saperstein's basketball team was more clearly promotional and comedic. Late in the game he would serve up a thirty-inch gopher ball to funnyman Meadowlark Lemon, who circled bases only he could see. Before and after, Satchel would sign autographs and wave to the crowd. His title was assistant business manager but his real role was in PR, landing in towns before the team did and doing whatever it took to gin up fan and press interest.

His unwritten assignment was as a role model. "We were in California at a Sambo's pancake house, having lunch," recalls Lee Talboys, a white musician who did promotional work for the Globetrotters alongside Satchel. "A guy looked at us, a mixed race group of players and staff sitting in a booth, and said, 'You've got to be careful anymore what you say. You can't use that "nigger" word anymore.' I had some rings on and I very quietly slipped them off, expecting a fight. Satchel very slowly shook his head from side to side and said, 'No altercations, Lee.' Suddenly two friends of the loud-mouthed guy grabbed him, saying, 'Let's get him out of here.'

"Abe Saperstein had told us he didn't ever want to pick up a paper and read about someone affiliated with the Trotters involved in some altercation. That would defeat the whole purpose of our spreading a little good feeling across the country," adds Talboys. Satchel understood that without being told. It was what he had been doing for even longer than the Globetrotters.

Playing for laughs with the Clowns and Trotters was not the work

Satchel had anticipated for his golden years. He knew he was too old to return to barnstorming, but also knew he had more pitching acumen than anyone in the game. In 1963 he got *Sports Illustrated* to publish his phone number—Wabash 1-2684—and his offer that "if any of those big league boys want to call they can reverse the charges." Two years later he, Lahoma, and his eldest child, Pamela, sent out letters to everyone in baseball asking for work. Anything at all, from player to manager to coach. "You wanta know how many even answered my letters about a steady job?" he asked. "Just one. That's Mr. Charles O. Finley."

Finley had more in mind than Satchel's three-inning performance against the Red Sox that summer of 1965. He knew the pitcher was just 158 days shy of the five-year requirement to collect a Major League pension, and he knew how much that monthly check of $250 would mean to him. So he proposed keeping Satchel on with the Athletics as a pitching coach. Finley had to drop the offer when he realized that Satchel already had legal commitments to Saperstein and the Anchorage owners, but the A's owner helped his favorite charity case pay back cash he had withdrawn from the pension plan so that he was paid up for his four-plus years of service. Veeck also did what he could, asking every team in baseball to hire Satchel as a coach. None would, even when Veeck offered to share the cost. "You know what some of them said to me? They said 'he's eccentric,' " Veeck recounted to columnist Jimmy Breslin. "I told them, 'He's not wealthy enough to be an eccentric.' "

A new sugar daddy stepped up in 1968. William Bartholomay was a Chicago insurance executive who in 1962 bought the Milwaukee Braves and in 1966 moved them to Atlanta. Bartholomay cared about Satchel enough to hire him as a pitcher-coach-trainer for long enough to meet his pension needs. In case there was any doubt about what he was doing, he assigned Satchel number 65, the age at which his retirement salary would kick in. "Baseball would have been guilty of negligence should it not assure this legendary figure a place in the pension plan," the owner said at the signing in 1968. Looking back forty years on, Bartholomay says Satchel justified his faith by performing sensationally as a goodwill ambassador, the way he had for Saperstein and his other benefactors.

He did it partly by signing autographs and spending time with fans. The team was new to Atlanta, and its fans were new to the team and often to baseball itself. Satchel helped with the adjustment. An even richer dividend from hiring him came during the summer of 1968, when riots were raging and cities burning in the wake of Martin Luther King, Jr.'s assassination. Having a bridge builder such as Satchel was reassuring to Atlanta and to the Braves. He was not the only black on the team, just the best known and most trusted. He had suffered the Jim Crow injustices King railed against and embodied the preacher's dream of an integrated America. "He came to us four months after the King funeral in Atlanta," says Bartholomay. "Those were pretty tough times for African Americans and the country in its entirety. Satchel understood that. He helped in a way that went way beyond baseball."

Life with Satchel brought new touches to Atlanta's start-up franchise. A rocking chair was installed in front of his locker. He had young teammates toting his fishing gear and serving as gophers. Names were more twisted than ever, intentionally or otherwise. "He called me Daffy," says Dusty Baker. "I said, 'My name is Dusty.' He said, 'Daffy, I know what your name is.' " In spring training Satchel lived with friends, as was his wont, but this time it was at a funeral home. On the bus he broke the mournful quiet after painful losses, getting the team laughing with tales of Cool Papa Bell hitting a pop-up so high that it took a full day for it to fall back to earth. On the plane he still carried his typewriter, along with a suitcase, garment bag, and attaché case. Phil Niekro, the world's most accomplished knuckleballer, recalls Satchel sitting at the back of the plane by himself with his case on the pullout tray. "I was going to the bathroom and he said, 'Niekro, sit down for a second. Do you drink?' I said that I have one now and then and he said, 'What would you like?' Anything I wanted was there in his little case." What impressed the Torre brothers was Satchel's attitude about life. "He was always sort of being thankful for just being alive. He was thankful he got the opportunity to play in the Majors even as late as he got it," says Frank, who had played first base for the Braves back when they were in Milwaukee. "It was all about life and Satchel enjoyed living," agrees Joe, a catcher and first baseman for Atlanta who is now the manager of the Los Angeles Dodgers. "Satchel never stopped thinking young."

They called Satchel a trainer, but "he didn't do any training," recalls Dave Pursley, the Braves' real trainer. What he wanted to do was pitch. Bartholomay was concerned about his eyesight, "which was going pretty rapidly. We worried that he wouldn't see a line drive coming back to him." But Satchel proved that even at the age of sixty-two the crack of a bat was enough to tell him where the ball was headed, and he pitched a couple of innings in an exhibition game for the Braves' highest-level minor league team, Triple-A Richmond, when they played the parent club. It was a face-off for the ages when Atlanta outfielder Hank Aaron stepped to the plate: history's greatest hurler against its greatest hitter. Satchel was smiling as he unleashed his first one, a slow arcing pitch. Hank had stepped out of the box, but too late. Strike one. The next was slower still. Hank dropped his bat into the dirt in disgust. Strike two. The future home run champ checked his swing on the following pitch, making the count one ball, two strikes. "Now Aaron, still glowering at his old friend, stepped forward in the box as far as rules would allow," Wilt Browning, who covered the Braves for *The Atlanta Journal,* remembered years later. "Again Paige's pitch came floating toward the plate out of the fading light of early evening. Aaron tried to time the pitch. He made a mighty swing. The ball clicked weakly against the top of Aaron's bat and flew softly, with little arc, to the waiting third baseman for the out. The old man pounded his bony fist into his glove with the sort of youthful joy all of us could understand."

Satchel's time with the Braves was a last hurrah in baseball. It made him one of only three black coaches in the Major Leagues. Yet just as Satchel was qualifying for the five years of service that baseball required for a pension, baseball lowered the threshold to four years. It was the story of his life: the rules changed for the better, but it generally occurred too late for him to benefit.

His dream was to be the first black manager, or at least a serious pitching coach. He wanted players to value him for what he knew rather than owners for his fan appeal. He never got that chance. His last jobs in baseball were ever more about puffery. In 1976 A. Ray Smith, an owner in the bigger-than-life style of Bill Veeck and Charlie Finley, hired Satchel as vice president for sales and promotion of his Triple-A Tulsa Oilers. Satchel moved with Smith and the team to

New Orleans, where they became the Pelicans, then to Springfield (Illinois), where they changed their feathers to Redbirds, and finally to Louisville. Whatever the city and title, Satchel's duties were the same: set up operations at a red-and-white table tucked between the beer machine and popcorn maker, preach to anyone who would listen about the sanctity of the double steal and the blessedness of the bunt, and give away autographed business cards inscribed on the back with his Rules for Livin' the Good Life. He was, in the words of *New York Times* columnist Dave Anderson, "vice president in charge of himself."

At least Satchel was able to stay connected to the game, which remained out of reach for most of his fellow stars of blackball. After he stopped playing, Cool Papa Bell spent twenty-one years as a custodian and night watchman at city hall in St. Louis. John Henry "Pop" Lloyd, the greatest shortstop and perhaps the greatest all-around player in Negro Leagues history, became a janitor in the post office and public schools in Atlantic City. Ted Page, a standout on the Homestead Grays and Pittsburgh Crawfords, ran a bowling alley in Pittsburgh and was beaten to death with a baseball bat during a burglary at his home. While some Negro Leaguers translated their baseball experiences into careers as preachers, teachers, or coaches, more ended up in the bottom-tier jobs that were the bane of black males.

Between baseball jobs Satchel tried anything he could to cash in on his celebrity in a way that fed, clothed, and housed his family. His most far-fetched venture was as a deputy in the civil division of the sheriff's office serving Kansas City. Everything he knew about police work was as an offender, not an enforcer. He had been arrested as a youth. He was stopped repeatedly by the police as an adult, for offenses ranging from speeding (guilty as charged) to murder (flattered to have been asked, since the real murderer was less than half his age). None of that mattered to longtime sheriff Arvid "Hippo" Owsley, who in 1968 hired Satchel on the spot when he asked for work and paid him $300 a month plus a $75 car allowance. "He can wrap up the papers he serves and throw them like baseballs, if he wants to," the rotund sheriff told reporters. Satchel did not stay at the job long but while there he counseled youthful inmates on how to use their time behind bars constructively, the way he had. Even his work as a process server became an adventure: "I figure some of them are going to be mad about having to appear in court. But after I show them my deputy sheriff's identification card they push court action out of their minds. They want to stand there for hours and talk baseball with me."

A week before he signed on with the sheriff he filed to run for the Missouri legislature. A white political boss figured he could exploit Satchel's popularity to unseat the incumbent, who ran a black political organization and, like Satchel, was a hero in black Kansas City. Heroism was one thing, but begging for votes and keeping to a campaign schedule were too much for a man genetically programmed to disregard calendars, clocks, and political politesse. "I've got about as much right in politics," he said, "as a mule has in a garage." So clumsy was Satchel's bid that he filed in the wrong district, then took a job with the sheriff despite merit system rules limiting the political activity of county workers. No one seemed to care, least of all the white sheriff, who said that "the merit system doesn't mean anything." Reporting on what it called Satchel's "reluctant" candidacy, the black-focused magazine *Jet* wrote that "he is not making any speeches. He does not have radio and TV broadcasts telling you how great it would be if he were elected, but when you drive through Kansas City you do see posters with pictures of Paige on them and he is wearing a baseball uniform. Occasionally, you see a bumper sticker saying 'Let Satch Go To Bat For You.' " As expected, Satchel was trounced, garnering 382 votes to his opponent's 3,870. His mind was taken off his loss when, a week later, Bartholomay called with his offer to work for the Atlanta Braves.

Movies made more sense than politics. Satchel's entire life was a script in the making, so when Hollywood beckoned, he ran. The first call came in 1949, when Republic Pictures made a film about a wayward youth brought back to righteousness by the world champion Cleveland Indians. *The Kid from Cleveland* could have been about Satchel himself, except that the boy was white and in that pre–civil rights era the studio knew better than to build an all-American fable around a Negro. The cast featured a lineup of ballplayers playing themselves in bit roles, including the easiest to recognize, Satchel Paige.

He made it onto the screen again in the 1959 film *The Wonderful Country,* a Western starring Robert Mitchum and Julie London. The movie was packed with action as Mitchum, an aging gunslinger, escaped to Mexico after killing his father's murderer, then gave up his gunslinging for the love of London. Satchel played a minor and forgettable role as an army sergeant leading a black unit. To him, however, it was the start of a promising career in the motion picture industry, which he fittingly called "pitchers." He had never been on a horse before, served in the army, or acted. No problem. "A trick rider showed me how to ride a horse," he said. "I learn in a week an' a half." As for acting, "the director sent me the book and I learn my lines by heart. . . . He say I gotta learn to look sad, which I look sad all the time. He say I gotta learn to cry which is very hard for me, since nobody has seen me cry for a long time. But after I learn I find pitcher-makin' fascinatin'. I love it. I'd like to do more of it if they want me."

No one did. His cameo in the cowboy film had shown Hollywood that the stage where Satchel belonged was the pitcher's mound. Still, popular culture's interest in him kept expanding. One place he turned up was books, both fiction and nonfiction. He earned a full chapter, "The Travelin' Man," in Robert Peterson's 1970 *Only the Ball Was White,* the first in a series of titles that resurrected the wonders of Negro baseball. He was the centerpiece in other works, for children and adults, from *Josh and Satch,* which featured his on-field exploits, to *Don't Look Back,* which took in his whole life, to an entire treatise devoted to his wit and wisdom entitled *Satchel Sez.* Novelists used his life as a point of departure in books such as the 1992 *The Day Satchel Paige and the Pittsburgh Crawfords Came to Hertford, N.C.* and the 2007 *Satchel Paige: Striking Out Jim Crow.* No other Negro Leaguer came close to the written words devoted to Satchel.

Playwrights were equally enraptured. They wrote him into the intersection of sports and society, and of Jim Crow and the Black Panthers. "Life was for havin' fun," the Paige character said in a 1997 drama, *Satchel: A Requiem for Racism.* "I always thought that if you took things seriously, it was too easy to be hurt." Even composers knew that the mere mention of his name conjured up images they were after, of music and race and baseball, hence Oscar Peterson's 1974 collaboration with Count Basie entitled simply *Satch and Josh.* Bob Weir, the ex–Grateful Dead guitarist, is blending song and theater in a work designed to celebrate the birth of the blues, jazz, and the Negro Leagues. Satchel better than anyone, Weir says, ties together those strands of American culture.

It was onscreen that Satchel's story was told most often if not most accurately. He was a centerpiece in a stream of documentaries on the Negro Leagues and baseball generally, including Ken Burns's nine-part public television epic. He was the inspiration for Leon Carter, the high-paid pitcher whose delivery "had the whip action of a slingshot," in book and movie versions of *The Bingo Long Traveling All-Stars & Motor Kings.* He was featured on a segment of "This Is Your Life," the long-running TV series where host Ralph Edwards surprised celebrity guests with family, friends, and quick trips through their lives. NBC did a film about Satchel in 1949, and CBS did another more than thirty years later. There were perpetual teases over the years that he would be the focus of a feature film, with the leading role going to Stepin Fetchit. Step said he had the script (by default when a Hollywood studio took a pass), a title (*The Man Who Wouldn't Grow Old*), and a partner (Satchel). The movie never made it beyond the rumor mill and it is unlikely that Satchel, despite his friendship with Step, would have agreed to be played by the actor whose caricature became Satchel's nemesis.

The closest thing to a full-fledged film treatment of his career and life came in 1981, when ABC aired the made-for-TV *Don't Look Back,* based on Satchel's second memoir. It originally had all the makings of a major production. Hollywood icon George C. Scott was brought in to direct. The executive producer was Danny Arnold, who developed the hit TV series *Barney Miller,* and the producer was Stanley Rubin, who had made the movie *Babe,* about female sports pioneer Babe Didrikson. The actors were from the A-list of black talent: Ossie Davis, Cleavon Little, Clifton Davis, and, playing Satchel, Louis Gossett, Jr., who would win an Academy Award the following year for his role in *An Officer and a Gentleman.* Everyone involved with the film adored its subject. "Satch was a folk hero to me," Gossett said. Scott said he agreed to direct his first TV film because "I'm an old-time baseball fan who has idolized Satchel Paige since I was a boy. It would bring me enormous satisfaction to make viewers—especially people of a younger generation—appreciate and understand this incredible athlete."

Scott would never get that satisfaction and the public never got a film worthy of the pitcher's life and the director's talent. A couple of weeks into shooting Scott was fired for what he said was his unwillingness to go along with the network's shoestring budget and Rubin said was the director's unwillingness to follow orders. Arnold said the chaos surrounding the production was the most disillusioning experience of his long career in film. No one was more disappointed than Rubin, who had persisted with the project despite being turned down by every network—"they didn't want to do a film on the exclusion of a major black sports figure from major sports"—with ABC relenting only after Arnold, a proven moneymaker, was brought in. "I never got a feeling from Satchel that the film was satisfying him in any way," says Rubin, now ninety. "I never got even a cursory thank-you. I never, ever got it. I was pretty disappointed. All of us felt like we were doing something that was doing good."

What Rubin wanted was something Satchel could not deliver. "I wanted him to be on a soapbox about his having been excluded from the Major Leagues and having to play in the Negro Leagues," the producer says. It was what black militants wanted, too. Satchel had, in fact, been fighting Jim Crow for forty years the ways he knew how, by pitching as hard and for as long as he was able. It was the quiet but determined approach that he had learned from Booker T. Washington. By the time Rubin started shooting his film, Satchel was seventy-four years old and he was tired. What he wanted most was the $10,000 he was being paid as a "technical adviser" to the production. He also pressed to star in his story, but the moviemakers said no. The pitcher was less concerned about how the film condensed and trivialized his life—authors, journalists, and filmmakers had been doing that for two generations. He did have one worry. "When it says something about me having a woman in every town, you see, I couldn't have had a woman in every town and pitch like I did for 50 years. You understand, man?" he told the crew when he was on location in Hattiesburg, Mississippi.

The problem was, there was nothing in the script that made him out to be a philanderer. "He did not read the script thoroughly. He had overheard a reporter saying it was in there and he got very upset. The producer said, 'It's not true. It's not in the script,' " recalls Dean Williams, the official photographer on the set. "Satchel did not read and write very well," adds Williams, who, along with his wife, started helping Satchel read the scenes being shot every day. While he seemed like an old and "very, very lonely" man when he arrived in Mississippi, says Williams, "when he got on the set and was revered by people like George C. Scott, wow, you could see him come alive. His days of notoriety and glad-handing all came back to him."

AS HIS BASEBALL WORLD CONTRACTED, Satchel could finally spend the time at home that most fathers do and that he wanted to. He and Lahoma started having children when he was in his early forties, which in the 1940s was the age that many fathers were becoming grandfathers. He had his last child in 1965, when he was fifty-nine and his oldest children were thinking about having children. His early children got a dad with more energy to do the lifting and running that fatherhood calls for. His later ones got more of a full-time father, since he was no longer out with his teams nine or more months a year.

Satchel had dual personas as a father, the first being that of a drill sergeant. He was determined that his seven kids and his stepdaughter get the education he had not. It was, he told them, the key to survival. For his part, that meant earning money to keep them in school by hustling up pitching jobs and traveling the country long after his arm and legs had begun to wilt. For his children, it meant earning good grades or else. "If you brought bad grades home he would be the meanest person in the world," said Warren, the youngest. "He would bend over backwards to reward you for your great accomplishments."

If education was lesson number one, being humble and grounded was next. Satchel knew firsthand the pitfalls of arrogance. He knew, too, that his fame would not help his children earn a living or make it through life. "I didn't realize how famous he was until I graduated from high school," recalled Warren. Pamela, the firstborn, says Satchel "protected us. For many years, except in Kansas City, people did not know our father had children. He would talk about us in a way that was ambiguous or vague. He wanted us to be very grounded and understand that in life, you get what you give. He said, 'Always keep your nose clean. Roll up your sleeves.' . . . He may not have coined the statement, but he said, 'The crowd is fickle. You have your fifteen to twenty minutes of fame.' " There were only three sorts of people you could count on, Satchel said: brothers and sisters, husband or wife, and yourself.

There was one more thing Satchel tried to shield his children from: rumors of his cheating on his wives. It worked when they were young, but as they grew they heard the whispers. Some originated long before he settled down with Lahoma; others were more recent and involved women who lived in Kansas City not far from his family. There were hints over the years that Satchel had fathered children other than Lahoma's, and in one case there was a name attached. In 2007 the Illinois House of Representatives passed a resolution congratulating retired postal service manager George Paige on his fiftieth wedding anniversary and noting that he "is the son of legendary baseball pitcher Satchel Paige." That was news to the pitcher's Kansas City kids, who believe that any other children with verifiable claims would have come forward earlier, hoping to cash in on Satchel's estate if not his legacy. As for George, he will not discuss his supposed ties to the ballplayer, although the Kansas City children believe George may be the son of Satchel's first wife, Janet, and a father other than theirs.

The Paige kids for the most part got the college educations and other opportunities Satchel wanted for them, but he felt it was equally essential for them to appreciate what he had gone without and why. Every burner on the family stove was covered with a pot of rice, grits, or gumbo, and the children knew to take a spoonful as they walked by in tribute to his childhood hunger. They also knew to tell him it was the best ever. He lived through the worst years of the Cold War and kept the basement air-raid shelter stocked with gas masks, canned peaches and apples, C rations, homemade wine, and gigantic wind-up military radios. Most of all he wanted his kids to understand how their skin color would shape their world, even if their world was not as racially rancorous as his had been. The Paige children were not naïve about segregation; Pamela attended all-black Central High while her younger siblings grew up in a neighborhood from which almost every white had fled. Still, Satchel felt it was critical that they know about the safe houses he had relied on while navigating the byways of Jim Crow and the danger of being on the road after dark in Dixie. He had them spend time with Cool

Papa, Double Duty, and others of his blackball cronies. And he made sure they knew what it meant for a Negro Leaguer like him to make it to Cooperstown. "It was the happiest I've ever seen him," says Robert, his older son who was there at the Hall induction. "It's the only time in my life that I remember seeing him just break down. It was his crown of thorns from all the pain and suffering he had been subjected to throughout the Major Leagues."

If drilling lessons into his kids was Satchel's stiff and proper side, his flip side was soft as custard. They listened with him to Ray Charles and B. B. King and learned to dance the Itch and Chicago Chicken. Linda, Lula, and Rita Jean were mesmerized watching the gadget-loving baseball man take apart and reassemble his old Cadillacs out in the garage, using tools he made himself. Pamela watched the fights on TV with him, with Satchel pulling hard for Cassius Clay. Robert donned a receiver's mitt and mask and caught his father's pitches in the backyard. Warren ran to Satchel's room every time he rang the bell, fetching Fig Newtons, canned sardines, or whatever else the aging pitcher yearned for from the stash he kept locked in the basement. All the children and Lahoma went with Satchel on fishing trips, where they lined up nine old cane poles in a row of stands along the riverbank, waiting for a bite. The family, says Pamela, was "self-entertaining."

Each child had a nickname. Robert was "Bug," a testament to his fluttering around like a June bug. Pamela was "Spud," for the Russian Sputnik satellite launched a decade after she was born. Warren, the youngest and most vulnerable, was "Mr. Paige." By the time it came to his grandchildren, of which there were fourteen, Satchel stopped trying to remember their names or give them handles. He summoned them with a simple "boy" or "girl," much the way he had called his receivers "Catch."

While all his kids and grandkids understood his passion for baseball, he made it a point not to impose it on them. All but Robert. He looked too much like Satchel, and showed too much promise during their backyard tossing, for Dad not to dream. So what if Robert's real love was basketball; Satchel could hope, and Robert could shoot baskets without his father knowing. Robert did pitch once in Little League, an experience that still makes him wince. He walked the first batter on four balls. The second walked, too, as did the third, fourth, fifth, sixth, seventh, and eighth. The coach kept him in, amazed that the son of the all-time strikeout king could not find the strike zone. When Robert finally handed over the ball there were tears in his eyes. It was the last time he ever pitched.

The Paige home, located a block into what had been the whites-only section of Kansas City, became a guesthouse for weary relatives, itinerant ballplayers, and a collection of friends, from Globetrotter clown prince Goose Tatum to boxing dynamo Sugar Ray Robinson. It also was home to twenty-two hunting dogs, baying beagles mostly. The division of labor in caring for the dogs went like this: Satchel cooked up the chicken hash and rice, the kids carried it out to the yard in huge bowls, Lahoma cleaned up after everyone. The setting was decidedly urban, but it had the feeling of a farm with chickens, ducks, raccoons, cats, lizards, turtles, and, every Easter, a bevy of bunnies. The split of responsibilities was even clearer when it came to the peas, corn, potatoes, green beans, and wild onions in the forestlike garden out back. The kids and grandkids did the planting, with seeds laid at regular intervals along lines that had to be ever so straight. Satchel supervised from his lawn chair.

The house itself was three stories, the first made of brick while the second and third were white shingles. There was a long porch out front where the family could gather on steamy summer nights, and a dozen spacious rooms with rich hardwood floors and a feel of old money. It was just the feel Satchel was after. Two rooms especially pleased him. The first housed his Chippendales, Wedgwoods, and Chinese antiques assembled under the guidance of Mrs. J. L. Wilkinson. The other, his trophy room, held gold-bordered testimonials and gold-plated cups bestowed for forty years of pitching marvels. Other memorabilia—pictures of Satchel with Mickey Rooney and Martha Raye, balls autographed by Rapid Robert Feller and other barnstorming buddies, a poster promising that Satchel would strike out the first nine batters "or your money back"—was stacked in an old steamer trunk stored upstairs. He loved the kitchen, too, frying up catfish or sizzling burgers the way he had on the road.

Lahoma took charge of everything else involving the kitchen, kids, and household, starting with religion. Her attachment to the church became a passion when she joined the Jehovah's Witnesses, and it sustained her when Satchel's absences and infidelities tested her patience and soul. Hers was a joyful faith. She greeted the children every morning with church songs, sung at full throttle. On Saturdays, hymns reverberated through the house as kids did assigned chores. On Sunday, Mother led the way to church, with only Satchel getting to opt out. That was his day to pitch with the Monarchs or anyone who rented his services. In later years he preferred to spend the Lord's day and others at the corner gas station or nearby bowling alleys, shoe shines, and bars, where he was a celebrity. Hilton Smith and Buck O'Neil would drop by to talk. So would Ewing Kauffman, the pharmaceutical tycoon who owned the Kansas City Royals—successors to the A's—and who made sure Satchel had the best seats for the biggest games. People he knew and those he just met were eager to be regaled with stories.

His kids' favorite is the one about the chicken. Lahoma wanted to make fried chicken, so she asked Satchel for money. He gave her a hundred-dollar bill. When Lahoma and Robert got home Satchel asked his son, " 'Did you go to the store?' I said, 'Yah, we're back,' " Robert recalls. "He says, 'You and your mother went to the store. You know I gave her a hundred-dollar bill and you know she didn't bring me no change. I want you to pull back the window shades because I want to see the truck that is going to bring that chicken up. It has got to be the biggest chicken in Kansas City.' "

Money generally was not a laughing matter with the Paiges. Too little was coming in, and what did come was not steady. Just how deep-seated Satchel's financial troubles were became apparent when he signed in 1965 with the Kansas City A's, who paid him about $3,500 for his three innings. "When the announcement was made of his signing, creditors from all over the Kansas City area immediately started to file claims on his salary. I think there was a furniture store he owed quite a bit to, and others," remembers Hank Peters, a former executive with the club. Sportscaster Curt Gowdy realized how hard up Satchel was when he and sidekick Tony Kubek invited Paige to Boston as an expert analyst on an NBC Game of the Week. Satchel and Kubek took the same plane to Chicago the next day. "When Satchel reached up to put a couple of big paper sacks up above him, the bottom fell out and a mess of groceries came crashing down—eggs, vegetables, leftover pieces of steak from the night before," Gowdy recounted in his memoir. "Well, Paige was terribly embarrassed. Everything was laying there in the aisle. 'My family needs something to eat,' he explained to Kubek. 'So I ordered room service at the hotel and was going to take this home.' "

Satchel owed money to Bill Veeck and J. L. Wilkinson, neither of whom chose to collect. The desire to avoid creditors, along with worries about being hounded by fans, explains why he listed his home phone under the pseudonym James L. Jackson. It also may be why he bought his homes in the name of his mother, Lula Paige, and why he sent so little money back to her and his struggling siblings in Mobile. He tried to hold onto everything he earned in his later years, for the sake of the kids, but it was difficult to resist buying another sharkskin suit or to turn down a teammate asking for a loan. Two sources Satchel felt could add to his income were reporters and authors who hounded him for interviews yet never shared what they earned. He set his price high—from $200 an interview to $2,000 an hour. Some paid on the spot, throwing in a couple bottles of Scotch to show their goodwill; others refused based on their journalistic scruples or empty wallets. It was the free-agent experience all over again: Satchel recognizing his value at a time when other ex-players felt exploited but were unwilling or unable to do anything about it.

The children got direct evidence of how precarious family finances were every time the lights went out. "I would be at work. The children would call me and say, 'Mamma, they cut the lights off,' " Lahoma recounted. "I would call the light company and tell them that I was coming and bringing the monies, and would they please come back later on because we needed the lights. And the gentleman would come out to the house and meet me there." Satchel told his kids that while it was great to have money, they should not get used to it. "When he was not employed we adjusted," says Pamela. "Other years he did extremely well and we adjusted to that, too."

Lahoma joined Satchel on the road whenever she could during his playing days and later, when he traveled mainly to receive tributes. She was there to provide companionship, to care for his aging arm, and, like a mindful mother, to keep an eye on him. When Satch and Lahoma were out barnstorming, the older children looked after the younger ones, with help from Lahoma's sisters Helena, Nina, Beulah, and Carrie. "My aunties, they are the ones that stayed home and took care of the kids while my mom and dad traveled," recalled Warren. "They were actually like my parents' maids. They attended to the children, they kept their house while they were out of town. And like if we had people like the mayor or someone come to the house, they would all come and put on little aprons and be maids." Because he was the youngest, Warren was sometimes dragged along with his parents. "My mom said I was her legs, so I just ran and did all the errands for them when we were out of town." While Warren saw himself as a road warrior, some trips were a child's fantasy. They were flown to San Francisco on Joe DiMaggio's private jet for a meal at his restaurant, and they visited the homes of Hank Aaron and Willie Mays for long enough that Warren got to play with the ballplayers' children.

When they were small the older children, too, had been vagabonds. They were mainly chasing second-string teams, to faraway places, but to them all the destinations seemed like Oz and Satchel was the wizard. When he was away alone Satchel tried to write letters home, and he loved getting missives from the kids. He called, too, and although he was not much of a phone conversationalist the message came through: Dad was thinking of them.

One place the Paige children did not spend much time growing up was in Mobile, where most of Satchel's family still lived. Satchel would go infrequently during his playing days and a couple of times a year in later years, holding court on his sister Palestine's porch or in old friends' backyard beer halls. He loved Palestine's oyster loaf and her boiled crabs. He did not like getting stopped repeatedly by the police, who wondered why a black man was driving a late-model Cadillac and wearing all that jewelry. Sometimes Lahoma joined him and occasionally one or more of the kids, but generally he went alone. He stayed with his brother John and more often with Lula, who still called him Leroy and still treated him like another of her brood rather than a star.

Satchel relished being celebrated as the hometown boy who came from nothing but made it big. He liked even better escaping his fans and any talk of baseball by stealing away at night to fish with his great-nephew Chris Grove. "He knew I could hide him in this city and he could have his private time, his Satchel time," says Grove, whose grandmother was Satchel's youngest sibling. Grove would get a call out of the blue saying, "Nephew, I'm on my way. You know what to do." That meant tracking how the fish were running and knowing just which pier to go to. Grove would tell the proprietors who Satchel was, what this uncle and nephew were doing there in the dead of night, and how secrecy was essential since Satchel did not like a crowd when he was fishing. The pitcher did like to bring along wine, especially the cache he had distilled at home in Kansas City and packed in the trunk of his car next to the fishing tackle. "When he came here to Mobile," says Grove, "he wanted to fish, raise Cain, and have fun."

As fun as fishing was, visiting Mobile was not easy for Satchel. His nephew Leon Paige thinks the famous pitcher was embarrassed by his family's poverty and his native city's racially retrograde ways. He may have been, but it was more complicated. Being home reminded Satchel why he had wanted to escape. He saw the ghosts of what he might have become every time he looked at his siblings, none of whom had it easy. One brother drowned at sea. A sister had a nervous breakdown after her son was killed in a fight. Wilson, who according to family lore was an even better ballplayer than Satchel, turned to the bottle much the way their father had. "Uncle Satchel took Uncle Wilson up there to Kansas City," recalls Leon. "He died up there and it was three to four days before anyone knew it. He had gotten drunk and some people broke into his house, robbed it, and took his money."

Satchel knew that but for the intervention of men like Coach Byrd and Alex Herman, he could have ended up like Wilson—digging graves to earn a living, then ending up in his own early grave. It was not a comforting image for the returning baseball hero. Being a kid again, which is the way most people feel when they go home, was no more fun for Satchel the second time around than it had been the first. That was why he stayed away and, when he came home, it is why he spent so much time fishing with his grandnephew, carousing with new friends, and looking ahead rather than back.

Lula understood. She never told Satchel or anyone else but she knew that his success was as much serendipity as skill. Her son Wilson had the latter but not the luck. She surely cherished Satchel's success and his fame, but felt what he needed from her was not another acolyte but a reminder of core values and where he came from. So she never asked about the homes he was buying in her name in

Kansas City just as she had never asked him for the one he bought for her in Mobile. She only requested money when it was for one of Satchel's sisters or brothers. She was too proud to ask for more. She enjoyed spending time with her baseball hero son when he had it and liked even more being with his third wife, Lahoma, with whom she could talk about the burden of raising children and the grace of the Good Lord.

Lula was the one who kept the extended family together in Mobile and continued to mother her kids into their dotage. In her later years arthritis kept her rubbing liniment onto her knees just as Satchel did with his shoulder. At the end, her daughter Palestine and grand-daughter Lillian looked after her. Lula died in her sleep on New Year's Day, 1966, at what newspapers said was the age of 104 but census records suggest was 90. "Aunt Palestine went in to get her her coffee," remembers Leon, "and she was dead."

Over the years Satchel's relatives from Mobile reached out to him occasionally, but not as often as expected given his relative wealth and their pressing needs. Like Leon and Lula, they could have been too proud to ask and felt Satchel should have offered. Or maybe they heard what had happened to Wilson Jr. He went to Kansas City when he was fresh out of high school and looking for a job. He stayed in Satchel's home, taking in the scene from an upper stairwell as his uncle entertained guests "and listening to the music until somebody made me go to bed." He never did find work there, and Satchel "wasn't able to go with me to use his influence. It was during the off-season and he always had a lot of business to take care of."

OLD AGE ROBBED THIS SYMBOL of youth first of his health, then of his optimism. The only medical problems Satchel had through his first six decades were an arm that went dead temporarily, a stomach that acted up, and teeth that needed extracting. From age fifty-nine on the troubles were more diverse and unrelenting. In 1965 he got what he called "sinus trouble, bad," then he failed to show up at a scheduled pitching appearance because of an unspecified blood pressure disorder. In 1968, during his ham-handed campaign for the Missouri legislature, he was hospitalized for pneumonia. The next year he was back in the hospital for a week with what he labeled a bad cold and doctors said was puzzling. All the microbes, muscle aches, and mystery symptoms could mean only one thing: Satchel Paige was mortal, subject to the same damage and deterioration that afflicted the rest of humanity.

That did not mean he was graying. Every newspaper profile on him until he hit seventy marveled at his jet-black hair and a body without any discernible fat. But instead of sizing up batters from the vantage point of the mound, he was doing it sitting in front of the television set. He could still spot any weakness, but there was no one to tell now other than his adolescent children. He was at baseball stadiums a lot, but mainly to get another plaque, deliver a dinner talk, or receive the key to a city that not long before had banished him to "colored only" beaches, parks, and locker rooms. "People," he took to saying in those years, "think Satch is either rich or dead." He was neither, but he was getting old.

One group that honored him was the National Cartoonists Society. He had been supplying rich material to newspaper caricaturists for decades, and they wanted to say thanks in 1972 by giving him their top award during a dinner at New York's Commodore Hotel. It was a swell party, with sports celebrities ranging from Casey Stengel to Jack Dempsey and Howard Cosell. Event chairman Bill Gallo of the New York *Daily News* casually reminded the honoree to make himself at home during his visit, not appreciating that Satchel would do just that. "The Commodore was now a Grand Hyatt and they had stores and stuff on the bottom floors and he could sign for whatever he got," Gallo remembers thirty-five years afterward. "He got a suit, maybe two. He also bought a case of booze, I think it was Jack Daniel's. Of course we paid and didn't ask questions. What the hell? He was Satchel Paige and it was worth paying just for getting a kick out of it. For him I wouldn't call it outrageous. I would call it normal."

Likewise, Bowie Kuhn did not mind when Satchel used him as a personal complaint department after his inauguration into the Hall of Fame in 1971. "I had many calls from Satch grumbling about transportation and expense arrangements and other miscellaneous problems," the baseball commissioner recalled. "I doubt that it ever occurred to Satch that there was anything out of the ordinary about this procedure, and somehow I rather enjoyed it. It kept us in touch." Marty Appel was less amused when Satchel did something equally Satchel-like at an old-timers' event at Toots Shor's restaurant in Manhattan. "Satch walked away with a Monarchs uniform I let him wear," says Appel, the former Yankees PR chief. "He'd promised to guard it with his life but he never gave it back. It still bothers me thirty-five years later." What bothers him even more is how "very, very programmed" Satchel seemed. "It was a sad night. He didn't relax and swap stories. I think this was his life then. He traveled and was treated well. He got gifts, then it was on to the next town to do it over again."

It happens to lots of leading men as they fade into supporting roles. Loneliness sets in, along with sadness. There is more time to remember all you have achieved and to wonder why others have forgotten. There are endless hours to tally who stood by you, and who failed to. Satchel had suffered enough real indignities to keep anyone thinking for a very long time. He had always had a brooding side, but had concealed it with enchanting wit and perpetual motion. Now the mask was off.

Jim Bankes, the author of a history of the Pittsburgh Crawfords, remembers meeting Satchel for the first time in the mid-'70s, when he was working for the Redbirds: "I definitely did not feel this was the Satchel of the 1930s, with Jimmy Crutchfield's line about the sun coming out when he got to the park. He wasn't that way anymore. He would sit there and if you wanted to come up and talk to him, he would talk to you. But he was not especially friendly. He was cranky." Others used the words *touchy* and *distant, mercurial* and *petulant* and *bitter.* Even his voice, one sportswriter noted, had lost its smile.

Part of that was a response to his worsening health. Years of smoking had caught up with him, as had riding tens of thousands of miles along dusty roads in emission-spewing jalopies. The diagnosis, delivered in the late 1970s, was emphysema. Scar tissue was forming on his lungs. As it thickened, less and less oxygen reached his bloodstream. The condition had him in and out of the hospital, occasionally landing him in the surgical suite or intensive care unit, where nurses and doctors tended to his ailments then asked for his autograph. He would seem to get better, but a month or two later the troubles would resurface. Slowly, the illness was robbing Satchel of his capacity to breathe.

He followed his own timetable and marching orders even when it came to his emphysema. In the aftermath of a major lung operation Satchel sat in a rocking chair in his hospital room, hood pulled over his head and mood glum. His surgeon begged him to move around and cough as much as possible, which clears the lungs of sputum and can prevent infection. The pitcher nodded, then shooed away the doctor. On day six, the physician remembered, Satchel's door was closed. The doctor knocked, entered, and found his patient dressed in a suit and tie and looking robust. "Doctor," said Satchel, "I'm going home."

Sickness pushed this forward-thinking man to relive past glories—the no-hitters, the face-offs against the likes of Dizzy Dean and Slim Jones, the barnstorming and showboating and legend building. As he reran them, he focused more on the matter of race. There was less need now to censor himself the way blacks in America had been doing, as a matter of survival, since their days on the plantation. How far had Negroes come? a reporter asked in 1974. "We ain't all that far," answered Satchel. "If I get on a plane and there are four seats and I sit in one of 'em, won't nobody sit there less'n they have to. They'll circle the plane 15 times before they'll finally sit there. Shows [how] bad a condition we're in." How did he feel about the Cleveland Indians giving him only a token outing in the 1948 World Series and letting him go after the '49 season? "Of all the places I ever played in 47 years, Cleveland gave me the roughest deal."

He vowed never to go back to Cleveland, or to Cooperstown. While he broke both promises, his attitude toward the Hall of Fame reflected his understandable frustration. "It's a shame they kept us out because we're black, and it's an even bigger shame the way they treated us when we first got in," he said at a 1981 reunion of old Negro Leaguers in Ashland, Kentucky. "I told them at Cooperstown we had a lot of Satchels. We had top pitchers. We had quite a few men could hit the ball like Babe Ruth and Josh Gibson. I got in trouble in Cooperstown for saying we had players (in the Negro leagues) who didn't have to go to a farm club before they went to the major leagues."

Organizers of the Ashland reunion never expected Satchel to actually show up, and certainly not to dominate proceedings that featured contemporary stars like Willie Mays. They had sent him a plane ticket to a similar event two years earlier; he used the ticket, but not to fly to Kentucky. They also learned that Satchel was in such pain that he had recently turned down an invitation from President Reagan to a White House luncheon with other Hall of Famers. But he was seventy-four years old and knew that Ashland might be his last chance to be with his old blackball buddies and to have an audience with reporters from publications as prestigious as *The New York Times* and *The Sporting News.* So he and Lahoma made the trip, dragging along the portable oxygen pack he needed to breathe and the wheelchair he relied on to move. "I'm glad to be here in Ashland," he said at a news conference. "At my age, I'm glad to be anywhere." Having center stage again felt like the top of the world. In the best sign that age had slowed but not stopped him, Satchel ordered two bottles of whiskey at $38 each from room service and charged it to his hosts. "I remember saying, 'Please, Mr. Paige, don't order any more expensive whiskey,' " recalls Harry T. Wiley, one of the organizers. "He said, 'I didn't know.' "

Satchel last appeared in public on June 5, 1982, in Kansas City. The roar was gone from his voice as he addressed the crowd from his wheelchair, with an oxygen tube strapped to his face and his hand gripping a baseball. "I hope the next time you come out, I can stand up," he said hopefully as the thin crowd stood in his honor. The city was dedicating in his name a baseball stadium near his home. The ballpark was as decrepit as the old ballplayer, weeds poking through fresh-cut grass and wind pouring through breaches in the grandstand roof. Friends who knew Satchel's condition had rushed to organize the naming ceremony, hoping it would lift his spirits. But it would take more than that. "I am honored with the stadium being named for me. I thought there was nothing left for me," he said. "I've been in Kansas City 46 years and I can walk down the street and people don't know me."

Two days later Kansas City was battered by a rainstorm that felled trees and knocked out power. It was typical then for utility crews to work first on the tony neighborhoods along Ward Parkway, with power to black areas restored sometime later. The local newspaper got a tip that the Paige home had no electricity and that the aging ballplayer was suffering without his humidifier and fan. More grist, reporter E. A. Torriero recalls, for a story he was writing on how the community had forgotten the seventy-five-year-old pitcher.

Satchel woke that night with a headache. The next morning, the eighth of June, he could not find a comfortable position to lie or sit in. His shoulder was throbbing. He had the chills. Lahoma applied a hot water bottle and draped her jacket around him, then she headed to the store for ice to keep food from spoiling during the power outage. While she was gone, Carolyn, their second-oldest child, found Satchel in a daze. She fanned him, calling, "Daddy, daddy, can you hear me?" All he could manage was, "Ugh." His daughters called the paramedics, but their arrival was delayed by a fallen tree. In the meantime Lahoma got home and tried to resuscitate Satchel using the CPR she had learned as a nurse's aide. He was "limp as a dish rag," she said. His heart gave out for good in the ambulance and he was pronounced dead at 1:15 P.M. at Truman Medical Center. In the days just before "he knew he was going to pass on," Lahoma recalled. "We would try and not talk about it."

IN HIS LAST YEARS the world may not have paid Satchel the attention he craved, but it did upon his death. *The New York Times* called him "one of those wondrously endowed and worldly athletes who looms larger than any sports arena," adding that "it does not diminish the achievements of Jackie Robinson and other young blacks who broke baseball's color barrier to remember that Satchel Paige showed the way." *Washington Post* baseball bard Tom Boswell wrote that "the Paige tragedy is that, by his excellence, he proved that 50 years worth of black-league players had been wronged more severely than white America ever suspected." Buck O'Neil had a different message for white America. "Don't feel sorry for us," he said in his eulogy to Satchel. "I feel sorry for your fathers and your mothers, because they didn't get to see us play."

The funeral went just the way Satchel wanted. Buck, Slow Robinson, Hilton Smith, and other blackball buddies were honorary pallbearers, remembering only the good times. The Reverend Emanuel Cleaver, a pastor who would later become Kansas City's mayor, told the 150 celebrants that "from now on when you hear the thunder roll and the lightning flash across the skies, don't panic, it is probably the scoreboard of Heaven, signaling that Satchel just completed another big inning." The reigning mayor, Richard Berkley, asked Kansas Citians to lower their flags to half-mast as Satchel's body was transported to Forest Hills Cemetery. The right tone was struck even in the choice of a hearse: a Packard from 1938, the year Satchel's arm went dead and sportswriters wrote his premature obituaries. In a style befitting a king, Satchel was laid to rest in an isolated burial plot dubbed Paige Island.

In subsequent years a school in Kansas City would be named after him, with a lifesize wax replica in uniform. His picture was added to the champions celebrated on boxes of Wheaties breakfast cereal, and songs, poems, and trivia questions were composed in his honor. A Satchel statue now graces the grounds of the Hall of Fame Museum that once wanted to banish him to a Jim Crow corridor. His birth, far from being forgotten the way he feared, is listed by the Library of Congress as the most noteworthy event in American history on the seventh of July. The tribute he would have treasured the most is at Mount Meigs, where officials named a dormitory Paige Hall to inspire the boys living there to turn their lives around the way the reformatory's most acclaimed alumnus had.

But Satchel would not have wanted the media, the ministry, or even the Mount to have the last line on his legacy. Far better to leave that to Negro Leagues scholars, who unveiled a graveside memorial seven years after he died and three years after Lahoma did. The couple's pictures and his rules for staying young are etched into one side of a six-foot, seven-thousand-pound granite monument. "Thrilling millions with his extraordinary pitching feats," the historians wrote on the other side, Satchel became "the most celebrated moundsman in the history of our national pastime." And so it was, the marker adds in words he would have savored, that "Leroy became Satchel. And Satchel became a legend."

ACKNOWLEDGMENTS

WHAT COULD BE BETTER for a baseball lover than getting to call baseball work for two years, the way I just did? Just this: getting to write the biography of a baseball icon that is, at the same time, a biography of Jim Crow.

To do that I needed help, and as always I turned first to Jill Kneerim. She believed in this book even though the only baseball game she watches each season is the one I take her to at Fenway Park. She embraced my idea, edited my proposal, ginned up interest at publishing houses, and helped me find the right editor and publisher. That is what a good agent does. Jill did even more, editing my first draft with a red pencil and broad sweep.

My other early readers were as good as they get, each from a different perspective. Justin Kaplan is one of America's preeminent biographers and thinkers. Don MacGillis and Tom Gagen are top-tier journalists and savvy baseball watchers. No one knows and cares more about the Negro Leagues than Leslie Heaphy, who edits the journal *Black Ball* and teaches history at Kent State University.

Working with a new editor is a scary prospect, but Will Murphy of Random House exceeded even Jill's buildup. He offered feedback on the manuscript that reassured me and made the book crisper and fuller. Then he became the in-house advocate that every author craves and too few get. As anyone who has written a book knows, interactions with your publisher on things big and little are perpetual;

everyone should have someone like Courtney Turco to make them seem painless and seamless. Everyone also should have a production editor as gifted as Evan Camfield and a copy editor like Steven Meyers, who sorted out my grammar and punctuation and found just the right words and ideas when I came up short.

Closer to home I got advice, encouragement, and deft editing from my wife, Lisa Frusztajer, as well as newfound and much-appreciated interest in the game of baseball from Marina and Alec. My mother, Dorothy Tye, was where she always is in my work and life, front and center, and my uncle Ray Tye offered critical support. Sally Jacobs and Claudia Kalb, ace writer-reporters, helped me clarify my thinking and phrasing.

Every city I visited and every issue I probed turned up gaps in Satchel's life. I filled them with help from these authors, experts, and friends: Stephen Banker, Jim Bankes, David Brewer, Ed Bridges, Nick Cafardo, Jorge Colón Delgado, Gary Crawford, Phil Dixon, Raymond Doswell, Steve Fainaru, Tom Fredrick, Jim Gates, Ben Harry, Tommy Hicks, Jerome Carolyn Holmes, Jeff Idelson, Collette King, John Kurtz, Larry Lester, Steve Marantz, Tom Mason, William McNeil, Leigh Montville, Rod Nelson, Rob Neyer, Jim Overmyer, Layton Revel, John Richmond, Tim Rives, Winnie Robinson, Donn Rogosin, Rob Ruck, Brad Snyder, Bryan Steverson, Wayne Stivers, Ed Storin, Jose A. Vega Imbert, and Dick Wilkinson. Thanks, too, to the National Baseball Hall of Fame and Museum and to the Negro Leagues Baseball Museum.

I hired a stream of student researchers in Boston, Kansas City, Mobile, and other communities central to this story, to help with library searches, ballplayer searches, and other inquiries. The ones who stayed longest and put up most with my pestering were Guillermo Bleichmar, Angie Brewster, Daniel Coleman, Carolyn D'Aquila, Stewart Deck, Pam Hays, Kevin Hill, Michael Koplow, Clinton Lawson, Patrick McGrath, Caleb Peiffer, David Schneider, Rob Silverblatt, Rita Thompson, and Josh Willis. Jim Cahill, thanks for keeping my computers running and me online.

Satchel's family—especially Leon Paige, Wilson Paige, Julio Figueroa, and Chris Grove—was terrific. So were scores of retired ballplayers I interviewed from the Negro Leagues and Major Leagues. They shared stories of Satchel and themselves with a total stranger. I am grateful.

$\boxed{\text{APPENDIX}}$

Satchel by the Numbers

W/L: wins/losses
CG: complete games
IP: innings pitched
SO/BB: strikeouts/bases on balls
RPG: total runs—both earned and unearned—per nine innings pitched
ERA: earned runs per nine innings

NEGRO LEAGUES

YEAR	TEAM(S)	W/L	CG	IP	SO/BB	RPG
1927	Birmingham Black Barons	7-1	5	89.3	69/26	3.32
1928	Birmingham Black Barons	12-5	11	134.3	112/21	2.95
1929	Birmingham Black Barons	10-9	15	188.3	176/31	4.92
1930	Baltimore Black Sox	3-1	3	31.0	17/6	3.48
	Birmingham Black Barons	7-4	9	96.3	69/9	3.27
1931	Cleveland Cubs	1-2	1	32.7	18/4	3.31
	Pittsburgh Crawfords	0-1	1	8.0	0/1	3.38
1932	Pittsburgh Crawfords	10-4	12	132.7	92/35	3.19
1933	Pittsburgh Crawfords	5-7	8	95.0	55/12	3.69
1934	Pittsburgh Crawfords	14-2	15	154.0	144/26	2.16
1935	Kansas City Monarchs	0-0	1	9.0	11/1	0.00
1936	Pittsburgh Crawfords	5-0	5	47.7	47/9	3.21

NEGRO LEAGUES *(cont'd)*

YEAR	TEAM(S)	W/L	CG	IP	SO/BB	RPG
1937	Trujillo All-Stars	0-1	1	11.0	11/1	4.09
1940	Kansas City Monarchs	1-0	1	11.0	8/0	0.82
1941	New York Black Yankees	1-0	1	9.0	8/0	3.00
	Kansas City Monarchs	4-0	2	55.0	42/6	3.44
1942	Kansas City Monarchs	4-5	5	95.0	79/11	2.84
1943	Kansas City Monarchs	6-8	3	102.0	74/22	4.59
	Memphis Red Sox	1-0	0	5.0	7/2	0.00
1944	Kansas City Monarchs	4-5	5	82.7	76/13	1.96
1945	Kansas City Monarchs	2-4	2	51.7	54/14	5.05
1946	Kansas City Monarchs	5-1	2	47.0	45/3	2.11
1947	Kansas City Monarchs	1-1	2	19.0	17/0	0.95
Totals		103-61	110	1506.7	1231/253	3.31

Source: Compiled by Negro League researchers Larry Lester and Dick Clark for a study supported by Major League Baseball and the Hall of Fame, and published in *Shades of Glory,* 406–7. While historians continue to disagree on Satchel's statistics, these figures—including only league-sanctioned games where box scores were found—are the most authoritative available.

Satchel's records understate his wins because he often left the game after three or four innings, which was too short an appearance to be credited with a win but long enough to be stuck with a loss. There are no reliable records for 1938 and 1939, when he was injured and on the comeback trail with the Baby Monarchs.

EAST-WEST ALL-STAR GAMES

YEAR	W/L	CG	IP	SO/BB	RPG
1934	1-0	0	4.0	5/0	0.00
1936	0-0	0	3.0	0/0	3.00
1941	0-0	0	2.0	2/1	0.00
1942	0-1	0	3.0	2/2	9.00
1943	1-0	0	3.0	4/1	0.00
Totals	2-1	0	15.0	13/4	2.41

Source: Lester, *Black Baseball's National Showcase,* 445.

NORTH DAKOTA

YEAR	TEAM	W/L	CG	IP	SO/BB	RPG
1933	Bismarck	6-0	7	72.0	119/11	1.25
1935	Bismarck	29-2	18	229.2	321/16	1.96
Totals		35-2	25	301.2	440/27	1.79

Source: Assembled by author from newspaper records and box scores. Some clippings did not include complete stats.

CALIFORNIA WINTER LEAGUE

YEAR	TEAM	W/L	CG	IP	SO/BB
1931–32	Philadelphia Giants	6-0	6	58.0	70/NA
1932–33	Tom Wilson's Elite Giants	7-0	7	63.0	91/NA
1933–34	Wilson's Elite Giants	16-2	18	172.0	244/47
1934–35	Wilson's Elite Giants	8-0	7	69.0	104/20
1935–36	Wilson's Elite Giants	13-0	6	94.0	113/28
1943–44	Baltimore Elite Giants	3-1	1	36.0	39/10
1945	Kansas City Royals	1-1	1	27.0	27/12
1946	Kansas City Royals	0-2	0	15.0	21/7
1947	Kansas City Royals	2-1	1	35.0	60/14
Totals		56-7	47	569.0	769/138

Source: McNeil, *California Winter League,* 166, 269.

LATIN LEAGUES

YEAR	TEAM	W/L	IP	SO/BB	ERA
1929–30	Cuba, Santa Clara Leopards	6-5			
1938	Mexico, Agrario of Mexico City	1-1	19	7/12	5.21
1939–40:	Puerto Rico, Guayama Witches	19-3	205.0	208/54	1.93
1940–41	Puerto Rico, Guayama Witches	4-5		70/26	3.89
1947–48	Puerto Rico, Santurce Crabbers	0-3	34.0	26/13	2.91
Totals	Puerto Rico	23-11		304/93	

Sources: Figueredo, *Who's Who in Cuban Baseball; Mexican Encyclopedia of Baseball;* Jorge Colón Delgado; Angel Torres; and Ray Nemec.

MAJOR LEAGUES

YEAR	TEAM	W/L	IP	SO/BB	ERA
1948	Cleveland Indians	6-1	73.0	43/22	2.47
1949	Cleveland Indians	4-7	83.0	54/33	3.04
1951	St. Louis Browns	3-4	62.0	48/29	4.79
1952	St. Louis Browns	12-10	138.0	91/57	3.07
1953	St. Louis Browns	3-9	117.0	51/39	3.54
1965	Kansas City Athletics	0-0	3.0	1/0	0.00
Totals:		28-31	476	288/180	3.29

Source: Baseball Hall of Fame.

MINOR LEAGUES

YEAR	TEAM	W/L	IP	SO/BB	ERA
1956	Miami Marlins	11-4	111.0	79/28	1.86
1957	Miami Marlins	10-8	119.0	76/11	2.42
1958	Miami Marlins	10-10	110.0	40/15	2.95
Totals		31-22	340.0	195/54	2.73

Source: Ray Nemec.

NOTES

PREFACE

viii   THE ANSWER DEPENDED ON WHO WAS ASKING: "Leroy 'Satchel' Paige,"
       Colored Baseball & Sports Monthly; "Satchel the Great," *Time;* McAuley, "Life in the
       Majors, Part 1," *The Sporting News;* "Old Satch Paige," *The Washington Post;*
       "Satchel Paige, Ace Negro Pitcher," *The New York Times;* "Mother Says Satchel Is
       44," Cleveland *Plain Dealer;* Sterry and Eckstut, *Satchel Sez,* 18.

viii   "ON EITHER JULY 17": *1949 Cleveland Indians Sketchbook; Cleveland Indians
       1949 Press and Radio Yearbook.*

ix   "SAVED THE DAY AT WATERLOO": Lardner, "The Old Man in the Chair,"
       Newsweek.

ix   HIS DRAFT RECORD: Registrar's report, October 16, 1940.

ix   HIS SOCIAL SECURITY CARD: Application for Social Security Account Num-
       ber, January 31, 1940.

ix   HIS PASSPORT FILE: Affidavit of Birth with Application for American Pass-
       port, April 15, 1938.

x   DISPATCHED SATCHEL'S NEPHEW: Veeck said he sent a private detective to
       check Satchel's birth record. Leon says Veeck came himself, with Indians player-
       manager Lou Boudreau and a second companion Leon thinks was Indians ace Bob
       Feller. Author interview with Leon Paige.

x   "THEY WANT ME TO BE OLD": Paige and Lebovitz, *Pitchin' Man: Satchel Paige's
       Own Story.*

x   "I WANT TO BE THE ONLIEST": Anderson, "Satch Surveys Catfish and Ages,"
       The New York Times.

xi   SHE SUPPOSEDLY MIXED HIM UP: Lula Coleman Paige told the Associated
       Press in 1948 that Satchel was forty-four, which was several years older than he
       was admitting. "I remember something came up once about changing his age
       when he left to play ball in Chattanooga back about 1927," added the white-
       haired matriarch, who confessed to being seventy-eight. "But he's really 44." Not

so, a bemused Satchel fired back: "If she said it, she must have me mistaken with my oldest brother."

xi   "NOBODY KNOWS HOW COMPLICATED": Bilovsky, "Satchel Paige—Bittersweet Tale," Philadelphia *Sunday Bulletin.*

xi   "HOW OLD WOULD": www.baseball-almanac.com.

CHAPTER 1: COMING ALIVE

3   THE HURRICANE THAT BATTERED: Mathews and Browne, *Highlights of 100 Years in Mobile,* 67–69; "Mobile Buries Many Victims," *The Atlanta Constitution;* "West India Hurricane Strikes Mobile," Mobile *Press-Register;* "Storm Scenes Night and Day," Mobile *Press-Register;* "Rev. A. F. Owens Finds the Colored People Fared Very Badly," Mobile *Press-Register.*

4   MOBILE HISTORICALLY WAS A CENTER: Thomason, ed., *Mobile: The New History,* 1–2, 155–67.

5   LOOTING THE HOMES: "Negroes Looting Homes of Dead," Mobile *Press-Register.*

5   THE RISING TENSIONS TURNED VIOLENT: Alsobrook, *Alabama's Port City,* 167–76, 191; "Sheriff Overpowered and Two Negroes Lynched," Mobile *Press-Register;* "Alabama Negro Lynched," *The New York Times;* "Negro Is Lynched in Mobile Street," *The New York Times;* "Philip Fatch Loses Life," Mobile *Press-Register.*

6   "I WAS NO DIFFERENT": Paige and Lipman, *Maybe I'll Pitch Forever,* 16, 19.

7   HE HAD FIVE YOUNGER SIBLINGS: Public records and relatives' memories offer up other names for Satchel's siblings, including Samuel, although all agree that John and Lula had twelve children.

7   "IF YOU TELL A LIE": "Satch Surveys Catfish."

8   "I DON'T SEE WHY": "Ladies Discuss Negro Servants," Mobile *Press-Register;* Alsobrook, *Alabama's Port City,* 228.

8   "IT WAS POVERTY-STRICKEN": *Maybe I'll Pitch Forever,* 16.

9   "THIS IS MOBILE": Author interview with Mike Thomason.

9   "YOU LOOK LIKE": *Maybe I'll Pitch Forever,* 17–18.

9   FOURTEEN YEARS EARLIER: *Pitchin' Man,* 17.

9–10 "THEY STARTED TO CALL ME": Banker, *Black Diamonds: An Oral History of Negro Baseball,* Satchel Paige interview.

10   THE TAG WAS PINNED: Hoffman, *Back Home: Journeys Through Mobile,* 152; Curran, "Sister Shares Memories of Satchel Paige," Mobile *Press Register.* Satchel liked two other versions of how he got his nickname that he admitted were untrue: it was a natural fit because victory was in the bag when he took the mound, or it was a spinoff of Louis Armstrong's "Satchmo" because Satchel was as impressive blowing his fastball by batters as Armstrong was blowing his trademark trumpet.

10   "THAT'S WHEN I NAMED": Ribowsky, *Don't Look Back,* 28.

10   "PAGE LOOKED TOO MUCH": Glass, "How Old Is Satch?" *Sports Illustrated.*

10   "MY FOLKS STARTED OUT": *Maybe I'll Pitch Forever,* 14.

11   HE ARRIVED JUST AS MOBILE'S: Alsobrook, *Alabama's Port City,* 219–21.

11   "TO GET MARRIED": Leon Paige interview.

11   LIED ON HER MARRIAGE: Marriage, census, birth, and other records of Satchel's siblings.

11 PLAYING HOOKY: *Pitchin' Man,* 26.

12 "I CAN STILL SEE": Hoffman, *Back Home: Journeys,* 152.

12 "WHY, HE'D RATHER PLAY": "Mother Says Satchel Is 44."

12 "WE'D MAKE COTTON BALLS": Nick Wilson e-mail to author, May 5, 2007, with Wilson's interviews of Negro Leaguers.

12 SATCHEL GOT HIS FIRST TASTE: *Pitchin' Man,* 24–25; *Maybe I'll Pitch Forever,* 22.

13 MOBILE BAY JUBILEE: Fox, *Satchel Paige's America,* 82.

13 "GET OUT OF HERE": *Maybe I'll Pitch Forever,* 20.

13 BY THE HOUR HE HUNG: Fox, *Satchel Paige's America,* 21.

13–14 ONE TIME HE WAS AMBLING: Author interview with Floyd Nicholson.

14 "I CRIPPLED UP": *Maybe I'll Pitch Forever,* 18–19.

14 "I USED TO THINK": *Maybe I'll Pitch Forever,* 19–20.

15 "UNLESS YOU'VE GONE": *Maybe I'll Pitch Forever,* 22.

15 MRS. MEANIE: *Maybe I'll Pitch Forever,* 23–24.

16 MOUNT MEIGS: Author interview with Jerome Carolyn Holmes; Holmes, *Reflections into the Past;* Holmes, *Origin and History of the State Colored Women's Clubs;* Holmes, *History and Landmarks of Mount Meigs;* "The Negro Reformatory Problem," *Montgomery Advertiser;* General Laws of Alabama, 1911, An Act to Create Reform School for Training of Juvenile Negro Law-Breakers No. 336, H. 238; Hart, *Social Problems of Alabama.*

16 "WE WAS FREE TO GO": Rod Roberts's interview with Satchel Paige, Baseball Hall of Fame, June 20, 1982.

16 HAVING GROWN UP DEEP: Ribowsky, *Don't Look Back,* 35; *Maybe I'll Pitch Forever,* 24–25.

17 THEN THERE WAS BASEBALL: *Maybe I'll Pitch Forever,* 26; Ribowky, *Don't Look Back,* 34.

17 EDWARD BYRD: *Don't Look Back,* 34.

18 COACH BYRD EARNED HIS LIVING: Information is sketchy on Coach Byrd, with the only mention coming in *Don't Look Back* and the only reference to an Ed or Eddie Byrd coming from city directories. It is likely that he worked part-time as a coach at Mount Meigs.

18 "GIVE TO THE STATE": *Colored Alabamian,* July 25, 1908.

19 HARD WORK WAS THE CENTERPIECE: Washington's approach did little to challenge a racist system that saw the state appropriate nearly twice as much per child at the Industrial School for White Boys as it did at the Reform School for Juvenile Negro Law-Breakers. And its philosophy of acquiescence would not meet today's standards for fairness or justice, just as it disappointed DuBois and other activists in the early 1900s. Washington, however, wanted to be judged not by the social unrest he fomented but by his effect on individuals like Satchel Paige. By that measure, what he and Mount Meigs accomplished was monumental.

19 "THINK WHAT IT MEANS": Hart, *Social Problems of Alabama,* 31.

19 "EVERY DAY PRUNING": State Reform School for Negro Boys, *Program for Closing Session,* May 19, 1916.

19 "IN CASE OF SERIOUS": *By-Laws and Rules and Regulations of The Alabama Reform School for Juvenile Negro Law-Breakers,* Mount Meigs, Alabama, 1916, 13.

19 A DOZEN CHRISTMAS WREATHS: Letter from governor's secretary to J. R. Wingfield, Superintendent, December 11, 1922, Governor Kilby files; Return letter from Wingfield to W. A. Darden, secretary to Governor.

20   THE REFORM SCHOOL WAS IMPRESSED: Office of the Superintendent, State Reform School, December 31, 1923. Though his parole document was dated December 31, officials said it could take as long as a month for the state to inspect the home residents would return to. Satchel may not have left Mount Meigs until January 1924.

20   SATCHEL WALKED AWAY: Young, *Negro Firsts in Sports,* 91; "Satchel Hurls for Cleveland Indians," *Chicago Defender.*

20   WHICH HE DID NOT: Leftwich, registrar at Tuskegee, letter to author, July 5, 2007.

20   "THOSE FIVE AND A HALF": *Maybe I'll Pitch Forever,* 24, 26.

20   THE MOBILE SATCHEL RETURNED TO: Thomason, *Mobile: The New History,* 181–208.

21   "I'D BE A STOCKBROKER": Alsobrook, "Boosters, Moralists, and Reformers," *Alabama Review.*

21   DAVIS AVENUE, THE CITY'S BLACK BROADWAY: *Mobile: The New History,* 206; Author interviews with David Alsobrook, Mike Thomason, and Clarence Mohr.

21   SATCHEL KNOCKED ON DOORS: *Maybe I'll Pitch Forever,* 28.

21   "POPPED AGAINST": *Maybe I'll Pitch Forever,* 29.

22   "ALL THE GALS": *Maybe I'll Pitch Forever,* 30.

22   "WE SURE COULD USE": *Maybe I'll Pitch Forever,* 32.

22   EVEN FASTER THAN SATCHEL: "How Old Is Satch?" *Sports Illustrated,* 44.

22   "BUT HE LIKED THE GIRLS": Curran, "Sister Shares Memories of Satchel Paige," Mobile *Press-Register.*

22   THE TRUTH IS: Author interview with Wilson Paige, Jr.

22   MOST OF SATCHEL'S BROTHERS: City directories and U.S. Census records.

23   "ACUTE DETERIORATION": John Page, Alabama Center for Health Statistics, May 2, 2007.

23   "WE'D TAKE A HOE": Leon Paige interview.

23   "YOU WANT TO BE": *Maybe I'll Pitch Forever,* 15.

24   "SOMEBODY WAS GOING": *Maybe I'll Pitch Forever,* 34–35.

24   "WILD AS A MARSH HEN": Nick Wilson e-mail.

24   HERB AARON, HANK'S DAD: Notes of Jim Riley interview with Herb Aaron.

24   IN 1949 *SPORTS ILLUSTRATED:* "How Old Is Satch?" *Sports Illustrated.*

24   "DIDN'T LIKE BASEBALL": *Pitchin' Man,* 27.

24   "IT'S A TERRIBLE STRAIN": Fox, *Satchel Paige's America,* 31.

24   ALEX HERMAN: Herman said he owned the team. Others referred to him as a scout, or the player-manager, and he was listed in the box scores as an infielder in some games where Satchel pitched. The team's name also changed over the years—from White Sox to the Black Lookouts to the All-Stars.

24   "MY FATHER WAS DRIVING": Author interviews with Kirk Herman and Alexis Herman.

25   SATCHEL WAS UNDERAGE: *Pitchin' Man,* 83.

25   "YOUR PA AIN'T BEEN DEAD": *Maybe I'll Pitch Forever,* 36.

25   HERMAN KEPT PRESSING: *Pitchin' Man,* 27–28.

25   TALE TO RECITE: Alexis Herman interview.

CHAPTER 2: BLACKBALL

26 HE WAS GREEN AS A: *Maybe I'll Pitch Forever*, 30; Fox, *Satchel Paige's America*, 89.

26 HE LOOKED LIKE A RUBE: Shane, "Satchel Man," *Reader's Digest;* Shane, "Chocolate Rube Waddell," *The Saturday Evening Post.*

27 "HOLD THE MITT": *Pitchin' Man*, 28.

27 SODA POP BOTTLES: *Maybe I'll Pitch Forever*, 41.

27 "I TALKED WITH HIM": "How Old Is Satch?"

27 "[ALEX] WAS ALWAYS PUSHING": *Maybe I'll Pitch Forever*, 41.

27 LEFT SCENTED NOTES: Donovan, "The Fabulous Satchel Paige," *Collier's.*

27 "WE'D HUNT UP": *Maybe I'll Pitch Forever*, 45.

28 SO CLOSE WERE THE TWO: "How Old Is Satch?"

28 NEXT PAYDAY CAME: *Maybe I'll Pitch Forever*, 43.

28 HIS FIRST GAME: *Maybe I'll Pitch Forever*, 39–40.

28 "IN TWO YEARS": *Maybe I'll Pitch Forever*, 43.

28 "WAS A GREAT PITCHER": "How Old Is Satch?"

29 "OFFERED ME FIVE HUNDRED": *Maybe I'll Pitch Forever*, 44.

29 "ALEX FINALLY TALKED": *Maybe I'll Pitch Forever*, 44.

30 WILLIAM EDWARD WHITE: Fatsis, "Mystery of Baseball: Was William White Game's First Black?" *The Wall Street Journal.*

30 "THE UNFORTUNATE SON": Malloy, *Sol White's History of Colored Base Ball*, 137.

31 HARASSED FROM BOTH SIDES: Malloy, *Sol White's History*, 137–38.

31 THAT PITCHER NEVER GOT HIM: Malloy, *Sol White's History*, 139.

31 GRANT EVENTUALLY WENT: *Sol White's History*, 140.

31 THE BARRIER BREAKERS PERSEVERED: Hogan, *Shades of Glory*, 50–56; Jim Overmyer e-mail to author, 2008; list compiled by Bob Davids of Society of American Baseball Research; Fox, *Big Leagues*, 304.

32 "DARK OBJECTS": Delaney, "The 1887 Binghamton Bingos," *Baseball Research Journal.*

32 BARRING "ANY CLUB": Peterson, *Only the Ball Was White*, 16–17.

32 "APPROVE NO MORE CONTRACTS": Peterson, *Only the Ball Was White*, 28.

32 "DO NOT AGREE TO PLAY": Peterson, *Only the Ball Was White*, 28–29, 31.

32 "GENTLEMAN'S AGREEMENT": Povich, *All Those Mornings . . . at the Post*, 64.

32 ALL BUT FLEETWOOD WALKER: Peterson, *Only the Ball Was White*, 45–46.

33 DATING TO THE PLANTATION: Fox, *Big Leagues*, 301–3.

33 CUBAN GIANTS, WHICH BEGAN: Peterson, *Only the Ball Was White*, 35–36.

33 INTEREST IN A BLACK FEDERATION: Peterson, *Only the Ball Was White*, 26–27, 62.

33 CUBAN STARS: Two mixed-race teams called themselves the Stars, one playing in the East and the other the West. There were also two Cuban Giants, the first called simply the Giants while the second, composed of Giants defectors, was aptly known as the X-Giants. Riley, *Biographical Encyclopedia*, 202–4.

34 FOSTER MAINTAINED CONTROL: Peterson, *Only the Ball Was White*, 82–84, 110–11.

34 THE BLACK MAJORS: Peterson, *Only the Ball Was White*, 80–91.

35 DID NOT LIKE A CALL: There also were not enough umpires. In their heyday the Negro Leagues hired just two per game, one behind home and the other at first, which was too few to see all the action.

310 · Notes

35 NOT THE STRUCTURAL DEFECTS: Peterson, *Only the Ball Was White,* 3–15.

35 GIBSON, NOT RUTH: Peterson, *Only the Ball Was White,* 159–60.

36 "TY COBB, BABE RUTH": O'Neil, Wulf, and Conrads, *I Was Right on Time,* 25.

36 HIJACKING BEER TRUCKS: Holway, *Josh and Satch,* 37.

38 A TEAMMATE GOT OFF: Banker, *Black Diamonds;* William Jack Marshall interview.

38 "WHY ARE YOU": Donn Rogosin's taped interviews of Negro Leaguers for his National Public Radio broadcast in 1980 and his book *Invisible Men: Life in Baseball's Negro Leagues.*

39 "AS GOOD AS SEX": Hogan, *Shades of Glory,* 3.

39 "I GOT STRAWBERRIES": Bankes, *The Pittsburgh Crawfords: The Life and Times,* 110.

39 WIDESPREAD USE OF LIGHTS: Peterson, *Only the Ball Was White,* 124.

39 "JUST LOOKED UP": Ward and Burns, *Baseball: An Illustrated History,* 221.

40 EACH MANIPULATION: Adair, *The Physics of Baseball,* 63–64.

40 "WE HAD TO HIT": Francis, "Satch: The Life of Leroy 'Satchel' Paige," *From Delinquency to Diamond.*

40 COONSBERRY RULES: Ward and Burns, *Baseball: An Illustrated History,* 221.

40 DISREGARDED ITS LAWS: Bruce, *Kansas City Monarchs,* 51.

41 "SATCHELL, A NEW HURLER": "Chattanooga White Sox Beat Black Crackers," *Chattanooga News.*

41 HE WAS BACK IN THE PAPER: "Colored White Sox Beat Black Crackers," *Chattanooga News.*

42 "AFTER BREEZING THROUGH": "Negro White Sox Win Double-Header," *Chattanooga Times.*

42 "ALL I KNOW FOR SURE": "Satch Fools 'Em with Fast One," *Chicago Sun-Times.*

42 HIS SECOND SEASON IN CHATTANOOGA: *Pitchin' Man,* 28; *Maybe I'll Pitch Forever,* 46.

43 HIS FIRST BIG GAME: "Fight at St Louis Park Halts 3rd Game," *Birmingham Reporter.*

43 SATCHEL PUT A DIFFERENT SPIN: *Pitchin' Man,* 32; *Maybe I'll Pitch Forever,* 50.

43 "IT WAS WORTH HALF": Peterson, *Only the Ball Was White,* 133.

44 "SATCHEL WAS JUST AS FAST": Ray, "He's Just a Big Man from the South," *Los Angeles Times.*

44 "SEE, HE'D WIND UP": Holway, *Josh and Satch,* 7.

44 "PRACTICE, PRACTICE": Holway, *Josh and Satch,* 7.

45 BUT AFTER HE'D WHIPPED FIVE: *Maybe I'll Pitch Forever,* 49.

45 HE WON AT LEAST: Hogan, *Shades of Glory,* 406–7. Here as elsewhere with Negro League stats, Negro League historians differ on Satchel's record. John Holway says he went 8-3 in 1927, striking out eighty and walking just nineteen in ninety-three innings, with a total runs average of 3.27. *Josh and Satch,* 9.

46 UNJOINTED TURKEY: "The Fabulous Satchel Paige."

46 "WHEN SATCHEL GOT TO": Rogosin, *Invisible Men,* 100.

46 NORMAN "TURKEY" STEARNES: Author interview with Nettie Stearnes.

46 "RIGHT HANDED HITTERS": Nick Wilson e-mail to author.

46 THOU SHALT NOT STEAL: That, along with Satchel's etching of FASTBALL on his shoe, were cited regularly but never seen.

46 "HANDLED A PITCHER": *Maybe I'll Pitch Forever,* 47.

47 SATCHEL STRUCK OUT 112: Hogan, *Shades of Glory,* 406–7.

47 WORDS LIKE "HELPLESS": "Black Barons Win and Lose at Kansas City," *Birmingham Reporter.*

47 CALLED HIM "INVINCIBLE": "Detroit Has Hard Time to Beat Barons," *Chicago Defender.*

47 "THE MAN COULD THROW": John B. Holway, *Voices from the Great Black Baseball Leagues,* 236.

47 "TENDS TO DISAPPEAR": Peterson, *Only the Ball Was White,* 141.

47 "SO INFERNALLY FAST": Hogan, *Shades of Glory,* 252.

48 WON-LOST BREAKDOWN: Hogan, *Shades of Glory,* 406–7. Again there is disagreement. Historian Timothy Whitt says Satchel's 1929 record was 12-11 (*Bases Loaded with History,* 42), while Holway says it was 11-11 (*Josh and Satch,* 16).

48 "THIS BOY SATCHEL": "Wesley to Send Ace to Face Giants," *Chicago Defender.*

48 "SATCHEL WAS IN RARE FORM": "Birmingham Leads Series with Detroit," *Chicago Defender.*

48 LASTED ALL SEASON: Hogan, *Shades of Glory,* 406–7. Whitt says his total was 184. Holway says in one book that it was 184 and in another 194, which would have been an all-time Negro League record. *Bases Loaded with History,* 42; *Josh and Satch,* 16; and Holway, *Complete Book of Baseball's Negro Leagues,* 244.

48 BLACK BARONS PAYING HIM: Haupert, "Fair Pay for Fair Play."

48 ON ONE EXCURSION: Bak, *Turkey Stearnes,* 136.

49 "I GOT TICKETS FOR SPEEDING": *Maybe I'll Pitch Forever,* 49.

49 FISH FRY BONUS: "Satchel Man."

49 "YOU'D FORGIVE HIM": Peterson, *Only the Ball Was White,* 142.

49 "A MAN WHO'S GOT TO": *Maybe I'll Pitch Forever,* 137.

50 "I GUESS I SHOULD HAVE": *Maybe I'll Pitch Forever,* 22.

50 "EVERYBODY IN THE SOUTH": Peterson, *Only the Ball Was White,* 133.

50 "IT STILL WAS BETTER": *Maybe I'll Pitch Forever,* 51.

50 "WAVED PLENTY OF GREEN": *Maybe I'll Pitch Forever,* 54.

50 CARD GAME HAD TURNED UGLY: "Black Sox Player Jailed Following Fight in Cuba," *Afro-American.*

50 LOCAL PAPERS GAVE HIM: "The Great Big Man from the South," *Afro-American;* "1930 Edition of Black Sox Promises to Be Fast," *Afro-American;* "The Black Sox Guns are Ready to Boom," *Afro-American;* "Double Plays, Heavy Blows," *Afro-American;* "Black Sox Boast a Pair o' Kings," *Afro-American;* Gibson, "Hear Me Talkin to Ya'," *Afro-American,* April 19, 1930; "Black Sox Trim White Club," *Afro-American.*

51 WON SEVEN GAMES: *Shades of Glory,* 406–7. Whitt says he won twelve games for Birmingham, Holway says it was nine. *Bases Loaded with History,* 42; and *Josh and Satch,* 21.

51 REMAINDER OF 1930: Holway, *Complete Book,* 259–60.

51 FOUR OF HIS BLACK BARONS WINS: Baseball Hall of Fame, *Shades of Glory* statistics.

52 SORT OUT HIS ATTRACTION: Ribowsky, *Don't Look Back,* 17; 2007 e-mail to author from Richard Schweid, former reporter for the Nashville *Tennessean.*

52 "I'D LOOK OVER": *Maybe I'll Pitch Forever,* 57.

CHAPTER 3: THE GLORY TRAIL

54 WAS NOT EASILY DENIED: Ruck, *Sandlot Seasons*, 137–38.
54 GREENLEE SHOWED THE SAME GRIT: Ruck, *Sandlot Seasons*, 138–52; Metcalfe, *Game for All Races*, 101.
54 EVEN MORE EXPANSIVE: Ruck, *Sandlot Seasons*, 139–40; Bankes, *Pittsburgh Crawfords*, 23–25; James Bankes e-mail to author.
55 IN RECENT YEARS: Ruck, *Sandlot Seasons*, 46–62.
55 PITTSBURGH ITSELF WAS CHANGING: Ruck, *Sandlot Seasons*, 8–38.
55 SEEMED LIKE CHRISTMAS: Ruck, *Sandlot Seasons*, 152–57.
56 TO HAVE A NATURAL RIVAL: Ruck, *Sandlot Seasons*, 128–36, 153–54.
56 PUBLIC FACE OF THE GRAYS: Ruck, *Sandlot Seasons*, 124–28.
57 COURTING LEROY PAIGE: "The Fabulous Satchel Paige."
57 FOR A MERE $250: Satchel says in his memoir that he was offered $250 but Frank A. Young, the sports editor of the *Chicago Defender*, says Gus was paying $550 "and all expenses." Reisler, *Black Writers/Black Baseball*, 66.
58 "MASTERFUL AND SENSATIONAL": "Paige Stops Grays as Crawfords Cop," *The Pittsburgh Courier*.
58 "THEY HARDLY HIT": Ruck, *Sandlot Seasons*, 154.
58 "WE CELEBRATED LIKE": *Maybe I'll Pitch Forever*, 63.
59 WAITRESS STOOD OUT: *Maybe I'll Pitch Forever*, 63–64.
59 CAPITALIZED ON HIS HERO'S STATUS: *Maybe I'll Pitch Forever*, 64–65.
59 "YOU LOOK LIKE": *Maybe I'll Pitch Forever*, 65.
60 OUT OF THE NUMBERS: Danver, "Pittsburghesque, the Caliph of 'Little Harlem,' " *Pittsburgh Post-Gazette*.
60 HIGH-CLASS STADIUM: "Greenlee Field Data Released," *The Pittsburgh Courier; Sandlot Seasons*, 156.
60 THE FIELD'S GRAND OPENING: Ruck, *Sandlot Seasons*, 156–57; Marasco, "Lifting the Lid at Greenlee," The Diamond Angle, www.thediamondangle.com.
61 REVENGE CAME LATER: "Grays Win 1, Lose 3 to NY Black Yanks," *The Pittsburgh Courier*.
62 RECORD OF 23-7: Washington, "Sez Ches," *The Pittsburgh Courier*, January 28, 1933. The Crawfords were not in a league in 1932, their opponents varied widely in skill, and reconstructions of Satchel's record fluctuate even more than normal—from Holway's 14-8 to Hogan's 10-4 in *Shades of Glory*.
62 HIS WINDMILL WINDUP: It was a Paige trademark and offers a great show, but studies show it does not add force or power to a pitch. Author interview with Glenn Fleisig, American Sports Medicine Institute, Birmingham, Alabama.
62 "LIVED A DIFFERENT LIFE": Holway, *Josh and Satch*, 48.
62 "ALL OF US WERE LOOKING": Leonard and Riley, *Buck Leonard: The Black Lou Gehrig*, 42.
62 "WE COULD NOT USE SATCHELL": Posey, "Posey's Points," *The Pittsburgh Courier*, June 15, 1940.
63 HE FILLED THE STANDS: Ruck, *Sandlot Seasons*, 157.
63 TURNING OVER HIS PACKARD CONVERTIBLE: Bankes, *Pittsburgh Crawfords*, 35.
63 "THERE ALWAYS WAS A MOB": *Maybe I'll Pitch Forever*, 66–69.
64 "HAS 'THAT CERTAIN THING' ": Reisler, *Black Writers/Black Baseball*, 101,

104; Washington, "Sez Ches, Satchel's Back in Town," *The Pittsburgh Courier,* May 9, 1936.

64   "I ALWAYS SAY": O'Neil et al., *I Was Right on Time,* 117.

64   SUSPEND "INDEFINITELY": "Satchel Paige Is Warned to Report," *Chicago Defender.*

64   "A BAFFLING ROOK": "Willie Foster and Satchell Paige to Settle Ancient Feud," *The Pittsburgh Courier.*

65   "SATCHELL PRESIDED ON THE MOUND": "Satchell Supreme in Craw Victory," *The Pittsburgh Courier.*

65   "IT AIN'T SO MUCH": Vass, "A Paige in Baseball History," *Mobile Press.*

65   "BASES ON BALLS": Vass, "A Paige in Baseball History," *Mobile Press.*

65   "THROW STRIKES AT ALL TIMES": Veeck, "Satchel Paige Would Have Loved the Orioles," *Chicago Tribune.*

65   DUEL OF THE CENTURY: "Willie Foster and Satchell Paige to Settle Ancient Feud," *The Pittsburgh Courier.*

65   "FASTEST BALL LOOKS": Washington, "Sez Ches," *The Pittsburgh Courier,* July 1, 1933.

65   BEST SEASON OF HIS LIFE: Hogan, *Shades of Glory,* 406–7; author's search of box scores and other records; www.baseball-reference.com.

66   HIS 1934 RECORD SOARS: Author's search of records.

66   IN THE NEGRO LEAGUES: Hogan, *Shades of Glory,* 406–7.

66   JULY 4 JEWEL: Nunn, "Paige Hurls No-Hit Classic," *The Pittsburgh Courier.*

66   "THE UMPIRE TOOK A LOOK": Roberts, "Paige First Cranked-Up Arm at Mobile," *The Pittsburgh Courier.*

67   SHOOTING OFF FIRECRACKERS: *Maybe I'll Pitch Forever,* 81.

67   "THE STANDS WENT WILD": "Grays Win Second Holiday Tilt, 4-3," *The Pittsburgh Courier.*

67   "HOPE THEY NEVER COME BACK": "Crawfords Drub Giants," *Chicago Defender.*

68   "TODAY'S GAME WAS MORE": Nunn, "As 'Speedball' Satchell Paige Ambled into the East-West Game," *The Pittsburgh Courier.*

68   "WITH MEASURED TREAD": Burley, "Looking Back at the East-West Classic," *The Pittsburgh Courier.*

69   "THAT DIDN'T LEAVE ME": *Maybe I'll Pitch Forever,* 81.

69   "THE HOUSE OF SATCHELL": Washington, "Paige Fans 12 to Shade Jones," *The Pittsburgh Courier.*

70   "THOSE FOOTSTEPS THAT YOU HEARD": Harris, "Philadelphia Pitcher Muffles Craws Sluggers," *The Philadelphia Tribune.*

70   BACK FOR A REMATCH: "Satchell to Oppose Jones in Stadium," *The Pittsburgh Courier;* Bearden, "Cole's Giants and Philly Stars Lose," *Chicago Defender.*

70   "HEARD THE BOYS BRAGGING": *Maybe I'll Pitch Forever,* viii.

71   THE NIGHTCLUB WAS HEADQUARTERS: King, *All the Stars Came out That Night,* 115.

71   PUBLIC ACTION AT THE GRILL: Ruck, *Sandlot Seasons,* 139–40; Bankes, *Pittsburgh Crawfords,* 23–25; Bankes e-mail.

71   TAP-DANCED ON THE DUGOUT: Ward and Burns, *Baseball: An Illustrated History,* 201.

71   EVEN BIGGER FANS: Bankes, *Pittsburgh Crawfords,* 103; Tygiel, *Past Time: Baseball as History,* 122.

72 LOOKOUTS FOR HIS NUMBERS RUNNERS: Ted Page earned $15 a week for sitting in front of headquarters and, when he saw someone suspicious, pushing a buzzer to warn the counters to stash the cash. McNeil, *Black Baseball out of Season,* 3.

73 HE HAD SIGNED WITH THE GANGSTER: Greenlee told a reporter he got out of the numbers racket in 1931, earning a living through his four restaurants and baseball team. As part of this bid for respectability he moved to the suburbs, where he owned a beautiful home and raised three hundred white leghorn chickens. Danver, "Pittsburghesque, the Caliph of 'Little Harlem' "; "Gus Greenlee, Pioneer of Numbers Here, Dies," *Pittsburgh Post-Gazette.*

73 CONSOLING HIMSELF WITH BOOZE: Holway, *Josh and Satch,* 132.

74 "ALL THE WOMENS": Bankes e-mail.

74 WAITRESS'S VENERABLE ROOTS: "Talk of Town," *The Pittsburgh Courier,* December 20, 1941; Polk, "Mrs. Bernice Sutton Buried on Jan. 3," *The Pittsburgh Courier.*

74 "WE CAN'T JUST KEEP RUNNING": *Maybe I'll Pitch Forever,* 84.

74–75 ALL-NIGHT AFFAIR: *Maybe I'll Pitch Forever,* 86.

75 "IT WAS LIKE BEING A KID": *Maybe I'll Pitch Forever,* 70–75.

75 "AFTER THAT HONEYMOON": *Maybe I'll Pitch Forever,* 86.

76 "I GUESS GUS WAS MAD": *Maybe I'll Pitch Forever,* 87.

76 "WHERE'RE WE GOING": *Maybe I'll Pitch Forever,* 87.

CHAPTER 4: THE GAME IN BLACK AND WHITE

77 BISMARCK IN THE 1930s: Conrad, "A Paige in Bismarck's History," *The Bismarck Tribune.*

78 "IT WASN'T UNTIL": *Maybe I'll Pitch Forever,* 88.

79 JAMESTOWN STRUCK FIRST: "Bismarck Nips Jamestown 3-2 with Thrilling Rally," *The Bismarck Tribune;* "Capital City Club Defeated Locals," *The Jamestown Sun. The Sun,* while crediting Satchel with just seventeen strikeouts, added three inches to his height, inflated the crowd estimate by nearly a thousand, and said baseballs were flying out of his hand "so fast one could hardly see them."

79 FINDING A LANDLORD: *Maybe I'll Pitch Forever,* 88; author interview with Dan Heintzman. Others dispute the boxcar story, and Satchel's memory on his time in Bismarck was foggy on everything from how much he was paid to play to where he lived to what years he was in North Dakota.

79 TOOK OUT HIS DISPLEASURE: *Maybe I'll Pitch Forever,* 89–90.

80 HIS SALARY WAS FATTENED: "A Paige in Bismarck's History." Again, there was disagreement over what he was paid, with estimates ranging from $100 a game to $600 a month.

80 "I'D CRACKED ANOTHER": *Maybe I'll Pitch Forever,* 88.

80 THAT BARNSTORMING: Cole, "Ersatz Octobers: Baseball Barnstorming," in *Baseball History.*

81 BARNSTORMING SINCE THE 1880s: Peterson, *Only the Ball Was White,* 146.

82 HIS TIME ON THE ROAD: Jim Wheeler e-mail to author; John L. Clark, "Satchel Paige: The Life History of the Great Pitcher," *Chicago Defender; Satchel Paige's America,* 89.

82 "EVERY STATE IN THE": *Pitchin' Man,* 41.

82 BARNSTORMING WAS EASY: Silverman, "Satchel Paige Sounds Off," *Sport;* Durslag, "Speaking of Sports," *The San Francisco Examiner,* March 4, 1969; Young, *Great Negro Baseball Stars,* 86.

82 "WE HAD TO GO IN THE COLORED": "Satchel Paige Sounds Off," 44–59.

82 TESTING WHETHER AN EATERY: Glenn, *Don't Let Anyone Take Your Joy Away,* 41.

83 GYPSY BALLPLAYERS IMPROVISED: Rogosin, *Invisible Men,* 131.

83 HIGH SCHOOL TEAM IN SAN DIEGO: *Voices from the Great Black Baseball Leagues,* 214.

84 CROWD TURNED NASTY: Rogosin, *Invisible Men,* 121.

85 INVENTING HANDLES FOR PLAYERS: "The Fabulous Satchel Paige"; "Chocolate Rube Waddell."

86 THOSE RESULTS COME WITH CAVEATS: McNeil, *The California Winter League,* 239–40. There are many theories on why Commissioner Landis imposed those limits on interracial competition. He said it was to keep Major Leaguers from getting hurt by extending their seasons. Others say that he wanted to increase his ballplayers' dependence on their owners—and that his particular reticence about barnstorming against Negro Leaguers reflected the racism of the era.

86 THAT WAS NO SURPRISE: McNeil, *California Winter League,* 236–41.

87 EVEN MORE OTHERWORLDLY: McNeil, *California Winter League,* 165–66.

87 "LIKE WE INVENTED": Brashler, *The Story of Negro League Baseball,* 67.

87 JOHNNY PESKY: Author interview with Johnny Pesky.

87 "LIKE A SPECIALLY-BUILT": Washington, "Sez Ches," *The Pittsburgh Courier,* April 14, 1934.

87 "HERO OF THE BATTLE": "So Satchel Paige Shows Dizzy Dean How to Pitch," *Chicago Defender.*

88 TOOK TIME FROM HIS HONEYMOON: "Satchel Whiffs 17 Soapsters," *Los Angeles Times.*

88 "SATCHEL PAIGE STOOD": McNeil, *California Winter League,* 238.

88 RELIGIOUS COMMUNITY: www.houseofdavidmuseum.org and e-mail to author from Chris Siriano, House of David Museum, Benton Harbor, Michigan. Among the colonies' baseball teams was the Colored House of David, which was made up mainly of Cubans.

88 CLAIMING TO HAVE DREAMED UP: The House's claim as the originator of the pepper game is more widely accepted than its contention that it dreamed up the waffle cone and pinsetter.

89 WHISKERLESS DARK-SKINNED MEN: Satchel says he had a mustache; others say he donned a fake red beard.

89 CAME IN AS A RELIEVER: Cahn, "House of David Looks Strong in First Tournament Victory," *The Denver Post.*

89 "MAGIC FIREBALL": "Lexington, Colorado Ice and House of David Win," *The Denver Post.*

89 TWO NIGHTS LATER: Cahn, "House of David, United Fuel, Los Angeles Win," *The Denver Post.*

89 THIRD AND FINAL START: Cahn, " 'Satch' Wins 3 in Five Days in Big Denver Tourney," *The Pittsburgh Courier.*

89 MERCHANTS PARK IN DENVER: www.diamondintherox.com.

90 SERGEANT CAUGHT HIM: Gregory, *The Story of Dizzy Dean,* 32.

90 SHOWED IN GAME FOUR: Gregory, *Story of Dizzy Dean,* 225.

91 ARTHUR BRISBANE: Quoted in Gregory, *Story of Dizzy Dean,* 225.

91 OL' DIZ PITCHED SIX: Curt Smith, *America's Dizzy Dean,* 20–21.

91 HALL OF FAME FORM: "Satchell Outhurls Dizzy!" *The Pittsburgh Courier;* Finger, "Satchel Paige Dominates Game," Cleveland *Call and Post;* "Satchel Paige Hands Beating to Dizzy Dean," *Chicago Tribune;* "So Satchel Paige Shows Dizzy Dean How to Pitch," *Chicago Defender.*

92 BERGER REMEMBERS ONE DAY: Berger and Morris, *Wally: Freshly Remember'd,* 171.

93 "THE FANS WERE YELLIN' ": Gregory, *Story of Dizzy Dean,* 376.

93 SATCHEL YELLED: *Maybe I'll Pitch Forever,* 91–92.

93 "HE TOLD THE TRUTH": Barry Mednick e-mail to author, 2006, including interview he conducted with Bonnie Serrell.

93 "THEY'D GET YOU NERVOUS": Author interview with Red Moore.

93 THAT ACCOUNTING COMES: Veeck and Linn, *Veeck—as in Wreck,* 182.

94 "PLAYERS SWUNG FISTS": "Dizzy Dean Almost Turns Exhibition into Riot," United Press International.

95 "A BUNCH OF THE FELLOWS": Dean, " 'Satchel Greatest Pitcher'—Dizzy," *Chicago Defender.*

95 DIZZY RATCHETED UP: Cohane, "The Ancient Satchel," *Look;* Addie, "The Big Picture," *The Washington Post.*

95 "THEY WERE SAYING": *Maybe I'll Pitch Forever,* 91.

96 "HE HAD TROUBLE KEEPING": Holway, *Josh and Satch,* 84.

96 RALPH KINER: Vincent, *The Only Game in Town,* 209–10.

96 STRUCK HIM OUT THREE TIMES: Tim Gay email to author, 2009.

96 KU KLUX KLAN: Lieb, *Baseball as I Have Known It,* 57.

96 CAN YOU COME NORTH: "The Fabulous Satchel Paige."

96 NOW HERE THEY WERE: Murphy, "Daily Scribe Tells Majors of Value of Satchel Paige," *Chicago Defender; Josh and Satch,* 84; Holway, *Complete Book of Baseball's Negro Leagues,* 324.

97 DIMAGGIO ALL WE HOPED: "The Fabulous Satchel Paige."

97 "THE GREATEST BASEBALL": "Daily Scribe Tells Majors of Value of Satchel Paige."

97 PROVE HIS PROWESS: *Maybe I'll Pitch Forever,* 102–6.

97 "SATCH HAS A CURVE": Powers, "Umpire," *The Washington Post.*

97 THE ULTIMATE CLASH: *Maybe I'll Pitch Forever,* 58–59; *Pitchin' Man,* 44.

98 TELL A DIFFERENT STORY: Author interview with Julia Ruth Stevens.

98 1943 STORY CARRYING HIS: Paige and Dismukes, " 'Satch' Struck Out Josh Gibson for Biggest Thrill," *The Pittsburgh Courier.*

98 FIVE YEARS LATER: Cerf, "Try and Stop Me," *Atchison Daily Globe* (Atchison, Kansas).

98 BOB FELLER, WHO ONE DAY: Author interview with Bob Feller.

98 AS DID COOL PAPA BELL: Interview with and e-mail from Bankes.

98 LAST BABE-SATCHEL ACCOUNT: Jenkinson, *The Year Babe Ruth Hit 104 Home Runs,* 221; and author interview with Buck O'Neil.

99 WHAT KEPT HIM AWAY: Eriksmoen, "Churchill Brought Baseball's Best to Bismarck," *The Bismarck Tribune;* "Satchel Paige, Colored Hurler, Expected in Bismarck Next Week," *The Bismarck Tribune;* "Paige and Medlock, Colored Pitchers,

Have Not Arrived," *The Bismarck Tribune;* "Satchel Paige May Pitch for Locals Against American All-Stars," *The Bismarck Tribune;* "Satchel Paige or Chet Brewer Will Get Pitching Call," *The Bismarck Tribune.*

99 "SENT SHERIFFS LOOKING FOR": Monroe, "Lock 'Em Up Boys," *Chicago Defender.*

100 "PAIGE IS BEING DETAINED: "Satchell Paige Detained by Cops," *Afro-American.*

100 THE BISMARCK OWNER: "Neil O. Churchill, Ex-Mayor of City, Dies," *The Bismarck Tribune.*

101 LILY-WHITE NORTHERN PLAINS: Roper, "Another Chink in Jim Crow?" in *Nine: A Journal of Baseball History and Social Policy Perspectives.*

101 SATCHEL CAME TO BISMARCK: Shury, "Satch in Saskatchewan"; Donovan, "Satch Beards the House of David," *Collier's.*

101 SATCHEL WON SIX: Author's search of records.

102 THREATENED TO SLICE CHURCHILL: Author interview with Marc Conrad, relating story told by an employee at Churchill's car dealership who overheard Churchill's end of a phone conversation with Greenlee.

102 HE WON TWENTY-NINE GAMES: Box scores assembled by author. Other historians say Satchel won thirty games that season for Bismarck. McNary, *Ted "Double Duty" Radcliffe,* 123; and McNeil, *Cool Papas,* 203.

103 BISMARCK'S LAST HOME GAME: "Bismarck Overwhelms Twin City Giants," *The Bismarck Tribune.*

103 CHURCHILL SHOWED HIS APPRECIATION: *Pitchin' Man,* 49–50.

103 "SATCHEL WALKED INTO MY": Author interview with Neil Churchill, Jr.

103 JANET WAS LESS RECOGNIZABLE: How much Janet was around in 1933 and 1935 is unclear, because Satchel got the dates wrong in his memoir and told different stories to Richard Donovan and others. It is likely she was there in 1933, though not much in 1935. Janet did, however, send Cool Papa and Clara Bell a postcard from Bismarck in 1935, according to James Bankes.

104 "MAKE SURE THEY DON'T MESS": Author interview with Randy Churchill.

104 "QUINCY, I DON'T": Trouppe, *20 Years Too Soon,* 50.

104 SATCHEL GOT THE MESSAGE: McNary, *Ted "Double Duty" Radcliffe,* 109.

104 "SEND HIM TO THE MAYO CLINIC": Satchel acknowledged getting treatment at the Mayo Clinic, although not for a sexually transmitted disease. The clinic, for its part, won't say.

104 HONORARY TITLE "LONG RIFLE": "Satch Beards the House of David."

104 "THEY TOOK A REAL LIKING": *Maybe I'll Pitch Forever,* 97–98.

104 LEARNED THE REAL KEY: Trouppe, *20 Years Too Soon,* 55.

105 "THE CHAMP OF TODAY": Washington, "Sez Ches," *The Pittsburgh Courier,* April 20, 1935.

106 WHIFF OF MANURE: Conrad interview.

106 WON THE FOUR GAMES: McNary, *Ted "Double Duty" Radcliffe,* 260.

107 "IF PAIGE WAS SICK": "Bismarck Faces 'Crucial' National Tourney Test Tonight," *The Bismarck Tribune.*

107 AFTER THE DUST SETTLED: "Locals Play Post-Tourney Games, Get Good Publicity," *The Bismarck Tribune.*

107 "SOME OF THEM BASEBALL MANAGERS": *Maybe I'll Pitch Forever,* 98.

107 QUOTED ALMOST NEVER: Terrie Aamodt, "Cracking a Chink in Jim Crow: Satchel Paige and the Integration of Baseball," in Heaphy, ed., *Satchel Paige and Company,* 64–65.

107 BISMARCK'S SIX BLACK PLAYERS: Travis Larsen, "Satchel Paige and Hap Dumont: The Dynamic Duo of the National Baseball Congress Tournament," in *Satchel Paige and Company,* 92–95.

107 IT ALSO MADE HISTORY: "Cracking a Chink in Jim Crow," *Satchel Paige and Company,* 70.

107 "THEY SAID AT": Kelley, *Negro Leagues Revisited,* 11.

CHAPTER 5: SOUTH OF THE BORDER

108 IN 1929 TO CUBA: Satchel's record that winter was one of his most undistinguished ever—six wins and five losses—but it was enough to lead the Santa Clara Leopards in victories and was better than that of other Negro League stars pitching that season in Cuba.

108 IN 1933 TO VENEZUELA: What drew Satchel to Venezuela rather than back to Pittsburgh, where Janet and Gus were waiting, was that "I didn't have a topcoat." His first game there was almost his last, as he tells it. He was inserted into the outfield to let him catch his breath and acclimate to his surroundings, which included what looked like an iron pipe near the far fence. Minutes later a batter smashed a ball that rolled to the pipe. He went hoofing after it and just as he reached for the ball, the pipe moved. "I was looking at a boa constrictor. I lit out of there so fast the papers the next morning said Jesse Owens was in Venezuela posing as Satchel Paige." The runner ended up scoring, as did another a couple of days later when Satchel confronted a second snake in the grass. This time he picked up a stick and battled back. *Maybe I'll Pitch Forever,* 77–78; *Pitchin' Man,* 54.

108–9 SEEDS WERE PLANTED: "El Benefactor," *Time;* Turits, *Foundations of Despotism,* 5–6.

109 "IN AN ACT OF RESPECTFUL": *Listín Diario,* March 5, 1937.

109 PUBLICITY DEPARTMENT DISTRIBUTE: Clark, "Satchel Paige: The Life History."

110 HAD JUST THREE TEAMS: The names of the teams reflected their character. Estrellas Orientales means "Eastern Stars," which was the kind of beacon this noble outfit offered, while its nickname—Elefantes, or "Elephants"—prophesied its fall to the bottom of the standings. Águilas Cibaeñas means "Eagles of the Cibao," a northern province, and the team did soar in its challenge to the Dragones. As for the dictator's club, what better symbol than a fire-spewing dragon?

110 RECRUITING TRIPS OF THEIR OWN: Holway, *Josh and Satch,* 89–90; Bankes, *Pittsburgh Crawfords,* 127–29.

110 "WE WILL GIVE": *Maybe I'll Pitch Forever,* 117.

111 AYBAR CALLED A PRESS CONFERENCE: *Maybe I'll Pitch Forever,* 118–19.

111 TRUJILLO'S CORPORATE FRIENDS: "Charge American Sugar Co. Lured Players," *New York Age.*

111 "TRUJILLO RUNS THE WHOLE SHOW": *Maybe I'll Pitch Forever,* 119.

112 "EN LA CARCEL": Bankes, *Pittsburgh Crawfords,* 129.

112 PROTECTION NOT INTIMIDATION: Author interview with Bienvenido Rojas.

112 THE MENU AT CAFÉ LINDBERGH: Bienvenido Rojas interview.

112 "CHILDREN" AND "PIKININIS": *Listín Diario,* April 1937.

112 "IT WAS JUST REAL RELAXING": Bankes, *Pittsburgh Crawfords,* 129.

112 CAMPAIGN OF CARNAGE: Turits, *Foundations of Despotism,* 161–62.

113 PREPONDERANCE OF PROBLEMS: Luna, *Gentlemen's Baseball in Santiago,* 131, 141–42.

113 ACCORDING TO *LISTÍN DIARIO:* April 25, 1937; May 10, May 17, May 24, June 7, June 28, and July 10, 1937.

113 TOPS IN THE LEAGUE: Holway, *Josh and Satch,* 90–91; McNeil, *Black Baseball Out of Season,* 145; *Listín Diario,* July 10, 1937.

114 EIGHT DECISIVE GAMES: Most American historians have written that this was a seven-game playoff series. It looked that way, but Dominican authorities say it was the remaining games of the regular season. That season was scheduled to have up to forty-five games, but the last one was not needed given that the winner was clear after just forty-four.

114 "BOY, MY MOUTH": "Leroy Satchel Paige as Told to Earnest Mehl," in Carmichael, *My Greatest Day in Baseball,* 151–52.

114 BY THE SEVENTH INNING: "Leroy Satchel Paige as Told to Earnest Mehl," 152.

115 STAKES OF THAT TRIUMPH GREW: "Satch Beards the House of David"; *Maybe I'll Pitch Forever,* 120; "Wendell Smith's Sports Beat," *The Pittsburgh Courier,* July 24, 1965.

115 "I COULD SAY ANYTHING": Banker, *Black Diamonds,* Satchel Paige interview.

115 PRESERVE THE VICTORY: *Listín Diario,* July 12, 1937.

115 POINTS OF CONTENTION: *Pitchin' Man,* 56; *Maybe I'll Pitch Forever,* 120; *Listín Diario,* July 16, 1937; Paige, "Paige Says He Prefers Jungles to NNL Play," *Afro-American;* Satchel's Application for American Passport, April 15, 1938.

116 "AS UNDEPENDABLE AS": Washington, "Satch Should Be Barred," *The Pittsburgh Courier.*

116 SATCHEL SHOT BACK: "Paige Says He Prefers Jungles."

117 "PERHAPS THE MOST": "All-Stars to Play Before Legionnaires," *Chicago Defender.*

117 CAPTURED THE TITLE: Satchel's teammates supposedly resented him for joining them late and trying to steal their thunder, along with a $1,000 bonus, by winning what could have been the clinching game. So, according to an unnamed player interviewed by Donn Rogosin, they intentionally lost that game and won the next one with Leroy Madlock on the mound. Rogosin, *Invisible Men,* 140–41.

117 "UNTIL TODAY": "Satchel Made Victim of No-Hit Contest," *Chicago Defender.*

117 TAYLOR, A YOUNG BUCKSHOOTER: "Negro Stars Take No-Hit Game," *The New York Times;* Bostic, "Taylor's No-Hitter Tops Satchel Paige," *Afro-American.*

117 "THE SELECT CIRCLE": "Taylor's No-Hitter Tops Satchel Paige."

117 "WAS SHELLED": Bostic, "Johnny Taylor Is Shelled from Mound as Paige Wins," *Afro-American.*

117 "SWEET REVENGE": "Paige Beats Taylor, 9-5 in Star Tilt," *Chicago Defender.*

118 THROW ICE CUBES: Smith, "Smitty's Sports Spurts," *The Pittsburgh Courier,* April 16, 1938.

118 "I'M HOLDING OUT": " 'I'm Holding Out Because Joe DiMaggio Advised Me To,' " *The Pittsburgh Courier.*

118 GONE UPTOWN: *Maybe I'll Pitch Forever,* 122.

119 "WILL TELL OF HIS BASEBALL": "Negro Nines to Drill Today for All-Star Game," *Chicago Daily Tribune.*

119 "THE MYSTERY OF SATCHEL": "Satchell Paige Barred from Baseball," *New Jersey Herald News.*

119 "TO PUNISH HIM": Peterson, *Only the Ball Was White,* 137.

119 "I'VE FOUND FREEDOM": Smith, " 'Smitty's Sports Spurts," *The Pittsburgh Courier,* May 6, 1944.

120 " 'SPEAK ENGLISH, BOYS' ": *Maybe I'll Pitch Forever,* 55.

120 "WHEN A GUY DOWN THERE": *Maybe I'll Pitch Forever,* 123.

120 HIS FIRST MAJOR MALADY: *Pitchin' Man,* 57; "Satch Beards the House of David."

120 SOMEBODY HAD PINCHED: *Maybe I'll Pitch Forever,* 123–24.

120 "SQUEEZED LEMON": www.geocities.com.

120 RETREATED TO HIS HOTEL: *Maybe I'll Pitch Forever,* 125–26.

121 EXAMINED BY PHYSICIANS: *Maybe I'll Pitch Forever,* 126–27.

121 PULLING AT HIS SOCKET: Adair, *Physics of Baseball,* 68; Fleisig interview.

122 "I DIDN'T WANT TO SEE": *Maybe I'll Pitch Forever,* 128–29.

122 "I KNEW IF I COULDN'T": *Maybe I'll Pitch Forever,* 129.

123 SHORTSTOP QUIT: Posnaski, *The Soul of Baseball,* 137–38.

123 "I WAS THROWING": *Maybe I'll Pitch Forever,* 133.

123 WILKINSON HAD FIXED IT: Posnaski, *Soul of Baseball,* 138.

123 "HOW'D HE EVER GET": *Maybe I'll Pitch Forever,* 133–34.

123 NEVER STOPPED DIGGING: "Rumor Paige Arm Is 'Dead,' " *New Jersey Herald News.*

124 MORE POETIC VERSION: Johnson, "Satchel's Arm Was Dead," Kansas City Call.

124 "HE COULDN'T EVEN WIPE": Holway, *Josh and Satch,* 123.

124 "WASHED UP": Robinson and Bauer, *Catching Dreams,* 28.

124 "YOU BETTER BE READY": Robinson and Bauer, *Catching Dreams,* 31.

124 SATCHEL CALLED IT A MIRACLE: *Pitchin' Man,* 59.

124 MOMENT IT HAPPENED: Donovan, "Time Ain't Gonna Mess with Me," *Collier's.*

125 WHAT HE WAS BACK FROM: Author interview with Dr. John Richmond.

125 HIS GURGLING STOMACH: *Pitchin' Man,* 57.

125 HAPPENED ONE AFTERNOON: "Satchel's Arm Was Dead,"127

125 CAME ON A RAINY DAY: Mednick e-mail.

126 HE CALLED "YELLOW JUICE": Posnaski, *Soul of Baseball,* 140.

126 HE PROVED HIMSELF: Van Hyning, *Puerto Rico's Winter League,* 73–74.

127 "PAIGE THREW ASPIRIN TABLETS": Van Hyning, *Puerto Rico's Winter League,* 74.

127 "IT TOOK SPECIAL EYES": Author interview with Ramón "Nica" Bayron.

127 "THE BEST I'VE EVER SEEN": Author interview with Luis Olmo.

127 THE MANAGER CAME RUNNING OUT: *Buck Leonard: The Black Lou Gehrig,* 124.

127 BY SEASON'S END: McNeil, *Baseball's Other All-Stars,* 62.

128 PREPARED HIM FOR GUAYAMA: Author interviews with Luis Guillermo Garcia and others in Guayama, Puerto Rico.

128 LUCY, AS SHE LIKED: Author interview with Julio Figueroa; interviews with Garcia and others in Guayama.

129 "FINE WOMAN": *Maybe I'll Pitch Forever,* 140.

129 GOLD CADILLAC BROUGHT BY SHIP: Julio Figueroa agrees that Satchel drove a big car but says it was a yellow-and-brown 1941 Chevrolet driven by Felix Banks, who owned the car and worked for the Witches.

129 "HE WAS SO BIG": Author interview with Desiderio de León.

130 "GO HAVE FUN": Julio Figueroa interview.

130 SATCHEL AND LUCY MET: Julio Figueroa interview.

130 LUCY'S FAMILY WAS NEVER RICH: Julio Figueroa interview.

131 "ONE OF THE NICEST": Irvin and Riley, *Nice Guys Finish First*, 83.

131 THE WEDDING: Author interviews with Julio Figueroa, Desiderió de León, and Frankie Figueroa.

132 "THEY AIN'T LETTING": *Maybe I'll Pitch Forever*, 110.

132 AS HIS FIANCÉE: "Satchel Paige, Negro Ballplayer, Is One of Best Pitchers in Game," *Life*.

132 "HAD A HANKERING": *Maybe I'll Pitch Forever*, 139–40.

132 JULIO QUESTIONS SATCHEL'S REWRITE: Julio Figueroa interview.

133 ONE HOT NIGHT DURING: "Satch Beards the House of David."

133 ONE DUSTUP INVOLVED: Echevarría, *The Pride of Havana*, 185.

134 WAS PLAYING THE SAME FILM: Irvin and Riley, *Nice Guys Finish First*, 85.

134 SATCHEL WAS UNCONCERNED: Irvin and Riley, *Nice Guys Finish First*, 84–85.

134 THAT SAME TORTOISE'S PACE: Larry Lester, "This Day on the History Pages," in *9th Annual Jerry Malloy Negro League Conference*, 86; "Baseball in Brief," March 22, 1941, *Chicago Defender;* "Smitty's Sports Corner," August 2, 1941.

134 ADVICE SATCHEL OFFERED: Author interview with Monte Irvin.

135 ESPECIALLY BALMY OIL: de León interview.

CHAPTER 6: KANSAS CITY, HERE I COME

137 HAD ITS ARCADIAN FLAVOR: Vaughan, "The Most American of All Cities," *The Kansas City Star.*

137 THE ALL-BLACK MONARCHS: Bruce, *Kansas City Monarchs*, 21.

137 "IT WAS THE AMBITION": Bruce, *Kansas City Monarchs*, 40. Jesse Williams was the Monarchs' shortstop.

138 J. L. WILKINSON MADE RUBE FOSTER: Bruce, *Kansas City Monarchs*, 14–18.

138 THE ONLY WHITE AMONG: Wilkinson's partner, Tom Baird, also was white, but few other Negro League executives knew Baird in the early years or thought of him as a founding father.

139 BUT THE RIGHT ONE: Author interviews with Dick Wilkinson and Tom Fredrick; Christian, "James Leslie Wilkinson: The Iowa Years, 1878–1916"; Bruce, *Kansas City Monarchs*, 14–15.

139 HIS NEXT VENTURE: "James Leslie Wilkinson: The Iowa Years"; Bruce, *Kansas City Monarchs*, 15–17.

140 JOHN DONALDSON HAD: Riley, *Biographical Encyclopedia*, 242.

140 WILBUR "BULLET JOE" ROGAN: Peterson, *Only the Ball Was White*, 214–15.

140 ONE OF THE LEADING TEAMS: Curtright, "O'Neil Recalls Negro Leagues, Days in Wichita," *Wichita Eagle;* Peterson, *Only the Ball Was White*, 257–88; Tim Rives, "Tom Baird: A Challenge to the Modern Memory of the Kansas City Monarchs," *Satchel Paige and Company*, 144.

140 NOSE FOR MONEY: Bruce, *Kansas City Monarchs,* 68-76.

140 TO ALLOW NIGHT GAMES: Wilkinson actually did that resurrection even earlier, in his days managing the team of lady ballplayers. By 1912 he was using
powerful electric lights that, when strung around the field, were said to make it
"light as day."

140 "THE MOST SIGNIFICANT": Washington, "Sez Ches," April 21, 1934.

141 HIS PLAYERS ADORED HIM: Bruce, *Kansas City Monarchs,* 78.

141 "EVERY YEAR HE'D": Dick Wilkinson interview.

141 AND WERE GRATEFUL: Bruce, *Kansas City Monarchs,* 19.

142 KU KLUX KLAN: "Tom Baird: A Challenge to the Modern Memory," 144–54.

142 THERE FROM THE START: Wilkinson took Baird in as a partner in the Monarchs in 1919, sold him half the team in 1937, and sold him the rest in 1948. Tom
Fredrick e-mail to author, 2008.

142 TIM RIVES: Rives's evidence starts as circumstantial: a "T. Baird" showing up on
KKK membership rosters from Kansas. Step by step, Rives makes it clear this
person is the Monarchs' owner. Baird lived near, worked alongside, and associated
socially and politically with confirmed Klansmen. He ran a pool hall and maintained an office in the building where the Klan was headquartered. His racial
views, confirmed in his own papers, coincided with those of the racist organization.

142 "ABOVE THE AVERAGE": Letter from Tom Baird to Jack Sheehan, Chicago
Cubs, April 29, 1949, T. Y. Baird Collection, University of Kansas Libraries.

142 "TOP HEAVY": Letter from Harry C. Jenkins, Boston Braves, to Tom Baird,
March 9, 1951, Baird Collection.

142 "IS AN INTELIGENT": Letter from Baird to Jenkins, February 19, 1951, Baird
Collection.

142 COMBINATION OF FACTORS: "Tom Baird: A Challenge to the Modern Memory," 144–54; Tim Rives e-mails to author, 2008.

143 "SILENT PARTNER": Dick Wilkinson interview.

143 BAIRD DID PLAY A BIG ROLE: Rives e-mails.

143 BAIRD'S HEIRS, NOT SURPRISINGLY: Author interviews with Tom Wickstrom and Doris Hill.

143 "WINTER TOUR OF THE SOUTH": "City Fetes Manager of Bismarck's U.S.
Semi-professional Champions," *The Bismarck Tribune.*

143 "SMOKED THE BALL": Burley, "Paige Fans 8, but Giants Beat Monarchs,"
Chicago Defender.

144 "HULA-HIPPED HARLEM BEAUTY": "Josh the Basher," *Time.*

144 EFFA REVEALED ANOTHER SECRET: Marshall, "Mrs. Effa Manley Interview," Chandler Oral History Project, 69.

144 "I EXPECT EACH OF YOU": Letter from Effa Manley to B. B. Martin and
Thomas T. Wilson, June 2, 1940, from Newark Eagle Files, Newark (NJ) Public
Library.

144 "I DON'T KNOW WHETHER": Marshall, "Mrs. Effa Manley Interview," 24–25.

145 WHAT SATCHEL ACTUALLY WROTE: Letter from Satchel to Effa Manley, sent
from Guayama, Puerto Rico, undated, Newark Eagle Files; Overmyer, *Effa Manley and the Newark Eagle,* 156–57.

145 WILKINSON WELCOMED HIM HOME: "Baseball War Brews over Satchel
Paige," *The Pittsburgh Courier.*

145 "KNEW THAT AS LONG": Robinson and Bauer, *Catching Dreams,* 48, 50.

145 "HE TOLD SATCHEL": Robinson and Bauer, *Catching Dreams,* 49.

146 SO THEY TOOK IT: It is unclear whether Abe Manley ever got back the $5,000 he paid for Satchel; Effa told an interviewer in 1977 that he probably did not. Wilkie pretended that his hands were clean in the Satchel affair, saying it was his brother Lee who owned the Baby Monarchs and signed Satchel. Marshall, "Mrs. Effa Manley Interview"; Carter, "From the Bench," *Afro-American,* June 15, 1940.

146 "I THOUGHT HE WAS": Bruce, *Kansas City Monarchs,* 82; *Josh and Satch,* 136.

146 "POPPED IN TOWN": Burley, "Famed Hurler Quits Kay See," *Amsterdam News.*

146 "WHEN LEROY (SATCHEL) PAGE": Burley, "Confidentially Yours," *Amsterdam News,* May 17, 1941.

147 "BLINDIN' SPEED": *Pitchin' Man,* 63.

148 "WHEN YOU STAY AROUND": *Maybe I'll Pitch Forever,* 150.

148 "I WAS LEADING OFF": Holway, *Voices from the Great Black Baseball Leagues,* 334.

148 "THE PITCH ZIGZAGGED": Motley and Motley, *Ruling over Monarchs,* 84–89.

148 JOHN "MULE" MILES: Author interview with John "Mule" Miles.

149 "WHERE HE WANTS IT": Lewis, *It Takes All Kinds,* 182.

149 "GIVES THE REST OF 'EM": Lewis, *It Takes All Kinds,* 182.

149 "I SEEN THE TIME": *Pitchin' Man,* 63.

149 ART "SUPERMAN" PENNINGTON: Author interview with Art "Superman" Pennington.

150 WILLIE "CURLEY" WILLIAMS: Author interview with Willie "Curley" Williams.

150 HE ENDED THE 1941 SEASON: Hogan, *Shades of Glory,* 406–7.

151 DREW CROWDS LARGER: Hogan, *Shades of Glory,* 1.

151 A BLACK SCRIBE CREDITED PAIGE: Burley, "Confidentially Yours," August 9, 1941.

151 "THERE WAS A MIGHTY": *Maybe I'll Pitch Forever,* 146–48.

152 "HE HAD PLENTY OF SPEED": "Kansas City Monarchs Win World Championship," *Chicago Defender.*

152 "A CASE OF 'TOO MUCH PAIGE' ": Gay, "15,000 Brave Cold," *The Philadelphia Tribune.*

152 "SATCHEL WAS ALWAYS": Holway, *Black Diamonds,* 21–22.

153 "YOU STAY WITH HIM": Sumner, *Legacy of a Monarch,* 79–89.

153 "ABOUT THE ONLY THING": Robinson and Bauer, *Catching Dreams,* 40–41.

154 "WE HAD SOMEWHERE": Dick Wilkinson interview.

154 "YOU AIN'T GOING TO TAKE": Irvin and Riley, *Nice Guys Finish First,* 57.

154 "PAIGE THOUGHT HE WAS": Peary, "Max Manning on Satchel Paige," in *Cult Baseball Players,* 304.

154 HERBERT BARNHILL WAS PUSHED AWAY: Kelley, *Negro Leagues Revisited,* 73–74.

155 "SATCHEL CALLED HIMSELF": Reisler, *Black Writers/Black Baseball,* 126.

155 "THEY PICKED ME": Author interview with Ross Davis.

156 SATCHEL'S FAVORITE MONARCH: Author interview with Bill "Youngblood" McCrary.

156 DIFFERENT SORT OF MENTORING: Author interview with Louis Clarizio.

157 NEVER LIVED TO SEE: Hilton Smith was voted into the Hall of Fame in 2001, eighteen years after he died.

157 "REALLY HURT ME": Holway, *Voices from the Great Black Baseball Leagues,* 281–82.

157 FISHING BUDDIES AND FRIENDS: Author interview with DeMorris Smith.

157 "YOU'RE ALWAYS SAVING": Bruce, *Kansas City Monarchs,* 95.

CHAPTER 7: MASTER OF THE MANOR

158 PAIGE DAY AT WRIGLEY FIELD: "Divorce Summons Darkens Satchel's Brilliant 'Day,' " *Chicago Defender.*

158 "I DON'T WANT": *Maybe I'll Pitch Forever,* 154–55.

159 JANET'S COMPLAINT LAID OUT: Decree, petition, and complaint for divorce and court divorce proceedings, August 4, 1943, Circuit Court of Cook County, Illinois.

159 "THERE WASN'T ANY TRUTH": *Maybe I'll Pitch Forever,* 153. By the time he published that second memoir Satchel had been remarried for fifteen years and was anxious to paper over his past misdeeds and indiscretions.

160 "WAS THERE TO WATCH": Galbreath, "The Women Take to East vs. West Baseball Classic," *Chicago Defender.*

160 PICTURE OF THE COUPLE: "Satchel Paige, Negro Ballplayer, Is One of Best Pitchers in Game," *Life.*

160 "I DON'T KNOW WHAT SHE DID": Irvin and Riley, *Nice Guys Finish First,* 83.

160 STORY DID NOT END THERE: Julio Figueroa interview.

161 GOSSIP COLUMNISTS CARRIED: Clark, "Wylie Avenue," *The Pittsburgh Courier,* December 22, 1945; "Wylie Avenue Here and There," *The Pittsburgh Courier,* January 2, 1965. A newspaper story on their divorce said Janet was married before to a "Mr. Howard" and they had a nine-year-old son. Howard, however, is her maiden name and it's unclear whether she ever had a child or was married to anyone other than Satchel. "Divorce Summons Darkens Satchel's Brilliant 'Day.' "

161 "I'D WON A LOT OF": *Maybe I'll Pitch Forever,* 140, 155.

161 "I COULD TELL RIGHT OFF": *Maybe I'll Pitch Forever,* 142.

161 DREW HIM TO LAHOMA BROWN: Lahoma, like Satchel, spelled her name differently depending on circumstances or whim. Sometimes it was LaHoma, other times Lahoma, which is how Satchel spelled it in his memoir. City directories in Kansas City offered another variation: La Homa.

162 HER BOSS TOOK HIS SIDE: *Maybe I'll Pitch Forever,* 143–44.

163 "I RACED THAT BUGGY": *Maybe I'll Pitch Forever,* 155–56.

164 "[SATCHEL] WILL PITCH": Contract between Kansas City Monarchs and Homestead Grays, May 26, 1942, Baird Collection.

164 DEMANDING TOP DOLLAR: "Fair Pay for Fair Play."

164 "THE HIGHEST-PAID PLAYER": Povich, "This Morning," *The Washington Post,* May 19, 1944.

164 "THE 'EARNINGEST' BASEBALLER": Wolf, "Sportraits," *Los Angeles Times,* February 16, 1950.

164 "WAS ROLLING IN": *Maybe I'll Pitch Forever,* 168.

165 "IT WAS A SIGN": *Pitchin' Man,* 74; *Maybe I'll Pitch Forever,* 144–45.

165 "FOUR CLOSETS FULLA SUITS": *Pitchin' Man,* 76. In today's dollars, his suits would cost $750 to $1,500 each.

165 SURELY THE MOST DRESSED: Considine, "On the Line," *The Washington Post,* July 20, 1941.

165 "SATCHEL WASN'T A FINANCIAL MAN": Dick Wilkinson interview.

165 "IT SEEMED LIKE": *Maybe I'll Pitch Forever,* 168–69.

166 "THAT WAS THE END": *Maybe I'll Pitch Forever,* 170–71.

166 "I DID A GREAT DEAL OF": " 'Satch' Struck Out Josh Gibson for Biggest Thrill."

166 "COURSE, THERE WASN'T": *Maybe I'll Pitch Forever,* 169–70.

166 REAL ESTATE TRANSACTIONS: Documents from Jackson County, Missouri, courthouse showing Satchel's house purchases and sales; author interview with and e-mails from Kansas City attorney John Kurtz.

167 HE ADMITS AS MUCH: *Maybe I'll Pitch Forever,* 225.

167 "THE LORD'LL PUNISH": *Maybe I'll Pitch Forever,* 113.

167 HE GOT AN IDEA: *Maybe I'll Pitch Forever,* 113–14.

168 "WHEN THIS SEASON IS OVER": *Pitchin' Man,* 22.

168 "YOU WOULD THINK": Leon Paige interview.

169 AS BUCK O'NEIL TELLS IT: O'Neil et al., *I Was Right on Time,* 13–15; *Soul of Baseball,* 128; author interview with O'Neil.

170 FELLER DREAMED UP: Feller and Gilbert, *Now Pitching, Bob Feller,* 136–44; Sickels, *Bob Feller: Ace of the Greatest Generation,* 149–61; Flaherty, "Feller's Bonanza Tops Ruth's Richest 'Take,' " *The Sporting News;* Old, "Tour Hikes '46 Income to $175,000," *The Sporting News.* Feller interview.

172 FELLER'S PRESS RELEASE: Sickels, *Bob Feller,* 152.

172 "A CREDIT TO THE RACE": "Bob Feller's All-Stars," Souvenir Program from Bob Feller Museum.

172 "THE WHOLE TRIP WAS BECAUSE": Feller interview.

172 "OLD SACHMO' DISDAINED": "Feller, Satchel in Scoreless Three Inning Mound Stints," *Council Bluffs* (Iowa) *Nonpareil.*

173 FINISHED WITH FIVE WINS: There were different stats on the tour results, from *The Sporting News's* November 6, 1946, account showing the whites ahead 13-5 to John Sickels's 17-5. The most complete accounting was provided to the author by baseball historian Rob Neyer, who includes two games in California at the end of the tour when Satchel was backed by less able teammates.

173 FIFTY-FOUR FRAMES: Those statistics do not include the last game of the tour, a Paige defeat in October in Los Angeles, because newspaper accounts did not include a box score.

173 "THEY ALL BORE DOWN": Feller, "The Trouble with the Hall of Fame," *Saturday Evening Post.*

173 FARED MUCH BETTER: In five face-offs in 1947, Satchel had a 1.00 runs-per-game average with forty-four strikeouts and one walk, compared with Feller's average of 4.50 runs. In the big face-off on November 2, both agreed to pitch all nine innings. Satchel struck out fifteen, allowing four hits and no runs. Feller was touched for eight runs. Sickels, *Bob Feller,* 178–79.

173 "HAVEN'T SEEN ONE": "250,000 See Feller-Paige Teams Play," *The Sporting News.*

173 "NOT EVEN JACKIE": "The few times I faced Feller has made me confident that the pitching I have hit in the Negro American League was as tough as any I will have to face if I make it at Montreal," Jackie replied in a November 10, 1945,

story in *The Pittsburgh Courier.* Feller and Robinson took repeated shots at each other, with the animus stemming in part from what Robinson felt was Feller's shortchanging him and other blacks during a 1946 barnstorming tour.

174 "PERFECT CONTROL": Feller and Rocks, *Bob Feller's Little Black Book of Baseball Wisdom,* 59–60.

174 "ONE OF THE TOP FIVE": Feller interview.

174 "THE MOST PROFITABLE": "Tour Hikes '46 Income to $175,000."

174 "THAT WAS THEIR PROBLEM": Feller interview.

175 "THE CASE FOR SATCHEL": Feller and Gilbert, *Now Pitching, Bob Feller,* 140.

175 TEN MILLION READERS: *The Post's* circulation was three million. The assumption of three readers per copy is conservative for that Depression era, when people did not order magazines unless they intended to read them and there were far fewer other options for entertainment.

175 SHANE GAVE THEM A SATCHEL: "Chocolate Rube Waddell."

176 "FOR THE FIRST TIME": Holway, *Josh and Satch,* 136.

176 "IN THE SAME WAY": O'Neil et al., *I Was Right on Time,* 107–8.

177 "SATCHELFOOTS": "Satchelfoots," *Time.* Josh Gibson got his own profile in the July 19, 1943, issue of *Time,* headlined "Josh the Basher." While it lauds him, it ran three years after the Paige piece and could not resist comparing Josh to Satchel, whom it called "Negro baseball's No. 1 attraction." Josh made no similar appearance in the *Time* story on Satchel.

177 THAT ATTENTION BY PRESS: Bruce, *Kansas City Monarchs,* 98–100; *Only the Ball Was White,* 93.

178 "THOSE WOUNDED BOYS'D": *Maybe I'll Pitch Forever,* 162–63.

178 "THEY WERE JUST PIECES": *Maybe I'll Pitch Forever,* 163.

178 "IS PAIGE TRYING TO FOOL": Young, "Paige Gets Himself Fired from Role as Pitcher in East-West Classic," *Chicago Defender.*

178 "HE WAS MISSED": Harmon, "Sportorial," Kansas City *Call,* August 18, 1944.

179 SELECTIVE SERVICE RECORDS: Registrar's Report: Leroy Paige, October 16, 1940.

179 "YOU GOT TO HELP": *Maybe I'll Pitch Forever,* 162.

179 DEFENDING HIS COUNTRY: Some press accounts at the time said he was rejected for being too old; others said he was available for service throughout World War II. One author suggested he was deferred for flat feet, but there is no evidence of that. "Draft Parade Passes a Few Sports Notables," *Chicago Daily Tribune;* "Satchel Paige, Ace Negro Pitcher, Signed by Indians," *The New York Times;* Dyer, "The Sports Parade," *Los Angeles Times,* March 12, 1944; Ward, "In the Wake of the News," *Chicago Tribune,* March 30, 1944; Ribowsky, *The Power and the Darkness,* 227.

179 "WITH ALL OF THEM": *Maybe I'll Pitch Forever,* 171–72.

CHAPTER 8: BASEBALL'S GREAT EXPERIMENT

180 "THAT THE END": Tygiel, *Baseball's Great Experiment,* 74.

180 "WE LIVE HAPPIER": Tygiel, *Baseball's Great Experiment,* 74.

180 "WERE A WHITE MAN": Tygiel, *Baseball's Great Experiment,* 76.

181 "THEY DIDN'T MAKE A MISTAKE": "Rickey Cites Wire to Refute Critics," *The New York Times.*

181 JACKIE SHOWED DISDAIN: Jackie Robinson, "What's Wrong with Negro Baseball?" *Ebony.*

182 "I'D BEEN THE GUY": *Maybe I'll Pitch Forever,* 173.

182 "THEY TOOK THAT KID": *Maybe I'll Pitch Forever,* 173.

183 "HIDEOUS MONSTER": Peterson, *Only the Ball Was White,* 172.

183 WESTBROOK PEGLER: Witwer, "Westbrook Pegler and the Anti-union Movement," *The Journal of American History; The Sporting News,* November 5, 1931, 4. In an unexpected turn in his later years, Pegler became a supporter of the right-wing John Birch Society and a critic of the civil rights movement.

184 "MAJOR LEAGUE BASEBALL DOES NOT": "Smith's Sports Spurts," *The Pittsburgh Courier,* May 14, 1938.

184 TWENTY-FIVE-YEAR-OLD LESTER RODNEY: Silber, *Press Box Red,* 53–54.

185 TACTICS DIFFERED DEPENDING: Duffy, "Red Rodney," *The Village Voice;* Wiggins, "Wendell Smith, the *Pittsburgh Courier-Journal* and the Campaign to Include Blacks in Organized Baseball," *Journal of Sport History;* Bruce, *Kansas City Monarchs,* 109.

185 LIBERAL POLITICIANS GOT INTO: Peterson, *Only the Ball Was White,* 183–85; Wiggins, "Wendell Smith." Muchnick has been accused of promoting integration to curry favor with his black constituency in Dorchester. There is one problem with those accounts: Dorchester was 99.5 percent white at the time.

186 HE TRIED TO BUY: Veeck and Linn, *Veeck—as in Wreck,* 171.

186 SCHOLARS STILL ARGUE: Jordan, Gerlach, and Rossi, "A Baseball Myth Exploded: The Truth About Bill Veeck and the '43 Phillies," *National Pastime;* Tygiel, "Revisiting Bill Veeck and the 1943 Phillies," *Baseball Research Journal.*

187 AND HE FAILED TO USE: Wiggins, "Wendell Smith."

187 "IF A BLACK BOY": Polner, *Branch Rickey,* 175.

187 CHANDLER'S FILES TELL: "Chandler Files Reveal Segregation Died Hard," *The Sporting News.*

187 HANGING FROM THE BRANCH: Author interview with Carl Long.

187 HAD AN AIR HOSE: Rogosin, *Invisible Men,* 128–29.

187–88 JAKE POWELL TOLD A RADIO: Powell not only was a racist, he apparently was a liar, too. Historian Chris Lamb reports that Powell was never a law officer in Dayton, Ohio, as he claimed, or anywhere else. His actual encounter with the law, Lamb says, was being arrested a decade later for allegedly writing bad checks and, while locked up in a Washington police station, killing himself with a gun. Lamb, "L'Affaire Jake Powell," *Journalism and Mass Communication Quarterly.*

188 "POWELL GOT HIS CUE": Pegler, *Chicago Daily News,* August 4, 1938.

188 ROOKIE OF THE YEAR: The Baseball Writers' Association of America started giving out the award in 1947, with one for all of baseball. In 1949 it began naming one Rookie of the Year in the National League and another in the American.

188–89 DESPERATE FOR A PLACE: Chadwick, *When the Game Was Black and White,* 80–81.

189 "WITHOUT THE BROOKLYN DODGERS": "An Interview with Lester 'Red' Rodney, the Man Who Helped Integrate Baseball." Quote as recalled years later by Rodney.

189–90 PERSONA OF THE SHIFTLESS STEP: Perry, who claimed he borrowed his stage name from a racehorse, was the first black actor to become a millionaire but his free-spending ways eventually led him to bankruptcy.

190 SATCHEL CHALLENGED COURTNEY: Broeg, "Old Satch Left Behind Some Great Memories," *St. Louis Post-Dispatch.*

190 "ONE DAY I NOTICED": Boswell, "Satchel Paige: 'Best I Ever Saw'—Veeck," *The Washington Post.*

191 "THE WAY HE WALKED": Author interview with George "Meadowlark" Lemon.

191 HE SET CLEAR CONDITIONS: Peterson, *Only the Ball Was White,* 142-43; Bankes interview.

191 "THE BEST OF THE ROOMS": Banker, *Black Diamonds,* Satchel Paige interview.

192 "IF ANYONE GAVE ME": Author interview with Arthur Richman.

192 LISTED SATCHEL ALONGSIDE: Brascher, "Thoughts for To-Day," *Chicago Defender,* January 17, 1942.

192 "AN OLD COLORED WOMAN": "Satchel Man."

192 HANDLE A STICKY QUESTION: Author interview with Bill Gleason.

192 SATCHEL PROPOSED THREE EXPERIMENTS: "Paige Asks Test for Negro Stars," *Daily Worker;* author interview with Lester Rodney.

193 HIS BUREAU FILE: "The FBI Files of Leroy 'Satchel' Paige."

193 "AND CONSIDERING IT STRICTLY": "Paige Not in Favor of Negro in Big Leagues," *Chicago Tribune.*

194 PAIGE NOT IN FAVOR: "Paige Not in Favor of Negro in Big Leagues."

194 PAIGE SAYS NEGROES: "Paige Says Negroes Not Ready for Big Leagues," *Chicago Defender.*

194 "I WANT YOU TO KNOW": " 'Was Misquoted,' Says 'Satchel,' " *The Pittsburgh Courier.*

194 "POINTLESS STATEMENT": Art Carter, "From the Bench," *Afro-American,* August 22, 1942.

194 PARROTING BACK SATCHEL'S ARGUMENT: Lanctot, *Negro League Baseball,* 445.

195 "WE STOOD THERE 30 MINUTES: O'Neil interview; O'Neil et al., *I Was Right on Time,* 100–1.

196 "HE WON MORE GAMES": Monroe, "It's News to Me," *Chicago Defender,* October 28, 1939.

196 "MAKES ME ILL": Lanctot, *Negro League Baseball,* 106.

196 "I DON'T OWN PAIGE": Monroe, "It's News to Me."

197 "THOSE OTHER PLAYERS": *Maybe I'll Pitch Forever,* 69.

197 "IF IT DON'T BE": Author interview with Raydell Maddix.

198 "WE ALL WANTED TO JOIN": O'Neil interview; O'Neil et al., *I Was Right on Time,* 48–49.

198 "MY FIVE SHORT MONTHS": "What's Wrong with Negro Baseball?"

199 "HE COULDN'T COME UP": Banker, *Black Diamonds,* Newt Allen interview.

199 "AN AVERAGE FIELDER": Rogosin, *Invisible Men,* 203.

199 "HAD A WHOLE LOT BETTER": Rogosin, *Invisible Men,* 203.

199 STAYED BACK AT THE HOTEL: Rogosin, *Invisible Men,* 203.

199 "I HAD NOT APPROACHED": Undated transcript, Jerome Holtzman interview with Wendell Smith.

200 SMITH HAD HIS REGRETS: Dolgan, "Universal Connection," Cleveland *Plain Dealer.*

200 "I MIGHT HAVE SET": "Satchel Paige Sounds Off."

200 "NO SIRREE, BOB": Banker, *Black Diamonds,* Satchel Paige interview.

200 "HIS HAIR'S WHITE": Berkow, "Jackie Robinson: Hope by Example," in Stout and Johnson, eds., *Jackie Robinson: Between the Baselines,* 175.

200 "THE GREATEST NEGRO PITCHER": Robinson, "Jackie Says," *The Pittsburgh Courier.*

200 "JACKIE DETESTED SATCH": Moore, *Pride Against Prejudice,* 169.

201 "WE WON'T TAKE IT": "Will Appeal to Chandler," Associated Press.

201 HE HAD BEEN "MISQUOTED": "Rickey Cites Wire to Refute Critics," *The New York Times.*

201 "THE NEGRO ORGANIZATIONS": "Rickey Takes Slap at Negro Leagues," *The New York Times.*

202 "WHILE IT IS TRUE": "Griffith Backs Monarchs," Associated Press.

202 WATCHED THEIR WORLD CRUMBLE: Peterson, *Only the Ball Was White,* 201–3.

202 FAR FEWER NEGROES: Hogan, *Shades of Glory,* ix.

203 VETERAN NEGRO LEAGUER: Author interview with Minnie Minoso.

CHAPTER 9: AN OPENING AT LAST

204 IS IT TIME FOR ME TO COME?: Veeck and Linn, *Veeck—as in Wreck,* 183.

204 ALL THINGS IN DUE TIME: Veeck and Linn, *Veeck—as in Wreck,* 183.

205 BASEBALL'S OLD GUARD: Veeck and Linn, *Veeck—as in Wreck,* 183.

205 "DAD CALLED ME ON THE PHONE": Dick Wilkinson interview.

205 "AFTER TWENTY-TWO YEARS": *Maybe I'll Pitch Forever,* 196. Saperstein tells a slightly different version, one that puts him at center stage and has Satchel moving at the pace of his hesitation pitch: It was he who persuaded a reluctant Veeck to give Satchel a serious look. He then contacted Satchel in Washington State, telling him to fly to Chicago, then head straight to Cleveland. Instead, Satchel hung around Chicago for a week, playing pool and waiting for Saperstein to get back and accompany him to Cleveland. "Wendell Smith's Sports Beat: Saperstein Directed 'Satchel' to Big Dough," *The Pittsburgh Courier.*

206 "BILL CALLED ME AT HOME": Boudreau and Fitzgerald, *Player-Manager,* 162.

206 "WHERE'S THE KID?": Veeck and Linn, *Veeck—as in Wreck,* 184.

206 "YOU KNOW, MR. LOU": *Maybe I'll Pitch Forever,* 197. The men involved, and the writers who covered it, differ on the details of Satchel's tryout but agree on the general circumstances.

206 "AGAINST PAIGE, HE BATTED": Veeck and Linn, *Veeck—as in Wreck,* 184.

207 "VEECK HAS GONE TOO FAR": Spink, "Two Ill-Advised Moves," *The Sporting News.* Veeck had the perfect reply—fourteen years later, in his autobiography: "If Satch were white, of course, he would have been in the majors twenty-five years earlier, and the question would not have been before the house." *Veeck—as in Wreck,* 185.

207 "THE SIGNING OF SATCHEL": Meany, "$64 Question: Paige's Age," *New York Star.*

207 "NO OTHER ANCIENT": Roberts, "An Open Letter to J. Taylor Spink," *The Pittsburgh Courier.*

208 STILL, HE WAS NERVOUS: *Pitchin' Man,* 1.

208 "AM I PLAYING THE FOOL": *Pitchin' Man,* 1.

208 "DON'T BE SCARED IF THEY": *Pitchin' Man,* 2.

208 "I ALWAYS HAD PRETTY GOOD": Author interview with Chuck Stevens.

209 THE FULL REPERTOIRE: "Paige Hurls Two Scoreless Innings," Cleveland *Plain Dealer;* Sauerbrei, "Flash Bulbs Pop, but Old Satch Just Hurls," Cleveland *Plain Dealer.*

209 A SPECTACLE THAT DREW: McAuley, "Tribe Raises Turnstile Sights, Now Aims at Two Million Gate," *Cleveland News.*

209 AS HE PROVED AGAIN: "Chicago's Surge to See Ol' Satch Collapses Gates," *The Sporting News;* Veeck and Linn, *Veeck—as in Wreck,* 186–87; Kaiser, *Epic Season,* 141.

210 JUST BEFORE THE GAME: Veeck and Linn, *Veeck—as in Wreck,* 187.

210 EQUIVALENT OF SAINTHOOD: "Paige Is Baseball's Greatest Drawing Card," *Chicago Defender.*

210 BENCHMARK FOR EVENING CROWDS: Night baseball came to the Major Leagues starting in 1935, in Cincinnati, and slowly spread to other ballparks.

211 "THE MISERIES WERE DOING": *Maybe I'll Pitch Forever,* 8.

211 PAIGE PITCHING—NO RUNS: Spink, "Robinson vs. Paige—Rookies," *The Sporting News.*

211 "SELDOM HAS THIS WRITER": Dunmore, "80,403 Awed as Paige Blanks White Sox," *The Pittsburgh Courier.*

212 VETERAN UMPS STEPPED OUT: "Paige Ranks Near Top Say 2 Veteran Umpires," *The New York Times.*

212 BILL SUMMERS: Coincidentally or not, Bill Summers was the name of the family goat that Satchel said ate the Bible with his birth records. "Satch Surveys Catfish."

212 "GLANCING OVER AT HIM": Author interview with Dom DiMaggio.

212 "ALL THIS RAISES": "Robinson vs. Paige—Rookies."

212 "I WASN'T SURE WHAT YEAR": Sterry and Eckstut, *Satchel Sez,* 91.

213 "THAT BLANKETY-BLANK": "Hesitation Pitch Most Effective," *Independent Record* (Helena, Montana).

213 RULED THE PITCH ILLEGAL: "Satch's Pitches to Nats 'Illegal' Rules Harridge," *The Washington Post;* " 'Hesitation Pitch' Is a Balk with Men On—Harridge," Cleveland *Call and Post.*

213 NONETHELESS BE REMEMBERED: Daley, "There's Life in the Old Boy Yet," *The New York Times.*

213 "I'D BEEN IN A WORLD SERIES": *Maybe I'll Pitch Forever,* 224.

214 "THEY'LL HAVE TO COME OUT": *Maybe I'll Pitch Forever,* 231–33. Teammates, friends, and reporters thought Satchel's dental woes were exaggerated if not invented, especially when he linked them to his stomach and arm troubles. But the latest research suggests he might have been as spot-on in diagnosing and treating his teeth as he was his shoulder. Gum disease and tooth decay can lead to infection and a buildup of acids that spawn serious problems in the stomach and other organs.

215 THEIR BARBERSHOP QUARTET: Moore, *Pride Against Prejudice,* 79.

215 "SATCHEL WAS A VERY HUMBLE GUY": Author interview with Eddie Robinson.

215 FELLER GOT SATCHEL: Feller and Gilbert, *Now Pitching,* 140.

215 GULPED DOWN TWO MEALS: Veeck and Linn, *Veeck—as in Wreck,* 182.

216 CLASHING WORLDS AND ERAS: Young, *Great Negro Baseball Stars,* 80; Moore, *Pride Against Prejudice,* 77–78; Vincent, *The Only Game in Town,* 187.

216 SATCH ASKED LARRY: Young, *Great Negro Baseball Stars,* 80; Moore, *Pride Against Prejudice,* 77–78; Vincent, *The Only Game in Town,* 187.

216 "SATCH NEVER RODE": Dyer, "Sports Parade, Lou Reveals 'Saga of Satch,' " *Los Angeles Times.*

217 "LOU BOUDREAU DIDN'T WANT HIM": Braham, "Greenberg, Boudreau Answer Satchel's Gripes," *Cleveland Press.*

217 SATCHEL'S KIND OF GUY: Lebovitz, *The Best of Hal Lebovitz,* 80–81; Eskenazi, *Bill Veeck: A Baseball Legend,* 1–2.

217 SATCHEL REPORTEDLY RECEIVED: "Ol' Satch Cost Just $55,000 Paper Figures," *The Washington Post.* Satchel denied he was paid a bonus but affirmed Veeck's generosity, saying he ended up with a "much smoother figure" than he would have earned in blackball. Other reporters put his salary for three months between $10,000 and $40,000. *Pitchin' Man,* 5.

218 DEVOTION TO INTEGRATION: Beck, "Working in the Shadows of Rickey and Robinson," *The Cooperstown Symposium on Baseball and American Culture.*

218 HE TREATED SATCHEL: The father-son relationship was a bit awkward, since Paige was eight years older than Veeck.

218 "THAT CURLY-HAIRED FELLOW": *Pitchin' Man,* xxiv.

218 THE OWNER REPEATEDLY LOANED: Author interview with Mike Veeck.

218 "INTERRACIAL AND UNIVERSAL": Veeck and Linn, *Veeck—as in Wreck,* 181.

218 "I'M GONNA PITCH": *Pitchin' Man,* xxiv.

218 SHAVED OFF HIS MUSTACHE: *Pitchin' Man,* 42–43.

218 "I MUSTA SLEPT": *Pitchin' Man,* 14–15.

219 "[SATCHEL] DIDN'T KEEP": Braham, "Greenberg, Boudreau Answer Satchel's Gripes," *Cleveland Press.*

219 "A MAN," HE SAID: *Maybe I'll Pitch Forever,* 181.

219 "YOU KNOW WHAT": *Maybe I'll Pitch Forever,* 182.

220 SWORN TESTIMONY: *LaHoma Paige v. Kansas City Power & Light Company,* 16.

220 NO RECORD OF SATCHEL: Information provided to author by officials in Hays, Kansas, and Kansas City, Missouri.

220 "NO PLACE TO SLEEP": Rogosin, *Invisible Men,* 126–27.

220 "THEY DIDN'T EVEN WANT": Rogosin, *Invisible Men,* 99.

221 "I WOULD LEAVE THE BALL PARK": Rogosin, *Invisible Men,* 99.

221 "SETTLED-DOWN LIFE": *Maybe I'll Pitch Forever,* 182.

221 "IT'S LIKE THIS": Veeck and Linn, *Veeck—as in Wreck,* 182.

221 "AND EVERY DAY A DIFFERENT": Veeck and Linn, *Veeck—as in Wreck,* 182.

221 "AND HE PULLS OUT": Author interview with Ned Garver.

221 "TO TWO DIFFERENT WOMEN": Author interview with Jack Spring.

221 "HE SAID, 'I DON'T' ": Author interview with Duane Pillette.

222 "DON'T LET ANYBODY TELL YOU": *Maybe I'll Pitch Forever,* 182.

222 "HE ALWAYS EITHER": Sue Durney e-mails to author. Her father was with Satchel on the St. Louis Browns and Miami Marlins.

222 "HAD THIS CHARACTER": Mike Veeck interview.

222 "IT REALLY STAGGERED": *Maybe I'll Pitch Forever,* 182.

223 "WHEN THINGS DON'T": *Maybe I'll Pitch Forever,* 184.

223 "HIS BOOK EARNINGS": Author interview with David Lipman.

224 "YOU WONT KNOW": Letter from Satchel to Hal Lebovitz, December 21, 1948, provided to author by Hal's son Neil.

224 MALLARDS OF MINOT: Swanton, *The ManDak League*, 14.

224 PRINCELY RATE OF TWO THOUSAND: Gould, "Satch Hits Jackpot in Exhibitions," *The Sporting News*.

224 "GOING BACK TO BARNSTORMING": *Maybe I'll Pitch Forever*, 237.

224 RESURRECTION ONCE AGAIN: *Bill Veeck: A Baseball Legend*, 97–99.

224 "THEY THOUGHT HE WAS HUMAN": Kerrane, *The Hurlers*, 108.

225 DID NOT EXPECT SATCHEL: Author interview with Buddy Blattner.

225 THE YEAR VEECK TOOK OVER: Eshkenazi, *Bill Veeck: A Baseball Legend*, 98–104.

225 MORE SURPRISING TO VEECK: Hufford, "Minoso One of the Oldest," *Baseball Research Journal*; Swaine, *The Black Stars Who Made Baseball Whole*, 43.

226 "ANYBODY AND EVERYBODY": "Satchel Paige Is Browns' 'Untouchable,' " *Jet*.

226 "THE BEST RELIEF PITCHER": Veeck and Linn, *Veeck—as in Wreck*, 188.

226 LONGEST SHUTOUT OF THE SEASON: Greene, "Old Man Paige Throws Book at Tigers," *The Detroit News*.

226 THROW A COMPLETE GAME: "Minoso One of the Oldest."

226 "HIS SLOW BALL": McSkimming, "Paige Puts on His Greatest Show," *St. Louis Post-Dispatch*.

226 FISH WOULD FIGURE: Broeg, "Satch Would Be Ready Tonight," *St. Louis Post-Dispatch*.

227 "THROUGHOUT THIS DISASTER": "Time Ain't Gonna Mess with Me," 55.

227 DATE OF BIRTH AS: "The Brainiest Man in Baseball," *Ebony;* Geyer, "Writer Reviews Nation's Unusual Sports Happenings During 1953," *Los Angeles Times;* Aron, *Did Babe Ruth Call His Shot?*, 99.

227 "DATE UNKNOWN": *1953 St. Louis Browns Press, Radio & TV Guide*.

227 "GET THE RUNS NOW": "The Fabulous Satchel Paige."

227 "SATCHEL WOULD BE": Author interview with Joe DeMaestri.

228 "PEERED IN THE BUCKET": Author interview with Ted Lepcio.

228 "THEY STILL TALK OF THE BLACK": Kaese, "A Living Legend in Cooperstown," *The Boston Globe*.

228 TOSS A BAR OF SOAP: "Satch Beards the House of David."

228 "IT WAS FOUR FEET LONG": Author interview with J. W. Porter.

228 EXPERIMENT OF HIS OWN: "Seeing-Eye Pitcher," *Sports Illustrated*.

229 HAD SATCHEL FIGURED OUT: Author interview with Steve Greenberg. Once when Williams struck out against Satchel, he reportedly threw a lineup of bats onto the field and tore up the dugout bathroom. Another version had Ted striking out, then splintering the bat by cracking it on the dugout railing. The broken bat was sent to the Hall of Fame, which says the incident took place in 1951.

229 WHO WAS THAT?: "Time Ain't Gonna Mess With Me," 56.

229 "HE SAID NONE": Author interview with Matt Batts.

230 "LET HIM ROLL OVER": "Paige Late Again; Marion Gives Okay," *Jet*.

230 "THE BOSS," HE SAID: Condon, "Veeck Took Credit; I Got Raps: Hornsby," *Chicago Tribune*. Marion and Hornsby should have talked to Buck O'Neil, who was Satchel's teammate and manager with the Monarchs. "You don't manage Satchel

Paige," Buck said. "You manage the team he happens to be on." *I Was Right on Time,* 132.

230 "HORNSBY DIDN'T CARE": Author interview with Lou Sleater.

230 "HORNSBY SAID, 'NEXT TIME' ": Garver interview.

230 THREE TAXIS IN THE WHOLE: In some cities, Veeck hired limousines to shuttle Satchel around so he would not face problems with taxis. Author interview with Neil Berry.

230 BEHIND THE CURTAIN OF RACE: Duane Pillette interview.

231 HIT BLACK BATTERS: White pitchers called that "taking their power away." The theory was that black players lacked the fortitude to dig back in. Satchel's hard-slugging buddy Luke Easter took it as a challenge, often knocking the next pitch out of the park. Hodermarsky, ed., *The Cleveland Sports Legacy: Since 1945,* 24.

231 VIRGIL TRUCKS DID NOT: Author interview with Virgil Trucks.

231 "FLAPPING HIS ARMS": Keane, "Rookie Piersall Teases Ole Satch," *The Boston Globe.*

232 QUESTION THAT NIGHT: Author interviews with Jimmy Piersall and Garver; Kaese, "Paige Had Arm, and the Nerve," *The Boston Globe.*

232 "OLD MAN PREJUDICE": *Maybe I'll Pitch Forever,* 243

232 "ONE TIME SATCHEL": Garver interview.

233 "THE NEW BOSSES": *Maybe I'll Pitch Forever,* 264.

233 "I WAS IN THE BLUE ROOM": *Maybe I'll Pitch Forever,* 265–66.

234 "I AM STILL ONE OF THE BEST": "Paige Signs to Pitch for Trotter Nine," *Chicago Defender.*

234 THE NEXT YEAR HE WAS: "Satchel Signs $40,000 Monarch Contract," *Jet.*

234 ONCE-REGAL TEAM: Tom Baird to Dr. J. B. Martin, December 9, 1955, Baird Collection; *Kansas City Monarchs,* 125–26; "T. Y. Baird Now Sole Owner of K.C. Monarchs," *Kansas City Kansan.*

234 BREATHTAKING FIRST ACT: Kelleher, "Paige of Gimmickry," *The Miami Herald.*

234 "I WAS SO SCARED": *Maybe I'll Pitch Forever,* 267.

234 "HE DIDN'T COME DOWN HERE": Veeck and Linn, *Veeck—as in Wreck,* 188–89.

235 CHARITY GAME AGAINST COLUMBUS: Czerwinski, "Paige Added to Legacy During Stint in Minors," www.mlb.com.

235 DURING THREE SEASONS: McNeil, *Baseball's Other All-Stars,* 65.

235 THE WORD GAME GHOST: "When Batters Wobble," *Newsweek.*

235 "HE KNEW BOTH": Author interview with Bo Mason.

236 "I WAS TOTALLY PETRIFIED": Author interview with Tom Qualters.

236 "I ALMOST FEEL LIKE AS BIG": *Maybe I'll Pitch Forever,* 269.

236 SATCHEL WAS SUSPENDED: "Satchel's Out at Miami," *Chicago Tribune;* "Satchel Paige Walks Out on Miami Marlins," *Chicago Defender.*

237 BEAVERS IN PORTLAND: Marasco, "The Traveling Man Goes to Portland," *The Diamond Angle.*

237 "IT WAS OBVIOUS": Author interview with Dwight Jaynes.

237 "I'VE ALWAYS WANTED TO GREET": "Satchel Paige Greeted by Unexpected Visitor," *Anchorage Daily News.*

237 "THERE ISN'T A BETTER": "Wendell Smith's Sports Beat: Satchel Paige Still a Man of the Road," *The Pittsburgh Courier.*

237 "AL WANTS ONLY THE PLAYERS": Veeck and Linn, *Veeck—as in Wreck,* 335.

238 "TOO OLD": Scouting Report, Nap Reyes, September 11, 1956, Satchel Paige File, Baseball Hall of Fame.

238 "SLIPPING (WASH-OUT)": Scouting Report, Reyes, July 21, 1957, Hall of Fame.

238 "SLEEP TOO MUCH": Scouting Report, Tony Pacheco, October 2, 1958, Hall of Fame.

238 "THE BEST CONTROL PITCHER": Scouting Report, Reyes, July 30, 1958, Hall of Fame.

238 "I THOUGHT THEY": "Satch Paige Joins A's at 'Shade over 50,' " *Los Angeles Times.*

239 ONE CHECK FOR $3,500: Author interview with Hank Peters, former general manager for the Kansas City Athletics. Peters says Finley paid Satchel between $3,000 and $4,000, which was a "decent payday in the 1960s."

239 "AT MY AGE": "Rocking Chair For A's Satch," *Chicago Defender.*

239 "A GIMMICK": Page, "Baseball Is Left Holding the Satchel," *Los Angeles Times.*

239 EVENING'S DRAMA MAY HAVE BEEN: Author interviews with Carl Yastrzemski, Bill Monbouquette, Ed Charles, Lee Thomas, and Eddie Bressoud.

240 WALKED OFF THE FIELD: "Satch Can Still Get 'Em Out," *The Kansas City Star; I Was Right on Time,* 221.

240 "WE HAD A LOT OF SATCHEL PAIGES": Banker, *Black Diamonds,* Satchel Paige interview.

CHAPTER 10: CRAFTING A LEGEND

242 DWIGHT D. EISENHOWER: Lebovitz, *The Best of Hal Lebovitz,* 218.

242 "ONE CANNOT HELP": "Paige Had Lot More Than Curveball, Physician Says," *Los Angeles Times.* In 2007, a century after Satchel's birth and quarter century after his death, the American Association of Retired Persons was still citing "Don't look back; something may be gaining on you" as encapsulating the spirit of forward thinking that could invigorate all older Americans. "Forget science, forget steroids, forget modern training techniques . . . Paige relied on his head, his heart and his savvy," the group wrote. "We need more Satchel Paiges."

242 HE SWORE HE DID: *Maybe I'll Pitch Forever,* 80; *Pitchin' Man,* 76.

242 TOLD A SPICIER STORY: Fox, *Satchel Paige's America,* 18–20.

242 AN AMIABLE CAMEL: Grayson, *They Played the Game,* 132.

242 "ETERNAL RESTER": *Maybe I'll Pitch Forever,* 149.

242 "RISING GENTLY": "The Fabulous Satchel Paige."

242 THERE WAS A DISSENTING VIEW: Clark, "Satchel Paige: The Life History."

242 THEY COULD BE ALTERED: Daley, "Don't Look Now But," *The New York Times;* Kahn, "Hacking a Path Through the High-Tech Jungle," *The Wall Street Journal.*

243 "IF YOU WANT TO LIVE": "Midnight Rider" chapter in *Baseball: A Film by Ken Burns,* PBS.

243 TO THE EISENHOWER WHITE HOUSE: The five rules sent to the president were (1) Avoid fried meats, which angry up the blood; (2) If your stomach disputes you, lie down and pacify it with cool thoughts; (3) Keep the juices flowing by jangling around gently as you move; (4) Go very light on the vices, such as car-

rying on in society. The social ramble ain't restful; (5) Don't look back, something may be gaining on you. A sixth rule, included in the original *Collier's* list but not the White House version, was, Avoid runnin' at all times.

243 **THE PRESIDENT WROTE BACK:** Letter from President Eisenhower to Dr. Franklin D. Murphy, Chancellor, University of Kansas, April 25, 1955, Dwight D. Eisenhower Records as President, White House Central Files, 1953–1961.

243 **"I FOUND NO EVIDENCE":** 2007 e-mail to author from Herbert L. Pankratz, archivist, Eisenhower Library.

243 **THE WORDS DONOVAN'S:** Jack Smith of the *Los Angeles Times* made public that arrangement twenty-seven years later. He said that Donovan, then a story developer with Bing Crosby Productions, had confessed it to him in the '50s. "I don't like to wake sleeping dogs," Smith wrote in his sports column, "especially since I am a disciple of Satchel Paige, and am especially respectful of his last rule: 'Don't look back. Something might be gaining on you.' . . . Indeed, to learn that Paige had nothing to do with the composition of his rules would be as great a disillusionment as learning that Abraham Lincoln didn't write the Gettysburg Address or that Sam Goldwyn didn't say 'Gentlemen—include me out.' "

Sadly, Donovan died four months after Smith's columns. His obituary in the *Los Angeles Times* led by referring to him as "the journalist who put 63 immortal words in Satchel Paige's mouth." Satchel, it added, "took the quotes as his own after the *Collier's* article appeared and continued to sprinkle them throughout his speeches and public appearances." The reason Smith gave for exposing the ruse so many years after he learned of it is that he had been called to task for misquoting one of the rules. "It is not with any thought of excusing my sin," he penned, "but simply in the pursuit of literary truth that I raise the question of whether Paige was actually the author of those widely quoted precepts."

Satchel had come clean—sort of—years before. He had a "whole system" for staying healthy, he wrote in his 1962 memoir, and "some sports guy on the East coast heard me talking about them once and then he went and turned them into a bunch of rules for me on how to stay young. I just adopted them." Satchel listed all six, adding, "that last one [don't look back] that fellow wrote was my real rule." How many of the others were Satchel's phrasing or thinking? He never said and reporters never asked. The result: Satchel got all the credit, Donovan none.

Jack Smith, "Living by the Goldwyn Rule," *Los Angeles Times;* Smith, "A Paige out of the Past," *Los Angeles Times;* "He Added a Few 'Paiges,' " *Los Angeles Times; Maybe I'll Pitch Forever,* 227; "Scorecard," *Sports Illustrated,* June 21, 1982.

244 **DID IT FOR THE FIRST TIME:** *Maybe I'll Pitch Forever,* 34–35.

244 **BIG-LEAGUE BASHERS:** Heintzman interview.

245 **"WITH TWO DOWN":** "Paige Pitches and 19,178 See Kay Cees Win," *Chicago Defender.*

245 **"I SAW HIM DO THIS":** "Area Residents Recall Pitcher's Magical Displays," *News Journal* (Mansfield, Ohio).

245 **"YOU CAN CALL THEM IN":** Author interview with Bob Motley.

245 **"WHILE MY OUTFIELD":** "Satch Beards the House of David."

245 **BIG AS A MATTRESS:** Baseball historian W. Bryan Steverson has put numbers behind those feats. A foil chewing-gum wrapper placed horizontal, he found, amounts to 17 percent of home plate and it is just 10 percent if it is folded. An unfolded matchbook takes up 22 percent.

246 **"I NEVER WORRIED":** Mednick e-mail.

246 "HE DIDN'T MISS": Author interview with Joe Scott.
246 TENPENNY-NAIL ACT: Pepe, "The Satchel Paige Legend," New York *Daily News.*
246 NET IN HIS BASEMENT: Mednick e-mail.
246 TOSSING QUARTERS: Pamela Paige O'Neal at the Kansas City conference of the Society of American Baseball Research.
246 ONE NIGHT IN 1957: Author interview with Whitey Herzog. Herzog wasn't the only one who remembered. So did Ed Storin, a baseball writer then for *The Miami Herald,* and two other Marlins, Ray Semproch and Tom Qualters. All three recall Satchel drilling the ball through the hole on his first try.
247 EQUALLY AMAZING WAS THE NIGHT: Herzog interview.
247 MADE A SIMILAR BET: W. Bryan Steverson, "Satchel: Ruse and Reality," *Satchel Paige and Company,* 29–31.
247 POINTED TO FIELDERS: Robert Smith, *Pioneers of Baseball,* 141.
247 TWITCHING OF FINGERS: Mednick e-mail.
247 "SATCHEL PUT HIS GLOVE": Garver interview.
248 CROSSES THE PLATE: Jordan, "The Hardest Stuff," *The New York Times; Physics of Baseball,* 56.
248 "LORD, MY HAND WAS SO": Author interview with Art Williams.
248 TWO-DOLLAR STEAK: Eckberg, "A Paige in History," *Heartland USA.*
248 "THE GNARLIEST": Motley and Motley, *Ruling over Monarchs,* 89.
248 "MAKING BELIEVERS OUT OF": O'Neil et al., *I Was Right on Time,* 119.
249 "I RAN OUT OF THE PARK": *Maybe I'll Pitch Forever,* 81.
249 SCORE A BIG WIN: Larry Lester, David Marasco, and Patrick Rock, "The Historical Satchel Paige: True Stories and Tales Truly Told," *Satchel Paige and Company,* 35–41; Holway, *Josh and Satch,* 59.
249 "UP COME JOSH GIBSON": *Pitchin' Man,* 46–47.
250 WHEN SATCHEL FIRST WROTE ABOUT IT: " 'Satch' Struck Out Josh Gibson for Biggest Thrill."
250 IN HIS 1948 MEMOIR: *Pitchin' Man,* 46.
250 ANTE WAS UP TO THREE: *Maybe I'll Pitch Forever,* 152.
250 "SATCHEL DRANK IT": O'Neil et al., *I Was Right on Time,* 134–35.
250 ALL THE MAJOR BLACK PAPERS: "Kaysees Win 2nd Tilt," *Afro-American;* Smith, "Third Straight Loss Dooms Grays Hopes," *The Pittsburgh Courier;* "The Historical Satchel Paige: True Stories and Tales Truly Told," 35–41; "Grays Lose as Paige Fans Gibson in Clutch," *Pittsburgh Sun-Telegraph;* "Kansas City Whips Grays Second Time," *Chicago Defender;* Sell, "Late Spurt by Monarchs Beats Grays," *Pittsburgh Post-Gazette.*
251 "A VERY IMPORTANT ITEM": Williams, ed., *The Joe Williams Baseball Reader,* 199.
251 LOW AS TWENTY: Finch, "Satchel Still Going Strong," *Los Angeles Times.*
251 HIGH AS A HUNDRED: *Maybe I'll Pitch Forever,* 57.
251 "SO MANY . . . I DISREMEMBER": *Pitchin' Man,* 41.
251 "I NEVER BATTED LESS": *Pitchin' Man,* 54.
251 HIS CAREER NEGRO LEAGUES: Baseball Hall of Fame; Hogan, *Shades of Glory,* 394–95; and author research.
252 SOME PITCHERS WERE BRILLIANT: Metcalfe, *A Game for All Races,* 95–96.
253 ONE BASEBALL STATISTICIAN: Merritt Clifton e-mail to author, 2007.

253 ANOTHER IMAGINED A BIG-LEAGUE: Doolittle, "The Stat Guy: Imagine What Satchel Paige Could Have Done in the Majors," *The Kansas City Star.*

253 THE MIGHTY HANK AARON: Aaron and Wheeler, *I Had a Hammer: The Hank Aaron Story,* 270.

253 HISTORIAN BILL JAMES: James, *The New Bill James Historical Baseball Abstract,* 360–61.

253 "DESERVES TO RANK": James, *The New Bill James Historical Baseball Abstract,* 193.

253 "HOW GOOD WAS SATCHEL": McGuire and Gormley, *100 Greatest Baseball Players,* 98.

254 "WE WERE OUT IN WYOMIN' ": Kelley, *Voices from the Negro Leagues,* 100.

254 MIAMI MAGISTRATE PUNISHED: "The Pitching Man," *Sports Illustrated.*

254 KANSAS IN 1972: "Satchel Writes Off Parking Fine," *The Kansas City Times.*

254 "THEY FOLLOWED HIM": Author interview with Frank Evans.

255 "SMART BLACK": Roberts, "Policeman Socks Satchel Paige," *The Pittsburgh Courier.*

255 "PAIGE WAS BROODING": "Cop Socks Satchel Paige," Cleveland *Call and Post.*

255 "I WAS RIDIN' 'ROUND": *Pitchin' Man,* 75.

255 "I WAS ON A JACKASS": "Time Ain't Gonna Mess with Me."

256 "METHUSELAH WAS MY FIRST": Sterry and Eckstut, *Satchel Sez,* 23.

256 "IT SEEMS IT'S AS IMPORTANT": *Pitchin' Man,* 6.

256 COPY OF HIS BIRTH CERTIFICATE: Glass, "How Old Is Satch?" *Sports Illustrated.*

257 ORIGINAL GRAVESTONE: That gravestone was donated. Satchel's family was grateful for the donation but not for the perpetuation of the ruse over the pitcher's age.

257 CHLOROFORM LINIMENT: Broeg, "Satch Would Be Ready Tonight," *St. Louis Post-Dispatch.*

257 KEROSENE AND OLIVE OIL: "Satch Beards the House of David."

257 "PLAIN, OLD-FASHIONED": Daley, "Satch Finally Makes It," *The New York Times.*

257 "HIS PITCHING ARM": Berry interview.

258 "HE PUT HIS ARM": Author interview with Yogi Berra.

258 "STAY OUT OF THAT TRAINING ROOM": Author interview with Dusty Baker.

258 "A MAN," HE SAID: Fox, *Satchel Paige's America,* 19–20.

258 "SOME SAID HE DRANK": Young, "An 'Old Man' Makes Baseball History," *Ebony.*

259 "SATCHEL WOULD OFTEN DRINK": Walker, "Playing Ball with the Great Satchel Paige."

259 "I JUST BLOW IT": "Sporting Life," *Time,* September 17, 1953, 51.

259 GERONTOLOGICAL CONGRESS: "The Fabulous Satchel Paige."

259 "I JUST EXPLAINED": Assuming he had anything real in mind, Satchel was probably referring to the fibula and tibia, both of which are in the leg.

259 "YOU BORN WITH SPEED": Banker, *Black Diamonds,* Satchel Paige interview.

259 "I WAS BORN ABLE": *Pitchin' Man,* 24.

260 HE TOLD ONE GULLIBLE TEAMMATE: McDermott and Eisenberg, *A Funny Thing Happened on the Way to Cooperstown.*

260 "GOSSIPMONGERS": "An 'Old Man' Makes Baseball History."

260 TRICK THE TRICKSTER: Bankes, *Pittsburgh Crawfords,* 59; Bankes interview.

260 NO, ALTHOUGH THEY KNEW: Banker, *Black Diamonds,* Satchel Paige interview.

260 NO, THEY HAD BEEN: James, *The New Bill James Historical Baseball Abstract,* 178.

260 "NO, UNH-UNH": Dick Wilkinson interview.

261 EVEN MORE SUPERSTITIOUS: Posnanski, *Soul of Baseball,* 144–46.

261 HIT A HAWK: Irvin and Riley, *Nice Guys Finish First,* 84.

261 "I GRABBED A .22": O'Neil et al., *I Was Right on Time,* 114–15.

261 "STORIES ABOUT SATCHEL": O'Neil et al., *I Was Right on Time,* 113.

261 "WRITING A BOOK ABOUT": Feller interview.

262 "DON'T PRAY WHEN IT RAINS": Sterry and Eckstut, *Satchel Sez,* 60.

262 "AIN'T NO MAN": Sterry and Eckstut, *Satchel Sez,* 60.

262 "WORK LIKE YOU": Sterry and Eckstut, *Satchel Sez,* 62.

262 "I AIN'T EVER HAD": www.baseball-almanac.com.

262 "I GOT BLOOPERS": *Pitchin' Man,* 64.

263 "I DON'T KNOW WHAT": Greene with Holway, "I Was Satchel's Catcher," *Journal of Popular Culture.*

263 "HE HAD A WAY OF NAMING": Robinson and Bauer, *Catching Dreams,* 33.

263 "THERE WEREN'T THAT MANY": Author interview with Tom "Satch" Sanders.

263 "THERE WAS SOMETHING": Aaron and Wheeler, *I Had a Hammer,* 271.

264 "WILKSON": The pitcher was not even sure about the spelling of his own nickname—sometimes he wrote it with one *l* and other times with two. As for the name he was born with, typically he wrote "Leroy" but sometimes "LeRoy."

264 "I WAS A REGULAR TRAVELIN' MAN": *Pitchin' Man,* 30.

264 SATCHEL CHOSE WHITE COLLABORATORS: His first book was supposed to have a black ghostwriter, but Satch backed out of that deal, according to black sportswriter Doc Young, who might have wanted to be that writer. Lester Rodney, the sports editor of the Communist Party's *Daily Worker,* says he was Satchel's first choice as cowriter but Satchel was talked out of it by his agent. Zirin, "An Interview with Lester 'Red' Rodney, the Man Who Helped Integrate Baseball."

264 "IF I TAPED HIM": Fox, *Satchel Paige's America,* 140.

265 "I JUST KNEW HOW HE SOUNDED": Author interview with William Price Fox.

265 "IN SUCH PSYCHOLOGICAL": Smith, "Living by the Goldwyn Rule."

265 HE HAD INTERNALIZED: Fox interview.

265 "MUCH OF THE MEMOIR": Lipman interview.

CHAPTER 11: MAYBE I'LL PITCH FOREVER

267 NIXON'S CONGRATULATIONS: Telegram from Herbert G. Klein, director of communications for the executive branch, August 19, 1971, Satchel Paige File, Baseball Hall of Fame.

268 "THAT SATCHEL PAIGE AND": Durso, "Stengel and Williams Inducted into Baseball Hall," *The New York Times.*

268 "IF YOU BELIEVE": Fitzgerald, "Let's Get Old Satch into the Hall of Fame," *Sport.*

268 "THIS NOTION OF JIM CROW": Murray, "Baseball's Injustice," *Los Angeles Times.*

268 "I'M PROUD TO BE": Povich, "Even in Back Room, Paige Brightens Hall," *The Washington Post.*

268 "SOME DARK NIGHT": Povich, "Even in Back Room, Paige Brightens Hall."

269 "THANK YOU, COMMISSIONER": Satchel Paige induction speech, Baseball Hall of Fame, Cooperstown, New York, August 9, 1971.

269 HIS REMARKS WERE TOUCHING: Satchel Paige induction speech.

269 INTERRUPTED THIRTEEN TIMES: Moore, *Pride Against Prejudice,* 168.

269 HEART TOOK OVER: "Satchel 'Proudest Man on Earth,' " *Los Angeles Times.*

270 "THEY ASKED ME TO": Grimsley, "Satchel Paige: Baseball Still Doing My People Wrong," *Staten Island Advance.* Satchel says his return visit to Cooperstown was in 1972, Hank Greenberg says it was in 1975, and newspaper clippings suggest it was in 1974.

270 SATCHEL'S CATCHER TOLD LOGAN: Author interview with Bill Clark.

271 "BIG OLD BOY": Clark identifies the player as Rich Alberts and says he is sure Alberts struck out. Alberts remembers things differently, saying he almost "took [Satchel's] head off with a base hit back through the middle of the diamond. I don't remember what Satchel said, I was so damn tickled to get that hit. He was a dandy."

271 "EVERYONE THOUGHT THAT SATCH": Shury, "Satch in Saskatchewan"; author interview with Bob Joyce.

271–72 "SATCHEL CLAIMED ME": Author interview with Sherman Cottingham.

272 PENINSULA PILOTS: *Carolina League Media Guide and Record Book.*

272 "THE REASON THIS STORY": Author interview with and e-mails from Jerry McGinn; McGinn, " 'Satchel' Paige Still Had Pitching Savvy, Scribe Discovers," *Chicago Defender.*

272 HE READILY ADMITTED: Shury, "Satch in Saskatchewan."

273 "I AIN'T NO CLOWN": *Pitchin' Man,* 16.

273 "HOW WE GONNA WORK IT": Heward and Gat, *Some Are Called Clowns,* 81.

274 "SIXTY YEARS OLD": Heward and Gat, *Some Are Called Clowns,* 82.

274 "THE CLOWN INFIELDERS": Bilovsky, "Bittersweet Tale of a Sad 'Clown,' " Philadelphia *Sunday Bulletin.*

274 "[SATCHEL] SQUINTED": Plaisted, "Satch Blows Stack," *The Sporting News.*

274 "SIT ALL THE WAY": Author interview with James Alderman.

274 "ONE TIME SATCHEL": Heward and Gat, *Some Are Called Clowns,* 266.

275 "I'M JUST AN ASSOCIATE": "Satchel Blasts Clowns," *Chicago Defender.*

275 SIGN AUTOGRAPHS AND WAVE: In the years after his Hall induction, when demand skyrocketed for his signature, Satchel reportedly used at least one ghostwriter to replicate his John Hancock. None was very good at it, which explains why so many variations of his autograph are being bought and sold today. Keating and Kolleth, *The Negro Leagues Autograph Guide,* 152.

275 WAS AS A ROLE MODEL: Author interview with Lee Talboys.

276 "IF ANY OF THOSE": "Scorecard," *Sports Illustrated,* March 11, 1963.

276 "YOU KNOW WHAT SOME": Breslin, "Here's a Prime Opportunity for Baseball to Redeem Itself," *New York Herald Tribune.*

276 "BASEBALL WOULD HAVE BEEN": "Satch Is Back," *Time.*

276 LOOKING BACK FORTY YEARS: Author interview with William Bartholomay.

277 "HE CALLED ME DAFFY": Baker interview.
277 "I WAS GOING": Author interview with Phil Niekro.
277 "HE WAS ALWAYS SORT OF": Author interviews with Joe and Frank Torre.
278 "HE DIDN'T DO": Author interview with Dave Percley.
278 "NOW AARON": Browning, " 'Baseball' Might Have Missed This."
279 SATCHEL'S DUTIES WERE THE SAME: McGuire, "Satchel Paige: Retired Pitcher Leroy Paige Has Opinions as Stinging as His Once-Great Fastball," *St. Louis Post-Dispatch.*
279 "VICE PRESIDENT IN CHARGE": Anderson, "Satchel Paige Finally Looks Back," *The New York Times.*
279 "HE CAN WRAP UP": Bulger, "Owsley Signs Satchel Paige to Staff," *The Kansas City Times.*
279 "I FIGURE SOME": Haggerty, "Satch Makes Political Pitch," *The Kansas City Star.*
280 "I'VE GOT ABOUT": "Ageless 'Satch' Earned Fame," *News Journal* (Mansfield, Ohio).
280 FILED IN THE WRONG DISTRICT: Sigman, "Error Before His First Pitch," *The Kansas City Times.*
280 "THE MERIT SYSTEM DOESN'T": Bulger, "Owsley Signs Satchel Paige to Staff," *The Kansas City Times.*
280 "HE IS NOT MAKING": Harrison, "Satchel Paige Runs for Missouri Legislature," *Jet.*
281 "A TRICK RIDER": Friedlander, "A Mythical Character Named Satchel Paige," *New York Post.*
281 "LIFE WAS FOR": Fred Newman, *Satchel: A Requiem for Racism.*
281 GRATEFUL DEAD GUITARIST: Author interview with Bob Weir.
282 "HAD THE WHIP ACTION": Brashler, *The Bingo Long Traveling All-Stars & Motor Kings,* 67.
282 STEP SAID: Morten, "Stepin' Fetchit Eyes Movie on Satchel Paige," *Chicago Defender.*
282 "SATCH WAS A FOLK HERO": "Ball Club Exec Wins Starring Role—Playing Himself," *News World* (New York).
282 "I'M AN OLD-TIME": "Ball Club Exec Wins Starring Role—Playing Himself."
283 DISILLUSIONING EXPERIENCE: Beck, "Satchel Paige Movie May Not Have the Right Stuff," *Chicago Tribune.*
283 "THEY DIDN'T WANT TO DO": Author interview with Stanley Rubin.
283 "ON A SOAPBOX": Rubin interview.
283 BY THE TIME RUBIN STARTED: Burnes, "The Legend Gains on Satchel Paige," *The Kansas City Star.*
283 "HE DID NOT READ": Author interviews with Dean Williams and Marlene Clark.
284 "IF YOU BROUGHT": Negro Leagues Baseball Museum interview with Warren James Paige, Kansas City, Missouri, undated.
284 "I DIDN'T REALIZE": Negro Leagues Baseball Museum interview with Warren Paige.
284 "PROTECTED US": Paige family presentation at Society for American Baseball Research conference in Kansas City, Missouri, Negro Leagues Committee, July 8, 2006.
285 "IS THE SON OF LEGENDARY": House Resolution HR0100, State of Illinois House of Representatives, February 22, 2007; author interview with Larry Lester.

285 THE PAIGE KIDS: Paige family presentation at SABR conference.

286 FLIP SIDE WAS SOFT: Paige family presentation at SABR conference.

286 ROBERT DID PITCH: Posnanski, *Soul of Baseball,* 147.

287 DOZEN SPACIOUS ROOMS: Later stories said his house had twenty-one rooms, which could have been a different way of counting and was more likely Satchel embellishing. Lahoma, as always, was more modest in her appraisal, saying the house had twelve rooms.

288 ONE ABOUT THE CHICKEN: Paige family presentation at SABR conference.

288 "WHEN THE ANNOUNCEMENT": Author interview with Hank Peters.

288 "WHEN SATCHEL REACHED UP": Gowdy and Powers, *Seasons to Remember,* 71–72.

289 UNDER THE PSEUDONYM: *LaHoma Paige v. Kansas City Power & Light Company,* 42–43.

289 HE SET HIS PRICE HIGH: Satchel's kids followed his lead, granting few interviews and generally asking to review materials prepublication and be paid a fee. "Now that we're at this period of life, most of us are able to take the time to do these things that we feel is the best way to manage ourselves," says Pamela, in explaining why she and her siblings hope to write their own book about their father. "Everyone is writing these books because it is lucrative." Author phone conversation with Pamela Paige O'Neal.

289 LIGHTS WENT OUT: The Paiges were overcharged for at least fourteen years because the Kansas City Power & Light Company thought they were running a rooming house or other business from their home. In 1984 Lahoma filed a complaint with the state Public Service Commission, and the next year she received a settlement from the utility believed to be $20,000. Kava, "Accord Reached on Bills," *The Kansas City Times.*

289 "WHEN HE WAS NOT EMPLOYED": Paige family presentation at SABR conference.

289 "MY AUNTIES": Negro Leagues Baseball Museum interview with Warren Paige.

290 STOPPED REPEATEDLY: Finding records of what the police did is hard. At the end of the civil rights era, many such records were believed to have been purged to eliminate evidence of misconduct.

290 "HE KNEW I COULD HIDE HIM": Author interview with Chris Grove.

291 EMBARRASSED BY HIS FAMILY'S: Leon Paige interview.

292 WHAT NEWSPAPERS SAID: Lula's birth information is almost as enigmatic as Satchel's. U.S. Census records for 1900, 1910, 1920, and 1930 show her as born in 1875, which would have made her ninety when she died. Her obituaries and death record said she came into the world in 1861 and left it 104 years later. That would have made her nearly eighteen years older than her husband and had her delivering her last child at the extraordinary age of fifty-five, or even fifty-six.

292 "AUNT PALESTINE WENT IN": Leon Paige interview.

292 "AND LISTENING TO": Wilson Paige, Jr., interview.

293 "PEOPLE," HE TOOK TO SAYING: "Scorecard," *Sports Illustrated,* January 27, 1964.

293 "THE COMMODORE WAS NOW": Author interview with Bill Gallo.

293 "I HAD MANY CALLS FROM SATCH": Kuhn, *Hardball,* 111.

294 "SATCH WALKED AWAY WITH A MONARCHS": Author interview with Marty Appel.

294 "I DEFINITELY DID NOT FEEL": Bankes interview.

294 EVEN HIS VOICE: Condon, "In the Wake of the News," *Chicago Tribune,* August 21, 1968.

295 MAJOR LUNG OPERATION: McGuff, "More Insight Is Developed into Paige," *The Kansas City Star.*

295 "WE AIN'T ALL THAT FAR": Murray, "They'll Never Catch Up with Satch," *The Oakland Tribune.*

295 "OF ALL THE PLACES": Braham, "Paige Ends Silence, Rips Indians," *Cleveland Press.*

295 "IT'S A SHAME": "Reunion Toasts Bell, Paige," *The New York Times;* Holway, " 'They Made Me Survive,' Mays Says," *The Sporting News.*

296 "I'M GLAD TO BE": Holway, "Negro League Reunion: Paige and Pals," *The Washington Post;* " 'They Made Me Survive,' Mays Says."

296 "PLEASE, MR. PAIGE": Author interview with Harry T. Wiley.

296 SATCHEL LAST APPEARED: Torriero, " 'We Lost Satchel,' " *The Kansas City Times;* Abel, "After Honors, 'Satchel' Paige Dies," Kansas City *Call.*

296 IT WAS TYPICAL: E. A. Torriero, e-mail to author, 2007.

297 SATCHEL WOKE THAT NIGHT: " 'We Lost Satchel.' "

297 LAHOMA RECALLED: Lahoma did not have it easy after Satchel's death. Money was tight and she had to borrow against the house to pay for a car and living expenses. Taking care of Satchel and the kids had been her mission; now he was gone and they were grown. She had grown heavier but still had her melting smile. Her daughter Linda in Detroit urged her to move there, while Robert wanted her to come to Illinois. Sustained by her faith as well as her other children and grandchildren, she stayed in Kansas City. She died four years after Satchel. Their kids mainly inherited debts, although they also got Satchel's trophies, glove, ball, and other cherished memorabilia.

297 "ONE OF THOSE WONDROUSLY": "Satchel," *The New York Times,* June 10, 1982.

297 "THE PAIGE TRAGEDY": "Satchel Paige: 'Best I Ever Saw'—Veeck."

297 "DON'T FEEL SORRY FOR US": Remarks by O'Neil at Satchel's funeral.

297 "FROM NOW ON": Paige eulogy by the Reverend Emanuel Cleaver II, June 12, 1982.

298 IN SUBSEQUENT YEARS: While he would have delighted in the tributes he received, Satchel also would have counted and compared those he didn't. Hank Aaron was memorialized by his hometown of Mobile with, among other things, a sports stadium; Satchel plays second fiddle there, as elsewhere, with his name attached to a mere road outside the stadium.

298 "THRILLING MILLIONS": Satchel and Lahoma's graveside memorial, designed by baseball historian Phil Dixon and others.

BIBLIOGRAPHY

*For a more complete listing of articles
and other sources, go to www.larrytye.com.*

Aaron, Hank, and Lonnie Wheeler. *I Had a Hammer: The Hank Aaron Story.* New York: HarperPaperbacks, 1992.
AARP Bulletin. "Maybe I'll Work Forever." April 2007.
Abel, Rick E. "After Honors, 'Satchel' Paige Dies." *The Call.* June 11–17, 1982.
Adair, Robert K. *The Physics of Baseball.* New York: Perennial, 2002.
Addie, Bob. "The Big Picture." *The Washington Post.* February 21, 1971.
Adomites, Paul, et al. *The Golden Age of Baseball.* Lincolnwood, Ill.: Publications International, 2003.
Advocate (Baton Rouge, La.). "Postal Service Honors Legend." July 7, 2000.
Afro-American (Baltimore and Washington). "Black Sox Boast a Pair o' Kings." May 3, 1930.
———. "The Black Sox Guns Are Ready to Boom." April 19, 1930.
———. "Black Sox Player Jailed Following Fight in Cuba." February 8, 1930.
———. "Black Sox Trim White Club." June 28, 1930.
———. "Double Plays, Heavy Blows, Feature Two Sox Victories." May 3, 1930.
———. "The Great Big Man from the South." March 22, 1930.
———. "Kaysees Win 2nd Tilt, 8-4." September 19, 1942.
———. "Satchell Paige Detained by Cops." June 2, 1934.
Ainslie, Peter. "In Kentucky: Memories of Black Baseball." *Time.* August 10, 1981.
Ajemian, Bob. "Paige Okay Now—New Store Teeth." *The Sporting News.* July 19, 1950.
Alabama, State of. "An Act to Create Reform School for Training of Juvenile Negro Law-Breakers." 1911. No. 336, H. 238
Allen, Lee. *The American League Story: A Colorful and Exciting History.* New York: Hill & Wang, 1962.
Allen, Maury. *Jackie Robinson: A Life Remembered.* New York: Franklin Watts, 1987.
Alsobrook, David E. *Alabama's Port City: Mobile During the Progressive Era, 1896–1917.* Ph.D. diss., Auburn University, 1983.
———. "The Mobile Streetcar Boycott of 1902: African American Protest or Capitulation?" *The Alabama Review,* April 2003.

Amsterdam News (New York, N.Y.). "Paige Faces N.N.L. Ban." May 21, 1938.
———. "Report Satchel Paige with K.C. Monarchs." May 6, 1939.
———. "Satchel Paige Hauled into Court by Manley." April 23, 1938.
———. "Satchel Paige Restrained from Going to South America." April 30, 1938.
Anchorage Daily News. "Paige Says He'll Boss Anchorage Earthquakers." August 27, 1965.
———. "Satchel Paige Greeted by Unexpected Visitor." August 26, 1965.
Anderson, Dave. "Satch Surveys Catfish and Ages." *The New York Times.* October 12, 1976.
———. "Satchel Paige Finally Looks Back." *The New York Times.* May 31, 1981.
Anderson, Russell. "The Truth About Satch's Age." *The American Weekly.* March 15, 1953.
Armstead, Emmet. "Paige Helps Crawfords Divide Pair with Grays." *Chicago Defender.* July 11, 1936.
Armstrong, Jim. "Negro League's Hidden Talent Labored on Fields of Dreams." *The Denver Post.* March 28, 1999.
Armstrong, Linda. "Satchel . . . A Story Which Should Be Told." *Amsterdam News* (New York). January 22–28, 1998.
Arnold, Millard. "Negro Leagues Revisited." *The Washington Post.* July 10, 1971.
Aron, Paul. *Did Babe Ruth Call His Shot? and Other Unsolved Mysteries of Baseball.* New York: John Wiley & Sons, 2005.
Associated Press. "Griffith Backs Monarchs." *The New York Times.* October 25, 1945.
———. "How Really Great Was Satchel?" *The New York Times.* August 10, 1971.
———. "Will Appeal to Chandler." *The New York Times.* October 24, 1945.
Athens Messenger (Ohio). "Feller's Team Wins." October 3, 1946.
Atlanta Constitution, The. "Mobile Buries Many Victims of Hurricane." October 1, 1906.
Baird, T. Y., Collection. Kenneth Spencer Research Library. University of Kansas.
Bak, Richard. *Turkey Stearnes and the Detroit Stars: The Negro Leagues in Detroit, 1919–1933.* Detroit: Wayne State University Press, 1994.
Baker, Ray Stannard. *Following the Color Line: An Account of Negro Citizenship in the American Democracy.* Williamstown, Mass.: Corner House Publishers, 1973.
Baltimore Sun. "Satch's Fast Ball Was Elusive as a 'Shadow.' " June 27, 1982.
Bamberger, Michael. "Man of a Century." *Sports Illustrated.* July 15, 2002.
Banker, Stephen. *Black Diamonds: An Oral History of Negro Baseball.* Washington, D.C.: Tapes for Readers, 1978.
Bankes, James. *The Pittsburgh Crawfords: The Lives & Times of Black Baseball's Most Exciting Team!* Dubuque, Iowa: Wm. C. Brown Publishers, 1991.
Barnes, Walter. "The Broadcast." *Chicago Defender.* May 1, 1937.
Barthel, Thomas. *Baseball Barnstorming and Exhibition Games, 1901–1962: A History of Off-season Major League Play.* Jefferson, N.C.: McFarland & Company, 2007.
Bartlett, Charles. "Little to Play at North Shore for Caddy Fund." *Chicago Tribune.* September 20, 1935.
Baseball: A Film by Ken Burns. "The Fifth Inning: Shadow Ball." DVD. Directed by Ken Burns. U.S.: PBS, 1994.
Baseball Almanac. www.baseball-almanac.com (accessed repeatedly).
Baseball Classics: 1948 World Series, Cleveland Indians vs Boston Braves. DVD. Rare Sportsfilms, Inc., 1988.
Baseball Library. www.baseballlibrary.com (accessed repeatedly).

Baseball Reference. www.baseball-reference.com (accessed repeatedly).

Beale, Harry. "Local Sports Slants." *The Pittsburgh Courier.* November 17, 1934.

Bearden, Bessye. "Cole's Giants and Philly Stars Lose Before 25,000." *Chicago Defender.* October 6, 1934.

Beck, Marilyn. "Satchel Paige Movie May Not Have the Right Stuff." *Chicago Tribune.* December 2, 1980.

Beck, Peggy. "Working in the Shadows of Rickey and Robinson: Bill Veeck, Larry Doby and the Advancement of Black Players in Baseball." *Cooperstown Symposium on Baseball and American Culture, 1997.* Jefferson, N.C.: McFarland & Company, Inc., 2000.

Bell, J. Walter. Letter to the editor. *The New York Times.* August 7, 1948.

Bellingham Herald, The. (Washington). "Hit-Starved Bells Lose to Clowns." July 27, 1967.

Benfield, Robert F. "Our Indians . . . 1949 Champions in Baseball . . . and Democracy?" Cleveland *Call and Post.* April 23, 1949.

Berger, Wally, and George Snyder. "An Encounter with the Great Satchel Paige." *The Diamond Angle.* Winter 2001.

Berger, Walter Anton, and George Morris Snyder. . . . *Freshly Remember'd.* Redondo Beach, Calif.: Schneider/McGuirk Press, 1993.

Berkow, Ira. "Ryan, Paige and Rules for Keeping Young." *The New York Times.* March 9, 1992.

———. "Satchel Paige: 'New General Is Taking Over.'" Chillicothe *Constitution-Tribune* (Missouri). March 31, 1969.

Bilovsky, Frank. "Satchel Paige—Bittersweet Tale of a Sad 'Clown.'" Philadelphia *Sunday Bulletin.* August 14, 1966.

Birmingham Reporter, The. "Black Barons Win and Lose at Kansas City." July 7, 1928.

———. "Fight at St Louis Park Halts 3rd Game; Near Riot as Mitchell Chases Paige with Bat." July 2, 1927.

———. "Satchel Strikes Out 17; Barons Split Series." July 20, 1929.

Bismarck Tribune, The. "Bismarck Faces 'Crucial' National Tourney Test Tonight." August 20, 1935.

———. "Bismarck Nips Jamestown 3-2 with Thrilling Rally Late in Game." August 14, 1933.

———. "Bismarck Overwhelms Twin City Giants in Final Home Game, 21-6." August 12, 1935.

———. "How Can They Hit Safely When They Can't See 'Em?" August 24, 1935.

———. "Locals Play Post-tourney Games, Get Good Publicity." August 31, 1935.

———. "Neil O. Churchill, Ex-mayor of City, Dies at Age 78." September 30, 1969.

———. "Paige and Medlock, Colored Pitchers, Have Not Arrived." May 12, 1934.

———. "Satchel Paige, Colored Hurler, Expected in Bismarck Next Week." January 24, 1934.

———. "Satchel Paige May Pitch for Locals Against American All-Stars." September 26, 1934.

———. "Satchel Paige or Chet Brewer Will Get Pitching Call." October 3, 1934.

Bivens, Shawn A. *Mobile, Alabama's People of Color: A Tricentennial History, 1702–2002.* Vol. 1. Victoria, B.C.: Trafford Publishing, 2004.

Bjarkman, Peter C. *Baseball with a Latin Beat: A History of the Latin American Game.* Jefferson, N.C.: McFarland & Company, 1994.

———. *A History of Cuban Baseball, 1864–2006.* Jefferson, N.C.: McFarland & Company, 2007.

Black, Joe. "Black Gives Rundown on Majors' 1st Negro Players." *Chicago Defender.* February 18, 1963.

Blackmon, Lou. "Bring Series South." *Newark Daily News.* September 24, 1938.

Blackwell, Lee. "Off the Record." *Chicago Defender.* April 28, 1958.

Blackwood, Kendrick. "Stealing Home." *Pitch Weekly.* February 3, 2005.

Bloomberg News Service. "Leonard, Paige Top Negro League Stars." June 8, 1999.

Blumenstock, Kathy. "Paige Dies, Legendary Pitcher, 75." *The Washington Post.* July 9, 1982.

Bolden, Ed. "League Chairman Answers Critics of Negro Baseball." *The Pittsburgh Courier.* October 31, 1936.

Bordman, Sid. "Books 1st to Paige." *The Kansas City Star.* June 5, 1973.

Bostic, Joe. "Johnny Taylor Is Shelled from Mound as Paige Wins." Baltimore *Afro-American.* October 2, 1937.

———. "Taylor's No-Hitter Tops Satchel Paige." *Afro-American.* September 25, 1937.

Boston Globe, The. "Record-Breaking Heat Wave Due to Smother City Today." August 25, 1948.

———. "Thousands Fail to Get into Park to See Sox Game." August 25, 1948.

Boswell, Thomas. "Satchel Paige: 'Best I Ever Saw'—Veeck." *The Washington Post.* June 9, 1982.

Boudreau, Lou. "What's Ahead for Baseball." *Chicago Tribune.* April 13, 1958.

Boudreau, Lou, and Ed Fitzgerald. *Player-Manager.* Boston: Little, Brown and Company, 1952.

Boudreau, Lou, and Russell Schneider. *Covering All the Bases.* Champaign, Ill.: Sagamore Publishing, 1993.

Bowman, Larry. "Moses Fleetwood Walker: The First Black Major League Baseball Player." In *Baseball History: An Annual of Original Baseball Research,* edited by Peter Levine. Westport, Conn.: Meckler, 1989.

Braham, Jim. "Greenberg, Boudreau Answer Satchel's Gripes." *Cleveland Press.* April 17, 1971.

———. "Paige Ends Silence, Rips Indians." *Cleveland Press.* April 16, 1971.

Brands, Edgar G. "Also-Rans Place Seven on 11-Man All-Star Squad." *The Sporting News.* October 27, 1948.

Brascher, Nahum Daniel. "Thoughts for To-Day." *Chicago Defender.* January 17, 1942.

Brashler, William. *The Bingo Long Traveling All-Stars & Motor Kings.* Chicago: University of Chicago Press, 1993.

———. *Josh Gibson: A Life in the Negro Leagues.* Chicago: Ivan R. Dee, 2000.

———. *The Story of Negro League Baseball.* New York: Ticknor & Fields, 1994.

Breslin, Jimmy. "Here's a Prime Opportunity for Baseball to Redeem Itself in the Case of Satchel Paige." *New York Herald Tribune.* July 14, 1968.

Broeg, Bob. *Baseball's Barnum: Ray "Hap" Dumont, Founder of the National Baseball Congress.* Wichita, Kansas: Wichita State University Center for Entrepreneurship, 1989.

———. "Old Satch Left Behind Some Great Memories." *St. Louis Post-Dispatch.* June 9, 1996.

———. "Satch Would Be Ready Tonight." *St. Louis Post-Dispatch.* October 16, 1979.

Brooklyn Bulletin. "Satchel Paige, a Man to Remember." June 23, 1982.

Brown, Dave. "Just How Good Are Race Ball Players?" *Chicago Defender.* September 12, 1936.

Brown, Sam. "American League Stars Lose to Paige and Mates." *Chicago Defender.* October 4, 1941.

Browning, Wilt. " 'Baseball' Might Have Missed This." Greensboro *News & Record* (North Carolina). September 20, 1994.

Bruce, Janet. *The Kansas City Monarchs: Champions of Black Baseball.* Lawrence: University Press of Kansas, 1985.

Buffalo Courier. "The Colored Ball Match." August 22, 1870.

Bulger, William W. "Owsley Signs Satchel Paige to His Staff." *The Kansas City Times.* May 4, 1968.

Burgos, Adrian, Jr. "Playing Ball in a Black and White 'Field of Dreams': Afro-Caribbean Ballplayers in the Negro Leagues, 1910–1950." *The Journal of Negro History* 82, no. 1 (1997): 67–104.

Burley, Dan. "Confidentially Yours." *Amsterdam News* (New York). May 17, 1941.

———. "Confidentially Yours." *Amsterdam News* (New York). August 9, 1941.

———. "Famed Hurler Quits Kay See to Come Here." *Amsterdam News* (New York). May 3, 1941.

———. "Looking Back at the East-West Classic in Chi." *The Pittsburgh Courier.* September 8, 1934.

———. "Paige Fans 8, but Giants Beat Monarchs Anyhow." *Chicago Defender.* September 28, 1935.

Burnes, Brian. "The Legend Gains on Satchel Paige." *The Kansas City Star.* July 20, 1980.

Burns, Edward. "Feet Didn't Start Name of 'Satchel.' " *Chicago Tribune.* August 29, 1948.

Butler, Rosemary Braziel. *Rosemary's Journey: Surviving Segregation with Privileged Pizzazz.* Mobile, Ala.: self-published, 2005.

Cahn, Leonard. "House of David Looks Strong in First Tournament Victory." *The Denver Post.* August 4, 1934.

———. "House of David, United, Fuel Los Angeles Win." *The Denver Post.* August 9, 1934.

———. " 'Satch' Wins 3 in Five Days in Big Denver Tourney." *The Denver Post.* August 18, 1934.

Call and Post (Cleveland). "Cop Socks Satchel Paige." August 18, 1945.

———. " 'Hesitation Pitch' Is a Balk with Men On—Harridge." July 31, 1948.

———. "Indians Vote Full Share to Satchel." October 16, 1948.

Call, The (Kansas City). "Satchel Is Sorry About 10th Pitch." October 19, 1951.

———. "Services Saturday for Lahoma Paige; Was Wife of Baseball Legend." September 26, 1986.

Calvin, Floyd. "It's News to Me." *Chicago Defender.* May 16, 1936.

Campanella, Roy. *It's Good to Be Alive.* Boston: Little, Brown, 1959.

Cannon, Jimmy. "Endless Road for Satchel." *New York Post.* August 16, 1955.

Capozzi, Joe. "Smith Knows Importance of Past." *The Palm Beach Post.* August 20, 2000.

Carmer, Carl Lamson. *Stars Fell on Alabama.* Rahway, N.J.: Quinn & Boden Company, 1934.

Carmichael, John P. *My Greatest Day in Baseball.* Lincoln: University of Nebraska Press, 1996.

Carter, Art. "From the Bench." Baltimore *Afro-American.* June 15, 1940.

———. "From the Bench." Baltimore *Afro-American.* August 22, 1942.

Carter, Booker H., Jr. "Michigan." *Chicago Defender.* October 4, 1941.

Carter, Richard. "Baseball as Usual: If You're Black, Get Back." *Amsterdam News* (New York, N.Y.). December 1, 1999.

Casey, Lawrence "Larry." "Sports Ledger." *Chicago Defender.* August 15, 1966.

Catlin, Roger. "Staging Satchel: A Grateful Dead Member's Salute to a Baseball Great." *The Record* (Hackensack, N.J.). November 6, 1997.

Cerf, Bennett. "Try and Stop Me." *Atchison Daily Globe* (Kansas). November 22, 1948.

———. "Try and Stop Me." *Chicago Defender.* April 12, 1960.

Chadwick, Bruce. *When the Game Was Black and White: The Illustrated History of Baseball's Negro Leagues.* New York: Abbeville Press, 1992.

Chamberlain, John. "Reading for Pleasure." Review of *The Fireside Book of Baseball,* by Charles Einstein, ed. *The Wall Street Journal.* October 22, 1956.

Chandler, A. B. Oral History Project. University of Kentucky Library.

Chapin, Dwight. "Ol' Satch: After All These Years, He's Ailing." *Los Angeles Times.* April 27, 1969.

———. "Satchel Paige Came to My Hometown." *San Francisco Chronicle.* July 19, 2001.

Chattanooga News. "Chattanooga White Sox Beat Black Crackers." May 7, 1926.

———. "Colored White Sox Beat Black Crackers." May 10, 1926.

Chattanooga Times. "Negro White Sox Win Double-Header." August 9, 1926.

Cherokee, Charley. "National Grapevine." *Chicago Defender.* June 13, 1942.

Chicago Defender. "All-Stars to Play Before Legionnaires." September 11, 1937.

———. "Baseball in Brief." March 22, 1941.

———. "Birmingham Leads Series with Detroit." July 20, 1929.

———. "Crawfords Drub Giants." July 14, 1934.

———. "Detroit Has Hard Time to Beat Barons." September 15, 1928.

———. "Divorce Summons Darkens Satchel's Brilliant 'Day.' " July 24, 1943.

———. "Kansas City Monarchs Win World Championship." October 10, 1942.

———. "Kansas City Whips Grays Second Time." September 19, 1942.

———. "Paige Beats Taylor, 9-5 in Star Tilt." October 2, 1937.

———. "Paige Is Baseball's Greatest Drawing Card." August 28, 1948.

———. "Paige Pitches and 19,178 See Kay Cees Win." July 12, 1941.

———. "Paige Says Negroes Not Ready for Big Leagues; White Writer Hits Landis." August 15, 1942.

———. "Paige Signs to Pitch for Trotter Nine." May 15, 1954.

———. "Rocking Chair for A's Satch." September 29, 1965.

———. "Satchel Blasts Clowns." July 1, 1967.

———. "Satchel Hurls for Cleveland Indians." July 17, 1948.

———. "Satchel Made Victim of No-hit Contest." September 25, 1937.

———. "Satchel Paige Is Warned to Report." April 22, 1933.

———. "Satchel Paige Walks Out on Miami Marlins." August 16, 1958.

———. "So Satchel Paige Shows Dizzy Dean How to Pitch." November 3, 1934.

———. "Wesley to Send Ace to Face Giants." May 11, 1929.

Chicago Sun-Times. "Satch Fools 'Em with Fast One." August 8, 1949.

Chicago Tribune. "Paige Not in Favor of Negro in Big Leagues." August 7, 1942.

———. "Satchel Paige Hands Beating to Dizzy Dean." October 22, 1934.

———. "Satchel's Out at Miami." August 6, 1958.

Christian, Ralph. "James Leslie Wilkinson: The Iowa Years, 1878–1916." Presentation at SABR Negro League Committee Conference. Harrisburg, Penn., August 2000.

Chronicle-Telegram, The (Elyria, Ohio). "Satch Still up to His Old Tricks." June 18, 1980.

Clark, Dick, and John Holway. "1930 Negro National League." *Baseball Research Journal* 89: 81–86.

Clark, John L. "Satchel Paige: The Life History of the Great Pitcher." *Chicago Defender.* June 20, 1942.

———. "Wylie Avenue." *The Pittsburgh Courier.* December 22, 1945.

Clarke, Caroline V. "It's Nothin' but a Number." *Black Enterprise.* April 2004.

Cleveland Indians. *1949 Cleveland Indians Sketchbook.*

———. *1949 Cleveland Indians Press and Radio Yearbook.*

Cleveland Press. "Satchel Isn't Bitter, He's Just Happy." February 10, 1971.

Clivelle, Doyle. "Owners Should 'Sell' That Fost-Page Diamond Feud." *Chicago Defender.* June 17, 1933.

Cobbledick, Gordon. "Cobbledick Writes About Satchel Paige." Cleveland *Call and Post.* December 4, 1948.

———. "Ol' Satch Wins an 'Oscar' and Melillo Loses a Coke." Cleveland *Plain Dealer.* March 30, 1949.

Cohane, Tim. "The Ancient Satchel." *Look.* April 7, 1953.

Cohen, Haskell. "18,000 See Satch' Win, Grays Lose." *The Pittsburgh Courier.* July 20, 1946.

Cohen, Robert W. *A Team for the Ages: Baseball's All-Time All-Star Team.* Guilford, Conn.: The Lyons Press, 2004.

Cole, Robert. "Ersatz Octobers: Baseball Barnstorming." In *Baseball History 4: An Annual of Original Baseball Research,* edited by Peter Levine. Westport, Conn.: Meckler, 1991.

Colored Baseball & Sports Monthly. "Leroy 'Satchel' Paige." October 1934.

Conderacci, Greg. "Defeating Inflation, Alas, Is Not as Easy as Writing Letters." *The Wall Street Journal.* October 23, 1978.

Condon, David. "In the Wake of the News." *Chicago Tribune.* August 21, 1968.

———. "Veeck Took Credit; I Got Raps: Hornsby." *Chicago Tribune.* June 13, 1952.

Conrad, Marc. "A Paige in Bismarck's History." *The Bismarck Tribune.* June 1997.

Considine, Bob. "On the Line." *The Washington Post.* July 20, 1941.

Constitution-Tribune (Chillicothe, Mo.). "Satchel Paige . . . a True American Hero." June 10, 1982.

Coshocton Tribune (Ohio). "Feller All-Stars Edge Satch." October 3, 1946.

Costello, Rory. "Twilight at Ebbets Field." In *The National Pastime: Review of Baseball History.* Cleveland: SABR, 2006.

Cottrell, Robert Charles. *The Best Pitcher in Baseball: The Life of Rube Foster, Negro League Giant.* New York: New York University Press, 2001.

Coughlin, Gene. "Daily Scribe Speaks of Jim Crow in the Majors." *Chicago Defender.* July 13, 1935.

Court-martial of Jackie Robinson, The. DVD. Directed by Larry Peerce. 1990; Atlanta: Turner Home Entertainment, 1991.

Cowans, Russ J. "Glory Comes Late to Ol' Satch via His Untiring Arm." *Chicago Defender.* October 9, 1948.

———. "Old Satch Says He's on Last Legs." *Chicago Defender.* March 21, 1953.

Crasnick, Jerry. "Post Tourney Preceded Robinson." *The Denver Post.* April 14, 1997.

Crassweller, Robert D. *Trujillo: The Life and Times of a Caribbean Dictator.* New York: Macmillan, 1966.

Craw, Don. *The Forgotten Tribe: 1948 World Champion Cleveland Indians.* Brandon, Manitoba: Leach, 1999.

Cuhaj, Joe, and Tamra Carraway-Hinckle. *Baseball in Mobile.* Charleston, S.C.: Arcadia, 2003.

Cummiskey, Joe. "Baseball's Greatest Drawing Card: Ol' Satchmo at 38 Still Biggest Diamond Attraction." *Negro Digest.* August 1944.

Curran, Eddie. "Sister Shares Memories of Satchel Paige." Mobile *Press-Register.* April 1, 1990.

Curtright, Bob. "O'Neil Recalls Negro Leagues, Days in Wichita." *The Wichita Eagle.* September 21, 1994.

Czerwinski, Kevin. "Paige Added to Legacy During Stint in Minors." www .minorleaguebaseball.com (accessed June 23, 2008).

Dade, Lawrence. "Foster, Page Open Game." *Chicago Defender.* September 9, 1933.

Daily Independent (Monessen, Penn.). "Dizzy and Daffy Coming to Pittsburgh." October 18, 1934.

Daily Nonpareil, The (Council Bluffs, Iowa). "Feller, Satchel in Scoreless Three Inning Mound Stints." October 13, 1946.

Daily Worker (New York). "Old Satch Still Has It, Says Monarchs Owner." July 3, 1948.

———. "Paige Asks Test for Negro Stars." September 16, 1937.

Daley, Arthur. "The Big Cat Makes It." *The New York Times.* June 18, 1953.

———. "Don't Look Now But—." *The New York Times.* January 11, 1961.

———. "Forever Is a Long Time." *The New York Times.* September 4, 1968.

———. "A Master at His Trade." *The New York Times.* December 10, 1954.

———. "Ol' Satch Looks Back and Gains." *The New York Times.* February 10, 1971.

———. "Satch Finally Makes It." *The New York Times.* July 8, 1948.

———. "There's Life in the Old Boy Yet." *The New York Times.* October 11, 1948.

Daly, Maggie. "Reagan Presented Tribune Cartoon." *Chicago Tribune.* May 20, 1981.

Dancer, Maurice. "Tan Manhattan." *Chicago Defender.* August 2, 1941.

Danver, Charles F. "The Caliph of 'Little Harlem.' " *Pittsburgh Post-Gazette.* October 10, 1932.

Darnell, Tim. *The Crackers: Early Days of Atlanta Baseball.* Athens, Ga.: Hill Street Press, 2005.

Davis, Chuck. "Chuck-a-Luck." *Chicago Defender.* July 29, 1950.

Davis, E. N. "Chicago Plays Kansas City in St. Louis, July 4." *Chicago Defender.* July 5, 1941.

Day, Franklin. "Satchel Paige Magic Is Still Bright." *Daily Worker* (New York). October 8, 1961.

Day, John C. "50,000 See East Humble West at Chicago." *Chicago Defender.* August 2, 1941.

Dean, Dizzy. " 'Satchel Greatest Pitcher'—Dizzy." *Chicago Defender.* September 24, 1938.

Debono, Paul. *The Indianapolis ABCs: History of a Premier Team in the Negro Leagues.* Jefferson, N.C.: McFarland & Company, 1997.

Delaney, James, Jr. "The 1887 Binghamton Bingos." *Baseball Research Journal* 82: 89–115.

Denver Post, The. "Lexington, Colorado Ice and House of David Win Monday in Post Tourney." August 7, 1934.

———. "Negro League Stars Win Post Tourney Title." August 12, 1936.

Destination Freedom: "The Ballad of Satchel Paige." CD. Museum of Broadcast Communications.

Dial, Lewis E. "The Sport Dial." *New York Age.* September 14, 1935.

Dickson, Paul. *The New Dickson Baseball Dictionary.* New York: Harcourt Brace, 1999.

Dismukes, William. "Retrospective and Prospective." *The Pittsburgh Courier.* December 31, 1932.

———. " 'Satch' Struck Out Josh Gibson for Biggest Thrill, by Satchel Paige." *The Pittsburgh Courier.* May 8, 1943.

Dixon, Phil S. *The Monarchs 1920–1938: Featuring Wilbur "Bullet" Rogan.* Sioux Falls, S.D.: Mariah Press, 2002.

Doby, Larry. "Larry Doby's Exclusive Story." *The Pittsburgh Courier.* October 16, 1948.

Dodson, Dan W. "The Integration of Negroes in Baseball." *The Journal of Educational Sociology* 28, no. 2 (1954): 73–82.

Dolgan, Bob. *Heroes, Scamps and Good Guys: 101 Colorful Characters from Cleveland Sports History.* Cleveland: Gray & Company, 2003.

———. "Universal Connection." Cleveland *Plain Dealer.* June 23, 1997.

Donovan, Richard. "The Fabulous Satchel Paige." *Collier's.* May 30, 1953.

———. "Satch Beards the House of David." *Collier's.* June 6, 1953.

———. "Time Ain't Gonna Mess with Me." *Collier's.* June 13, 1953.

Don't Look Back: The Story of Leroy "Satchel" Paige. DVD. Directed by Richard A. Colla. 1981; USA: The Triseme Corporation and Warner Home Video, 1984.

Doolittle, Bradford. "The Stat Guy: Imagine What Satchel Paige Could Have Done in the Majors." *The Kansas City Star.* July 13, 2007.

Doyle, James E. "The Sports Trail." Cleveland *Plain Dealer.* July 8, 1949.

Drebinger, John. "86,288 See Braves Beat Indians, 11-5, to Prolong Series." *The New York Times.* October 11, 1948.

DuBois, Barney. "Paige to Lead City's Team." *Anchorage Daily News.* August 27, 1965.

Dunmore, Al. "80,403 Awed as Paige Blanks White Sox 3-0; Has Drawn 201,829." *The Pittsburgh Courier.* August 28, 1948.

Durslag, Melvin. "Speaking of Sports." *The San Francisco Examiner.* March 4, 1969.

Durso, Joseph. "Satchel Paige, Black Pitching Star, Is Dead at 75." *The New York Times.* June 9, 1982.

———. "Stengel and Williams Inducted into Baseball Hall." *The New York Times.* July 26, 1966.

Dyer, Braven. "The Sports Parade." *Los Angeles Times.* March 12, 1944.

———. "The Sports Parade: Lou Reveals 'Saga of Satch.' " *Los Angeles Times.* June 5, 1960.

Ebony. "The Brainiest Man in Baseball." August 1952.

Echevarría, Roberto González. *The Pride of Havana: A History of Cuban Baseball.* New York: Oxford University Press, 1999.

Eckberg, John. "A Paige in History." *Heartland USA.* Fall 1992.

Einstein, Charles, ed. *The Fireside Book of Baseball.* New York: Simon & Schuster, 1956.

Elderkin, Phil. "Hurler Satchel Paige: Pitching Wonder Who Never Looked Back." *The Christian Science Monitor.* June 14, 1982.

Eriksmoen, Curt. "1935 Bismarck Team Was One of the Best." *The Bismarck Tribune.* January 21, 2007.

————. "Churchill Brought Baseball's Best to Bismarck." *The Bismarck Tribune.* January 14, 2007.

Eskenazi, Gerald. *Bill Veeck: A Baseball Legend.* New York: McGraw-Hill, 1988.

————. "Mets' Wounds of Past Turn into Today's Grins." *The New York Times.* June 25, 1972.

Etkin, Jack. *Innings Ago: Recollections by Kansas City Ballplayers of Their Days in the Game.* Kansas City: Normandy Square Publications, 1987.

Evans, Willard. "Sports Snapshots." Baltimore *Afro-American.* November 16, 1935.

Evening Tribune, The. (Albert Lea, Minn.). "Rowe, Mates Lose to KC Monarchs." October 17, 1935.

Falkner, David. *Great Time Coming: The Life of Jackie Robinson, from Baseball to Birmingham.* New York: Simon & Schuster, 1995.

Fatsis, Stefan. "Mystery of Baseball: Was William White Game's First Black?" *The Wall Street Journal.* January 30, 2004.

Feller, Bob. "The Game." *The Saturday Evening Post.* January 27, 1962.

Feller, Bob, and Bill Gilbert. *Now Pitching.* New York: Citadel Press, 2002.

Feller, Bob, and Edward Linn. "The Trouble with the Hall of Fame." *The Saturday Evening Post.* January 27, 1962.

Feller, Bob, and Burton Rocks. *Bob Feller's Little Black Book of Baseball Wisdom.* Lincolnwood, Ill.: Contemporary Books, 2001.

Fields, Wilmer. *My Life in the Negro Leagues: An Autobiography.* Westport, Conn.: Meckler, 1992.

Figueredo, Jorge S. *Who's Who in Cuban Baseball, 1878–1961.* Jefferson, N.C.: McFarland & Company, 2003.

Finch, Frank. "Satchel Still Going Strong." *Los Angeles Times.* July 15, 1958.

Finger, Bill. "Satchel Paige Dominates Game." Cleveland *Call and Post.* October 27, 1934.

Fitts, Robert K. "Baseball Cards and Race Relations." *The Journal of American Culture* 17, no. 3 (1994): 75–83.

Fitzgerald, Ed. "Let's Get Old Satch into the Hall of Fame." *Sport.* November 1952.

Flaherty, Vincent X. "Feller's Bonanza Tops Ruth's Richest 'Take.' " *The Sporting News.* November 6, 1946.

Fleming, Gordon H. *The Dizziest Season: The Gashouse Gang Chases the Pennant.* New York: William Morrow and Company, 1984.

Florence, Mal. "Satch Ready to Make His Pitch for A's Again." *Los Angeles Times.* January 25, 1966.

Flory, Ishmael P. "The People Speak." *Chicago Defender.* August 19, 1958.

Forbes, Frank. "Kansas City Monarchs Go Down Before Black Yankees." *Chicago Defender.* July 13, 1946.

Foster, Willie. "Brown, Satchell Paige, Jones Lead." *The Pittsburgh Courier.* August 25, 1934.

Fox, Stephen. *Big Leagues: Professional Baseball, Football, & Basketball in National Memory.* Lincoln: University of Nebraska Press, 1998.

Fox, William Price. "Conversations with Satchel Paige." *Holiday.* August 1965.

————. *Satchel Paige's America.* Tuscaloosa: University of Alabama Press, 2005.

Fraley, Oscar. "What's This About Ol' Archie Moore?" *Chicago Defender.* January 6, 1959.

Francis, C. Philip. "Satch: The Life of Leroy 'Satchel' Paige, from Delinquency to Diamond." February 16, 2007. www.chatterfromthedugout.com.

Fredrick, Tom. "JL Wilkinson: The Man Behind the Monarchs (and the Globetrotters)." *The Kansas City Star.* January 4, 2004.

Freedman, Lew. *Diamonds in the Rough: Baseball Stories from Alaska.* Kenmore, Wash.: Epicenter Press, 2000.

Freeman's Journal, The (Cooperstown, N.Y.). "Satchel Paige 62 Years Old, Allen Says." August 21, 1968.

Fresno Bee, The. "Dean Loses 'Quick.' " March 18, 1935.

Frey, Jennifer. "Pinch-hitting Historian: John Holway Turned His Obsession with the Negro League into a New Career." *The Washington Post.* August 18, 2001.

Friedlander, Sid. "A Mythical Character Named Satchel Paige." *New York Post.* October 4, 1959.

Friedman, Dan. "Satchel Paige: Life and Times of an Ordinary Man." *The Record* (Hackensack, N.J.). February 9, 1998.

Frommer, Harvey. "Satchel Paige: World's Greatest Pitcher." July 10, 2002. www.baseballlibrary.com.

Fuller, Edmund. "Can It Be Frivolous if It's Therapeutic?" *The Wall Street Journal.* March 26, 1979.

Fuster, John E. "Organized Gangs of Hoodlums Riding Doby, Paige." Cleveland *Call and Post.* September 24, 1949.

Galbreath, Elizabeth. "The Women Take to East vs. West Baseball Classic." *Chicago Defender.* August 2, 1941.

Gallagher, Tom. "Lester Rodney, the Daily Worker, and the Integration of Baseball." *The National Pastime: A Review of Baseball History* 19 (1999): 77–80.

Gallo, Bill. "Taking a Paige out of Satch's Book." New York *Daily News.* May 20, 2001.

Gant, Eddie. "I Cover the Eastern Front." *Chicago Defender.* January 3, 1942.

Gardner, Robert, and Dennis Shortelle. *The Forgotten Players: The Story of Black Baseball in America.* New York: Walker and Company, 1993.

Gartner, Michael. "Who Said 'Even Napoleon Had His Watergate?' " *The Wall Street Journal.* June 19, 1979.

Gay, Eustace. "15,000 Brave Cold, See Paige Baffle Grays as K.C. Monarchs Win Series Contest." *The Philadelphia Tribune.* October 3, 1942.

Gergen, Joe. "The Legend of Satchel Paige." *Newsday* (Long Island, N.Y.). June 9, 1982.

Germanotta, Tony. "A Labor of Love: Portsmouth Native Thomas Burt Looks Back at His Negro League Career." Norfolk *Virginian-Pilot.* July 18, 2004.

Gettysburg Times. "Colored Stars Beat Bob Feller's Team." October 1, 1946.

Geyer, Jack. "Baseballers Steal Grid Lunch 'Spot.' " *Los Angeles Times.* October 21, 1952.

———. "Writer Reviews Nation's Unusual Sports Happenings During 1953." *Los Angeles Times.* January 4, 1953.

Gibson, Bill. "Hear Me Talkin' to Ya.' " Baltimore *Afro-American.* April 19, 1930.

Gietschier, Steve. "New Bio Brings Satch out of the Shadows." *The Sporting News.* August 29, 1994.

———. "The Short, Sweet Indian Summer of Satchel Paige." *Timeline.* April–May 1989.

Gilbert, Thomas W. *The Good Old Days: Baseball in the 1930s.* New York: Franklin Watts, 1996.

Gillespie, Ray. "Ol' Satch Winds Up, Fires Back at Critics." *The Sporting News.* August 15, 1951.

———. "Satch Signs '150th' Pact, Cuts Another Year from His Age." *The Sporting News.* February 20, 1952.

———. "Where Veeck Goes, Satch Will Follow." *The Sporting News.* September 30, 1953.

Girard, Fred. "He's 64!" *St. Petersburg Times.* March 9, 1971.

Glass, Arthur P. "How Old Is Satch?" *Sports Illustrated.* February 1949.

Glenn, Stanley. *Don't Let Anyone Take Your Joy Away: An Inside Look at Negro League Baseball and Its Legacy.* New York: iUniverse, Inc., 2006.

Goff, Brian L., Robert E. McCormick, and Robert D. Tollison. "Racial Integration as an Innovation: Empirical Evidence from Sports Leagues." *The American Economic Review* 92, no. 1 (2002): 16–26.

Goldstein, Patrick. "The Black Shadow." Review of *Don't Look Back* by Mark Ribowsky. *Los Angeles Times.* May 22, 1994.

Goldstein, Warren. "The Legend of Satchel Paige." *The New York Times.* April 10, 1994.

———. "Unfair Play: Black Athletes Have Had to Overcome More Than Their Opponents, and Still Do." Review of *$40 Million Slaves* by William C. Rhodes. *The New York Times.* July 23, 2006.

Gosselin, Rick. "Paige's Legend Will Live On." *The Chronicle-Telegram* (Elyria, Ohio). June 13, 1982.

Gould, Ben. "Satch Hits Jackpot in Exhibitions." *The Sporting News.* July 19, 1950.

Gould, Jay. "Race Track Gossip." *Chicago Defender.* March 7, 1936.

Gould, Stephen Jay. "Good Sports & Bad." *The New York Review of Books.* March 2, 1995.

Gowdy, Curt, and Al Hirshberg. *Cowboy at the Mike: The Autobiography of a Great Sports Announcer.* Garden City, N.Y.: Doubleday & Company, 1966.

Gowdy, Curt, and John Powers. *Seasons to Remember: The Way It Was in American Sports, 1945–1960.* New York: HarperCollins, 1993.

Grady, Sandy. "Atlanta Flags Satch's Train." *Philadelphia Daily News.* August 13, 1968.

Grayson, Harry. *They Played the Game: The Story of Baseball Greats.* New York: A. S. Barnes and Company, 1944.

Green, Ben. *Spinning the Globe: The Rise, Fall, and Return to Greatness of the Harlem Globetrotters.* New York: Amistad, 2005.

Green, Michelle Y. *A Strong Right Arm: The Story of Mamie "Peanut" Johnson.* New York: Puffin Books, 2004.

Greenberg, Hank, and Ira Berkow. *Hank Greenberg: The Story of My Life.* Chicago: Triumph Books, 2001.

Greene, James "Joe," and John B. Holway. "I Was Satchel's Catcher." *The Journal of Popular Culture* 6, no. 1 (1972): 157–170.

Greene, Sam. "Old Man Paige Throws Book at Tigers: 12 Frames for Satch." *The Detroit News.* August 7, 1952.

Gregory, O. Gray. "Umpires Put Race Entry into Major Leagues up to J." *Chicago Defender.* August 22, 1936.

Gregory, Robert. *Diz: The Story of Dizzy Dean and Baseball During the Great Depression.* Harmondsworth, Middlesex, England: Penguin, 1993.

Griffin, John. "Satchel Paige and Amoros May Return to Leagues." *Chicago Defender.* November 22, 1958.

Grimsley, Will. "Satchel Paige: 'Baseball Still Doing My People Wrong.' " *Staten Island Advance.* December 4, 1978.

Gustkey, Early. "Paige Breaks Own Rule, Looks Back." *Los Angeles Times.* May 12, 1979.

Gutman, Dan. "Satchel Paige's Age Eludes Us, Yet His Wisdom Is Timeless." *USA Today.* July 5, 2006.

Gwartney, James, and Charles Haworth. "Employer Costs and Discrimination: The Case of Baseball." *Journal of Political Economy* 82, no. 4 (1974): 873–81.

Haag, I. C. "Boudreau Talks Pennant at 1948 Spring Training." *Chicago Tribune.* January 27, 1970.

Haggerty, Michael. "Satch Makes Political Pitch." *The Kansas City Star.* June 16, 1968.

Halberstam, David, and Tate Donovan. *The Teammates: A Portrait of a Friendship.* New York: Hyperion, 2003.

Hammond Times (Indiana). "Paige Fans 11 in 5 Frames." July 5, 1946.

Hanssen, Andrew. "The Cost of Discrimination: A Study of Major League Baseball." *Southern Economic Journal* 64, no. 3 (1998): 603–27.

Harmon, Willie Bea. "Sportorial." Kansas City *Call.* August 18, 1944.

Harper, Lucius C. "Dustin' Off the News." *Chicago Defender.* August 3, 1940.

Harris, Ed R. "Philadelphia Pitcher Muffles Craws Sluggers." *The Philadelphia Tribune.* September 15, 1934.

Harris, Elliott. "Quick Takes." *Chicago Sun-Times.* August 9, 2006.

Harrison, Roscoe. "Satchel Paige Runs for Missouri Legislature." *Jet.* August 8, 1968.

Hart, Hastings H. *Social Problems of Alabama: A Study of the Social Institutions and Agencies of the State of Alabama as Related to Its War Activities.* New York: Russell Sage Foundation, 1918.

Haupert, Michael. "Fair Pay for Fair Play: A Preliminary Analysis of Race-based Wages in MLB and the Negro Leagues." In *Outside the Lines.* Cleveland: SABR Business of Baseball Committee, January 26, 2007.

Hauser, Christopher. *The Negro Leagues Chronology: Events in Organized Black Baseball, 1920–1948.* Jefferson, N.C.: McFarland & Company, 2006.

Hawkins, Dave. "Satchell to Oppose Jones in Stadium." *The Pittsburgh Courier.* September 29, 1934.

Hawkins, Jim. "Eye of the Hawk." *Sports Collectors Digest.* June 13, 1997.

Hawkins, Joel, and Terry Bertolino. *The House of David Baseball Team.* Chicago: Arcadia Publishing, 2000.

Hawn, Jack. "Beradino Looks Back." *Los Angeles Times.* May 31, 1981.

Heaphy, Leslie A. *The Negro Leagues, 1869–1960.* Jefferson, N.C.: McFarland & Company, 2003.

Heaphy, Leslie A., ed. *Satchel Paige and Company: Essays on the Kansas City Monarchs, Their Greatest Star and the Negro Leagues.* Jefferson, N.C.: McFarland & Company, 2007.

———. *9th Annual Jerry Malloy Negro League Conference, July 6–9, 2006.* Jefferson, N.C.: McFarland & Company, 2006.

———. *10th Annual Jerry Malloy Negro League Conference, June 14–17, 2007.* Jefferson, N.C.: McFarland & Company, 2007.

Heaton, Chuck. "Paige Makes Pitch for Spot as Coach." Cleveland *Plain Dealer.* April 17, 1971.

Hecht, Henry. "Satchel: All-time Great Dead at '75.' " *New York Post.* June 9, 1982.

Helem, John A. "Take Ten." *Chicago Defender.* October 2, 1965.

Henry, Bill. "Louis Deadly Calm as Zero Hour Approaches." *Los Angeles Times*. September 22, 1935.

Herzog, Whitey, and Kevin Horrigan. *White Rat: A Life in Baseball*. New York: Harper & Row, 1987.

Hess, Vince. "Satchel's Marriage, Like Age, Apparently to Remain a Mystery." *The Hays Daily News* (Kansas). June 18, 1982.

Heward, Bill, and Dimitri V. Gat. *Some Are Called Clowns: A Season with the Last of the Great Barnstorming Baseball Teams*. New York: Thomas Y. Crowell, 1974.

Hickok, Ralph. *A Who's Who of Sports Champions: Their Stories & Records*. Boston: Houghton Mifflin Company, 1995.

Hicks, Tommy. "Mobile Baseball: Did You Know?" Mobile *Press-Register*. July 25, 2004.

Higbe, Kirby, and Martin Peter Quigley. *The High Hard One*. Lincoln: University of Nebraska Press, 1998.

Higgins, Frank. " 'Don't Look Back' May Be Best Work on Baseball Legend." Review of *Don't Look Back* by Mark Ribowsky. *The Kansas City Star*. February 20, 1994.

Hill, Justice B. "1931 Homestead Grays Best Ever." MLB.com. March 4, 2007. www.mlb.com.

———. "Paige Family Remembers Satchel." July 8, 2006. www.mlb.com.

Hoard, Greg. *Joe: Rounding Third and Heading for Home*. Wilmington, Ohio: Orange Frazer Press, 2004.

Hodermarsky, Mark, ed. *The Cleveland Sports Legacy: Since 1945*. Cleveland: Cleveland Landmarks Press, 1991.

Hoffbeck, Steven R., ed. *Swinging for the Fences: Black Baseball in Minnesota*. St. Paul: Minnesota Historical Society Press, 2005.

Hoffman, Roy. *Back Home: Journeys Through Mobile*. Tuscaloosa: University of Alabama Press, 2001.

Hogan, Lawrence D. *Shades of Glory: The Negro Leagues and the Story of African-American Baseball*. Washington, D.C.: National Geographic Society, 2006.

Hogan, Lloyd. "Playin' the Game." *Chicago Defender*. December 27, 1969.

Holbrook, Bob. "Satchel Paige to Face Red Sox Tonight." *Boston Evening Globe*. August 24, 1948.

Holmes, Jerome Carolyn. *History and Landmarks of Mount Meigs Campus*. Self-published, 2002.

———. *Origin and History of the State Colored Women's Clubs*. Self-published, 2002.

———. *Reflections into the Past*. Self-published, 2002.

Holsey, Morgan. "Scalpers and Politics Mar East-West Game." *Chicago Defender*. August 28, 1948.

Holway, John B. *Black Diamonds: Life in the Negro Leagues from the Men Who Lived It*. Westport, Conn.: Meckler, 1989.

———. *Blackball Stars: Negro League Pioneers*. New York: Carroll & Graf Publishers, 1992.

———. *The Complete Book of Baseball's Negro Leagues: The Other Half of Baseball History*. Fern Park, Fla.: Hastings House, 2001.

———. *Josh and Satch: The Life and Times of Josh Gibson and Satchel Paige*. New York: Carroll & Graf Publishers/Richard Gallen, 1992.

———. "KC's Mighty Monarchs." *Missouri Life*. March–June 1975.

———. "The Kid Who Taught Satchel Paige a Lesson." *Baseball Research Journal* 16 (1987): 36–44.

————. *The Last .400 Hitter: The Anatomy of a .400 Season.* Dubuque, Iowa: Wm. C. Brown, 1992.

————. "Negro League Reunion: Paige and Pals." *The Washington Post.* June 28, 1981.

————. "Paige Helped Change Baseball, and World." *The Washington Post.* June 13, 1982.

————. "Paige's 'Four-day Rider' Does Job." *The Washington Post.* July 7, 1991.

————. "Satchel Paige." *TV Guide.* May 30, 1981.

————. " 'They Made Me Survive,' Mays Says." *The Sporting News.* July 18, 1981.

————. *Voices from the Great Black Baseball Leagues.* New York: Da Capo Press, 1992.

Home Movies: Baseball Game with Satchel Paige. DVD. Academy of Motion Picture Arts and Sciences, 1948.

Hoppel, Joe. "Paige Enjoyed Acclaim—But Was Stymied, Too." *The Kansas City Star.* June 9, 1982.

Horst, Craig. "Satchel—Baseball 'Giant'—Laid to Rest." Mobile *Press-Register.* June 13, 1982.

Hufford, Tom. "Minoso One of the Oldest." *Baseball Research Journal* 77:30.

Humphrey, Kathryn Long. *Satchel Paige.* New York: Franklin Watts, 1988.

Independent (Long Beach, Calif.). "Bob Lemon Outpitches Satchel Paige in L.A." October 28, 1946.

Independent Record (Helena, Mont.). "Hesitation Pitch Most Effective Against Yankees." July 29, 1954.

Inoa, Orlando, and Hector J. Cruz. *Baseball in the Dominican Republic: Chronicle of a Passion.* Santo Domingo, D.R.: Verizon, 2006.

Irvin, Monte, and Phil Pepe. *Few and Chosen: Defining Negro League Greatness.* Chicago: Triumph Books, 2007.

Irvin, Monte, and James A. Riley. *Nice Guys Finish First: The Autobiography of Monte Irvin.* New York: Carroll & Graf, 1996.

Isaacs, Stan. "Why Doesn't Baseball Put Paige in Front of the Hall?" *Newsday* (Long Island, N.Y.). February 5, 1971.

Isley, Bliss. "Kansan Runs Sandlot Baseball Tourney into Big League Business." *The Wall Street Journal.* August 17, 1948.

Jackson, Harold. "46,000 See West Win All-Star Classic, 7-4." Baltimore *Afro-American.* August 19, 1944.

Jackson, Hayward. "Paige vs. Barnhill in New Orleans Easter." *Chicago Defender.* April 8, 1944.

Jackson, Jay. "So What?" *Chicago Defender.* May 25, 1944.

Jackson, Scoop. "SI Forgot Paige and Clemente." www.sports.espn.go.com (accessed October 12, 2006).

James, Bill. *The New Bill James Historical Baseball Abstract.* New York: Free Press, 2001.

James, Bill, and Rob Neyer. *The Neyer/James Guide to Pitchers: An Historical Compendium of Pitching, Pitchers, and Pitches.* New York: Simon & Schuster, 2004.

Jamestown Sun, The. (North Dakota). "Capital City Club Defeated Locals Sunday." August 14, 1933.

Jarrett, Vernon. "Business Acumen of Satchel Paige." *Chicago Tribune.* August 13, 1971.

————. "Paiges Torn from History." *Chicago Tribune.* July 18, 1982.

Jauss, Bill. "Veeck Blasts Other Club Owners." *Chicago Tribune.* February 25, 1976.

Jenkins, David. *Baseball in Chattanooga.* Charleston, S.C.: Arcadia, 2005.

Jenkins, Lee D. "Gold Doors Open for Paige." *Chicago Defender.* February 10, 1971.

Jenkinson, Bill. *The Year Babe Ruth Hit 104 Home Runs: Recrowning Baseball's Greatest Slugger.* New York: Carroll & Graf, 2007.

Jet. "Paige Late Again; Marion Gives Okay." July 3, 1952.

———. "Satchel Paige Is Browns' 'Untouchable.' " June 19, 1952.

———. "Satchel Signs $40,000 Monarch Contract." June 16, 1955.

———. "Ted Williams Boosts Paige for Hall of Fame." January 22, 1953.

———. "'Why Negro Baseball Stars Feud." October 9, 1952.

Johnson, John I. "Satchel's Arm Was Dead." Kansas City *Call.* March 11, 1949.

Johnson Publishing Company. Negro League Cereal Box. March 4, 1996.

Joplin Globe, The. (Missouri). "Kansas City Monarchs Win Opening Contest." September 18, 1946.

Jordan, David M., Larry R. Gerlach, and John P. Rossi. "Bill Veeck and the 1943 Sale of the Phillies: A Baseball Myth Exploded." *National Pastime,* 18 (1998).

Jordan, Pat. "The Hardest Stuff." *New York Times Magazine.* September 14, 2003.

Journal of Blacks in Higher Education, The. "Where Have You Gone, Jackie Robinson? In College Baseball the Diamonds Are Almost All White." 32 (2001).

Judge, Walter. "House of David Wins Post Tournament." *The Denver Post.* August 14, 1934.

Kaegel, Dick. "Inside Corner." *The Sporting News.* June 3, 1967.

Kaese, Harold. "Paige Had Arm, and the Nerve." *The Boston Globe.* August 14, 1968.

———. "Pre-game Barrage Fails to Worry Satchel Paige, Loss of $500 Does." *The Boston Globe.* August 25, 1948.

Kahn, Herbert L. "Hacking a Path Through the High-tech Jungle." *The Wall Street Journal.* March 25, 1985.

Kaiser, David E. *Epic Season: The 1948 American League Pennant Race.* Amherst: University of Massachusetts Press, 1998.

Kansas City Kansan, The. "T. Y. Baird Now Sole Owner of K.C. Monarchs." February 2, 1948.

Kansas City Star, The. "Paige Is 65, Honest." October 4, 1971.

———. "Satch Can Still Get 'Em Out." September 26, 1965.

Kansas City Times, The. "Fame Arrived Late for Paige After Obscure Beginning." June 9, 1982.

———. "Hall of Fame's Halfway House." February 13, 1971.

———. "Paiges Are Everywhere." June 10, 1982.

———. "Satchel Paige's Greatness." June 10, 1982.

———. "Satchel Writes Off Parking Fine." May 3, 1972.

———. "Satchel's Old Eyes Look Ahead." September 25, 1965.

Kava, Brad. "Accord Reached on Bills." *The Kansas City Times.* July 12, 1985.

———. "KCP&L Charged Paiges Too Much, Complaint Says." *The Kansas City Times.* October 5, 1984.

———. "PSC Says Paige Widow Was Overcharged." *The Kansas City Times.* May 16, 1985.

———. "Satchel Paige Home Overcharged for Electricity, Widow Tells PSC." *The Kansas City Times.* November 8, 1984.

Keane, Clif. "Rookie Piersall Teases Ole Satch." *The Boston Globe.* June 12, 1952.

Keating, Kevin, and Michael Kolleth. *The Negro Leagues Autograph Guide.* Richmond, Va.: Tuff Stuff Books, 1999.

Keisser, Bob. "Baseball Segregated, Later Integrated for One Overriding Reason—Money." Long Beach *Press-Telegram* (California). May 18, 1997.

Kelleher, Terry. "Paige of Gimmickry: Marlins Trotted Out an Ageless Pitcher." *The Miami Herald*. April 22, 1979.

Kelley, Brent P. *The Negro Leagues Revisited: Conversations with 66 More Baseball Heroes.* Jefferson, N.C.: McFarland & Company, 2000.

————. *Voices from the Negro Leagues: Conversations with 52 Baseball Standouts of the Period 1924–1960.* Jefferson, N.C.: McFarland & Company, 1998.

Kemp, Jon. "Satchel Paige, 75, Master of Mound and Bon Mot, Dies." *Los Angeles Times.* June 9, 1982.

Kerrane, Kevin. *The Hurlers: Pitching Power and Precision.* Alexandria, Va.: Redefinition, 1989.

Keyes, Ralph. "A Plea for Keeping the National Pastime a Soothing and Restful Sport." *Los Angeles Times.* April 5, 1973.

Kid from Cleveland, The. DVD. Directed by Herbert Kline. Old Time Entertainment, 1949.

Kidson, Dick. "Farmers Market Today." *Los Angeles Times.* February 3, 1954.

King, Kevin. *All the Stars Came Out That Night.* New York: Dutton, 2005.

Kings of the Hill: Baseball's Forgotten Men. DVD. Pittsburgh: San Pedro Productions, Ltd., 1993.

Kirkland, Kevin. "Penn Hills Man Helped History Play Out in Negro League." *Pittsburgh Post-Gazette.* February 6, 2007.

Kirshenbaum, Jerry, ed. "A Most Unnatural Natural." *Sports Illustrated.* June 21, 1982.

Kirwin, Bill, ed. *Out of the Shadows: African American Baseball from the Cuban Giants to Jackie Robinson.* Lincoln: University of Nebraska Press, 2005.

Kisseloff, Jeff. *Who Is Baseball's Greatest Pitcher?* Chicago: Cricket Books, 2003.

Klein, Alan M. *Sugarball: The American Game, the Dominican Dream.* New Haven, Conn.: Yale University Press, 1991.

Kleinknecht, Merl. "Blacks in 19th Century Organized Baseball." *Baseball Research Journal* 7 (1977): 118–27.

————. "Integration of Baseball After World War II." *Baseball Research Journal* 12 (1983): 100–6.

Koppett, Leonard. "Looking Back, Paige Says He's Proud." *The New York Times.* August 10, 1971.

Kountz, Mabe. "Major Leagues Honor Aliens; Bar Negroes." *Chicago Defender.* March 28, 1942.

Kozicharow, Eugene. "His Ageless Arm Still Awes." *The Kansas City Star.* August 22, 1966.

Kuhn, Bowie. *Hardball: The Education of a Baseball Commissioner.* New York: Times Books, 1987.

Lacy, Sam, and Moses J. Newson. *Fighting for Fairness: The Life Story of Hall of Fame Sportswriter Sam Lacy.* Centreville, Md.: Tidewater Publishers, 1998.

LaHoma Paige v. Kansas City Power & Light Company. Case No. EC-84-274, Public Service Commission of Missouri, May 15, 1985.

LaMar, Lawrence F. "Paige Outpitches Feller; Loses." *Chicago Defender.* October 13, 1945.

Lamb, Chris. "L'Affaire Jake Powell: The Minority Press Goes to Bat Against Segregated Baseball." *Journalism and Mass Communication Quarterly* 76, no. 1 (1999): 21–34.

———. "What's Wrong with Baseball: The *Pittsburgh Courier* and the Beginning of Its Campaign to Integrate the National Pastime." *The Western Journal of Black Studies* 26, no. 4 (2002): 189–92.

Lanctot, Neil. *Negro League Baseball: The Rise and Ruin of a Black Institution.* Philadelphia: University of Pennsylvania Press, 2004.

Lardner, John. "Lardner's Week: X Equals How Much?" *Newsweek.* February 17, 1958.

———. "Sport Week: Recollections of Old Satch." *Newsweek.* September 30, 1946.

———. "Sport Week: The Old Man in the Chair." *Newsweek.* July 7, 1952.

Larsen, Travis. "Leroy 'Satchel' Paige and Raymond 'Hap' Dumont: The Dynamic Duo of the National Baseball Congress Tournament." Presentation at the Jerry Malloy Conference of the Society for American Baseball Research. July 7, 2006.

Lautier, Louis. "Stewart Calls Satch a Dirty Name." Cleveland *Call and Post.* September 11, 1948.

Lawson, Ed. "20,000 See 'Satch's' Team Lose in 12th." *The Washington Post.* August 14, 1942.

Lebovitz, Hal. *The Best of Hal Lebovitz: Great Sportswriting from Six Decades in Cleveland.* Cleveland: Gray & Company, 2004.

———. "Paige Paying Trunk Rates on Huge Carry-all Satchel." *Cleveland News.* August 18, 1948.

———. "Strange Faces Put Paige on Indian Bench." Cleveland *Plain Dealer.* December 22, 1948.

———. "Summer of '48." Cleveland *Plain Dealer.* January 22, 1974.

Leonard, Buck, and James A. Riley. *Buck Leonard: The Black Lou Gehrig.* New York: Carroll & Graf, 1995.

Leonard, William. "As Actor, 'Satchel' Paige Comes of Age." *Chicago Tribune.* October 18, 1959.

Lester, Larry. *Baseball's First Colored World Series: The 1924 Meeting of the Hilldale Giants and Kansas City Monarchs.* Jefferson, N.C.: McFarland & Company, 2006.

———. *Black Baseball's National Showcase: The East-West All-Star Game, 1933–1953.* Lincoln: University of Nebraska Press, 2001.

Lester, Larry, and Sammy J. Miller. *Black Baseball in Kansas City.* Chicago, Ill.: Arcadia, 2000.

———. *Black Baseball in Pittsburgh.* Charleston, S.C.: Arcadia, 2001.

Lester, Larry, and John "Buck" O'Neil. "Satch vs. Josh: A Legendary Meeting of Legends." *National Pastime.* June 1933.

Leventhal, Josh, ed. *Baseball, the Perfect Game: An All-Star Anthology Celebrating the Game's Greatest Players, Teams, and Moments.* Stillwater, Minn.: Voyageur Press, 2005.

Levitt, Ed. "Satch & the Suit." *The Oakland Tribune.* May 24, 1970.

Lewis, Dave. "Once Over Lightly." *Independent* (Long Beach, Calif.). October 16, 1946.

Lewis, Franklin. *The Cleveland Indians.* New York: G. P. Putnam's Sons, 1949.

———. "Fast or No, It's Still Satchmo." *Baseball Digest* as condensed from the *Cleveland Press.* September 1951.

Lewis, G. D. "Sports Squibs." *Chicago Defender.* June 6, 1935.

Lewis, Lloyd. "Hesitation Ball." *Negro Digest.* November 1944.

———. *It Takes All Kinds.* New York: Harcourt Brace, 1947.

Lieb, Fred. *Baseball as I Have Known It.* Lincoln: University of Nebraska Press, 1996.

Life. " 'Satch' Makes the Majors." July 26, 1948.

————. "Satchel Paige, Negro Ballplayer, Is One of the Best Pitchers in Game." June 2, 1941.

Lima News, The (Ohio). "Satch Signs Pact and Satchel Proves 'Softie.' " August 13, 1968.

Lind, Angus. "Saluting 'Satchel' Paige." New Orleans *Times-Picayune.* July 6, 2005.

Lipsyte, Robert. "A Little Rusted Up." *The New York Times.* February 11, 1971.

————. "Satchel: 'Enshrined' and Diminished." *Sports of the Times.* August 14, 1971.

Litke, Jim. "The Best Pitcher You Never Saw Turns 100 (Maybe)." Associated Press. October 10, 2001.

Littlefield, Bill. *Champions: Stories of Ten Remarkable Athletes.* Boston: Little, Brown and Company, 1993.

Livingstone, Charles. "Satchel Paige Aging, but Stays in There Pitching." *Chicago Defender.* September 21, 1965.

Los Angeles Times. "Feller, Awaiting Game, Nibbles Birthday Cake." October 26, 1945.

————. "He Added a Few 'Paiges.' " May 5, 1980.

————. "Paige Had Lot More Than Curveball." July 7, 1977.

————. "Satch Paige Joins A's at 'Shade over 50.' " September 11, 1965.

————. "Satchel 'Proudest Man on Earth' After Hall of Fame Induction." August 10, 1971.

————. "Satchel Whiffs 17 Soapsters, Nine in Row." December 17, 1934.

————. "Satchel's Widow Complains She Was Overcharged." November 8, 1984.

Lovelace, Franklin. "Attorney Scores Arthur Brisbane for Article on Joe." *Chicago Defender.* October 19, 1935.

Lovell, John, Jr. "Pitcher of the Age." *The Journal of Negro Education* 32, no. 3 (1963): 255–57.

Loverro, Thom. *The Encyclopedia of Negro League Baseball.* New York: Checkmark Books, 2003.

Low, Nat. "Satchel Is Willing." *Daily Worker* (New York). November 16, 1947.

Lowry, Paul. "Satchel Paige on Mound at Gilmore Today." *Los Angeles Times.* October 31, 1943.

Lowry, Philip J. *Green Cathedrals: The Ultimate Celebration of Major League and Negro League Ballparks.* New York: Walker & Company, 2006.

Luna, Andres Barbour. *Gentlemen's Baseball in Santiago, 1903–2003: A Century of History.* Santiago, D.R.: 2003.

Lustig, Dennis. "Whatever Happened to . . . Satchel Paige." Cleveland *Plain Dealer.* February 15, 1974.

Lyons, Leonard. "The New Yorker." *The Washington Post.* July 15, 1940.

Mabley, Jack. "No Voice, No Raise—and That's No Good." *Chicago Tribune.* September 29, 1975.

Macht, Norman L. *Satchel Paige (Baseball Legends).* New York: Chelsea House, 1991.

Maher, Charles. "A Special Category." *Los Angeles Times.* February 5, 1971.

Malloy, Jerry. *Sol White's History of Colored Base Ball with Other Documents of the Early Black Game, 1886–1936.* Lincoln: University of Nebraska Press, 1995.

Maney, Richard. "Lloyd Lewis' Colorful Grab-bag of Americana." *The New York Times.* August 24, 1947.

Manley, Effa, and Leon Herbert Hardwick. *Negro Baseball . . . Before Integration.* Edited by Robert Cvornyek. Haworth, N.J.: St. Johann Press, 1976.

Marasco, David. "Lifting the Lid at Greenlee." www.thediamondangle.com (accessed July 1, 2008).

———. "The Traveling Man Goes to Portland." www.thediamondangle.com (accessed November 12, 2006).

Mardo, Bill. "Paige Signed by Cleveland." *Daily Worker* (New York). July 8, 1948.

Margolies, Jacob. *The Negro Leagues: The Story of Black Baseball.* New York: Franklin Watts, 1993.

Margolis, Bill. " 'Peanuts' Davis Is the Beloved Diamond Imp." *Chicago Defender.* August 1, 1942.

Marion Star, The (Ohio). "Feller Beats Paige." October 18, 1946.

Marsh, Irving T., and Edward Ehre, eds. *Best Sports Stories: A Thrilling Panorama of Sports.* New York: World Publishing, 1946.

Marshall, William. *Baseball's Pivotal Era, 1945–1951.* Lexington: University of Kentucky Press, 1999.

"Martin Dihigo Faces Satchel Paige." www.geocities.com/martindihigo (accessed July 2, 2008).

Martini, Stephen. *The Chattanooga Lookouts & 100 Seasons of Scenic City Baseball.* Cleveland, Tenn.: Dry Ice Publishing, 2005.

Mathews, Charles Elijah, and Anderson Browne. *Highlights of 100 Years in Mobile.* Mobile, Ala.: First National Bank of Mobile, 1965.

Matthews, Les. "Sportslight." *Chicago Defender.* October 16, 1956.

Mayer, Gerry. "Voice of the People." *Chicago Tribune.* August 20, 1968.

Mazer, Bill, Stan Fischler, and Shirley Fischler. *Bill Mazer's Amazin' Baseball Book: 150 Years of Tales and Trivia from Baseball's Earliest Beginnings Down to the Present Day.* New York: Zebra Books, 1990.

McAuley, Ed. "Life in the Majors with Satchel Paige: Part 1." *The Sporting News.* September 22, 1948.

———. "Life in the Majors with Satchel Paige: Part 2." *The Sporting News.* September 29, 1948.

———. "Snake in the Grass—in Venezuela—Ended Paige's Play in the Outfield." *The Sporting News.* July 14, 1948.

———. "Tribe Raises Turnstile Sights, Now Aims at Two Million Gate." *Cleveland News.* August 11, 1948.

McDermott, Mickey, and Howard Eisenberg. *A Funny Thing Happened on the Way to Cooperstown.* Chicago: Triumph Books, 2003.

McDonald, Neil. "Daily Writer Tells What Is Wrong with Baseball." *Chicago Defender.* August 10, 1935.

McGinn, Gerald A. "Satchel Paige Shows He Still Has His Stuff." *The Washington Post.* July 6, 1966.

———. " 'Satchel' Paige Still Had Pitching Savvy, Scribe Discovers." *Chicago Defender.* July 9, 1966.

McGuff, Joe. " 'Inner' Paige Usually a Closed Book." *The Kansas City Star.* June 9, 1982.

———. "More Insight Is Developed into Paige." *The Kansas City Star.* June 15, 1982.

———. "Paige Made Pitching the Consummate Show." *The Kansas City Star.* June 9, 1982.

McGuire, John M. "Satchel Paige: Retired Pitcher Leroy Paige Has Opinions as Stinging as His Once-great Fastball." *St. Louis Post-Dispatch.* February 15, 1981.

McGuire, Mark, and Michael Sean Gormley. *The 100 Greatest Baseball Players of the 20th Century Ranked.* Jefferson, N.C.: McFarland & Company, 2000.

McKenzie, Rob. "Boy, Could Satchel Ever Talk." *National Post* (Canada). July 23, 2005.

McKissack, Patricia, and Fredrick McKissack. *Satchel Paige: The Best Arm in Baseball.* Hillside, N.J.: Enslow Publishers, 1992.

McLemore, Henry. "The Lighter Side." *Los Angeles Times.* August 1, 1951.

McNary, Kyle P. *Black Baseball: A History of African-Americans & the National Game.* London: PRC Publishing, 2003.

————. *Ted "Double Duty" Radcliffe: 36 Years of Pitching & Catching in Baseball's Negro Leagues.* St. Louis Park, Minn.: McNary Publishing, 1994.

McNeil, William F. *Baseball's Other All-Stars: The Greatest Players from the Negro Leagues, the Japanese Leagues, the Mexican League and the Pre-1960 Winter Leagues in Cuba, Puerto Rico and the Dominican Republic.* Jefferson, N.C.: McFarland & Company, 2000.

————. *Black Baseball Out of Season: Pay for Play Outside of the Negro Leagues.* Jefferson, N.C.: McFarland & Company, 2007.

————. *The California Winter League: America's First Integrated Professional Baseball League.* Jefferson, N.C.: McFarland & Company, 2002.

————. *Cool Papas and Double Duties: The All-time Greats of the Negro Leagues.* Jefferson, N.C.: McFarland & Company, 2001.

McNichol, Dustan. "New Future in Store for Old Stadium." *The Kansas City Star.* June 2, 1982.

McSkimming, Dent. "Paige Puts on His Greatest Show Beating Tigers in 12 Innings." *St. Louis Post-Dispatch.* August 7, 1952.

Meany, Tom. "$64 Question: Paige's Age." *New York Star.* July 21, 1948.

Mehl, Ernest. "Satchel Paige Pitched His Best Game for Title Down in Old Santo Domingo." *The Kansas City Times.* March 26, 1943.

Merchant, Larry. "The Barnstormers." *New York Post.* September 3, 1968.

Metcalfe, Henry. *A Game for All Races: An Illustrated History of the Negro Leagues.* New York: MetroBooks, 2000.

Mickelson, Ed. *Out of the Park: Memoir of a Minor League Baseball All-Star.* Jefferson, N.C.: McFarland & Company, 2007.

Mihoces, Gary. "Tapes Recall Era of Black Players." *USA Today.* October 28, 1992.

Mims, Linda. "The Great 'Satchel' Paige: One of the Best Pitchers Ever to Play the Game." *The Sacramento Observer.* August 23, 1995.

Minshew, Wayne. "Braves Corral a New Hurler; Name Is Paige." *The Sporting News.* August 24, 1968.

Modesto Bee, The. "Negro Pitcher Strikes Out 17." March 19, 1935.

Moffi, Larry, and Jonathan Kronstadt. *Crossing the Line: Black Major Leaguers, 1947–1959.* Lincoln: University of Nebraska Press, 2006.

Monroe, Al. "It's News to Me." *Chicago Defender.* October 28, 1939.

————. "Lock 'Em Up Boys, They're Bunch of Jumping Players." *Chicago Defender.* June 16, 1934.

Montgomery Advertiser. "The Negro Reformatory Problem." February 27, 1911.

Montgomery, George F. "Murray's Claim Disputed." *Los Angeles Times.* March 4, 1978.

Moon, Elaine Latzman. *Untold Tales, Unsung Heroes: An Oral History of Detroit's African American Community, 1918–1967.* Detroit: Wayne State University Press, 1994.

Moore, James (Red). "Baseball's Oldest Rookie." *Newsweek.* October 25, 1999.

Moore, Joseph Thomas. *Pride Against Prejudice: The Biography of Larry Doby.* New York: Praeger, 1988.

Morten, Baker E. "Stepin' Fetchit Eyes Movie on Satchel Paige." *Chicago Defender.* May 2, 1960.

Motley, Bob, and Byron Motley. *Ruling over Monarchs, Giants and Stars: Umpiring in the Negro Leagues & Beyond.* Champaign, Ill.: Sports Publishing, 2007.

Munhall, Jack. "Paige, Grays Beat Stars, 8-1 Before 22,000." *The Washington Post.* June 1, 1942.

Murphy, Eddie. "Daily Scribe Tells Majors of Value of Satchel Paige." *Chicago Defender.* February 8, 1936.

Murray, Jim. "Baseball's Injustice." *Los Angeles Times.* February 14, 1971.

———. "They'll Never Catch Up with Satch." *The Oakland Tribune.* August 14, 1974.

Nathan, Daniel A. "Bearing Witness to Blackball: Buck O'Neil, the Negro Leagues, and the Politics of the Past." *Journal of American Studies* 35 (2001): 453–69.

Negro League Baseball Players Association. www.nlbpa.com (accessed repeatedly).

Negro Leagues Baseball Museum. Interview with Warren James Paige, Kansas City, Missouri, undated.

New Jersey Herald News. "Rumor Paige Arm Is 'Dead.' " December 3, 1938.

———. "Satchell Paige Barred from Baseball 'For Life.' " September 24, 1938.

New York Age. "Charge American Sugar Co. Lured Players from Negro League to South America." May 29, 1937.

New York News World. "Ball Club Exec Wins Starring Role—Playing Himself." September 5, 1980.

———. "Boudreau Recalls Satchel." June 10, 1982.

———. "Satchel Paige—Bigger Than Stats." June 11, 1982.

New York Post. "Satch Says Larsen Can Win 20 Games." August 3, 1953.

———. "Satchel Paige's Big Win." June 10, 1982.

New York Times, The. "Alabama Negro Lynched." September 23, 1907.

———. "Negro Is Lynched in Mobile Street." January 24, 1909.

———. "Negro Stars Take No-hit Game." September 20, 1937.

———. "Paige Ranks Near Top Say 2 Veteran Umpires." September 1, 1948.

———. "Reunion Toasts Bell, Paige." June 24, 1981.

———. "Rickey Cites Wire to Refute Critics." October 26, 1945.

———. "Rickey Takes Slap at Negro Leagues." October 25, 1945.

———. "Satchel." June 10, 1982.

———. "Satchel Paige, Ace Negro Pitcher, Signed by Indians for Relief Role." July 8, 1948.

———. "Satchel Paige's Mother, 104." January 6, 1966.

———. "Travels by Own Plane." July 9, 1946.

———. "Wichita Café Ends Segregation." December 29, 1961.

New Yorker, The. "Slow." September 13, 1952.

Newark Daily News. "Paige Antics Puzzle Moguls at Philly Meet." May 6, 1939.

———. "Same Ole 'Satch.' " July 2, 1938.

———. "Satchel Paige Must Report to Newark Eagles by July 15." July 9, 1938.

News Journal, The (Mansfield, Ohio). "Ageless 'Satch' Earned Fame." February 14, 1971.

———. "Feller's All Stars Win Before Crowd of 20,000." October 3, 1946.

Newsday (Long Island, N.Y.). "Satchel Paige Pitchin' Opinions." February 1, 1981.

Newsham, Brad. "How Satchel Paige Helped Break Baseball Color Bar." *San Francisco Chronicle.* May 19, 1994.

Newsweek. "Ageless Satchel Sneaks a Look Back." June 1, 1981.

——. "When Batters Wobble." July 14, 1958.

Newton, James. "Satchel Paige Unbeaten on Coast; Hero of League." *Chicago Defender.* February 2, 1935.

Nixon, Richard. "Baseball Fan Nixon Picks All-time All-Stars." *Los Angeles Times.* July 2, 1972.

Nogowski, John. *Last Time Out: Big-League Farewells of Baseball's Greats.* Lanham, Md.: Taylor Trade Pub., 2005.

Norfolk Journal and Guide (Virginia). "Paige Deal Hangs Fire with Owners." April 23, 1938.

——. "Satchell Paige Will Be Barred from N.N. League." May 8, 1937.

Nunn, William G. "As 'Speedball' Satchell Paige Ambled into the East-West Game and Simply Stole the Show: 'Satch' Stops 'Big Bad Men' of West Team." *The Pittsburgh Courier.* September 1, 1934.

——. "Paige Hurls No-hit Classic." *The Pittsburgh Courier.* July 7, 1934.

Oakland Tribune, The. "All-Stars Blank Negro Royals, 5-0." October 18, 1946.

——. "Feller Beats Paige." October 17, 1946.

Oleksak, Michael M., and Mary Adam Oleksak. *Beisbol: Latin Americans and the Grand Old Game.* Indianapolis: Masters Press, 1996.

O'Neil, Buck. Interview with Bob Edwards. *NPR Morning Edition.* October 22, 1997.

——. "Unforgettable Satchel Paige." *Reader's Digest.* April 1984.

O'Neil, Buck, Steve Wulf, and David Conrads. *I Was Right on Time: My Journey from the Negro Leagues to the Majors.* New York: Fireside, 1997.

O'Neill, Shane. "Like His Contemporary, Casey, Paige Has 'Inimitable Speech.' " *Anchorage Daily News.* August 28, 1965.

O'Toole, Andrew. "Satch the Sage: Satchel Paige." *The Best Man Plays: Major League Baseball and the Black Athlete, 1901–2002.* Jefferson, N.C.: McFarland & Company, 2003.

Otto, Solomon, and John Solomon Otto. "I Played Against 'Satchel' for Three Seasons: Blacks and Whites in the 'Twilight' Leagues." *The Journal of Popular Culture,* vol. 2, no. 4: 797–803.

Otto, Wayne K. "Satch at Best—Handcuffs Dean's Stars." *Chicago Herald-American.* May 24, 1942.

Overmyer, James. *Effa Manley and the Newark Eagles.* Metuchen, N.J.: Scarecrow Press, 1993.

Page, Don. "Baseball Is Left Holding the Satchel." *Los Angeles Times.* September 25, 1965.

——. "Satchel Paige: His Bag Is Pitching." *Los Angeles Times.* August 17, 1968.

Paige, Satchel. Collection at National Baseball Hall of Fame and Museum. Cooperstown, New York.

Paige, Satchel, and Hal Lebovitz. *Pitchin' Man: Satchel Paige's Own Story.* Westport, Conn.: Meckler, 1992.

Paige, Satchel, and David Lipman. *Maybe I'll Pitch Forever: A Great Baseball Player Tells the Hilarious Story Behind the Legend.* Lincoln: University of Nebraska Press, 1993.

Paige, Satchell. "Paige Says He Prefers Jungles to NNL Play." Baltimore *Afro-American.* July 31, 1937.

Parker, Virgil. "I May Be Wrong." *Lincoln Journal* (Nebraska). June 7, 1973.

Peary, Danny, ed. *Cult Baseball Players: The Greats, the Flakes, the Weird, and the Wonderful.* New York: Fireside, 1990.

———. *We Played the Game: 65 Players Remember Baseball's Greatest Era, 1947–1964.* New York: Hyperion, 1994.

Pedulla, Tom. "Negro League Stars Grace Wheaties Box." *USA Today.* February 21, 1996.

Penn, Franklin. "Crawfords Divide Pair with Bushwick." *The Pittsburgh Courier.* September 3, 1932.

Penn, Steve. "A Grave Baseball Mystery." *The Kansas City Star.* April 13, 2006.

Pepe, Phil. "Everybody Talked Satch but Jackie Was 1st." New York *Daily News.* February 12, 1971.

———. "The Satchel Paige Legend." New York *Daily News.* February 11, 1971.

Peterson, Robert W. "Baseball's Legendary Satchel Paige." *Boys' Life.* February 1, 2000.

———. *Only the Ball Was White: A History of Legendary Black Players and All-Black Professional Teams.* New York: Oxford University Press, 1992.

———. "Paige Rides Back of 'Hall's' Bus." *San Francisco Chronicle.* April 12, 1971.

Philadelphia Tribune, The. "Craws Charge Dominicans in Player Snatch." April 29, 1937.

———. "Satchel Panics Philly Fans." July 24, 1941.

Phillips, Larry. "Area Residents Recall Pitcher's Magical Displays of Talent." *News Journal* (Mansfield, Ohio). August 17, 1998.

Phoenix & Times Democrat (Muskogee, Okla.). "Satchel Paige Was Trailblazer." June 1, 1982.

Picou, Tommy. "Tommy's Corner." *Chicago Defender.* July 19, 1961.

Piersall, Jim, and Al Hirshberg. *Fear Strikes Out: The Jim Piersall Story.* Lincoln: University of Nebraska Press, 1999.

Pietrusza, David. *Judge and Jury: The Life and Times of Judge Kenesaw Mountain Landis.* South Bend, Ind.: Diamond Communications, 1998.

Pinckney, Paul. "Paige Yields 1 Hit in 5 Frames; Kay Cees Win." *Chicago Defender.* July 4, 1942.

Pittsburgh Courier, The. "Baseball War Brews over Satchel Paige as 2 Teams Claim His Services." June 1, 1940.

———. "Grays Win 1, Lose 3 to NY Black Yanks." July 16, 1932.

———. "Grays Win Second Holiday Tilt, 4-3." July 7, 1934.

———. "Greenlee Field Data Released." July 9, 1932.

———. " 'I'm Holding Out Because Joe DiMaggio Advised Me To,' Says Satchel Paige." April 23, 1938.

———. "Paige Stops Grays as Crawfords Cop, 10 to 7." August 8, 1931.

———. "Satchell Outhurls Dizzy!" October 27, 1934.

———. "Satchell Supreme in Craw Victory." June 10, 1933.

———. "Satchell to Oppose Jones in Stadium." September 29, 1934.

———. "Talk of Town." December 20, 1941.

———. " 'Was Misquoted,' Says 'Satchel.' " August 22, 1942.

———. "Willie Foster and Satchell Paige to Settle Ancient Feud When They Oppose Each Other on Mound July 8." July 1, 1933.

———. "Wylie Avenue, Here and There." January 2, 1965.

Pittsburgh Post-Gazette. "Gus Greenlee, Pioneer of Numbers Here, Dies." July 8, 1952.

Pittsburgh Sun-Telegraph. "Grays Lose as Paige Fans Gibson in Clutch." September 11, 1942.

Plain Dealer, The (Cleveland). "Mother Says Satchel Is 44 Years of Age." July 18, 1948.
———. "Paige Hurls Two Scoreless Innings, but Browns Upset Indians, 5-3." July 10, 1948.
Plaisted, Ed. "Satch Blows Stack—Clowns Aren't Funny." *The Sporting News.* July 15, 1967.
Polk, Alma A. "Mrs. Bernice Sutton Buried on Jan. 3." *The Pittsburgh Courier.* January 10, 1953.
Pollock, Alan J. *Barnstorming to Heaven: Syd Pollock and His Great Black Teams.* Tuscaloosa: University of Alabama Press, 2006.
Polner, Murray. "Don't Look Back." Review of *Don't Look Back* by Mark Ribowsky. *The Nation.* April 4, 1994.
Porter, David L., ed. *Biographical Dictionary of American Sports, Baseball.* Westport, Conn.: Greenwood Press, 2000.
Porter, G. L. "Same Teams Play Benefit Game in Cleveland, Aug. 18." *Chicago Defender.* August 15, 1942.
Porter, L. E. " 'Satchel' a Flop in 'Frisco." *Chicago Defender.* May 30, 1936.
Posey, Cum. "Posey's Points." *The Pittsburgh Courier.* June 15, 1940.
Posnanski, Joe. "Paige Proves Truth Can Be Inconvenient." *The Kansas City Star.* July 2, 2006.
Povich, Shirley. *All Those Mornings . . . at the Post: The Twentieth Century in Sports from Famed Washington Post Columnist Shirley Povich.* New York: PublicAffairs, 2005.
———. "Clowning Delayed Negroes' Stars in Majors." *The Washington Post.* May 11, 1953.
———. "Satchel Paige a Very Special Case in Baseball." *The Washington Post.* May 18, 1953.
———. "This Morning." *The Washington Post.* May 19, 1944.
———. "This Morning: Even in Back Room, Paige Brightens Hall." *The Washington Post.* February 10, 1971.
Powers, Francis J. "Dizzy Duels with Satchel." *The Sporting News.* July 19, 1945.
Prell, Edward. "Jones Reveals He Took Page out of Satch's Book." *Chicago Tribune.* May 14, 1955.
Press-Register (Mobile, Ala.). "How 'Satchel' Got His Name." December 5, 1982.
———. "Ladies Discuss Negro Servants." March 6, 1912.
———. "Negroes Looting Homes of Dead." October 1, 1906.
———. "Philip Fatch Loses Life." January 22, 1909.
———. "Rev. A. F. Owens Finds the Colored People Fared Very Badly." September 28, 1906.
———. "Sheriff Overpowered and Two Negroes Lynched." October 7, 1906.
———. "Storm Scenes Night and Day." September 28, 1906.
———. "Was Mobile-born Satchel Paige the Greatest Pitcher Who Ever Lived?" June 9, 1982.
———. "West India Hurricane Strikes Mobile." September 28, 1906.
Progress, The (Clearfield, Penn.). "Colored Giants Beat Houtzdale, 4-1, in Exhibition." July 29, 1946.
Rampersad, Arnold. *Jackie Robinson: A Biography.* New York: Alfred A. Knopf, 1997.
Rathet, Mike. "Paige Inducted into Fame Hall." Mobile *Press-Register.* August 10, 1971.
Ray, Bob. "He's Just a Big Man from the South." *Los Angeles Times.* November 12, 1933.

Reichler, Joe. "Paige Admits Paige Best Relief Hurler." *Los Angeles Times.* June 20, 1953.

Reisler, Jim. *Black Writers/Black Baseball: An Anthology of Articles from Black Sportswriters Who Covered the Negro Leagues.* Jefferson, N.C.: McFarland & Company, 1994.

Retrosheet play-by-play accounts. www.retrosheet.org (accessed repeatedly).

Rhea, Cortland R. "Johnson City." *Chicago Defender.* July 7, 1962.

Rhoden, William C. "Cool Papa Is Anointed by Wheaties." *The New York Times.* February 17, 1996.

Ribowsky, Mark. *A Complete History of the Negro Leagues, 1884 to 1955.* New York: Carol Publishing Group, 1995.

———. *Don't Look Back: Satchel Paige in the Shadows of Baseball.* New York: Simon & Schuster, 1994.

———. *The Power and the Darkness: The Life of Josh Gibson in the Shadows of the Game.* New York: Simon & Schuster, 1996.

Richman, Milton. " 'Satch' a Softie." *Houston Chronicle.* August 14, 1968.

———. "Satchel Was a Friend Who Loved a Challenge." *Los Angeles Times.* June 9, 1982.

Riley, James A. *The Biographical Encyclopedia of the Negro Baseball Leagues.* New York: Carroll & Graf, 1994.

———. *Dandy, Day, and the Devil.* Cocoa, Fla.: TK Publishers, 1987.

———. "Dave Barnhill." *Baseball Research Journal* 81: 56–59.

———. *The Negro Leagues.* Philadelphia: Chelsea House, 1997.

Roberts, M. B. "Paige Never Looked Back." November 11, 1999. www.sports.espn .go.com.

Roberts, Ric. "An Open Letter to J. Taylor Spink." *The Pittsburgh Courier.* July 24, 1948.

———. "Paige First Cranked-up Arm at Mobile, Back in 1924: Present Tour with 'Clowns' 42nd Season." *The Pittsburgh Courier.* August 14, 1965.

———. "Policeman Socks Satchel Paige in Washington." *The Pittsburgh Courier.* August 18, 1945.

Robertson, Mark. "On Pitching Better." *Better Investing.* May 2004.

Robinson, Frazier "Slow," and Paul Bauer. *Catching Dreams: My Life in the Negro Baseball Leagues.* Syracuse, N.Y.: Syracuse University Press, 1999.

Robinson, Jackie. *Baseball Has Done It.* Philadelphia: Lippincott Publishing, 1964.

———. "Jackie Says." *Pittsburgh Courier.* October 16, 1948.

———. "What's Wrong with Negro Baseball?" *Ebony.* June 1948.

Robinson, Major. "Satchel Paige Hurls 5-hit Ball for Yanks." Baltimore *Afro-American.* May 17, 1941.

Rock, Patrick. "Rube Foster's 'Bunts in the Mud' Strategy: Storytelling and Truth in Negro League History." Presentation at Jerry Malloy Conference of the Society for American Baseball Research. July 7, 2006.

Rodney, Lester. "On the Scoreboard." *Daily Worker* (New York). July 8, 1948.

———. "On the Scoreboard." *Daily Worker.* October 20, 1952.

Rogosin, Donn. *Invisible Men: Life in Baseball's Negro Leagues.* New York: Atheneum, 1983.

———. "Satch vs. Josh—Classic Duel Was a Lark." *The Sporting News.* July 18, 1981.

Rollow, Cooper. "Satchel Says He Made It with Six Rules." *Chicago Tribune.* February 14, 1971.

Roper, Scott. "Another Chink in Jim Crow? Race and Baseball on the Northern Plains, 1900–1935." *Nine: A Journal of Baseball History and Social Policy Perspectives* 2, no. 1 (1993): 75–89.

Roseboro, John, and Bill Libby. *Glory Days with the Dodgers and Other Days with Others.* New York: Atheneum, 1978.

Rosengarten, Theodore. "Reading the Hops: Recollections of Lorenzo Piper Davis and the Negro Baseball League." *Southern Exposure* 5 (1977): 62–79.

Royster, Vermont. "Thinking Things Over." *The Wall Street Journal.* December 19, 1976.

Rubin, Robert. *Satchel Paige: All-time Baseball Great.* New York: Putnam, 1974.

Ruck, Rob. *Sandlot Seasons: Sport in Black Pittsburgh.* Urbana: University of Illinois Press, 1987.

————. *The Tropic of Baseball: Baseball in the Dominican Republic.* Lincoln: University of Nebraska Press, 1999.

Rusinack, Kelly E. "Baseball on the Radical Agenda: The *Daily Worker* and *Sunday Worker* Journalistic Campaign to Desegregate Major League Baseball, 1933–1947." In *Jackie Robinson: Race, Sports & the American Dream,* Joseph Dorinson and Joram Warmund, eds. Armonk, N.Y.: M. E. Sharpe, 1998.

Rusk, Howard A. "Executives' Health." *The New York Times.* May 14, 1981.

————. "The Waste of the Aged." *The New York Times.* August 25, 1968.

Russo, Neal. "Ol' Satch Wins for Browns in 17th." *St. Louis Post-Dispatch.* June 4, 1952.

Rust, Art. *Get That Nigger off the Field!: An Oral History of Black Ballplayers from the Negro Leagues to the Present.* Brooklyn, N.Y.: Book Mail Services, 1992.

Rust, Art, and Michael Marley. *Legends: Conversations with Baseball Greats.* New York: McGraw-Hill, 1989.

Rust, Art, and Edna Rust. *Art Rust's Illustrated History of the Black Athlete.* Garden City, N.Y.: Doubleday, 1985.

Sailer, Steve. "How Jackie Robinson Desegregated America." *National Review.* April 8, 2006.

Salwen, Kevin G. "Stocks Overcome Rise in Rates to Pass Mark." *The Wall Street Journal.* January 6, 1989.

San Antonio Express. "Satchel Paige Reported Hurt in Florida Auto Accident." November 2, 1953.

Sanford, Jay. *The Denver Post Tournament: A Chronicle of America's First Integrated Professional Baseball Event.* Cleveland: Society for American Baseball Research, 2003.

San Mateo Times, The. "Bob Feller Wins for L.A. All Stars." October 17, 1946.

Sauerbrei, Harold. "Flash Bulbs Pop, but Old Satch Just Hurls in Usual Cool Manner." Cleveland *Plain Dealer.* July 10, 1948.

Sayama, Kazuo. " 'Their Throws Were Like Arrows'—How a Black Team Spurred Pro Ball in Japan." *Baseball Research Journal* 16 (1987): 85–88.

Schneider, Russell. *The Boys of the Summer of '48.* Champaign, Ill.: Sports Publishing, 1998.

Schudel, Matt. "Robert Peterson: Historian of Negro Leagues Baseball." *The Washington Post.* February 18, 2006.

Schwarz, Alan. *The Numbers Game: Baseball's Lifelong Fascination with Statistics.* New York: Thomas Dunne Books, 2004.

Schweid, Richard. "Great Blacks Denied Chance: Nashville's Elite Struck Out on Shot at White Big League." Nashville *Tennessean.* August 31, 1987.

Seeman, Bruce Taylor. "Health Advice from the Legendary 'Satchel' Paige Has Stood Test of Time." Newhouse News Service. April 1, 2004.

Segreti, James. "Satchel Paige Pitches, Grins and Conquers." *Chicago Tribune.* September 23, 1940.

Sell, Jack. "Late Spurt by Monarchs Beats Grays." *Pittsburgh Post-Gazette.* September 11, 1942.

Shane, Ted. "Chocolate Rube Waddell." *The Saturday Evening Post.* July 27, 1940.

———. "Satchel Man." *Reader's Digest.* June 1949.

Shannon, Mike. *The Day Satchel Paige and the Pittsburgh Crawfords Came to Hertford, N.C.: Baseball Stories and Poems.* Jefferson, N.C.: McFarland & Company, 1992.

Sheinin, Dave. "DC's 'Boojum' Gets His Day in Hall of Fame." *The Washington Post.* July 31, 2006.

Shirley, David. *Satchel Paige: Baseball Great.* New York: Chelsea House, 1993.

Shury, Dave, ed. "Satch in Saskatchewan." Saskatchewan Baseball Hall of Fame, 1996.

Sickels, John. *Bob Feller: Ace of the Greatest Generation.* Washington, D.C.: Brasseys, 2004.

Siegel, Morris. "Ageless Satchel Paige Beats Nats in 17th, 3-2." *The Washington Post.* June 4, 1952.

Sigman, Robert P. "Error Before His First Pitch." *The Kansas City Times.* May 1, 1968.

Silber, Irwin. *Press Box Red: The Story of Lester Rodney, the Communist Who Helped Break the Color Line in American Sports.* Philadelphia: Temple University Press, 2003.

Silverman, Al. "Satchel Paige Sounds Off." *Sport.* January 1972.

Simmons, R. S. "Negro American League Busy in Spring Camps." *Amsterdam News* (New York). April 18, 1942.

Smith, Alfred E. "Adventures in Race Relations." *Chicago Defender.* September 4, 1948.

———. "Capital Crystal." *Chicago Defender.* August 28, 1976.

Smith, Curt. *America's Dizzy Dean.* St. Louis: The Bethany Press, 1978.

Smith, Garfield L., Jr. "Good Times Roll into Cleveland Aboard the World Series Train." *Chicago Defender.* October 16, 1948.

Smith, Jack. "Living by the Goldwyn Rule." *Los Angeles Times.* January 7, 1980.

———. "A Paige out of the Past." *Los Angeles Times.* January 16, 1980.

Smith, Red. "A Luncheon at the Reagans' House." *The New York Times.* March 27, 1981.

———. "Satch Paige, Man with Immortal Arm." *Houston Post.* August 12, 1963.

Smith, Robert. *Pioneers of Baseball.* Boston: Little, Brown and Company, 1978.

Smith, Wendell. "Smith's Sports Spurts." *The Pittsburgh Courier.* May 14, 1938.

———. "Smitty's Sports Spurts." *The Pittsburgh Courier.* April 16, 1938.

———. "The Sports Beat: Satchel Paige Still a Man of the Road." *The Pittsburgh Courier.* May 21, 1960.

———. "Third Straight Loss Dooms Grays' Hopes." *The Pittsburgh Courier.* September 19, 1942.

———. "Wendell Smith's Sports Beat." *The Pittsburgh Courier.* July 24, 1965.

———. "Wendell Smith's Sports Beat: Saperstein Directed 'Satchel' to Big Dough." *The Pittsburgh Courier.* April 7, 1962.

Smitherman, Dennis. "Mobile's First Native Son Inductee!" Mobile *Press-Register.* January 13, 1972.

Snider, Steve. "The Sports Patrol." *Chicago Defender.* September 8, 1958.

Snyder, Brad. *Beyond the Shadow of the Senators: The Untold Story of the Homestead Grays and the Integration of Baseball.* New York: McGraw-Hill, 2003.

Society for American Baseball Research. SABR 36th Convention Program. St. Louis: July 26–29, 2007.

Soul of the Game. DVD. Directed by Kevin Rodney Sullivan. New York: HBO Home Video, 1996.

Spatz, Lyle, ed. *The SABR Baseball List & Record Book: Baseball's Most Fascinating Records and Unusual Statistics.* New York: Scribner, 2007.

Spink, J. G. Taylor. "Robinson vs. Paige—Rookies." *The Sporting News.* September 1, 1948.

————. "Two Ill-advised Moves." *The Sporting News.* July 14, 1948.

Sporting News, The. "250,000 See Feller-Paige Teams Play." October 30, 1946.

————. "Chandler Files Reveal Segregation Died Hard." February 25, 1978.

————. "Chicago's Surge to See Ol' Satch Collapses Gates." August 25, 1948.

Sports Illustrated. "The Pitching Man." July 28, 1958.

————. "Scorecard." March 11, 1963.

————. "Scorecard." January 27, 1964.

————. "Scorecard." June 21, 1982.

————. "Seeing-Eye Pitcher." March 22, 1971.

St. Louis Post-Dispatch. "Profiles of Prominent Negro-Leaguers: Leroy 'Satchel' Paige." February 4, 2001.

————. "Ump Suspended for His Actions Toward Press." August 8, 1952.

Stanton, Tom. *Hank Aaron and the Home Run That Changed America.* New York: Perennial Currents, 2005.

Staten Island Advance. "Pitcher Satchel Paige Dies of Heart Attack in Mo." June 9, 1982.

Staten, Vince. *Ol' Diz: A Biography of Dizzy Dean.* New York: HarperCollins, 1992.

Sterry, David, and Arielle Eckstut. *Satchel Sez: The Wit, Wisdom, and World of Leroy "Satchel" Paige.* New York: Three Rivers Press, 2001.

Stewart, Milton D. "Satchel Paige: Another Man for All Seasons." *Inc.* December 1982.

Stineman, Darrin. "Negro Leagues: More than Ball." *Salina Journal* (Salina, Kan.). March 20, 2006.

Storin, Ed. "Satchel Paige: His Lifelong Dream Finally Fulfilled." *The Miami Herald.* February 10, 1971.

Stout, Glenn, and Dick Johnson. *Jackie Robinson: Between the Baselines.* San Francisco: Woodford Press, 1997.

Stubbs, Lewis St. George. *Shoestring Glory: Semi-pro Ball on the Prairies, 1886–1994.* Winnipeg: Turnstone Press, 1996.

Sudyk, Bob. "Too Bad They Can't Bend Rules for Satchel." *The Sporting News.* December 19, 1964.

Sugar, Bert Randolph. *Baseball's 50 Greatest Games.* North Dighton, Mass.: JG Press, 1994.

————, ed. *The Baseball Maniac's Almanac.* New York: McGraw-Hill, 2005.

Sullivan, Michael John. *Top 10 Baseball Pitchers.* Hillside, N.J.: Enslow Publishers, 1994.

Sumner, Jan. *Legacy of a Monarch: An American Journey.* Denver: JaDan Publishing, 2005.

Sunday Record, The (Middletown, N.Y.). "Free Agent Deals Astonish Paige." December 26, 1976.

Swaine, Rick. *The Black Stars Who Made Baseball Whole: The Jackie Robinson Generation in the Major Leagues, 1947–1959.* Jefferson, N.C.: McFarland & Company, 2006.

Swanton, Barry. *The ManDak League: Haven for Former Negro League Ballplayers, 1950–1957.* Jefferson, N.C.: McFarland & Company, 2006.

Sylvester, Robert. "Everything's in a Good Gumbo Including Satch Paige's Age." *The Detroit News.* August 25, 1953.

Syracuse Herald. "Sandlotter Pulls Waddell's Stunt, Retiring Rivals." August 22, 1935.

Tammeus, William D. "Oddly Apt Memorial." *The Kansas City Star.* June 11, 1982.

Taylor, Jim. "Taylor Says Poor Umpiring, Bad Management Harmful." *Chicago Defender.* February 22, 1936.

Theofield, Myrtle. "Metropolitan Oakland Newsettes." *Chicago Defender.* August 19, 1940.

There Was Always Sun Shining Someplace: Life in the Negro Baseball Leagues. DVD. Directed by Craig Davidson. Westport, Conn.: Refocus Productions, 1984.

Thomas, Janie R. "Defends 'Ole Satch.' " Letter to the editor. *Chicago Defender.* March 4, 1950.

Thomas, Landon, Jr. "Parallel Paths Diverging Sharply: Longtime Ally of Conrad Black Floats atop New York Society as He Tries to Avoid Prison." *The New York Times.* May 17, 2007.

Thomason, Michael V. R., ed. *Mobile: The New History of Alabama's First City.* Tuscaloosa: University of Alabama Press, 2001.

Thompson, Rita K. "An American Tragedy: Lynching in Mobile, Alabama, 1891–1910." Unpublished research paper. University of Southern Alabama, Mobile.

Thorn, John, et al. *Total Baseball: The Official Encyclopedia of Major League Baseball,* 6th ed. New York: Total Sport, 1999.

Time. "Baseball: Satch Is Back." August 23, 1968.

———. "El Benefactor." July 30, 1951.

———. "Josh the Basher." July 19, 1943.

———. "Satchel the Great." July 19, 1948.

———. "Satchelfoots." June 3, 1940.

———. "Sporting Life." September 17, 1953.

Torriero, E. A. " 'We Lost Satchel': KC Neighbors Shed Tears as Legendary Baseball Pitcher Dies." *The Kansas City Times.* June 9, 1982.

Trouppe, Quincy. *20 Years Too Soon: Prelude to Major-League Integrated Baseball.* St. Louis: Missouri Historical Society Press, 1995.

Trucks, Virgil, Ronnie Joyner, and Bill Bozman. *Throwing Heat: The Life and Times of Virgil "Fire" Trucks.* Dunkirk, Md.: Pepperpot Productions, 2004.

Tucker, Frank. "Sportbeams." *Newark Daily News.* August 6, 1938.

Turits, Richard Lee. *Foundations of Despotism: Peasants, the Trujillo Regime, and Modernity in Dominican History.* Stanford, Calif.: Stanford University Press, 2003.

Tye, Larry. Author interviews or correspondence with Negro Leaguers, Major Leaguers, Paige family and friends, and others: Hank Aaron, Bill Acree, Red Adams, Rich Alberts, James Alderman, Dewey Alexander, David Alsobrook, Joel Alterman, George Altman, Don Amon, Rodney Anderson, Marty Appel, Robert Baab, John Bagley, Otha Bailey, Dusty Baker, Stephen Banker, James Bankes, Ernie Banks, Bill Bartholomay, Matt Batts, Hank Baylis, Bijan Bayne, Ramón Bayrón, Jim Becker, Aaron Bell, William Bell, Yogi Berra, Neil Berry, Peter Bjarkman, Buddy Blatner, Ike Bohn, Carl Boles, Milton Bolling, Rich Booker, Ed Bouchee, Jim Boudreau, Lou Boudreau, Jr., Bob Bowman, Robert Boyle, Eddie Bressoud, Ed Bridges, Alvin

Brooks, Connie Brooks, Bobby Brown, Clifford Brown, Henry Lee Brown, Wilt Browning, Janet Bruce, Billy Bryan, Sidney Bunch, Thomas Burt, Hewitt Burton, Tommy Byrne, Don Cardwell, Ed Catron, Gladys Catron, Wayne Causey, Orlando Cepeda, Cliff Chambers, Ed Charles, Boyd Christenson, Neil Churchill, Jr., Randy Churchill, Louis Clarizio, Allie Clark, Bill Clark, Dave Clark, Marlene Clark, Brian Cohen, Frankie Cole, Jerry Coleman, Angel Colón, Jorge Colón Delgado, Jim Colzie, Marc Conrad, Cuqui Cordova, Sherman Cottingham, Billy Coward, Gary Crawford, Andy Crichton, Bernice Maxwell Cross, Max Croster, George Crow, Lloyd Dalager, Craig Davidson, Charlie Davis, Ross Davis, Desiderio de León, Joe DeMaestri, Bill DeWitt, Paul Dickson, Bob Didier, Harrison Dillard, Dom DiMaggio, Phil Dixon, Ray Doswell, William Dulaney, Melvin Duncan, Georgia Dwight, Roberto González Echevarría, Bert Eichold, Curt Eriksmoen, Frank Evans, Lionel Evelyn, Willis Everett, Norm Felde, Billy Felder, Bob Feller, Oliver Ferguson, Audrey Wilmer Fields, Frankie Figueroa, Jorge Figueredo, Julio Figueroa, Rom Fimrite, Glenn Fleisig, William Price Fox, Emile Francis, Herman Franks, Tom Fredrick, Owen Friend, Bill Gallo, Luis Guillermo Garcia, Ralph Garr, Ned Garver, Ollie Gates, John Gibbons, Walter Gibbons, Sean Gibson, Bill Gleason, Stanley Glenn, Herald Gordon, Peggy Gray, William Greason, Dallas Green, Steve Greenberg, Chris Grove, Sonny Gulsvig, Ray Haggins, Harold Hair, Joe Hamper, Chuck Harmon, Tex Harrison, Dorothy Harshbarger, Ernie Harwell, Roy Hawes, Lester Hecht, James Hefner, Clara Heintzman, Dan Heintzman, Rollie Hemond, Joe Henry, Alexis Herman, Kirk Herman, Fred Hermann, Whitey Herzog, John Hetki, Tommy Hicks, Jay Higginbotham, Doris Hill, Bill Hoeft, Larry Hogan, Ulysses Holliman, Jerome Carolyn Holmes, Doc Horn, Willie Horton, Mamie Hughes, Bill Humber, Chuck Humphrey, Earl Hunsinger, Billy Hunter, Monte Irvin, James Ivory, Jerry Izenberg, Steve Jacobson, Dave Janowsky, Pat Jarvis, Dwight Jaynes, Robert Jenkins, Bill Jenkinson, Babe Jenning, Bill Jennings, Dick Johnson, Mamie Johnson, Ben Jones, Cleon Jones, Bob Joyce, Cecil Kaiser, David Kaiser, Bud Kane, Jerry Kassirer, Dave Kemp, Norwood Kerr, Alton King, Collette King, Hal King, Scotty Kirkland, Jerry Kirshenbaum, George Kissell, Lou Kretlow, Dick Kryhoski, John Kurtz, Rene Lachemann, Tim Lacy, Ed Lahr, George Lang, Jack Lang, Tommy Lasorda, Neil Lebovitz, Silas Lee, Willie Lee, Meadowlark Lemon, Don Lenhardt, Ted Lepcio, Larry Lester, Dwight Lewis, David Lipman, Robert Lipsyte, Winston Llenas, Curtis Lloyd, Carl Long, Rosemary Lowe, Lee Lowenfish, Norman Lumpkin, Raydell Maddix, Bob Maisel, Irene Marcus, Bill Mardo, Marty Marion, Enrico Maroto, Dan Martin, Henry Mason, Luis Mayoral, Clinton McCord, Bill McCrary, Jerry McGinn, Ira McKnight, Kyle McNary, William McNeil, Barry Mednick, Bob Micellota, Ed Mickelson, John Miles, Minnie Minoso, Bob Mitchell, Jesse Mitchell, Clarence Mohr, Bill Monbouquette, Leigh Montville, Joseph Thomas Moore, Monte Moore, Red Moore, Wicky Moore, Less Moss, Bob Motley, Don Motley, Chaguin Muratti, Emilio Navarro, Lyle Nelson, Rod Nelson, Rob Neyer, Roy Nicely, Floyd Nicholson, Phil Niekro, Odell Norris, Cliff Nygard, Luis Olmo, Gilbert Olson, Buck O'Neil, Jesse Outlar, James Overmyer, Leon Paige, Wilson Paige, Jr., Mel Parnell, Art Pennington, Phil Pepe, Dave Percley, Johnny Pesky, Hank Peters, Peggy Peterson, Tom Peterson, Duane Pillette, Don Pollock, Jerry Pollock, Andrew Porter, J. W. Porter, Hank Presswood, Charlie Pride, James Proctor, Tom Qualters, Ron Reed, Layton Revel, Arthur Richman, John Richmond, Jim Riley, Jim Rivera, Tim Rives, Eddie Robinson, Winnie Robinson, Patrick Rock, Lester Rodney, Michael Roe, Jesse Rogers, Donn Rogosin, Bienvenido Rojas, Bob Roselli, Al Rosen, Stanley Rubin, Rob Ruck, Deeb Salem, Satch Sanders, Carlos Santiago, Frank Saucier, Russ Schneider, Richard Schweid, Ed Scott, Joe Scott, Eugene Scruggs, Ray Semproch, Neill Sheridan, Roy Sievers, Al Silverman, Charlie Silverra, Bert Simmons, Silas Simmons, Herb Simpson, Chris Siriano, Seymour Siwoff, Lou Sleater, Nathan Smalls, DeMorris Smith, Wyonella Smith, Brad Snyder, Burt Solomon, Al Spearman, Jack Spring, Dick Starr, Nettie Stearnes, Chuck Stevens, Julia Ruth Stevens, Tom Stevens, Bryan Steverson, Wayne Stivers, Tom Stoltz, Ed Storin, Lou Stringer, Mickie Stubblefield, Bert Sugar, Marianne Sutton, Lee Talboys, Sam Taylor, Ron Teasley, Bud Thomas, Lee Thomas, Mike Thomason, Frank Torre, Joe Torre, Quincy Trouppe, Jr., Virgil Trucks, Bob Turley, Thomas Turner, Jules Tygiel, Armando Vasquez, Mary Francis Veeck, Mike Veeck, Jose A. Vega Imbert, Mickey Vernon, Fay Vincent, George Walden, Jimmy Walker, Johnny Walker, Bunny Warren, Johnny Washington, Levi Washington, Reg Waterton, Bud Watkins, Bob Weir, Isaac Welch, Ernie Westfield, Sonny Weston, Jim Wheeler, Charles Whitehead, Larry Whiteside, Tom Wickstrom, Harry Wiley, Dick Wilkinson, Helen Wilkinson, Dean Williams, Franklin Williams, Larry Williams, Marty Williams, Walter Williams, Willie Williams, Artie Wilson, Lyle Wilson, Yvonne Wilson, Kearney Windham, Kenneth Wood, Walter Wood, Bryan Woolley, Hubert Wooten, Carl Yastrzemski, Jim Zapp, Vertes Zeigler.

Tygiel, Jules. *Baseball's Great Experiment: Jackie Robinson and His Legacy.* New York: Oxford University Press, 1997.

———. *Extra Bases: Reflections on Jackie Robinson, Race, and Baseball History.* Lincoln: University of Nebraska Press, 2002.

———. *Past Time: Baseball as History.* New York: Oxford University Press, 2000.

———. "Revisiting Bill Veeck and the 1943 Phillies." *Baseball Research Journal* 35 (2007): 109–114.

United Press International. "Dizzy Dean Almost Turns Exhibition into Riot." October 24, 1934.

U.S. Department of State. Affidavit of Birth to Be Submitted with Application for American Passport: Leroy Satchel Paige. April 15, 1938. Provided by Department of State, October 10, 2007.

U.S. Federal Bureau of Investigation. The FBI Files of Leroy "Satchel" Paige," File # 100-7002-A. Provided at Jerry Malloy Negro League Conference, Kansas City, Missouri, July 7–8, 2006.

U.S. Selective Service System. Registrar's Report: Leroy Paige. October 16, 1940. Local Board No. 4, Kansas City, Missouri. Provided by Selective Service System, June 22, 2007.

U.S. Treasury Department. Application for Social Security Account Number, Internal Revenue Service: Leroy Satchel Paige. January 31, 1940. Provided by Social Security Administration, May 24, 2007.

USA Today Baseball Weekly. "Life-size Satchel Paige Statue Unveiled at School." March 21–27, 2001.

Van Dellen, T. R. "How to Keep Well." *Chicago Tribune.* March 14, 1960.

Van Hyning, Thomas E. *Puerto Rico's Winter League: A History of Major League Baseball's Launching Pad.* Jefferson, N.C.: McFarland & Company, 1995.

———. *The Santurce Crabbers: Sixty Seasons of Puerto Rican Winter League Baseball.* Jefferson, N.C.: McFarland & Company, 1999.

Vass, George. "A Paige in Baseball History." Mobile *Press-Register.* June 9, 1982.

Vaughan, Bill. "The Most American of All Cities." *The Kansas City Star.* June 4, 1950.

Vaughan, Irving. "51,013 Watch Paige Blank White Sox, 5-0." *Chicago Tribune.* August 14, 1948.

———. "Record 78,382 See Mr. Paige Blank Sox, 1-0." *Chicago Tribune.* August 21, 1948.

Vecchione, Joseph J., ed. *The New York Times Book of Sports Legends.* New York: Times Books, Random House, 1991.

Veeck, Bill. "The Ageless Nomad of Baseball." *Chicago Tribune.* March 25, 1962.

———. "Baseball's Own Paul Bunyan: Satchel Paige." *Chicago Tribune.* July 20, 1962.

———. "Satchel Paige Would Have Loved the Orioles." *Chicago Tribune.* October 14, 1983.

Veeck, Bill, and Ed Linn. *The Hustler's Handbook.* New York: Fireside, 1965.

———. *Veeck—as in Wreck: The Chaotic Career of Baseball's Incorrigible Maverick.* New York: Putnam, 1962.

Verdi, Bob. "He Can Barely Hear or Walk but Even Roasted . . ." *Chicago Tribune.* April 24, 1976.

Vincent, Fay. *The Only Game in Town: Baseball Stars of the 1930s and 1940s Talk About the Game They Loved.* New York: Simon & Schuster, 2006.

Wade, Dick. "Satchel Looks Back." *The Kansas City Star.* August 9, 1971.

Walker, Roy. *Playing Ball with the Great Satchel Paige, Christmas 1989.* Self-published.

Wall Street Journal, The. "Thinking Things Over." December 29, 1976.

———. "What's News." June 9, 1982.

Ward, Arch. "In the Wake of the News." *Chicago Tribune.* March 30, 1944.

Ward, Geoffrey C., and Ken Burns. *Baseball: An Illustrated History.* New York: Alfred A. Knopf, 1994.

Washington Post, The. "Another Fish Story? Paige Admits 47 Age." June 24, 1952.

———. "Ol' Satch Cost Just $55,000 Paper Figures." August 25, 1948.

———. "Old Satch Paige, Great Negro Pitcher Signed by Cleveland, Says 'Batters Can't Scare Me—I've Been Around Too Long.' " July 8, 1948.

———. "Satch's Pitches to Nats 'Illegal,' Rules Harridge." July 21, 1948.

———. "Signing of Negroes Can't Be Worked Out, Says Paige." August 7, 1942.

Washington, Chester L. "Paige Fans 12 to Shade Jones in Hot Mound Duel." *The Pittsburgh Courier.* September 15, 1934.

———. "Sez Ches." *The Pittsburgh Courier.* January 28, 1933.

———. "Sez Ches." *The Pittsburgh Courier.* July 1, 1933.

———. "Sez Ches." *The Pittsburgh Courier.* April 14, 1934.

———. "Sez Ches." *The Pittsburgh Courier.* April 21, 1934.

———. "Sez Ches." *The Pittsburgh Courier.* April 20, 1935.

———. "Sez Ches: Satchel's Back in Town." *The Pittsburgh Courier.* May 9, 1936.

Washington, Hazel A. "This Is Hollywood." *Chicago Defender.* November 13, 1958.

Waters, Enoc P. "Adventures in Race Relations." *Chicago Defender.* January 14, 1950.

Watson, Frank. "Jest Sports." *Chicago Defender.* September 25, 1965.

Waukesha Daily Freeman (Wisconsin). "Feller's All-Stars Cop 6-5 Victory." October 3, 1946.

Weaver, Bill L. "The Black Press and the Assault on Professional Baseball's 'Color Line,' October 1945–April, 1947." *Phylon* 40, no. 4 (1979): 303–17.

Webber, Harry B. "Satchell Paige in Puerto Rico, Not with Eagles." Baltimore *Afro-American.* May 11, 1940.

Weir, Tom. "Negro Leagues Had Talent, but Fans Left to Follow Robinson." *USA Today.* April 16, 1997.

White, Gordon S., Jr. "Mr. Paige Keeps 'Em Low and Away at Stadium." *The New York Times.* August 21, 1961.

————. "Satch (52?) Strikes a NEW Blow for Aging Players." *The New York Times.* August 21, 1961.

White, Lonnie. "Three for a Show: Remembering the Negro Leagues." *Los Angeles Times.* July 30, 2006.

Whiteside, Larry. "Veeck's Day in the Sun." *The Boston Globe.* August 1, 1991.

Whitt, Timothy. *Bases Loaded with History: The Story of Rickwood Field, America's Oldest Ballpark.* Birmingham, Ala.: The R. Boozer Press, 1995.

Whittaker, Andrea, and Rick Reilly. "Paige out of History." *Sports Illustrated for Kids.* July 2002.

Wiebusch, John. "Torre Absent, but Life Goes on in Braves' Camp." *Los Angeles Times.* March 10, 1969.

Wiggins, David K. "Wendell Smith, the *Pittsburgh Courier-Journal* and the Campaign to Include Blacks in Organized Baseball, 1933–1945." *Journal of Sport History* 10, no. 2 (1983): 5–29.

Williams, Harry A. "Our Rhythmic Negro Athletes." *Los Angeles Times.* September 22, 1935.

Williams, Joe, and Peter Williams, ed. *The Joe Williams Baseball Reader.* Chapel Hill, N.C.: Algonquin Books, 1989.

Williams, Marty. "Satchel Paige Encounter Is a Fond Memory." *Dayton Daily News.* April 15, 1997.

Williams, Ted, and Jim Prime. *Ted Williams' Hit List: The Best of the Best Ranks the Best of the Rest.* Chicago: Contemporary Books, 2003.

Wilson, Nick. *Voices from the Pastime: Oral Histories of Surviving Major Leaguers, Negro Leaguers, Cuban Leaguers and Writers, 1920–1934.* Jefferson, N.C.: McFarland & Company, 2000.

Wilson, W. Rollo. "Boldenmen Trip 'Craws' Twice to Take Top Rung of League Flag Ladder." *The Pittsburgh Courier.* July 21, 1934.

Winnipeg Free Press. "Third Strike-outs Seen in Game Here—Maroons Hold Substantial Lead: Satchel Paige Fans Seventeen While Brewer Turns Back Thirteen Batters." June 7, 1935.

Winter, Jonah. *Fair Ball! 14 Great Stars from Baseball's Negro Leagues.* New York: Scholastic, 1999.

Witwer, David. "Westbrook Pegler and the Anti-union Movement." *The Journal of American History* 92, no. 2 (2005): 527–52.

Wolf, Al. "Sportraits." *Los Angeles Times.* February 16, 1950.

Wonderful Country, The. DVD. Directed by Robert Parrish. DRM Productions, 1960.

Woodward, Stanley. "Satchel's Ambition." *Negro Digest.* August 1943.

Woolley, Bryan. "Herbert Kokernot, Satchel Paige, and Me." In *Generations and Other True Stories.* El Paso: Texas Western Press, 1995.

Wyatt, Dick. "Postscripts." *The Washington Post.* February 12, 1945.

Wucker, Michele. "The River Massacre: The Real and Imagined Borders of Hispaniola." www.haitiforever.com (accessed August 16, 2008).

Yonkers, Bob. "Satch Is Gone, but Those Other Rumors Remain." *Cleveland Press.* February 11, 1950.

Young, A. S. "An 'Old Man' Makes Baseball History." *Ebony.* March 1969.

————. *Great Negro Baseball Stars and How They Made the Major Leagues.* New York: A. S. Barnes, 1953.

————. *Negro Firsts in Sports.* Chicago: Johnson Publishing, 1963.

Young, Dick. "Young Ideas." New York *Daily News.* February 11, 1971.

Young, Doc. "Is This a Yankee Fan or Is He Sore at the Cards?" *Chicago Defender.* April 10, 1943.

Young, Fay. "Paige Gets Himself Fired from Role as Pitcher in East vs. West Classic." *Chicago Defender.* August 12, 1944.

Young, Frank A. "39,500 See Paige Humble Chicago in Detroit." *Chicago Defender.* September 20, 1941.

Ziff, Sid. "Satchel's Day Okay." *Los Angeles Times.* September 13, 1965.

Zimmerman, Paul. "Sportscripts." *Los Angeles Times.* July 30, 1949.

Zinkoff, Dave, with Edgar Williams. *Around the World with the Harlem Globetrotters.* Philadelphia: Macrae Smith Co., 1953.

Zirin, Dave. "An Interview with Lester 'Red' Rodney, the Man Who Helped Integrate Baseball." *International Socialist Review* 35 (May–June 2004).

INDEX

ABOUT THE AUTHOR

LARRY TYE was an award-winning journalist at *The Boston Globe* and a Nieman Fellow at Harvard University. An avid baseball fan, Tye now runs a Boston-based training program for medical journalists. He is the author of *The Father of Spin, Home Lands, Rising from the Rails,* and *Shock.*

ABOUT THE TYPE

This book was set in Garamond, a typeface originally designed by the Parisian typecutter Claude Garamond (1480–1561). This version of Garamond was modeled on a 1592 specimen sheet from the Egenolff-Berner foundry, which was produced from types assumed to have been brought to Frankfurt by the punchcutter Jacques Sabon.

Claude Garamond's distinguished romans and italics first appeared in *Opera Ciceronis* in 1543–44. The Garamond types are clear, open, and elegant.